PLANS, SPECS AND CONTRACTS
for
BUILDING PROFESSIONALS

Waller S. Poage, AIA, CSI, CCS

R.S. MEANS COMPANY, INC.
CONSTRUCTION CONSULTANTS & PUBLISHERS
100 Construction Plaza
P.O. Box 800
Kingston, Ma 02364-0800
(617) 747-1270

The editors for this book were Mary P. Greene and Edward B. Wetherill; the production supervisor was Marion E. Schofield

Printed in the United States of America

10   9   8   7   6   5   4   3   2   1

Library of Congress Cataloging in Publication Data

ISBN 0-87629-068-3

To Elizabeth

For friendship, support, counsel and sacrifice, but most of all for sharing those things of no price which make life a worthwhile adventure.

Acknowledgments

Several AIA standard documents have been reproduced for the reader with the permission of the American Institute of Architects license number 87020. Because AIA documents are undergoing periodic changes, several of the documents included in this book will soon be superceded in 1987 by newer editions of those documents. The reader is strongly urged to obtain the most recent editions of the AIA documents by contacting a local AIA component chapter or the national AIA. To contact the national AIA, write to 1735 New York Ave., N.W., Washington, D.C., 20006.

We also wish to acknowledge the contributions of the following organizations: the Engineer's Joint Documents Committee, the Construction Specifications Institute, the American Society for the Testing of Materials, and the editors and staff of the R. S. Means Company who have made major contributions to the direction and content of this volume.

TABLE OF
CONTENTS

FOREWORD

Construction in the twentieth century has become a major industry on which a great part of society depends for its livelihood as well as its shelter. The effort required to construct the "built" environment incorporates many elements. Among them are the ambition of the owner, the art of the designer, and the ingenuity of the engineer, together with the leadership of the contractor, the skill of the tradesman, and the product of the manufacturer. The welfare and economy of the community are also major considerations. There are few human endeavors that require more coordination and communication skills than the work of today's construction professional who directs the profusion of trades and skills needed to erect a modern building. The common "touch-stone" relating owner, professional, manager, tradesman, and producer is that series of documents known in the industry as "Plans, Specs and Contracts".

Man has expanded his construction knowledge and ability more in the last hundred years than in the previous forty centuries of recorded history. The "built" environment has more than doubled in the last 50 years alone. Looking ahead, we can reasonably expect to see the collective work of construction more than double again in the twenty-first century. Present and future construction professionals have little time for the "trial and error" learning methods of their predecessors. The time has come to establish a better formula for using and controlling construction documentation.

Construction documents consist of drawings, technical specifications and other related material which include agreements, conditions of agreements, instructions and modifications. Such instruments are all necessary to the construction of modern building projects. They serve as the product or the tool of the modern construction professional. Design professionals will spend a great part of their professional lives preparing contract documents. Building professionals will spend a like amount of time interpreting and following such documents. Owners will spend large sums of money to have construction documents created and used.

After twenty years of professional practice, and five years dedicated to teaching the construction sciences, the author has recognized the need for a text that examines the subject of construction documents. This book, his response to that need, covers the preparation and use of documentation by owners, architects, engineers, contractors, subcontractors, material producers, and the many others that contribute to the construction industry.

Legal issues as well as legal documents and their use are discussed in this text. Much of the material included has important legal consequences and implications. It is the explicit recommendation of the author, editors, and publisher that an attorney should be consulted on all legal matters and that all construction documents receive a thorough and competent legal review.

INTRODUCTION

From the beginning, man has been an organizer, an inventor, a constructor, and an artist/designer. Like other creatures, his primary motivation was survival, but his competitive and challenging spirit set him apart. Not satisfied for long with the simple elements of survival, man designed shelter that reflected his personality and ego. Throughout his history, he has built an ever-expanding, complex, and colorful environment.

Construction has, over time, reached mammoth proportions, and growing along with it has been the requirement for documentation. As we investigate construction documentation today, it is appropriate to look back to the origins of this far-reaching venture.

Early Construction

The simple need for food and shelter required early man to become organized and to use teamwork. Clans were formed, and then tribes, each with established territories. The common need for food and shelter also led to specialization by trade. Members of the tribe were trained for different tasks and arts to become part of the community effort. Father taught son and master taught student. Available space in caves and other forms of natural shelter were outgrown as new generations increased the populations of the tribes. This population growth and the necessity to maintain communities led to the construction of shelter.

History did not record the first structure built by man, nor does it recognize the first architect or contractor. The first structure was probably a residence, made from the rough elements and materials available in the surrounding area. Archeological evidence suggests that the familiar coolness and safety of the cave prompted the first builders to excavate below the surface. Consequently, retaining and supporting walls had to be built, using stones of a size which could be hand carried, sometimes from great distances. The earliest roof structures were made from tree limbs lashed together with thatched reeds, bonded with a covering of mud.

Anthropologist/archaeologists pose an interesting theory as to how man may have emerged from nomadic hunter/gatherer to builder and dweller of permanent structured communities—the first towns and cities. The theory suggests that the discovery of wheat was an important factor. Unlike its ancestor grasses, the kernels of wheat are heavy and not easily blown by the wind from their stalks or place of growth. As a result, wheat grew near the place where it fell, creating natural fields of edible grain. About 10,000 years ago, as nomadic man came upon these "windfalls" of wheat, he remained nearby, without the need to continue roaming in search of food. From the wheat grains he made bread, and he baled and stored the stalks and leaves for his livestock. For this reason, it is thought that the first permanent villages were constructed near wheatfields, and that these early structures of stone and brick were the beginning of civilized community life. The town of Bethlehem, Israel, lies a few miles from the historical city of Jerusalem and is known to be one of the oldest places of man's continued inhabitance in the world. The name "Bethlehem", translated from the original Hebrew means "place of bread".

Early Documents

Man's first known documents were sketches drawn on cave walls, depicting the excitement of the hunt. These sketches can be seen in the caves of Lascaux located in the Vezere Valley in France. The first known record-keeping documents were clay tablets inscribed with symbols that communicated stories and made records of transactions. The excavation of the ancient city of Ebla, now in modern Syria, has uncovered thousands of these clay tablets. Their existence is evidence of man's having lived in permanent communities with documentary skills for more than 10,000 years.

About 4,000 years ago, in Egypt, man found that he could transform the pith of certain reeds that grew along the rivers into a crude form of paper that has come to be known as "papyrus". Using a brush made from animal hair, he could write on this medium with ink made from the carbon of burned organic matter. The first known "books" were actually scrolls written on long sheets of papyrus glued together.

Papyrus was used to record some of the first known construction documents in the Septiguent Bible, written in the Greek language and first transcribed around 300 B.C. One of the first specifications appears in the book of Genesis, describing the Ark, built to save a remnant of mankind and selected animal species from the Great Flood. Here we find divine instructions given to Noah as to how and of what material he and his sons were to construct the Ark.

Twentieth century man lives in a veritable sea of paper; its benefits to his knowledge and survival are many. The invention of the printing process in the sixteenth century gave man the ability to document his discoveries and knowledge, and stimulated achievement and understanding through writing, education, science, and invention.

The Master Builders

The traditional master builder is architect/engineer, artist, and contractor. He not only designed the building, but also directed or managed the construction. Although the master builder's job is now often divided into two professions, that of the design professional, and the contractor or project manager, this design/build approach still goes on in many parts of the world today, as it has for many centuries.

Master builders directed the construction of the pyramids of Egypt. These structures are among the world's oldest reminders of civilized man's early zeal to design and build on a grand scale. Although there is much speculation as to the methods by which the pyramids were constructed, it is evident by the structures themselves that their master builders were able to achieve a high degree of engineering accuracy, measurement, and control of form. By the Fourth Dynasty of Egypt (2575 B.C.) man's talent as a master builder was reaching classic proportions. The first true pyramids were built by the Egyptian ruler Snofru, who reigned from 2575 until 2551 B.C.

By far the most famous of the pyramids is the Great Pyramid of Khufu. The exactness of measurement, the relationship of the perimeter of the base (which is divisible by 2 pi), the obvious skill in scheduling the time of construction to match the lifetime of the monarch, and the management of the tremendous amount of material and manpower all indicate a highly developed architectural design, and some form of architectural documentation. The Great Pyramid contains an estimated 2,300,000 blocks of stone with an average weight of two and one half tons each. The volume of this structure could easily contain five or more of the great cathedrals of Europe, including St. Peter's in Rome, the largest church in Christendom. The pyramid has a nearly perfect square base with sides 756 feet long. It covers 13 acres of ground, equal to approximately ten New York City blocks. The four sides vary in length less than eight inches in overall dimension, an error of less than one in 1100. (Today we specify an acceptable error in masonry of one in 500.) The Pyramid's original height has been computed at 481 feet, about two thirds of the height of America's first high rise building, the Woolworth Tower in New York.

Throughout history, the master builder has considered it a duty and a privilege to train his understudies in the art and science of building design and construction. Until the early eighteenth century, and before the creation of the modern day school of architecture, much of the master builder's education consisted of actual practice in building skills such as masonry, stone cutting, concrete manufacture and placement, and carpentry. Training behind a drawing board was incidental to the main exposure, which thrust the student physically into learning the theory and science of building construction by doing. As we shall see, the professionalism of the master builder/architect, his training, and his participation in the building process (for reasons of ethics and other considerations) took a much different turn with the creation of the American Institute of Architects in the nineteenth century.

Unlike the traditional master builder, the American design professional (architect/engineer) has held himself apart from any financial or functional interest in the actual construction process. The intent was to keep his service and advice to the client free of any conflict of interest. Such conflicts could be potential profit from the production and marketing of materials, or from the construction process. Today, the American design professional concerns himself with the building design, its form, envelope, structure, site improvements, and mechanical and electrical service and function. He defines the work by creating certain professional documents. During construction, the architect or the engineer becomes an interested observer in the employ of the owner. He administers and interprets the intent of the Contract for Construction, and documents the flow of information throughout the process. From time to time, he is called on to express his judgment in the case of questions or disputes. Design professionals have recently become more entwined in the construction process in the roles of owner, developer, and construction manager. The same basic ethic prevails, but it has become more complicated, as we shall see in subsequent discussion.

The Age of Discovery
The development of the wheel gave man a revolutionary new tool with which to construct his buildings. The wheel provided the means to transport materials of great bulk and weight, and the pulley allowed the use of hoists, the block and tackle, and other labor saving devices such as the wheelbarrow. All of these are basic tools today. No one is certain

just when the wheel was invented, but it is clear that construction was not the primary motivation behind its development.

It is interesting to note that the inspiration behind most of these inventions and discoveries was not a desire to construct spectacular buildings. The structural use of the arch, for example, was the result of the experiments and discoveries of the Greek mathematician and scientist, Archimedes. Archimedes lived in the third century B.C. when Greek civilization was in its prime. It was this civilization that gave us art, drama, philosophy, and science, as well as having a great influence on the development of architecture as an art form. In addition to the arch, Archimedes gave us the mathematical relationship of the surface area of a sphere to its circumference, diameter, and volume. Despite the fact that Archimedes was not a builder, his discoveries led to major advancements in construction. The arch was used extensively by the Romans during the next five centuries. An understanding of the arch led to the development of the vault, the dome, and the flying buttress, all common elements in the great cathedrals of Europe from the fourth century A.D. well into the nineteenth century.

It was the invention of the steam engine by James Watt and the discovery of electricity around 1746 which would lead man, the master builder, to the achievement of his dream to build higher structures. Electricity produced safer and cheaper artificial lighting as well as the electric motor, without which we would not have mechanical ventilation, elevators, power tools, or communications. Modern blast furnaces produced steel, thereby allowing buildings to be constructed more quickly and cheaply, and to greater heights. The development of refrigeration provided air-conditioning for buildings. The Fourcault process allowed for the economical production of glass, and the Bayer process produced pure aluminum. The availability of electricity has enhanced almost every industry related to building construction—from the lumber sawmill to the modern brick and concrete kilns. It was the growth of technology that allowed the American builder to participate in the largest building boom in the history of mankind. In a brief period of 200 years, the North American continent would see as much building construction as had taken place in the whole of Europe and Asia in 4000 years.

Production of Materials

With the Industrial Revolution came the development of industries related to the extraction and refinement, or manufacture of building materials and systems of all kinds. In 1824, in England, Joseph Aspidin patented a hydraulic cement he called "Portland Cement", because of its resemblance to grey limestone mined on the isle of Portland. The development of energy resources such as coal and natural gas allowed for the production of great quantities of Portland Cement in furnaces or kilns. This material, one of the major ingredients of modern building, was introduced into the marketplace in Pennsylvania in 1872. The blast furnace was developed by Henry Bessemer in 1847, the open hearth furnace by the Siemens brothers of England in 1868, and the electric furnace in the United States in 1906—all for the production of steel. The Fourcault and Cobern processes were developed for producing sheet glass, and the Bayer process for aluminum.

All of these advances brought the building material industry into full focus in the early twentieth century. With such industries came the need for expanded engineering and technical drawing. The processes themselves brought about the need for technical specifications and new forms of labor specialization. The corresponding explosion of new building created the need for management and design techniques that would blend skill, labor, materials, and assemblies to create the complex buildings that so totally dominate the skyline of modern cities in the world today.

The Shaping of Technology

Throughout history, man's technological advancements have been reflected in his achievements in building construction. From the time of the Great Pyramids until just 200 years ago, building structures, tools, and techniques were evidence of the limitations of technology. However, from that time until today, man has been striving for larger and higher structures. That goal and dream has certainly been achieved in the present age, but the technology required to construct large, habitable buildings was slow to evolve. The pyramid builders produced spectacular structures, yet over the following 40 centuries, the most significant developments in building technology were the invention of the wheel, the arch, and the development of concrete. Consequently, architectural documents remained relatively uncomplicated for many centuries, and construction management was largely achieved by using simple drawings, verbal instructions issued on the job, and the most basic of technical specifications.

In Khufu's time, it took a quarter of a century to construct the Great Pyramid. Today, man is able to construct in less than three years a structure such as the World Trade Center in New York City, a remarkable 110 story building complex capable of housing more people than the total population of the average U.S. city.

In the early 1980's, a group of computer scientists finished compiling a data bank that listed biographical data on everyone in recorded history who had been known to have invented anything or made a major discovery. The evidence showed that almost 80% of all the people who had made such a contribution were still living. Indeed, the technical advancements related to science in general, and building construction in particular, have been rapid and far-reaching in the latter half of the twentieth century.

In the mid seventeenth century, the English mathematician and scientist, Issac Newton, developed the first major advances in mathematics and physics since Archimedes almost 2000 years before him. Newton gave us the theory of gravity, the mathematical principal of the lever arm, calculus, and differential equations. From Newton's work, we have derived the mathematical ability to analyze the structural behavior of buildings. One of the by-products of this technology is the need to create more detailed documents that would include structural calculations and requirements for the various sections and connections. A diagram of the building's structural assembly has also become a requisite.

From the time of the pyramids, it was about 4500 years before any portion of a man-made structure surpassed the record height of 482 feet achieved in the Great Pyramid of Giza. The Washington Monument, completed in 1884, is 555 feet high, and the Eiffel Tower of Paris, completed in 1889, is 984 feet high. While these monumental buildings will always hold a significant place in the history of architecture, it must be remembered that none of them was built for human habitation. It was the American "skyscraper", designed to house large numbers of people, which would finally surpass the height record set by the ancients. The first true high-rise building to be constructed in the United States was Cass Gilbert's 58-story Woolworth Building completed in New York City in 1913.

From the beginning, man has been a builder and a shaper of his environment. In solving the need for shelter over a period of some ten thousand years, he has become an inventor, artist, architect, engineer and constructor. In today's complex society, specializations have evolved to support the ambitions and creature comforts that characterize modern man. The construction industry recognizes and depends upon the coordination of talents, skills, trades, professions and products in order to continue constructing the built environment. The cord that binds the package is that collection of information we call "Professional Documents". Every individual who becomes part of the construction industry, no matter what his role, will spend more than half of his available time dealing with or preparing that package of information to which this book is dedicated.

Chapter 1
THE CONSTRUCTION INDUSTRY AND THE "OPC" RELATIONSHIP

The construction industry in the United States exerts an influence on practically every sector of the nation's economy. Total expenditures for building construction in the United States are far in excess of those produced by any other single industry. Since the end of World War II, the U.S. has produced more total building construction than in the first 175 years of its existence. Current predictions forecast that the period 1980–2000 will see the total built environment double again.

The building construction process has become a complex and diverse undertaking. The construction of a modern building can be likened to the performance of a symphony orchestra. The orchestra is composed of many different musical instruments, all of which must be scheduled to play at different times, in different combinations, and exactly on schedule. Like musical instruments, the various parts of a building's construction must be orchestrated together in harmony and on schedule, in order to produce a predictable and acceptable end result. In addition to the traditional triad of owner, design professional and contractor, many other persons or entities may be required to produce a modern building. Included in this list might be a multitude of manufacturers, fabricators, suppliers, and specialists in the installation and application of any number of systems and sub-systems. Also required are services in the following areas: engineering, transportation, communications, data processing, insurance, banking, legal and accounting, among others. Building construction consumes great quantities of labor, energy, and utilities of all descriptions. Modern construction requires vehicles of all sizes and shapes, tools of all varieties that range from simple hand tools to sophisticated power tools, plus a profusion of highly specialized equipment and technical processes.

The continual development of new materials and methods adds to the complexity of planning and estimating for construction. The growing influence of government, a decline in worker productivity, and rising inflation have all taken a toll on the quality and economy of building construction. Project costs have also been affected by spiraling land values, fluctuating interest rates, the need for more extensive professional services, and rising fee schedules. Prototype building projects constructed in the 1980's have more than doubled in cost for similar projects constructed in the 1960's.

At the beginning of this century, the ratio of privately to publicly owned new buildings was approximately five to one. In the final quarter of the twentieth century, the total expenditure of capital for construction in public versus private work has come to be almost equal. During periods of high inflation and high interest rates, expenditures for public work have actually exceeded those for private work by several percentage points. At the same time, government regulations, primarily more stringent building codes, have increased the requirements for professionally prepared documents. Project documentation has been further affected by the same factors that have contributed to higher building costs.

Early in this century, the desire to maintain quality and design control among owners and their architects and engineers produced the current accepted practice of competitive bidding for award of contract to build. This practice has maintained competition among constructors and has mandated a high degree of competency among those who have continued to be successful in the various trades. Over the years, a structured protocol, or procedure, has been developed for competitive bidding. Despite the complexity of social and economic forces, most contracts continue to be awarded by this process. There is, however, a growing tendency, especially among private owners, to award contracts selectively.

Industry Services

Since 1950, the construction industry has spawned many service organizations and institutions that have greatly improved communications and have made significant contributions to the health and welfare of the construction industry as a whole. Today, in the United States, plan rooms sponsored by service organizations are located in practically every major city and among some smaller communities. Plan rooms provide a convenient location for tradesmen and suppliers to review currently available bidding documents. Some plan rooms are sponsored by private companies, others by trade associations. Plan rooms generally advertise, display and provide facilities for the study of current bidding documents (provided by owners and architects) for local projects. Bidding documents are generally issued directly to primary bidders. Plan rooms make copies of the bidding documents available to manufacturers, fabricators, material suppliers and others who bid work to primary bidders.

Several of the service companies and trade organizations that provide plan rooms also publish journals, newsletters, and special reports. These reports keep subscribers informed as to the projects available for bidding, and the results (when publicly available) of competitive bid and negotiated bid awards. Information is also provided on the subject of technical innovations, new products, labor relations, and legislative and code changes. Most prominent among these organizations are the Associated General Contractors of America (AGC) and the F.W. Dodge Corporation.

The "OPC" Relationship

Building construction, by its nature and complexity, requires contractual relationships between owners who wish to build, architects and/or engineers called design professionals, and constructors who accomplish the actual building. The relationships that develop between owner, professional, and constructor are the subject of this chapter. In order to understand the Contract for Construction, we must first understand the parties to the contract and the role that each plays in the construction process.

In order for a project to be constructed, someone must identify the need, provide the location, or site, and establish the financing or means by which the cost of the project will be satisfied. The party who initiates the project and retains legal title to the building and its site is defined as the owner.

Unless the owner has the technical and artistic skills to design the building, establish a statement, or program, describing the functional requirements of the building, and make all of the decisions concerning the materials and methods of construction (including the building's conformity to local, state and federal building codes and other ordinances), he must employ the professional services of an architect and/or engineer—the design professionals.

Unless the owner or the architect/engineer has the skill, labor resources, and tools with which to construct the building, the owner must also employ the services of a constructor. The majority of building construction takes place through agreements between the owner and the design professional, and separately between the owner and the constructor. This text will frequently refer to the interactions between owner, design professional, and constructor as the "OPC Relationship" This relationship is illustrated in Figure 1.1.

The Owner

The owner can be an individual, a partnership, a corporation, a political subdivision, or any one of a number of agencies of state or federal government. The owner must be able to meet the minimum standards of competency defined by state law in order to execute a valid and binding contract, or agreement. As a practical matter, the owner should be able to fulfill all of his obligations under the agreement. Included are the ability to pay for the project, evidence title to the real property, arrange for insurance, make payment of interest, and to provide basic and relevant information. The owner must also have the ability to make binding decisions and approvals. These are most often the owner's primary contractual responsibilities in both an *Agreement between Owner and Architect* and an *Agreement between Owner and Contractor*.

Owner's Consultants
In addition to the design professional, the owner of a modern building project may employ the services of an attorney, an accountant, an insurance specialist, and a financial adviser, in addition to the architect or engineer. These professional services may be necessary to ensure that a proposed project will not only be successful, but lawful and profitable as well.

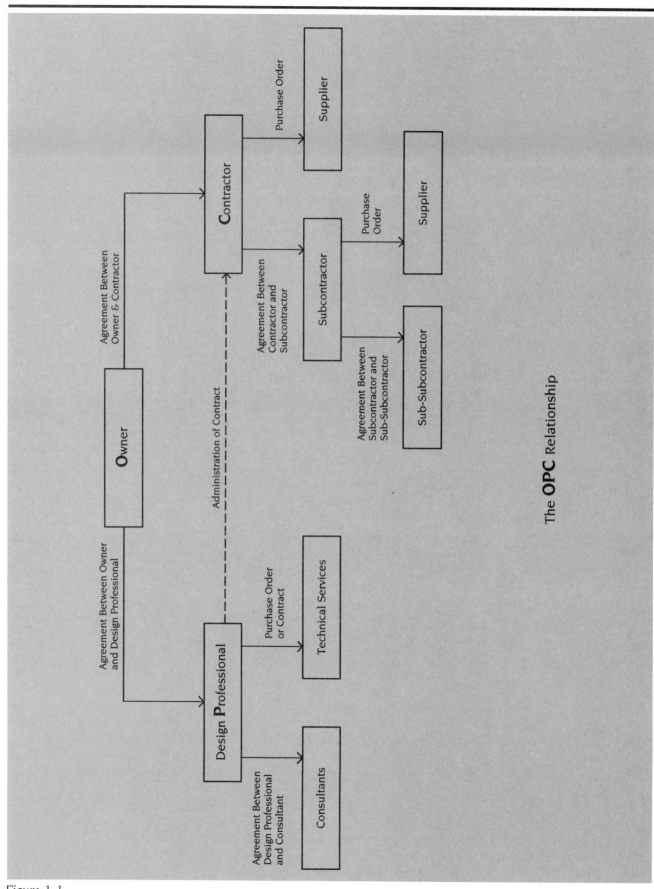

The **OPC** Relationship

Figure 1.1

4

The Architect/Engineer

An architect or engineer, under the laws of most states, can only act as an individual, since the state examines and certifies for practice only those individuals who meet the standards and requirements established by that state for professional practice. A partnership, corporation or joint venture, however, may practice professionally by virtue of the licensing of the partners, corporate executives or individual members of the joint venture who do business under the name of the partnership, corporation, or joint venture. Many state boards regulating the licensing of architects and engineers require the filing of an "Assumed Name Declaration", which establishes, as a matter of public record, the fact that an individual practitioner, jointly with others, is doing business in the name of the partnership, corporation, or joint venture.

The education and licensing requirements for architects and engineers vary from state to state. In the case of architects, the National Council of Architectural Registration Boards (NCARB), has established uniformity in the procedures for examining candidates for licensing as architects. NCARB membership consists of the boards regulating licensing of architects from each of the 50 states and other U.S. territories. Although the examination of architects is now uniform throughout the United States, each state may vary as to additional requirements and procedures that lead to acceptance and final licensing by that state. Many individuals have the advantage of being licensed in both architecture and engineering. In most cases, however, the architect and the engineer are separate individuals who may or may not be related by agreement in specific projects.

For most projects, the owner has the option to employ either an architect or an engineer to perform the prime professional service that is required. The Prime Design Professional—either the architect or the engineer—may hire other disciplines to act as consultants in the performance of the professional service. For the majority of buildings constructed in the United States, the owner hires the architect as the design professional, and the architect, in turn (with the approval of the owner), hires engineers and others of various disciplines to assist in the performance of the professional service. Engineers are usually hired as the design professional in construction projects involving utilities, streets, highways, drainage structures, bridges, municipal subdivisions, and similar projects requiring considerable engineering skill and experience. This text, however, deals chiefly with the architect as design professional in the design and construction of buildings.

Two or more architects and/or other related professionals may practice together in a partnership, a corporation, a professional corporation, or a joint venture. By virtue of his license to practice, the architect holds himself out as possessing the basic artistic and technical skills necessary to confirm the owner's program, prepare the building design, determine or recommend the materials and methods of construction, prepare the documents necessary for construction, assist the owner in the selection of a constructor, and to act as the owner's representative in the construction process.

In the OPC relationship for most building projects, the architect or the engineer provides a professional service to the owner as described in an *Agreement between Owner and Architect or Engineer*. There are instances where the professional is the owner, and others where the architect or engineer is employed by the constructor. These types of contracts will be discussed in subsequent chapters.

The Relationship of Architect to Engineer

In recent years, public sector owners, particularly agencies of the Federal Government, have referred by contract language to the "A/E", meaning "Architect/Engineer". Many contemporary documents refer to the Architect/Engineer. The two disciplines are quite different and are usually complementary rather than contradictory or competitive. In any event, the two are not interchangeable, nor is the existence of one necessarily dependent upon the other. Many professional firms present themselves as A&E firms, employing representatives of both disciplines. However, the majority of practitioners in the United States prefer to practice separately, each with the option to employ the other as a consultant when the need arises.

Unless the architect is part of a larger professional company employing both disciplines, the services of an engineering consultant will be procured for much of the technical design work, particularly the elements of structure; plumbing, heating, ventilating and air conditioning; electrical; and site work. Engineering consultants may be employed once the architect has been awarded the commission of a building or similar project to design.

In projects where engineering is the prime discipline involved, the engineer will employ the architect to design any buildings that may be part of the project. An example of this type of project would be a utility treatment plant requiring a building to house administrative and control functions.

The Constructor

This text applies the term Constructor to that entity most commonly known in the industry as the Contractor, Prime, or General Contractor. Technically, the constructor is not a contractor until he is a party to a contract; therefore, we will refer to him as "constructor" in the general sense and as "contractor" in the context of his contractual relationship to the owner.

The constructor can be an individual, a partnership, a corporation, or a joint venture. Many states require that constructors who act as general contractors for building projects must be licensed by the state for that purpose. The constructor demonstrates by his experience, education, and financial ability that he is equipped to provide the skills, labor, materials, equipment, and other resources necessary to construct the project required by the owner. Many constructors possess an educational background in engineering, business administration, law and/or a blending of those disciplines.

By the nature of building construction costs, considerable financial capability in the form of capital is required of the constructor. The large sums of money that flow through the constructor's hands as he fulfills his contractual duties require that he be financially sound and well capitalized.

The Subcontractor

The 20th century may be that era in man's history that will be referred to as the "Age of Specialization". In this highly specialized economy, the construction industry has recognized a series of specialized constructors, commonly referred to as subcontractors. These subcontractors have each developed a particular specialty within the scope of the "total project". These specialties usually occur in areas of the project that require individual licensing as well as special skills, tools, or techniques, and unique materials and applications. Subcontractors are employed to perform a defined portion of the construction of a building project. The subcontractor is usually employed directly by and at the discretion of the constructor in his role as prime or general contractor. The term "sub", used as a prefix to the term "contractor", connotes the usual subordinate role of the subcontractor.

Like the constructor, the subcontractor can be an individual, a partnership, a corporation, or a joint venture. Depending upon the needs and approach to construction chosen by the owner, the subcontractor can be employed directly by the general contractor, by the owner or construction manager, or by another subcontractor who may be in a contract relationship to the project through a separate entity.

In the case of the contractor–subcontractor relationship, the subcontractor is not in a direct agreement with the owner since he is not a party to the Contract for Construction, or "Agreement between Owner and Contractor", as it is sometimes called.

This is an important point for the professional who prepares the documents. It will be shown in subsequent chapters that in typical contract documents, where a single contract for construction is awarded, the language should be such as to enforce the contractor's total responsibility for the work to be done. In this instance, the subcontractor, although a recognized entity in the performance of the work, is not a part of the OPC relationship; he is responsible primarily to the contractor with whom he has an agreement, and indirectly to the owner.

The subcontractor is employed by the contractor, usually with the direct or indirect permission of the owner. The subcontractor is obliged to perform his work in accordance with the provisions of the contract between owner and contractor; therefore the conditions of that contract apply to the subcontractor as well.

When a company that normally performs work as a subcontractor is employed directly by the owner, the construction manager, or the project manager, that subcontractor is then identified as a "separate contractor". In this relationship, (although his work may be identical to that which he might perform under contract with a general contractor), the agreement provides a direct relationship with the owner and requires cooperation with other contractors under similar contracts with the owner.

Primary Subcontractors

Primary Subcontractors perform definable portions of the work that may require licensing by the state and/or subdivision responsible for issuing building or construction permit certificates. Primary subcontractors are generally identified as those who perform the work of providing and installing equipment and accessories related

to the following:
- Plumbing
- Heating, Ventilating and Air Conditioning
- Electrical
- Specialized Equipment, Design and Installation

Secondary Subcontractors

The list of secondary subcontractors is long and not as well defined as that of primary subcontractors. Secondary subcontractors perform definable portions of the work requiring special skills, applications, tools and/or equipment. However, secondary subcontractors are not generally required to possess special licensing by the state and/or subdivision. Secondary subcontractors could include but are not limited to work in the following areas:
- Earthwork and/or Paving
- Concrete Placement and Finishing
- Masonry
- Steel Erection
- Carpentry
- Moisture and Thermal Protection
- Insulation
- Sheet Metal
- Glass & Glazing
- Painting and/or Decorating
- Tile
- Flooring
- Ceiling

Sub-subcontractors

The sub-subcontractor is a separate entity in a contractual relationship with a subcontractor who is, in turn, in a contractual relationship with a contractor or other third party. Some examples of possible sub-subcontractors are listed below:
- Concrete Finishing
- Welding
- Gypsum Board Installation
- Finish Material Installation
- Special Carpentry
- Special Equipment Installation

Materialmen

In an entrepreneurial economy, such as that which exists in the United States, manufacturers of construction materials are subject to keen competition among their peers for the market of their goods and services. The demand for competitive prices coupled with the desire for quality and performance of building components and systems has given rise to the job of the architectural or engineering representative, more commonly referred to as the materialman. These manufacturers' representatives are usually persons who have developed a professional knowledge of the use, cost, and best application of a particular product or products manufactured by a certain company. The materialman is both salesman and expert in assisting the professional and constructor in the proper application of his product. The materialman will usually furnish catalogs and samples to users and purchasers of the wares he represents and is constantly on the alert for opportunities to sell his product.

This chapter has reviewed the major components and most prominent roles played in the wide and diversified construction industry. The importance of the OPC relationship has been noted, and the roles of those who serve each owner, professional, and constructor have been defined. Subsequent chapters describe the professional documents used by these participants, and outline the composition of the documents as well as the issues and concerns that commonly affect their use. As the world looks to the twenty-first century, we hope and trust that the "players" in the industry will see and note that excellence in communication is a key ingredient for continuing prosperity. Understanding the need for and content of professional documentation of building construction is an important step toward this goal—for professional documents are the common "touchstones"—perhaps the very essence of one of the largest industries and endeavors of the new century.

Chapter 2
THE HISTORY & INFLUENCE OF LABOR

The dawn of the machine age in Europe came at a time when young America was developing its first growing pains. In centuries past, the primary issue in building construction was not the time required for completion, but rather the quality of workmanship and degree of ornamentation, and the extent and complexity of the fenestration. The master builders of ages past could afford to use time to advantage. Competition among the trades and guilds was not as keen as it would become in later years. Burgeoning populations provided an excess of workers for the building process and the master builders could pick and choose, hire and fire, and set wage rates at levels that suited the budget, if not the needs of the worker.

The technology which has allowed man to build larger and more quickly has also created complications which have profoundly influenced the quality and quantity of Labor. Technology not only transformed man's ability to build, it drastically changed the availability and value of man's labor.

Before the discovery of labor-saving, energy intensive devices, building construction relied chiefly on man's brute strength to extract, refine, transport, and place the materials. The common laborer, more in demand for his brawn than for his brain or skill, was the mainstay of the building construction industry until the middle of the 20th century. With the advent of increasingly specialized machinery, brute force is no longer the chief qualification of the laborer in American construction.

Specialization

Organized labor as we know it today seems to have had its beginnings in the "collegia opificum", committees which began to emerge in the early days of the Roman Empire. According to Plutarch, the Greek historian of the first century, the emperor Numa Pompilius, the second king of Rome, distributed the workers by their trades into companies or guilds. There were at least 30 of these guilds, called "collegia", or "corporia" in Rome at the beginning of the third century A.D. Their existence was based upon statutory authority—the "lex collegii", and they were subject to the administration of "magistri". Thus we see not only the beginnings of labor law, but the origins of such institutions as the college, the corporation, and the magistrate, or judge. The fate of the collegia and the corporia after the fall of the

Western Roman Empire in 476 A.D. is largely unknown, but there seems no doubt that these Roman institutions were the forerunners of the medieval guild systems that predominated in Europe through the beginning of the eighteenth century.

The Labor Movement

The first labor unions and labor laws developed in the beginning of the eighteenth century, when the ability to harness natural energy led to manufacturing and employment opportunities for great masses of skilled and semi-skilled workers. The so called "Machine Age" came to the United States just as masses of immigrant workers were pouring into a "new land of opportunity". With the machines came employment, and with employment came abuses of employees by their employers.

The term, "Industrial Revolution", was first popularized by Arthur Toynbee in the late nineteenth century. He referred to the phenomena that accompanied the development of improved spinning and weaving machines, the steam engine, the factory, as well as an explosion of technological, economic, social, and cultural changes. The "Industrial Revolution" had its roots in eighteenth century England, but it is generally thought to have taken hold in the United States in the early nineteenth century. With the Industrial Revolution came new-found means of mass manufacture, as well as the ability to exploit natural forms of energy such as coal and natural gas. With natural energy, electricity could be produced; and electricity would change forever the focus upon manpower as a basic source of energy.

Industry's need for large numbers of workers and the corresponding abuses by greedy and unsympathetic employers brought the need for some form of collective bargaining by employee organizations. The history of labor organizations began when groups of tradesmen, who possessed some similar trade or craft, began organizing into groups that were called "guilds", "brotherhoods", or "mechanics societies". The initial objective of these organizations was to provide sickness and death benefits (unavailable from employers) to the widows and children of members. In addition, proficiency standards were developed among members of a particular trade or skilled group. From these standards have come definitions of achievement levels, such as "apprentice", "journeyman", and "master".

Because of employer opposition to any form of organization that might threaten profits and competition among industries, many of these early trade organizations were forced to operate in secret. As a result, they were often thought of as unlawful, illegal conspiracies that posed a danger to society. From the 1840's until the era of the "New Deal" in the early 1930's, the history of labor organizations was a continuing saga of confrontation between labor and management.

The *American Federation of Labor* (AFL) was organized by Samuel Gompers in 1886. Until that time, semiskilled and unskilled workers had little or no alternative but to work in "sweat shop" conditions of manufacturing plants. Despite the existence of small, independent trade organizations with names such as, "Industrial Workers of the World" and "Knights of Labor", labor was not collectively coordinated or organized, and aside from much active rhetoric, it had little effect in producing any sweeping changes in the plight of the average worker. The AFL was the first successful attempt to unite skilled craftworkers, such as cabinetmakers, blacksmiths, and leather tanners. The building trades department of the

AFL, organized in 1908, became the "umbrella" organization for the craft unions of the construction industry.

In the beginning, the AFL sought to bring the existing labor organizations under its influence, rather than allow rival groups to threaten its own existence. Inevitably, those groups representing the less skilled workers did not receive the same distinction as did those with the most developed skills. The resulting friction brought about the creation of the *Committee for Industrial Organizations* (CIO) in 1935, a move that was taken without the approval of the AFL board of directors. The CIO was branded a treasonous organization and was expelled from the AFL. John L. Lewis, then president of the United Mine Workers of America, a member of CIO, was elected its president. The CIO acted independently from the AFL until 1955, when personal and philosophical differences were put aside, and the two were merged into the AFL-CIO. This organization continues today as the major labor entity in the United States.

These new labor unions, as we have come to call them, could impose upon management the threat that all workers who were members of the union would "strike", or stay away from their jobs unless and until their demands were met. Since the AFL-CIO involved the greater majority of the trades or crafts, the collective ability to demand reform at threat of prolonged strikes became very effective in improving the situation of the average worker in the United States. The word "strike" would from that time have a new and more significant meaning to the average worker and management as well. The unions brought about many benefits other than increased wages; retirement benefits, insurance coverage, and cost of living increases are among them. Portions of annual dues paid by workers into the union organizations were set aside as a special fund, out of which benefits to striking workers could be paid. This fund provided the worker with considerable "staying power" during prolonged strikes and disputes over worker demands. The AFL-CIO and the management of large industries then began a policy of establishing blanket contracts for the conditions and time periods under which member workers would work, a practice which continues to this day.

The forces affecting labor have played no small part in shaping the construction industry, as labor practices and costs can often determine what will get built and what will not. The majority of legislation affecting the industry has come about because of labor. Legislation has invariably come into existence in order to correct some form of abuse or inequity.

Labor Legislation

The *Sherman Anti-Trust Act* of 1890 was enacted in order to check the growth of big business and to prevent industries from creating monopolies in certain areas of commerce. At that time, the oil and steel companies had joined together by forming giant cartels. The term "cartel" is defined as an international syndicate, combine, or trust generally formed to regulate prices and output in a field of business. A cartel acts as a kind "union" among producers. These cartels were designed to provide control of the major markets for unusual self advantage. In 1908, the Supreme Court ruled (in the Sherman Act) that the organization of labor constituted the formation of just such a cartel in that labor, once organized, could fix prices and therefore monopolize and control the wage level. For some time, management used the provisions of this ruling to gain judicial injunctions. In this way, the labor movement was prevented from organizing, and thereby growing.

In 1914, Congress enacted the *Clayton Act*; this legislation was intended to offset the negative effects of the Sherman Anti-Trust Act by allowing labor to organize and to negotiate with a single employer. Management then argued that the unions were organized and controlled by outsiders, not those actually seeking employment. As a result, the terms of the Sherman Act continued to be applied.

In 1931, during the height of the Great Depression, a piece of legislation was enacted that would have a profound effect on the construction and other industries. The *Davis-Bacon Act* provided that wages and fringe benefits on all federal or federally funded projects should not be less than the prevailing rate for each particular trade, as set by the Secretary of Labor of the United States. To ensure that these rates are paid, the bill further provided that a certified accounting of payrolls be submitted to the agency of contract for auditing.

The Davis-Bacon Act created a major advantage for union contractors because the rates set by the Labor Secretary are usually the highest of the latest rates to be negotiated by contract with the union(s) in a particular geographic area. Non-union contractors would usually not be allowed to compete under such circumstances.

Some employers, in order to avoid employing union employees, began a common practice involving the use of "yellow dog" contracts. A "yellow dog" contract was a statement, signed by the prospective employee, as a condition of his employment, stating that he was not, and would not subsequently become, a member of a labor union, nor would he—subject to immediate dismissal—participate in any activity in the organization of a labor union.

The *Norris-LaGuardia Act* in 1932 was the first piece of major legislation that would diminish the power of management over labor. This act, sometimes referred to as the "Anti-Injunction Act", accomplished what the Clayton Act failed to do. It specifically stated that the courts could not intercede on the part of management to prevent formation of labor organizations. It specifically curtailed the power of the courts to issue injunctions and protected the rights of employees to strike and picket peacefully. It declared the "yellow dog" contracts unlawful.

The *National Labor Relations Act* (NLRA), sometimes referred to as the "Wagner Act", was established in 1935. The Wagner Act became a standard framework of procedure and regulation as to the methods by which management-labor relations were to be conducted. Basically, the bill defined and forbade unfair practices by management and, among other provisions, made it unlawful for an employer to discriminate against a union employee for any reason.

Perhaps the most significant provision of NLRA was the establishment of the *National Labor Relations Board* (NLRB). Appointed by the President of the United States, the NLRB became the "clearing house" for management-labor disputes of all kinds. The act also established the concept of "Closed Shop", which characterized management hiring none but union members, as opposed to "Open Shop" practices where non union personnel could be employed as well. Later legislation in the form of the *Taft-Hartley Act* would change the "Closed Shop" concept to "Union Shop", for reasons that we shall see.

In 1938 came the *Fair Labor Standards Act*, commonly referred to as the "Minimum Wage Law". Originally passed in 1938, this law, which has been amended frequently in relation to the current purchasing power of the dollar, established a minimum wage for all workers, with the exception of agricultural workers. It also established a maximum 40 hour work week based on an eight hour day. For overtime, which is defined as any work done in a time frame beyond 40 hours in one week, the law provided for payment at a rate not less than one and one half times the normal hourly rate.

As organized labor became more powerful, a disreputable element began to infiltrate the union ranks. Just after World War II, in 1946, Congress enacted the *Hobbs Act*, sometimes called the "Anti-Racketeering Act". This legislation was designed to protect employers from having to pay "kickbacks" to unscrupulous union "bosses" in order to assure that workers would "show up" for work. To demand such bribes was declared a felony, punishable by time in prison.

Designed to complement the National Labor Relations Act, the *Labor Management Relations Act*, also known as the *Taft-Hartley Act*, was enacted in 1947. Taft-Hartley once more reversed the swing of the pendulum, still leaving labor in a position of power, but bringing the balance of power closer to center. This act was designed to "clean up" certain practices carried out by the management of organized labor, and included forced participation by workers in certain activities. The act also restructured the make-up of the National Labor Relations Board in an attempt to give management a stronger voice to balance that of labor during disputes. This law further provides for establishment of the *Federal Mediation and Conciliation Services*, a group which acts as a third party in mediating disputes. Under Taft-Hartley, the President of the United States can invoke a 90 day "cooling off" period which postpones the negotiations and restricts any action by either side for that period of time.

In the 1950's, there was evidence of widespread graft and corruption among the union executives. *The Landrum-Griffin Act* of 1959 required labor management to be responsible for the funds of union members, and subject to audit. This legislation, together with other federal tax laws, has had a significant impact on the administrative procedures of American business.

The Internal Revenue Act and FICA
The act creating the *Internal Revenue Service* (IRS) together with the *Federal Insurance Contributions Act* (FICA) enacted by Congress in the mid-1930's, mandated a series of income reporting and withholding procedures. This legislation, basic to the collection of federal income taxes and social security contributions, requires any employer in the United States to withhold appropriate sums from the wages of his employees and to pay those amounts directly to the federal government. The keeping of detailed financial records, employee data, time cards, and records of all financial transactions and payments has become fundamental to the process of building construction.

The Williams-Steiger Act (OSHA)
In 1970, the *Occupational Safety and Health Act* (OSHA), sometimes known as the *Williams-Steiger Act*, was passed by the Congress of the United States in order to improve job safety by providing enforcement through the U. S. Department of Labor. This legislation provided for the imposition of fines and penalties for non-conformance to specific

standards and regulations related to protective clothing, tools, equipment, construction procedures and other aspects of building construction. Sometimes known as the "Hard Hat Law" it was such OSHA regulations that made the wearing of construction helmets, commonly known as "hard hats" common practice on the job site.

Finally, in our summary of significant labor legislation, is the issue of Civil Rights. *Title IV of the Civil Rights Act*, enacted in 1964, established the concept of equal employment opportunity. This act expressly forbids discrimination by an employer on the basis of race, color, religion, sex, or national origin. This law is administered by the *Equal Employment Opportunity Commission* (EEOC) and applies to hiring, discharge, conditions of employment, and classification of workers. Executive Order 11246, issued by President Lyndon Johnson in 1965 amplifies Title IV by mandating affirmative action requirements regarding equal employment on all federal or federally funded construction projects. This rule is administered by the *Office of Federal Contract Compliance* (OFCC). This particular agency has been instrumental in ensuring minority contractor participation and opportunity in bidding for federal contracts. Executive Order 11375 extends 11246 by including reference to sex discrimination, thereby extending the minority contractor consideration to specifically include women.

Chapter 3
PROFESSIONAL PRACTICE

Professional practice in the construction industry has come into being for two primary reasons. First, public officials, in order to safeguard the public interest, have enacted licensing laws to govern those who design the built environment. Secondly, licensed practitioners have organized to promote a system of acceptable ethics and excellence in the work of their fellows.

Licensing Requirements

Since the middle of the twentieth century, all 50 of the United States have enacted licensing laws for architects and engineers. These registration procedures require those who wish to become professional practitioners of these disciplines to show explicit qualifications related to education, work place experience, and knowledge of building materials and methods. To these basic requirements are added comprehension of civil, structural, mechanical, and electrical design as well as an understanding of building codes and safety regulations. A candidate for licensing must exhibit, by written examination, a thorough knowledge of the community, the physical environment, and the law in the areas that apply to building construction. An architect or a professional engineer must be well versed in the many facets of labor and material cost, as well as having a good grasp of the amount of time that is required for project construction.

In order to survive in an extremely competitive, but often rewarding career, professionals in the science and art of building construction must be astute businessmen as well as technical experts. Today's professional must have the ability to competitively market services and experience while at the same time making decisions that require large expenditures of his client's money. Good judgment based on knowledge and experience is the professional's stock in trade. His success is generally measured by how well his judgment serves the needs, desires, and economic goals of his client. His survival will depend to a great extent, upon his ability to manage a staff of multi-disciplined personnel, while producing a profit under conditions that limit the fees he can charge for his services. This is why it is called "professional practice".

Industry and Professional Institutions

Professional societies have been formed in each discipline for the purpose of establishing and maintaining the highest of moral and professional ethics. A listing of Professional Societies and related organizations appears in the Appendix. Such professional societies include the American Institute of Architects, the National Society of

Professional Engineers, and others. Active membership in these societies is limited to those who have been licensed by the state(s) and who are in the mainstream of professional practice; associate memberships are available to those who are in the process of professional development. From such professional organizations have come published standards of practice, codes of ethics, suggested formats for the documentation of technical material, recommendations for business practice, and disclosures of advancements in technology for the continuing education of architects, engineers, and those in related fields of professional practice. Most professional societies publish magazines and other literature wherein practitioners share experience and judgment with their peers on technical solutions and other matters of mutual interest.

American Institute of Architects

Since 1857, the *American Institute of Architects* has provided its members with an increasing number of services and support. Its purpose is to foster and sustain functioning members in one of the most demanding of professions. In 1986, the AIA served more than 44,000 member architects in the United States. Membership is three tiered. A member belongs to the national organization, a state wide affiliate, and a local chapter. Thus, the entire membership of AIA is united in common cause with the profession at all levels of society and government. The AIA provides programs of professional development, member and component services, and liaison with government at all levels. Committees work on issues that include historic resources and preservation, regional and urban development, energy and housing. Special committees focus on such subjects as architecture for health, justice, education, and aging.

A primary service of the AIA is providing documents for use by the construction industry. Many of these documents are referenced and or reproduced in this text (by permission of the American Institute of Architects). These documents and their use have important legal consequences and implications. Any user of these documents (or of related information or recommendations in this text) must be fully aware of such consequences and implications. To assure this knowledge, consultation with an attorney is encouraged prior to the use of any documents.

Engineering Societies

Unlike the practice of architecture, professional engineering encompasses many varied and sometimes dissimilar disciplines under one broad subject. The disciplines that most often become involved in the design and construction of building structures are civil engineers, mechanical engineers, and electrical engineers. Out of civil engineering has come structural engineering. Over the years, there have been many different, often competing, often overlapping engineering societies. Among the most prominent of these organizations are the National Society of Professional Engineers (NSPE), the American Consulting Engineer's Council (ACEC), and the American Society of Civil Engineers (ASCE), to mention but a few. In recent years, work on professional engineering documents has been carried out by organizations, such as American Institute of Architects (AIA), Construction Specifications Institute (CSI), and Associated General Contractors (AGC), working together jointly. To create a common voice, the major engineering societies created an organization which has come to be called *Engineers Joint Contract Documents Committee* (EJCDC).

Associated General Contractors of America

Constructors, or those who manage the construction of buildings and related structures, have not yet been recognized with the same degree of professional status throughout the industry as have licensed architects and engineers. There is a growing trend in the industry today that may eventually change that image and status for contractors, general contractors, and subcontractors. Many states now require general contractors and those subcontractors who install mechanical and electrical systems in buildings to be licensed by the state. Just as professional societies have been organized around the various professional disciplines. Similar organizations have been created around various trade oriented groups. Such an organization is the *Associated General Contractors of America* (AGC).

Just as many professional societies began to appear at the end of the nineteenth century, building contractors also began to organize. In the early 1900's there were as many as 100 organizations dedicated to building construction alone. The AGC was organized in November 1918 in Chicago as a result of a meeting of prominent general contractors whose aim was to establish a single, strong, national organization of contractor members to act for the benefit of all. Today there are over 8,400 AGC members in 112 local chapters throughout the United States. Of these, 1,300 members serve on 70 national committees dealing with such varied issues as labor, collective bargaining, safety, health, infrastructure, taxation and a variety of other related subjects.

Construction Specifications Institute

There is one organization made up of members from all levels of the construction industry. The *Construction Specifications Institute* (CSI) is a non-profit technical organization dedicated to the improvement of professional documentation, more specifically to the improvement of specifications and building practices through service, education, and research. Founded in 1948, CSI provides a forum for architects, engineers, contractors, subcontractors, material manufacturers, suppliers, and others in the construction industry.

Before the days of organizations such as CSI, there was no universally accepted format for the preparation of professional documents in the United States. The language of construction varied from state to state, city to city. Often even the definitions of items commonly used in construction varied greatly. For example, a suspended ceiling in one locale might be a furred ceiling in another, a modular ceiling in yet another. The character and organization of the specifications was left to to the discretion of the individual specifier. As buildings and systems became more complex and interwoven through a maze of interrelationships of contractor, subcontractor, and supplier, the bidding process became more and more difficult, and disputes and misunderstandings became more common and acute.

The CSI was organized not to be just another in a profusion of self serving professional societies, but rather an organization which drew its membership from the whole of the construction industry. As an industry oriented organization, CSI has given a universally understood definition to the language of construction, and a common format to the writing of construction specifications. The contributions of CSI to the industry are many, but the improvements in communication and understanding of professionally prepared contract documents are among the most significant in the history of the industry.

Construction Management

A professional is defined as one who practices a learned skill or an art. There has always been a sharp distinction between the professional and the non-professional. Academicians, physicians, attorneys, architects, and engineers have been thought of as professionals. Constructors, mechanics, farmers, and merchants, on the other hand, have been considered non-professionals. Professionals have been distinguished by their degrees of learning (or education) and ability to use their knowledge in performing a service. Non-professionals have been characterized by the work that they do or the product that they produce. Professionals are compensated by a fee. Non-professionals are compensated by a wage or a price. The coming view of management of the construction process is seen as a service compensated by a fee, requiring expertise, knowledge and learning. At the beginning of the twentieth century, a wide distinction was made in the construction industry between professionals and non-professionals. Architects and engineers were considered professionals while contractors, subcontractors, manufacturer's representatives and tradesmen were generally thought of as non-professionals. Today, the greater majority of the latter group are well qualified by experience and education to be thought of a professionals. Further, many are trained and licensed as architects and engineers. Today, it is not uncommon for the construction process to be rendered as a service, managed and compensated on the basis of a fee.

Construction Management is a term that is becoming more prominent in the construction industry today. For almost two centuries, the general contractor has been looked upon as both constructor and manager of the construction process. The separation of the functions of design from implementation, or construction, has been viewed as an ethical as well as a practical matter. The idea has traditionally prevailed that the design professional is in a better position to advise his client if he has no financial interest or other bias in the construction process. At the same time, if the general contractor is an unsupervised manager of the construction process, there is the possibility that he might extract unusual profits by substituting inferior materials and methods in a building. Because of the potential for loss to the owner, the design professional has traditionally been employed—as an unbiased administrator—to represent the owner's interest during construction. This system of checks and balances has held in place a relationship between professional and constructor that, while adversarial in some respects, has been mutually respectful for many decades.

The growth of technology and the complexity of the modern commercial or institutional building structure require not only comprehension and ability on the part of the professional who conceives and documents the design, but also upon a high degree of skill, knowledge and education on the part of the constructor. Today, a very high percentage of the nation's constructors are themselves licensed professionals, either engineers or architects, by training and/or experience. Organizations such as the AGC and the CSI, and the ethical and supportive service that each provides have had much influence in raising the image of the constructor to a position of near professionalism. With the increasing growth of construction management, the awarding of multiple prime contracts, and the phased construction of buildings, the image and the responsibility of the constructor is changing. Many owners are successfully turning to the concepts of design/build or "fast track" contracts in order to save precious time as well as money. Since construction costs involve a significant percentage of the economy, the creation of a new discipline—the *Professional Constructor* may be near at hand.

Ethics and Protocol

Over the years, the primary method for selecting the constructor has been competitive bidding. By awarding a contract for construction to the low bidder, the owner is reasonably assured that his building will be delivered at the best available price. With the architect or the engineer to oversee the construction and to administer the terms of the contract including payment, the owner has further assurance that the building will be built according to the requirements of the contract documents. This balance of ethics and conventional protocol has served the construction industry reasonably well throughout its history in the United States. This "traditional" approach remains as a requirement by many public laws concerned with the expenditure of public funds.

For a general contractor to establish a secure and successful business, some unusual risks may be taken. History has shown that the contractor's expected profit is in the average range of two to seven percent of the total contract price. Any mistake made in preparation of the bid price could seriously affect the business' economic well being, particularly if the loss exceeds the expected profit. Survival in the field of building construction has become a game of wit and ingenuity as well as an art requiring great business acumen and daring. The ability of the American building contractor, as the low bidder, to take on a project and produce that project on time and profitably has become one of the absolute wonders of the world. The key to this phenomenon has been innovation. With innovative ideas such as "tilt wall" construction, the reusable "flying form", component prefabrication, labor saving tools, computerized scheduling, and many more new ideas and techniques, it has been the American contractor who has taught the rest of the world how to get a seemingly impossible job done, with a profit and on time. This is not to say, however, that *every* project is successful. There remains the possibility that the contractor might somehow become insolvent while in the process of fulfilling the contract requirements. In this event, the potential loss to the owner can be very high. Even though a great deal of care and expense may have been taken to prepare a complete and thorough set of contract documents, and despite the fact that the owner may recover damages for breach of contract, a money judgment against a financially irresponsible contractor is, at best, an inadequate remedy. For the owner's protection, a system has been established using certain types of bonds. These bonds can be purchased by the contractor (at the insistence of the owner) to protect the owner in the case of loss through the contractor's failure to perform. Chapter 5 deals in some detail with bid bonds, performance bonds and payment bonds as part of the industry-wide protocol of building construction contracting.

Supervision vs. Administration
There has been some confusion in the construction industry regarding the responsibility, or more specifically the liability, of the design

professional for supervision of the construction process. It should be made absolutely clear that under most commonly used forms of agreement, the role of the design professional during construction is one of administrative representation of the owner and not that of supervisor of the actual construction.

To rule out the possible misconception that the architect or engineer is responsible for the contractor's performance, the language of contract agreements and conditions has become very specific. The professional's responsibility to the owner and relationship to the contractor are both made very clear. Some have argued that because the architect or engineer is in a supervisory position, he should be responsible if the contractor fails in any way to meet the intention of the contract documents. Such is not the case for the following reasons. First of all, the professional is not a party to the contract between owner and contractor. Secondly, it is not the responsibility of the architect or engineer to conduct an exhaustive investigation of the contractor's work at the job site. Articles 1.5.3 and 1.5.4 of AIA Document B141— *Standard Form of Agreement Between Owner and Architect*, state:

> "1.5.3. The Architect shall be a representative of the Owner during the Construction Phase (of the project), and shall advise and consult with the Owner. Instructions to the Contractor shall be forwarded through the Architect. The Architect shall have authority to act on behalf of the Owner only to the extent provided by the contract documents unless otherwise modified by written instrument . . ."

> "1.5.4. The Architect shall visit the site at intervals agreed by the Architect in writing to become generally familiar with the process and quality of the work and to determine in general if the Work is proceeding in accordance with the Contract Documents. However, the Architect shall not be required to make exhaustive or continuous inspections to check the quality or quantity of the work . . ."

AIA Document A201—*General Conditions of the Contract for Construction*, has been drafted and otherwise approved by a joint committee of construction industry representatives. It is typical of such documents that accompany, modify, and are otherwise (by reference) a part of an Agreement between Owner and Contractor. Article 2.2.4 of AIA Document A201 states:

> "2.2.4. The Architect will not be responsible for and will not have control or charge of construction means, methods, techniques, sequences or procedures, or for safety precautions and programs in connection with the work; and he will not be responsible for the contractor's failure to carry out the Work in accordance with the Contract Documents. The Architect will not be responsible for or have control or charge of the acts or omissions of the Contractor, Subcontractors, or any of their agents, employees, or any other persons performing the work."

Such contract documents avoid use of the word, "supervise" in establishing the role of the professional. Further, the documents suggest that the professional will only discharge administrative kinds of duties. The language of an Agreement between Owner and Contractor will, in most instances, stipulate that the Architect or Engineer is not responsible for the actual means and methods of construction, nor for any undetected error that the contractor might make during construction.

Contract "protocol" has evolved along with the many "self-healing" remedies that are constantly incorporated into that body of documents we call the "Contract Documents". AIA Document A201—*General Conditions of the Contract for Construction*, has developed through a number of editions during the period 1857 to 1976. The most prominent of these editions have appeared in the years 1963, 1967, 1970 and the current edition dated 1976. Other forms, such as the *Standard General Conditions of the Construction Contract*, published by the Engineer's Joint Contract Documents Committee (EJCDC), have undergone similar revisions. Documents such as these have stood the test of time in usage, have been consistently revised to reflect solutions to common problems in the field, and have been recognized by the courts as reflecting accepted industry practice and thus as an aid in adjudicating disputes. Both the AIA form and the EJCDC documents have been debated, coordinated and negotiated by study/recommendation committees from a wide cross section of the industry, and therefore reflect the accepted thinking of the industry.

Chapter 7 deals specifically with the General Conditions of the Contract in greater detail. Chapter 6 addresses the Contract for Construction and will explore, in some depth, the elements that make up the Bidding Documents, the Contract Documents, and that combination of information we call the "Construction Documents".

Quality and Competition

Americans take pride in a spirit of competition and the fact that we have one of the most vital and powerful economies in the world today. Our success has been the product of ingenuity and energy, coupled with the competitive spirit by which we conduct our day-to-day business. Our system, however, is not without disadvantages. Building construction at the lowest price, if left purely to the demands of competition and without some kind of informed quality control, could suffer diminishing quality in both materials and labor. There must be some form of final authority responsible to the owner, who can act as the element of balance in project construction. This is the role of the design professional.

The quality of a product cannot always be determined from a cursory inspection by the architect or engineer. In order to give the professional the "tools" by which to measure quality, the construction industry has, over the years, created a number of industry organizations. These organizations establish and publish many varied standards of quality and performance for materials and methods. Such "Reference Standards", have become part and parcel of professionally prepared Contract Documents. These standards form not only a reference for information, but also a standard of quality by which items in dispute can be measured and judged.

Documentation: The Professional's Product

Before this century, it was not necessary to document every decision before the commencement of construction. The master builder could work out many details, answer questions and perform many of the design functions on the job site during the actual construction process. The age of machines turned time into the most valuable commodity on the job site. The cost relationship between materials and labor had been two to one at the beginning of the eighteenth century; by the nineteenth century, the ratio was one and a half to one. Currently, labor costs are exceeding material costs. While mass production has substantially reduced the cost of most material, labor laws have created a shorter work week without a reduction in pay; workers receive not only higher hourly wages, but more fringe benefits as well. Most cost estimators now know to expect that of the total net cost of a building, 45% will be materials and 55% will be labor.

The professional has had to become increasingly aware of cost relative to the designs that he produces. In the early stages of project development, programming according to budget is most important. Decisions made during this stage of project development set the parameters of the project and can seldom be extended. In the case of private projects, it is at the preliminary stage that the owner often consults with his banker or lender and receives a commitment which establishes the limit of finances (leverage) in the project. Public projects must be financed out of general funds or with general obligation bonds. This process may even require a public referendum which must be passed before any funds can be spent on the project. In any event, the budget is established in the early, conceptual phases of a project and must be respected and adhered to all the way from project development through construction.

The quality of professionally prepared documents is important to help keep a project within budget. If the documents are incomplete or contain errors, conflicts, or ambiguities, the bidder will be confused as he attempts to prepare a winning, low bid. In order to protect himself, the bidder may have to include enough money in the bid price to cover any flaws in the documents that may cause unexpected expense during the construction. Disorganized, haphazard documents also add "hidden", or unexpected cost because of the difficulty the contractor may have in following the requirements of the project.

It is important that the professional preparing the documents communicate effectively with those who use them. The constructor who is awarded the job is the person who will carry the total responsibility for seeing that the building is constructed; it is his convenience that should be uppermost in the preparer's mind. Next on the list of priorities are the subtrades. The information contained in the documents must be conveniently arranged so as not to confuse the tradesmen who bid to the contractor. Lastly, the manufacturers of products contained in the project must be kept in mind; data describing each product must be placed in such a way that the product can be conveniently estimated and quantities ordered during construction.

Communicating with the Estimator

The construction estimator is the constructor's first line of offense and defense. The constructor's ability to offer a total price for a project that is low enough to be accepted (in competition with his peers), and yet sufficient to produce a profit, requires a precise effort from the estimator.

The design professional preparing the contract documents (particularly drawings and specifications) should strive to make the job of the contractor's estimator as easy as possible. Typically, the design professional will spend months preparing his documentation while the estimator may only have a few weeks to study the documents and prepare a "take-off" or quantity survey of the work required to construct the project. Uniformity in the coordination and organization of the documents is extremely helpful to the estimator during the bidding or negotiation process. Considering the pressures of time and the volume of detail facing the estimator, the preparer of documents should present the information in such a way that it can be readily grasped and understood. The sixteen Division format (Masterformat) of the Construction Specifications Institute (CSI) is universally accepted in the industry and has proven to be extremely useful in the organization and presentation of data.

CSI has published, and continues to edit and upgrade the CSI *Manual of Practice*. This book, along with "Masterformat" are publications available from the Construction Specifications Institute, 601 Madison Avenue, Alexandria, VA 22314. (The preparation of the Project Manual is discussed in more detail in Chapter 8. The use of "Masterformat" is discussed in Chapter 9). The CSI *Manual of Practice* contains recommended procedures for preparing the Project Manual as the primary instrument of the Construction Documents. The guidelines offered in this manual are both industry endorsed and proven by usage in the field.

Communicating with the Contractor

The contractor has been identified as the primary resource for labor, material, and the implementation of the means and methods of construction. The contractor, acting under contractual agreement with the owner, depends upon documentation created by the professional, defining the work to be done. Professionally prepared construction documents provide the primary definition and control of the contractor's task. Good communication between the professional and the contractor is essential if a building project is to be constructed in a timely, profitable manner, to the mutual credit of the construction triad—owner, professional, and constructor.

Professional documentation should address the *contractor* (general or prime) only. While it is a worthy objective to identify the tasks of individual crafts and trades, it must be remembered that it is the contractor who is responsible to the owner. Thus, all information should be addressed to the contractor. The various trades, crafts, vendors and subcontractors look to the contractor to define the scope of their work and to coordinate their efforts. If the professional documents in any way circumvent the contractor's authority (by defining work that is rightfully the contractor's option to define and to contract for), the documents will not serve the purpose for which they are intended. Examples of proper and improper documentation are discussed in subsequent chapters of this text.

It is during the bidding or negotiation phases of project development that the communicative quality of professional documents plays a key role. The contractor's *estimator* is the first of many on the contractor's team who will come into contact with the work of the professional. The estimator must be able to quickly comprehend the scope of the work to be done, and with his staff, must be able to account for that work in both a quantitative and qualitative way. Quantities of materials must include allowances for the waste and loss that will invariably occur during construction. Labor must be measured—not only in terms of man-hours required to assemble or install the materials and systems, but also for scheduling the most efficient sequence and timing by which those items and elements must fit together. The estimator must decide what equipment, tools, and vehicles will be required; which available trades, crafts, and subcontracted services will be appropriate to the job; and the extent to which temporary services will be required. The estimator must also know the job requirements and cost of insurance premiums, building permits, taxes, temporary utilities, cartage fees, clean-up and trash removal, testing expenses, and other special services. The estimator's experience alone provides some understanding of the potential cost of delays, waste, human error, and coordination failures.

The contractor is called upon, in most cases, to deliver a project at a total cost which, when competitively bid, will be lower than that offered by his peers, yet sufficient to afford the quality of materials and workmanship demanded by the professional and the owner. Further, the project must be completed in a timely fashion according to the terms of the contract with the owner. Finally, the price must allow a profit for the contractor. It is little wonder that in the latter half of the twentieth century, the opportunity for success among general contractors is becoming limited. Professional documents that are disorganized, vague, incomplete, and contradictory are a major contributor to the early demise of many otherwise competent construction companies. It is incumbent upon the professional to constantly seek ways and means to improve the communicative quality of his documents, to better coordinate information, and to make a complete definition of the work to be done. To further these causes, such organizations as AIA, NSPE, CSI, and AGC have individually and collectively dedicated a significant effort toward the development of standard documents and manuals of practice.

Communicating with the Trades

It has been said that the professional documents should be addressed to the contractor. This in no way implies that indirect communication should not exist with the various trades, crafts, and subcontractor services that are appropriate to carry out major portions of the work. Being aware of the work of these trades can often determine the strategy by which the drawings are organized and the specifications sections written.

Just as the contractor's estimating staff develops a statement of the total work to be done for bidding and negotiating purposes, the various sub-trades will likewise review the documentation and isolate the work that is the specialty of each. Based on this evaluation, they will make their own proposal to the various constructors who are bidding the project. The documents should efficiently, yet indirectly accommodate the various sub-trades so that each can not only define the appropriate portions of the work, but also get a clear understanding of all of the associated costs.

Communicating with Construction Suppliers

Professional documents should clearly identify those manufacturers and products which are best suited, or which can be used as standards of quality by which to judge similar products to be used in the project. This task becomes more complicated when the owner (by law or for other reasons) requires that all material or labor items be open to the widest possible latitude of competitive bidding. Chapter 5 of this text deals with the bidding process in much more detail. The placement of copies of the bidding documents with "plan rooms" and through other construction information services and bureaus will assure the widest possible distribution and advertisement of bidding opportunities among the many manufacturers and vendors who supply the construction industry.

Economic Objectives and Considerations

The economic objectives of the owner should be of primary concern to the professional preparing the documents. An owner who has been well served will most certainly be willing to recommend or re-employ that professional. The owner's best interest is not only the ethical goal, but it also insures the professional's survival in business over future years.

Professional documents should define, demand, and reasonably ensure high quality standards, in keeping with the best interest of the owner. Standards which allow the use of inferior methods and materials (in the interest of assuring the lowest possible initial cost) are not always in the best interest of the owner. The professional must exercise judgment during the design and selection of materials and methods to benefit the owner—not only in terms of the construction budget, but during the defined life cycle of the project as well. Experience shows that the initial construction cost of a building may be only 10% to 15% of the cost to maintain and operate the building during its lifetime. Continuing energy, maintenance, and replacement costs are a tremendous factor when considered over a period of 25 to 30 years. The current science of value engineering deals with the economics of construction materials and methods when the initial cost is compared with the predictable, continuing costs of maintenance and replacement.

Economic Considerations of the Professional

In the early years of organizations such as the AIA, NSPE, and others, it was commonplace for professional societies to establish and publish minimum fee schedules. These schedules set forth standard minimum fees for defined professional services. These standards had been agreed upon by a majority of professionals within a common discipline and were generally accepted among owners in the private and public sectors. Professionals were largely exempt from having to compete with each other solely on the basis of fee. Competition was instead based on depth of experience, the quality of the staff, and the professional's ability to respond to an owner's needs quickly and efficiently. Many owners investigate the professional's background and success as measured by the quality of references provided by other clients.

In the late 1960's and early 1970's, several events occurred that would drastically change the competition among professionals. In several cases, a professional was selected on the basis of fees lower than called for by the minimum fee schedule. Several professional societies objected on grounds that the lowered fee was a violation of the basic code of ethics. The professionals who were challenged argued that for various reasons, their services required a much lower "overhead" cost than that of their competitors, and therefore, the lower fee was valid. Several cases were litigated and the results favored the position of the party opting for the lowered fee. The Supreme Court eventually ruled that the Minimum Fee Schedules maintained by the professional societies were unlawful in that they were a violation of "price fixing" provisions of the Sherman Anti-Trust Act.

Since the ruling on published fee schedules, professionals have come under increasing pressure to compete on the basis of fee as well as qualification. As a result, professional practitioners today are forced to "streamline" services in order to adequately serve the needs of clients—while remaining competitive in their fee structure.

Economic Considerations of the Contractor

Factors such as growing competition, regulation, and government and union wage controls have lead many constructors to avoid competitive bidding situations. For every successful bidder in the construction marketplace, there are usually several who are unsuccessful. The "cost" of entering the bidding competition has become extremely high. Those constructors who are unsuccessful must pass along to other projects the costs incurred by bidding, or be forced out of business. For these reasons, a growing number of successful construction organizations are opting to negotiate contracts, or to provide complete "turn-key", design-build services, thus avoiding competitive bidding. These types of contracts and their implications upon professionally prepared documents are discussed in greater detail in Chapter 6.

Economic Considerations of Subcontractors

The protocol and ethic that exists between the contractor and subcontractor is not as clear-cut as the owner-professional-constructor relationship in the competitive bidding or negotiating process. Bidding among subcontractors to general contractors is extremely competitive and unfortunately does not always exhibit the confidentiality and ethics that exist among general contractors bidding to owners. There is a growing tendency for many subcontractors to "build" a continuing relationship with a limited number of general contractors with whom an established degree of trust and mutual support has developed. These "alliances" offer advantages to both contractor and subcontractor for a number of reasons, not the least of which is mutual survival in a climate of increasing competition and economic uncertainty. Allied subcontractors who can depend upon a particular contractor for a predictable annual work volume can often be flexible enough in pricing to give the allied contractor considerable advantage in the competitive bidding process.

Although the contractor has the direct responsibility for the work of his subcontractors, owners and design professionals are becoming more concerned with the contractor's selection of subcontractors. In today's economy, it is not unusual for a higher and higher percentage of the total work to be performed by subcontractors. Major subcontractors such as the plumber, the mechanical (HVAC) contractor, and the electrician may collectively accomplish up to 50% of the work. Any failure of a major subcontractor who represents 15% or more of the work could cause a corresponding failure on the part of the prime contractor. For this reason, subcontractors are more and more often required to provide bonding, insurance and evidence of financial stability before being approved by the owner or design professional. Other subcontractor issues are discussed in subsequent chapters.

For centuries, the master builder was also the architect, engineer, artist, and construction manager. He was recognized and employed because of his years of training and apprenticeship. From the guild system of the middle ages came the modern day schools of engineering and architecture. Professional degrees were first awarded in the eighteenth and nineteenth centuries. In the twentieth century, government, recognizing the need to preserve the safety of the human environment, enacted licensing laws, with registration procedures for the disciplines of engineering and architecture.

The licensed professional of today must deal with an explosion of new technology, law, government involvement, and keen competition.

Although the conditions under which he must practice have changed along with his tools and methods, the product of his effort has not. His concern in the construction process is giving the building its form and supporting the project with professional documents. The remaining chapters of this book are dedicated to a better understanding of those documents—how they are created, and what functions they perform.

Chapter 4
LEGAL CONCERNS AND PROFESSIONAL INSURANCE

A construction worker is permanently injured from a fall off a scaffold from which he was working, when an erection clip, welded to the face of a steel column and supporting one end of the scaffold, fails. As a result of the accident, a man is confined to a wheelchair for the rest of his life. Who is responsible? How is the workman compensated for the loss of the use of his legs? At a high school under construction, thieves break in and steal some valuable laboratory equipment. Who pays for the loss? Does it come out of the contractor's profit? Does the owner have to pay for the equipment twice? Lightning sets fire to a building that is under construction. Who pays for the re-construction to repair the fire damage? A fire in the basement of a highrise hotel causes the death of several guests on another floor from smoke inhalation. A school child contracts lung cancer, a disease now associated with exposure to asbestos, a material once used in quantity to provide fire protection in the structure of elementary schools. These kinds of problems and many others can occur in the modern building construction process. Many have dramatic financial or physical effects, both on the parties to the contract and on others who are indirectly related to the project.

The capitalist economy of the United States is based in large part upon risk. A farmer risks the cost of seed, equipment, employees and his own labor against the forces of nature in order to produce a profitable crop. An owner risks his capital to build a commercial building in hopes that future tenants will prosper there, bringing a profitable return on investment in the form of increased rents and service charges. A constructor studies the contract documents prepared for an owner who has advertised for receipt of competitive bids. In preparing his bid, and in order to achieve the favored position of being the "low" bidder, the constructor takes a risk on profits and gambles on his ability to manage according to his estimate of cost and labor. The construction worker, injured in the fall, takes a calculated risk to work on a scaffold high in the air, though he does have a right to trust the tools that he was provided by his employer. A school board takes a calculated risk in awarding the contract for construction, based on trust of the contractor's ability to construct and protect the property during construction. The guest in the hotel takes a risk in selecting a hotel while away from home, but he has a right to trust the safety of the building's design.

The legal responsibilities surrounding the activities of the construction industry are of no small concern to owners, design professionals, contractors, subcontractors, material suppliers, manufacturers, skilled workers and other employees who rely upon the industry for their livelihood. Also involved are the various branches of government that serve the community, the state and the nation. From these mutual concerns, a series of laws has evolved. These laws are designed to accommodate and define the complex legal relationships of the construction industry.

The Agreement, or Contract for Construction, deals with the direct, or voluntary, legal responsibilities of the involved parties. The Contract Documents define the work to be done, the contractor agrees to do the work, and the owner agrees to pay. The contractor places purchase orders for materials and arranges subcontracts for certain defined work within his responsibility. These direct agreements are made on a voluntary basis and the covenant between the parties is reasonably clear.

The project also involves legal responsibilities that are indirect or involuntary. Take the case of the permanently injured construction worker. All 50 of the United States now require all employers to purchase Worker Compensation Insurance. This insurance provides (by a third party agreement) compensation to an injured worker for medical expenses and loss of income as a result of injury on the job. The third party in this case is a surety or insurance company. However, if the fall is proven to be the result of some form of negligence on the part of someone other than the injured worker's employer, such as the contractor, his employees, or subcontractor(s), the responsible party may be liable for the entire legal damages sustained by the worker. If the worker cannot recover his ability to work in the manner to which he was accustomed, the contractor's liability may extend to compensation in proportion to the loss of income and ability suffered by the worker for an extended period of time, as well as compensation for such intangible losses as pain and suffering. This liability on the part of the contractor is an involuntary legal responsibility. Likewise, if some portion of the building fails to properly function, and that failure results in a loss to the owner or a third party, the contractor and/or others may become involuntarily responsible. In many cases, the so-called negligence may be proved a contributory factor, that is, others involved in the construction process might be shown to have contributed in some part to the failure of the erection clip that caused the fall of the injured worker. In this case, the steel fabricator, under purchase order from the contractor, assembled and fabricated the structural steel components of the building. The erector, under subcontract to the contractor, erected the fabricated steel components and performed the welding of the erection clip to the face of the column flange. The testing laboratory, appointed by the owner, was commissioned to perform periodic testing of welds performed on the job and in the shop. Perhaps it can be shown that all of the parties to the construction process had some responsibility for the failure of the erection clip, and the ensuing injury to the worker. In such a case, the injured worker may seek to enforce his claim against any or all of the responsible parties. In most states, a party that pays more than its pro rata share of damages may seek "contribution" from the other parties responsible for the injury.

The amount of compensation finally paid to the injured worker could be a substantial sum. What is the value of a man's earning ability in the future? How many advancements would he have made in the course of years? How long would he remain able to work at capacity? What is a proper amount of compensation for those years, whatever their number? What is fair compensation for a permanent injury and a lifetime of pain and suffering? Agreement on these questions is not easily reached by the parties directly involved. Unlike commercial disputes involving contractual relationships which are often submitted to arbitration, liability claims involving personal injury often result in costly and time consuming lawsuits and expose the responsible parties to substantial and even ruinous damage awards following a jury trial.

Settlement of Disputes

The case of fair and equitable compensation for a permanently injured worker is but one example of the types of problems that can arise during the construction process. Disputes can arise for any number of reasons over the complicated relationships that exist in the construction process. For example, sometime after the building is completed, a severe roof leak causes considerable damage to the interior of the building and its contents. The owner looks to the contractor to repair the leak and to compensate him for the resulting damage and loss of use. The contractor, in turn, looks to the roofing subcontractor who installed the work surrounding the apparent failure. The roofing contractor points out that the leak happened because of damage done to his work by the mechanical subcontractor who installed the rooftop mechanical equipment after the roof was in place. The mechanical contractor claims that his work meets all of the requirements of the Contract Documents prepared by the design professional. The design professional looks to his consultant engineer who designed the system that was installed on the roof. Which individual was at fault? Did both subcontractors contribute to the problem? Was the building design somehow inadequate? Was the contractor's superintendent careless in not discovering the problem as the work was being done? Perhaps the mechanical contractor was at fault, but has since died or declared bankruptcy; what then? What if the general contractor was no longer in business?

Arbitration

One of the two methods of solving the dispute over who is responsible, who pays and how much is to be paid is the process of *arbitration*. Under this method, a panel is convened of knowledgeable, outside third parties to the dispute. This panel reviews the facts and makes a determination that is equitable to the parties that are concerned. Under the current Construction Industry Arbitration Rules of the American Arbitration Association, unless the parties to the dispute agree otherwise, each party appoints an arbitrator to the panel and the appointed arbitrators agree upon and appoint another arbitrator. The parties agree to be bound by the findings and determinations of the arbitrators, either by previous agreement in the body of the related agreements to the Contract for Construction, or by agreement prior to convening the Arbitration Panel. Arbitration is mentioned in AIA Document A201—*General Conditions of the Contract for Construction* and further defined in AIA Document A101—*Standard Form of Agreement between Owner and Contractor*. The facts of the case, the various contracts by which each is related to the other, the claims made by each, and other issues pertinent to the case are then studied and debated. Sworn testimony of witnesses is given and other evidence is presented by a variety of methods. Through this procedure, the opportunity is given to present all of the facts surrounding the issue. Once the facts are disclosed, each arbitrator privately presents an opinion to the panel. A common opinion is then arrived at among the panel of arbitrators and a recommended solution is delivered. Without a contract provision requiring arbitration, the parties to a dispute always have litigation in the courts as a final resort. However, many favor the arbitration process and tend to discourage litigation because of the time, expense, and likelihood that the results of any settlement derived from the courts would vary substantially from that found by a panel of unbiased experts.

Litigation

The second option in settling disputes is litigation. Litigation is determined by the filing of lawsuits and is decided in a court of law. This process is carried out according to the court rules of the state or other local jurisdiction. The court renders a judgment which is binding by law and can be enforced by officers of the court. A jury may be convened to hear the evidence and render a decision, or verdict. The judge in the case accepts the verdict of the jury and renders a judgment according to the law. If both parties so agree, some cases are heard by the judge alone, who then renders a judgment.

It is appropriate to avoid the settlement of disputes by litigation for a number of reasons. First of all, litigation is much more expensive than arbitration. Secondly, in most jurisdictions, the court dockets are overcrowded and it may be years before the case is actually heard by the court. Thirdly, there is no guarantee that the judge who presides over the case or the jurors who decide upon it will be at all knowledgeable of construction technology or the unique established relationships in the construction industry. In litigation, the initial burden of "educating" those who will judge construction related issues is both time-consuming and expensive. Each side to the dispute must parade a host of "experts" before the jury to present opinions on the issues. Obviously each party to the dispute will select experts whose testimony will support their position. Quite often the testimony is contradictory and confusing, and because of this, the results may be less than satisfactory to one or both of the disputants.

Compensation for Involuntary Responsibility

The process of achieving the contract sum for the construction of a modern building or other construction project is obviously not an exact science. The process of bidding and negotiating for the Contract for Construction is discussed in Chapter 5. The implications of such procedures are addressed in Chapter 6. The constructor who bids or negotiates the contract sum, may add a contingency in order to protect himself from unknown factors for which he may become responsible. Obviously he cannot include a contingency adequate to cover every possible unforeseen circumstance for which he may have an involuntary responsibility. Coverage of such unforeseen expenditures can be lessened to some degree by the purchase of insurance. Insurance is an agreement made by a third party that promises to pay for certain unforeseen, but designated misfortunes that may become the insured party's responsibility through a variety of predictable causes. Insurance, a necessary service in the construction and other businesses, has become a major industry in itself.

The Insurance Industry

The construction industry could not long survive the effects of its involuntary responsibilities without the insurance industry. Insurance companies offer, for a fee, to sustain the cost of certain unforeseen occurrences that may occur during the process of construction. While all conditions may not be insurable, the most common risks can be covered. Under the agreement, or policy, issued by the insurance company, covered risks are described. Specific exclusions, or items not covered, are also named and described. When and if the insured, in this case, the contractor, experiences a loss, he makes a claim to the insurance company. If the cause and conditions meet the terms of the policy, the contractor is compensated for the loss by the insurance company.

Although it cannot claim to be uniquely an invention of the American economy, the insurance industry today, certainly owes its collective prosperity and stature among other industries to the opportunistic nature of the capitalistic system of the United States. The insurance business is based on professional risk taking. The insurance industry, by the nature of it's service, has provided many of the answers to the dilemma of compensation for the injured worker, compensation for loss by theft, compensation for loss by natural disaster, compensation for loss or injury due to the negligence of those in positions of trust and other similar causes.

Insurance may be described as a service which provides the vehicle by which a large group of individuals, through a system of equitable contributions, may spread certain common measurable risks of economic loss among all members of the group. The primary purpose of insurance is to substitute a degree of certainty for absolute uncertainty as regards the economic loss that may be sustained by an individual due to some unforeseen accident, disaster, catastrophe, or other act or circumstance causing measurable loss. Its effect is to spread the cost of particular types of loss that otherwise would be sustained by the individual, to the many, who share the potential for such a loss, in an equitable manner that is relatively affordable to all.

The insurance industry had its beginnings in Europe in the latter 17th and early 18th century. The first known life insurance policy was written just as the Industrial Revolution began to change the world economy from one that was based upon individual production and agriculture, to one that was based on mass production, mass markets and rapid transportation. The first insurance companies were more like associations than specific business ventures, and often were formed by trade associations, such as the shipping industry, for the mutual protection of each member, where the collective losses of cargoes at sea, by a few, were sustained by the resources of all. With these protective associations, there came into being what has come to be known as Marine Assurance. As transportation of goods over land became a parallel industry to that of transportation by ships, another form of insurance known as Inland Marine Assurance came into being. From these early assurance associations has come the modern insurance industry which provides protective agreements, called policies, covering loss from practically every conceivable type of misfortune that could possibly beset an individual or established business. The famous Lloyd's of London Insurance Company is one of those European establishments that remains a major insurer in the modern world. For almost 300 years, Lloyd's has been willing to insure almost anything or anybody for a price.

It was the building owner in Colonial America who would ultimately inspire the creation of fire and casualty insurance companies. Most of the early structures in the United States were built of wood. Losses from fire were great and frequent and often involved large segments of the early villages in America. In New England early in the 18th century, following the European model of associated marine insurance associations, building owners would join local fire companies to which was paid an annual "premium" which went to sustain the cost of a fire station which housed firemen and steam-powered, horse-drawn fire engines capable of carrying and pumping large amounts of water. Each fire company had a symbol, or "fire-mark", which the member was entitled to prominently display on his house or place of business. When a fire alarm was sounded, the fire company responded with the common equipment. If the building had the proper fire mark, or the fire threatened a building with such a firemark, the company would endeavor to extinguish the flame. If there was no firemark, often the company would return to the station and the victim, who did not have the foresight to pay an annual "premium" into the fire "policy", would suffer his loss alone.

To this day, many of the major insurance companies, most of which were spawned in those early days prior to the Revolutionary War bear as their trademark, those same firemarks. The agreement of insurance is still referred to as the Policy, and the fee is referred to as the Premium.

Over the years, two major types of insurance companies have emerged. The Mutual Companies of today are still based on "mutual" assurance and are organized as co-operative enterprises. The other type of company, known as Stock Companies, are organized as private enterprises including individual underwriters, syndicates of underwriters, and corporations or joint-stock companies whose ownership and control is based on corporate stock ownership.

In today's economy, the premiums paid to insure one's life, property, business venture or potential liability are relatively inexpensive when compared to the potential losses that the policy may cover. In a widespread economy, the "Law of Averages" is to the advantage of the Insurer. Insurance companies are continually basing annual premiums, or fees for coverage, on relatively predictable mathematical models of probabilities of loss, which are based on well documented data bases of actual statistics recorded by historical fact. It follows that the probability of death to a young person 20 years of age is less likely that that of a person who is 80.

The insurance industry of today has four major components, all interlinked to make the cost of insurance, as well as its coverage and availability to be within the budget of almost every individual and business in the United States. There are (1) the insurers, those Mutual or Stock Companies whose principal function is to take the risk and provide the coverage, (2) the field organizations or agencies whose primary function is to maintain contact with the public for the writing of insurance and settlement of losses, (3) intercompany associations or bureaus whose function is the establishment of standards, making of rates, doing research, institutional advertising, dissemination of information, influencing legislation and other activities to promote the interest if the insurers, and (4) organizations of agents and brokers, called associations or boards, which perform many of the same functions as the bureaus, except in the greater interest of the agents and insurance men who make their living in the field.

The fire insurance companies no longer maintain the fire stations and equipment, a responsibility of local subdivisions and municipalities. Cities and Counties, in order to provide uniform protection to all citizens of the community, have assumed the responsibility of maintaining the fire companies, equipment and personnel. In the interest of protecting the public, laws and mandatory regulations have been enacted by the various branches of government in an attempt to prevent loss to the community, through such catastrophic events.

Codes and Standards

Municipal regulations, called Building Codes, have been established by ordinance to regulate building construction. These codes have become the law within the jurisdiction where construction procedures take place. Building codes are commonly administered by the local government and define buildings by type of construction and by type of human occupancy and function. Building codes regulate the design of the building and the use of construction materials and methods in such manner as to provide optimum protection to the the building's occupants, the property itself, the surrounding property and the public. Similar regulations and codes have been enacted to provide maximum protection to the persons who are employed in the construction of buildings.

Over the years, certain model codes and standards have evolved which are adopted as law (often with modifications) by many municipalities around the country. The model codes are written by panels of experts and are revised frequently. The most commonly accepted model codes include, but are not limited to the following:

The Uniform Building Code
Written by:
The International Conference of Building Officials (ICBO)
5360 South Workman Mill Road
Whittier, California 90601

The Standard Building Code
Written by:
Southern Building Code Congress, International (SBCCI)
900 Montclair Road
Birmingham, Alabama 35213

Basic Building Code
Written by:
Building Officials and Code Administrators (BOCA)
4051 West Flossmoor Road
Country Club Hills, Illinois 60477

National Code:
American Insurance Association
85 John Street
New York, New York 10038

Other codes which concentrate on specific disciplines of design and safety concerns are:

The National Electrical Code
Written By;
National Fire Protection Association
Batterymarch Park
Quincy, Massachusetts 12269

The National Plumbing Code
Written By:
Coordinating Committee for NPC
U. S. Department of Commerce
and
U.S. Department of Housing and Urban Development
Washington, D.C. 20410

National Fire Codes
Written By:
National Fire Protection Association
Batterymarch Park
Quincy, Mass. 02269

Several organizations are involved in keeping code administrators and other officials informed and advised. These organizations have an influence on the enforcement of building codes and have made major contributions in bringing uniformity to the content and format of various building codes that have been adopted around the nation. These advisory organizations include:

Council of American Building Officials (CABO)
5203 Leesburg Pike, Suite 708
Falls Church, Virginia 22041

National Conference of States on
Building Codes and Standards (NCSBCS)
481 Carlisle Drive
Herndon, Virginia 22070

Still other organizations have dedicated themselves to determining certain uniform standards of composition, quality, testing and installation of materials, assemblies and methods of construction. These published model standards have come into general use and are accepted by architects, engineers, contractors, code officials, and others involved in the construction industry. The following are among the most prominent of this group of agencies.

The American Society for Testing Materials (ASTM)
1961 Race Street
Philadelphia, Pennsylvania 10103

American National Standards Institute
1430 Broadway
New York, New York 10018

Underwriter's Laboratory
333 Pfingsten Road
Northbrook, Illinois 60062

Federal Specifications
Superintendent of Documents
U. S. Government Printing Office
Washington, D.C. 20402

General Liability

The potential for loss to businesses and individuals from claims of those who allege to have suffered injury or loss has become very great. The whole issue of liability is becoming a matter of national concern among professionals, legislators and insurers. Physicians, lawyers, architects, engineers, manufacturers, owners and other businesses are all being threatened by the devastating cost of malpractice lawsuits. Liability insurance, once commonly available and inexpensive, is in serious danger of becoming unaffordable to certain ''high-risk'' activities. The ramifications of such a development could be far reaching and damaging to the construction industry as well as to other elements of the economy.

The much publicized collapse of pedestrian bridges in a major hotel, and the resulting death and injury to several hundred persons has brought about a net liability claim to owner, architect, engineer and contractor of more than 3 billion dollars. In another instance, the apparent failure of code-required fire dampers in the supply ducts of another major hotel caused the death by smoke inhalation of a number of guests in the hotel. These are large scale examples of building design and construction-related calamities. It is these kinds of incidents that have caused the entire construction industry, the insurance industry, the legal community and legislative bodies to look to more responsible design of buildings, more stringent legislation and code requirements, and more rigid field enforcement of building codes.

The widespread use of asbestos in building construction, and the subsequent discovery of its cancer-causing properties is an example of the kind of large-scale problems that have contributed to the increased liability of the industry. The discovery of asbestos in the nineteenth century was heralded as a major scientific achievement. New building materials were made using this substance that would neither burn nor support combustion, with the goal of offering ''protection'' in the built environment. Practically every school, public building, and much private sector development used asbestos materials for ceilings, floors, and cladding of exterior walls and roofs. Asbestos was also used to insulate steam and hot water lines in major environmental systems, as fireproofing on structural systems, and even in clothing for firefighters and combat troops. When scientific evidence linked asbestos exposure to cancer, the results included not only the costly removal of asbestos from existing structures, but also liability claims forcing the asbestos companies into receivership. Governments and private owners alike were forced to spend many times more than the original cost of the building to either remove or encapsulate exposed asbestos fibers. An entire asbestos abatement industry has sprung up and prospered in just a few worrisome years.

History may record the latter two decades of twentieth century America as the generation of the ''Mega-Liability Claim''. The professional architect, engineer or constructor of the future will have to adopt an attitude so conservative that it will make his mid-twentieth century antecedents appear careless and reckless by comparison. Tomorrow's professional will have to be the student not only of science and technology, but also of law. If he is to survive in the business community, he must possess multiple skills, from those of a salesman and diplomat to scientist, writer, and financial advisor. The ability to design and construct a beautiful building may well be just one among these requirements.

Owner's Liability
Chapter 3 addresses the subject of professional practice as it relates to the construction industry. In the triad relationship of owner, design professional (architect and/or engineer) and constructor, the professional is related to the owner by separate agreement, and the

constructor (contractor) is related to the owner by yet another separate agreement. The professional is pledged by common ethic to be fair and impartial in rendering judgments that may affect the interests of both the owner and contractor. These relationships relate to legally binding agreements. In the OPC relationship, the prime architect or engineer is responsible for interpreting the intent of the agreement and for establishing the language of the Contract Documents. In the event that the professional's judgment is, for any reason, unacceptable to the parties to the Contract for Construction (or to those involved in related agreements such as subcontracts), the issue must be decided either by arbitration or litigation, seldom both. Chapter 6 explores the character and content of Contract Documents in more detail.

The owner's legal responsibility under the various agreements, and his liability as the proprietor of a property are two separate issues. For example, the owner of a proposed new commercial building may go to great trouble and expense to find an extraordinary architect. The achievement of certain aesthetic criteria may be so important that cost is no object. These goals may be achieved in an award winning design, with the community recognizing the building as a "landmark". The weak point of this masterwork may not be recognized until one rainy winter morning when the surface of the specially designed Italian marble plaza becomes dangerously slippery due to freezing rain above, and the warmth of a mechanical equipment room below. The result may be an injured pedestrian, perhaps resulting in a lifelong disability. The cost of the resulting lawsuit and the potential for another similar accident emphasize the importance of liability. Who must pay?—in all likelihood, the owner and the architect. The pedestrian will sue the owner who has primary responsibility, but the owner may have an action against the architect because of the choice of the terrazzo paving. The architect may in turn have an action against his engineering consultant because of the transference of undissipated heat through the plaza deck.

Design professionals must be ever aware of the potential for calamity relative to the design of buildings and their surroundings. Another example of the kinds of factors that must be considered is a glass panel in the all glass sheath of a new high-rise tower. This panel, "popping" out of its frame, causes damage or injury to pedestrians below. The temperature differential in the glass sheath of the building—depending upon the position of the sun and the time of year—creates a condition of expansion and contraction on any particular point of the building's exterior surface that is difficult to predict. With many more hours and resources invested in the design phase, the thermal conditions might be predicted with tremendous accuracy, thereby ensuring that such an accident could not occur. However, the owner would probably reject payment of the increased fee to cover all of this research. On the other hand, that particular pane of glass may simply have been cut incorrectly. In any case, the evidence would have been destroyed in the fall to the pavement.

An owner may experience severe budget limitations because of economic factors beyond his control. To build, he must borrow. The lender wishes to limit his exposure to loss and therefore places restrictions on the amount of money he is willing to advance for the project. The potential is great for "saving" money by overlooking or eliminating a construction feature that might prevent an accident or damage to a building. Following this course, however, can be a common "trap" for owner, lender and design professional alike.

All members of the OPC relationship must be ever aware of any foreseeable hazards during the planning process and should periodically advise the other members accordingly. This in no way implies that the professional should presume to give legal advice to his client, or that the owner or contractor should give design advice. Quite the contrary! The design professional, through his membership and participation in professional societies, through study of professional and trade journals, and through his own experience and the "shared" experience of others, must continually educate himself on "what went wrong" and "why" in his own projects, and others in the construction industry. The owner, on the other hand, should avail himself of the advice of competent legal, financial and insurance counsel in order to create the best available "umbrella" of protection for his circumstances. The contractor should also seek competent counsel, and should view current building and safety codes as protective tools, not bureaucratic obstacles.

The Design Professional's Liability

Professional offices commonly employ a number of different specialists who contribute to the creation of construction documents. The office structure may be such that a project architect or engineer may be assigned the task of administering several projects at the same time. This person must deal not only with each client and his needs and issues, but at the same time direct the activities of the office staff and of consultants who are located elsewhere. There are also building code issues to be settled with the municipality, land use issues to be resolved with the zoning commission, and environmental issues to be resolved with the Federal Government, to mention just a few of the daily complications faced by today's design professional.

As much as half of the project administrator's time is taken up with meetings, most of which may be outside of the office. The other half is occupied by decision making and the administration process in his own organization. The job captain, who is responsible for putting lines to paper to produce the project, has one or two persons under his supervision. The civil, structural, mechanical and electrical engineering design is commonly executed in another location. The Project Manual is usually prepared by the specification writer, and specialized portions of the design may be prepared by a variety of persons making up the project team. The Project Manual is the subject of Chapter 8. In today's medium to large professional office, there may be a number of other specialists involved in every project. Included might be the landscape architect, the interior designer, the specification writer, and the cost estimator. One can easily see the potential for human errors and omissions, and the necessity for professional liability insurance. There may also be inconsistencies between the drawings and the specifications. The specification writer may assume that an item to be included is in the drawings and vice-versa. The engineer may fail to take into consideration the depth of a beam when locating ducts and lighting fixtures. There may be mathematical mistakes in preparing dimensions. A typographical error in preparing the specifications may completely change the meaning of an item of work. On the other hand, the design professional might simply make a error in judgment. For example, a type of waterproofing that has proved satisfactory in a number of projects might fail when used in new work that is subjected to different soil conditions, however slight the variation. Or, an item may simply be left out of the documents. Perhaps the language used to describe a particular requirement is written unclearly and misunderstood. There are literally hundreds of circumstances that often lead to potential liability on the part of the professional.

Like members of other professions such as medicine and law, the design professional must protect himself with liability insurance coverage if he is to survive this age of "runaway" litigation. Lawyer's fees can become substantial in a very short time, and the cost of defense in court can easily surpass the design professional's total fee for the project. If for no other reason than the deferment of potential legal fees, most design professionals believe that "Errors and Omissions" insurance is worth the expense. The insurance company, by virtue of its covenant to protect the insured, is obliged to help in the defense of any allocation of error on the part of the design professional. Many insurance companies will provide legal services from within their own ranks. Others will allow the owner to select his own attorney, and then partially, if not totally reimburse the insured for any prepaid expense, depending upon the prior agreement in the policy as to deductible expense and liability under the coverage.

We have suggested that this period in history will be known for its massive number of lawsuits. Indeed, many cases against design professionals can be called "frivolous". In the early development of such documents as the General Conditions, the term "supervise" was commonly used to describe the activity of the design professional in pursuing his obligation as the owner's representative. Litigation and the quest to determine responsibility for "what went wrong" after the fact changed the implications of the term, "supervise". This term came to suggest responsibility on the part of the design professional for the sequences and means and methods of construction. Lawsuits naming the architect became common when owners' or contractors' bonding companies sought relief from the cost of a major building failure. Such lawsuits are still common. To a large degree, the design professional's responsibility remains misunderstood.

An example of that responsibility is demonstrated in the case of the collapse of a brick veneer exterior wall as a result of unusually high storm winds. It was found that the mortar used in the construction did not meet the specified strength requirements. Further, the wreckage revealed that an insufficient number of structural ties had been used in constructing the wall. To complicate matters, both the contractor who had constructed the building and the masonry subcontractor had gone out of business and could not be found to account for the deficiency. Searching for compensation, the owner decided that there may be liability on the part of the architect who designed the building and "supervised" the construction. The courts held that the architect had properly designed the building, specified the proper mortar strength and had called for a proper number of wall ties, and because he was not required to make "exhaustive or continuous on-site inspections to check the quality or quantity of the work", he should not be held accountable for the failure of the brick wall.

In a detailed review of the individual responsibilities of the design professional and the contractor, one finds the courts determining that only the contractor has the ultimate responsibility to construct the building according to "plans and specs.". As the design professional is not required to be on the job on a continual basis, he cannot be held responsible for seeing or guaranteeing that the construction is, in fact, constructed in every respect in accordance with the Contract Documents. Seeing this weakness in the recommended language of Contract Documents, the American Institute of Architects, in collaboration with other institutions related to the construction industry, brought about a change in the language describing in greater detail the limit of the design professional's role in the OPC relationship. In the modern document, the design professional is described as the "Administrator" (not Supervisor) of the contract and, "will have authority to act on behalf of the owner to the extent provided by the Contract Documents". See Article 2.2.2 of the *General Conditions of the Contract for Construction*—AIA Document A201 in Chapter 7.

The architect, by virtue of provisions in the General Conditions of the Contract for Construction, is not responsible for the ". . . *control or charge of construction means, methods, techniques, sequences or procedures, or for safety precautions and programs in connection with the work*". This statement, made with the joint cooperation of professional, industry and construction institutions, has stood the test of time and the courts. The courts have, in fact, ruled consistently against the claims that the design professional is responsible for the overall quality of the contractor's work. In order to further limit the design professional's legal liability, the term "supervise" has been omitted from all of the AIA's Standard Forms. The word "supervise" has the connotation that quality assurance and conformity with the contract documents are reasonably assured when, in fact, they are not! There are occasions where someone will sue the design professional on the basis that the "supervision" provided by the professional was inadequate and because of this, the building or some component in it failed. There remains the current misconception among some owners, attorneys and insurance companies that the design professional shares responsibility with the contractor for the quality of construction.

The previous discussion of the design professional's responsibility during construction is not to say that he cannot be held responsible for a failure in the design of a building. He can, and does, hold that responsibility. In the case of errors and omissions in the preparation of the contract documents, he can be held responsible to both owner and contractor, and if called upon to do so, may have to pay to remedy the error and for any resulting damage.

The design professional's ultimate protection from excessive liability will come from a combination of professional competence and continuing education, as well as the competence of personnel, consultants, and legal counsel. The other essential element is the purchase of insurance as it continues to be available. The days are gone when the architect or engineer is able to survive purely on competence, talent, training and sharpness of wit. The emphasis upon continuing education throughout the career of the design professional cannot be stressed strongly enough.

Contractor's Liability and Legal Responsibility

The contractor is the member of the OPC triad who bears the ultimate responsibility for safety, performance, quality of workmanship, organization of the construction process, payment for equipment, materials and labor, taxes, transportation, non-conforming work and labor, insurance, some miscellaneous fees, and any other cost that is required or implied by the Contract Documents.

Job safety has become not only a matter of law and propriety, but has also become a science requiring considerable experience, knowledge and special training. The potential for loss of life or limb during the process of construction is great as is the risk of other serious injury. In a highly competitive atmosphere where only the "low" bidder wins the contract, the potential expenditure for safety precautions naturally becomes a low priority in the quest for potential profit. It is because of such faulty reasoning that substantial changes have been brought about in the "system", including laws requiring protection of the worker in the work place. Chapter 2 addresses labor issues and points out the fact that frequent abuses on the part of employers brought about organized labor and the now powerful labor unions. By the same token, the failure of contractors to make necessary safety preparations has brought about such laws as mandatory Worker's Compensation insurance, and such federal organizations as the Occupational Safety and Health Act—OSHA and the Environmental Protection Agency (EPA). OSHA has brought about numerous changes in the procedures of construction, including the mandatory wearing of protective helmets (hard hats) and the use of safety equipment (goggles and shoes). OSHA has also brought about a number of innovations such as improved temporary safety railings and back-up safety supports. Other improvements involve lighting, graphics, and signs. OSHA makes periodic inspections of the work place and is empowered to levy heavy fines on employers who do not conform to its regulations.

Imposed safety regulations and the requirement of certain types of insurance still do not absolve the constructor of responsibility for many types of loss or damage claims. The role of the constructor is fast changing from "tradesman" to professional, that is, one who pursues an art requiring special training and talent. Today's constructor must constantly improve himself by means of experience, training, continuing education, and participation in construction oriented institutions and organizations.

Insurance for the Construction Process

We have noted the importance of insurance to the health of the construction industry. Indeed, few owners, professionals or constructors could maintain their normal business posture without it. Insurance specifically designed for the construction industry and its concerns is available in a variety of forms and services.

Worker's Compensation

The advent and frequency of personal injury in the workplace has brought about the statutory requirement that all employers in the United States purchase and maintain Worker's Compensation insurance. This type of insurance statute or law provides for compensation for any employee who is in any way injured and suffers loss of wages, medical expense and other hardships due to a mishap while discharging his or her duties as an employee. The statutory requirements are governed by state law in the United States, and therefore may vary in requirement (and cost) from jurisdiction to jurisdiction. All 50 of the United States require some form of Worker's Compensation Insurance. Premiums are generally based on a statutory formula that is derived by considering the amount of total payroll an employer sustains, the claims history for compensation under the coverage, the history of and amount of claims paid statewide, and other variable factors.

In the case of the injured worker who was victim of the failed erection clip, the contractor's Worker's Compensation policy would have paid for his medical and hospital expense and compensation for wages lost. However, as with any legitimate form of insurance, there is an inevitable limit as to how much, and under what circumstances the insurance company will pay. In our example, the injured worker would look to the contractor and anyone else who could possibly be liable for the failed erection clip. In this case, the worker sued the general contractor, the general contractor sued the steel fabricator, the steel fabricator sued the testing laboratory and the testing laboratory sued the architect. Each of the defendants in the series of lawsuits called upon their respective general liability insurance carriers to assist in their defense.

General Liability Insurance
Most mutual and stock insurance companies offer policies that provide many kinds of insurance that protect the insured from loss due to claims brought by third parties for property damage or personal injury. In this type of general insurance, the provisions of the policy are written to be exclusionary rather to be inclusive. The term "exclusionary" means that the policy will be interpreted to cover all forms of potential loss, up to the amount of money named as the extent of the coverage for each separate incident, unless a particular risk is specifically excluded from the coverage in writing. Inclusive coverage, by the same token, means that only specific acts which are specifically included or described in the policy are covered to the limits named. General liability may exclude acts of nature, coverage under Worker's Compensation, acts of war, and similar specific acts or related events.

Vehicle Liability
No construction project in the United States could be accomplished without the use of various vehicles. Much of the actual work, as well as material delivery and worker transportation, involves the use of vehicles. While the motor operated vehicle has changed the means and magnitude of modern construction, the use of vehicles has also created a special element of risk requiring specialized liability coverage. Vehicular liability coverage usually covers any form of injury to persons or property, operator or passengers in the vehicle to certain upper limits as stated on the face of the policy. Vehicle insurance is mandatory coverage as a matter of statute in most states.

Property Insurance
The contractor should carry insurance designed to cover the premises of the project that he is is constructing (for the time of construction). Sometimes called "Builder's Risk Insurance", this coverage would include possible perils such as fire, windstorm, hail damage and other inclusive risks. It would also provide compensation for itemized perils common to construction work. Under special endorsements, additional coverage may be written to include other items commonly excluded such as damage from falling aircraft, and from rising flood waters, lightning and other natural phenomena.

Theft from construction sites has become such a common occurrence in recent times that many insurance companies completely exclude compensation for theft of materials. In such cases, insurers are willing to insure against theft, but only for materials and equipment that have been actually installed into the job. Materials simply stored on the job are usually excluded.

All Risk Insurance

General liability coverage, vehicle liability, and property insurance may be combined into one single policy commonly called "All Risk" insurance. By creating one policy, the cost is somewhat less than the individual policies. This type of coverage is written almost exclusively for contractors.

Owner's Liability

It is advisable that the owner carry coverage against general liability during the process of construction. Risks such as injury to a pedestrian or to someone who wanders into the construction site are a possibility on any construction project, and the owner is likely to be named in a lawsuit because of property ownership. Generally, the design professional is also named in such coverage. The contractor may be required by the contract to provide additional liability coverage for the owner and the design professional.

Loss of Use Insurance

While property insurance will compensate the insured for loss due to defined perils, it does not compensate the owner for the delay in delivery that would be caused by a major fire or building collapse in a windstorm or the like. In such circumstances, the contractor would have a legitimate cause to ask for an extension on his deadline for project delivery, so that a claim for liquidated damages due to delay would not apply. Loss of use insurance adds additional coverage to benefit both owner and contractor and compensates the owner a reasonable amount for each day that the project is delayed through no fault of the contractor.

Bonds

A bond is defined as a sealed agreement or promise by a surety to take certain actions at a specified time, or to make a payment in case of certain events. Certain types of bonds are required for the owner's protection in case of default by the contractor. These bonds offer a "sure" guarantee of the covenant, or the "fruit" of the agreement between two parties. Bonds may be offered with some form of security by one or more parties to the agreement. Generally, a surety (a financial institution or an insurance company), as a third party, agrees to be financially responsible for the fulfillment of the covenants of the agreement at no loss of time or expense to the first party. Three common types of bonds are usually required of the contractor for the benefit of the owner. They are the Bid Bond, the Performance Bond and the Payment Bond.

Bid Bonds

When the competition is keen for the award of the construction contract, bids are sealed and confidential. When the other proposals are eventually revealed, any constructor submitting a bid or proposal may wish to withdraw his low bid for any number of reasons. The bid bond requirement, submitted to the owner along with the proposal, guarantees that the bidder will honor his proposal as a firm contract sum, and if asked by the owner to do so, will faithfully enter an Agreement between Owner and Contractor for the construction of the project, according to the Contract Documents. The Agreement indicates that the work will be done for a contract sum equal to the amount of his proposal. The alternative is to forfeit the amount of the bid bond to the owner as liquidated damages for failure to meet the conditions of the Invitation to Bid. Bid bonds are discussed in more detail in Chapter 5.

Performance Bonds

The Performance Bond is usually in the form of an agreement, parallel to the Contract for Construction. In this agreement, a third party surety, acceptable to the owner, guarantees that the contractor will faithfully perform the work of the Contract Documents in all respects with no loss of time or money to the owner. Under this agreement, if the contractor, for any reason, should default on the agreement with the owner, the surety will take full responsibility for the performance of the contract.

Payment Bonds

The third type of bond usually required of the contractor is a guarantee by a surety that all costs of construction, labor, materials and equipment, and all related incidentals will be paid by the contractor. The owner is subject to significant vulnerability in the Contract for Construction. He pays the contractor for work accomplished as certified by the design principal, but without the payment bond, he has no guarantee that the contractor will in turn, pay those who do the work or provide materials or equipment. There are statutes, now enacted by all 50 states, that protect the "mechanic" who does work on the property or premises of an owner. Essentially, these statutes allow a subcontractor or supplier to file a lien against the value of the owner's property to protect their right to be paid for work done or materials supplied. A mechanic's or materialman's lien is filed with the clerk of the county or parish where the property ownership is recorded in the official property records. This filing of lien effectively prevents the owner thereafter, from conveying title, or giving a Deed of Trust (mortgage) to that property until such time as the mechanic has been satisfied and agrees to release the lien. In other words, if an employee, subcontractor, material supplier or other party, engaged by the contractor, but with no direct contractual relationship with the owner were to remain unpaid, that person could, under the law, protect himself by filing a lien against the owner's property. With a lien against the property, the owner cannot, without paying the mechanic (thereby having to pay for the work twice), convey clear title to the property—either to a buyer or a lender (in the case of establishing a mortgage on the property). The Payment Bond assures the owner of the following: in the event that the contractor defaults on payments to others, the surety will satisfy all obligations to the relief of the owner. This is true provided the owner meets the obligation of paying the contractor for the work. There are instances where liens that are filed against the owner may prove to be invalid and have the potential of causing some actual damage or loss to the owner. Such cases often result from an unsettled dispute involving a third party to the contract for construction such as a subcontractor or a vendor. In the event that the point of Substantial Completion has been reached and agreed upon, and the contractor is unable to produce lien waivers from all of his subcontractors, sub-subcontractors, vendors and others (as required by the contract documents), the contractor should be required to post additional bonds to protect the owner. This is true regardless of how the dispute or other issue may be eventually settled. In the case of an arbitrary and groundless lien, the owner may also have some legal recourse for damages against the party filing the invalid lien.

Statutes of Limitation

Except in cases where federal or state legislation limits the time period during which third parties are responsible for specific acts, any or all of the parties in the OPC relationship may be subject to potential loss through liability at any time in the life of a building. Statutes of Limitation vary from state to state in their treatment of owners, architects, engineers, and contractors. However, even with such statutes the professional may bear some liability for periods of up to ten years. Careful coordination between legal and insurance advisors is required for any project by all parties concerned.

Chapter 5
PROCEDURES OF BIDDING AND NEGOTIATING

Thousands of decisions must be made, documented, and carried out during the construction process for even the simplest structure. For every decision, there may be several variables and possibilities for alternate choices. Each variable may have a different cost. For example, an owner wishes to construct a warehouse of 100,000 square feet. The architect or engineer advises that the cost history for such a building type has ranged from a low of $31 per square foot to a high of $52. The lower cost figure is for construction of a building with prefabricated steel components on a conventional foundation, and represents maximum economy. A more expensive choice might include a near-conventional foundation, light steel framing, and reinforced concrete walls that are formed and poured on the job site and lifted or "tilted" into place. The most expensive alternative requires walls constructed of conventional masonry and a structure that is custom designed to allow the addition of future floors. There might be other variations on these three basic examples. The roof could slope and might be finished with insulated metal; or, it could be flat and constructed of composite roof deck with a built-up membrane.

The difference between the high and low historical cost for this building type is $20 per square foot. Beginning with the lower cost of $31, the potential cost escalation could be 60% or more. If the higher cost of $52 is referenced, there is a possible $20 difference that could be returned to the owner in possible savings of annual energy and maintenance costs. At the same time, the most expensive building may be out of reach of the owner's budget. This budget figure may be determined by the economics of the business intended to use the building. Countless variables are tied into the decision making process that finally produces a building.

Most of the owner's dilemma regarding choices of cost can be resolved by the architect or engineer retained to accomplish the building design. As an added service, the professional may perform studies to identify choices of materials and systems that the owner may wish to consider. Life cycle analysis, if required, will provide the owner with performance criteria—in terms of both the initial cost of materials and systems *and* the projected annual costs of maintenance, replacement, energy consumption, security, environmental control, and other factors of economy and function.

Once the owner and the professional are in agreement on the basic choices, a well defined set of professional documents, drawings, and specifications is prepared. This information describes the proposed building and can reduce the "gap" in the construction estimate from 20% to 10%. The final contract price could still possibly vary from the estimate by 10% or more.

Neither the owner nor his professional consultant has control over all of the conditions that form or shape the exact contract price for which a constructor will be willing to deliver the completed building. The total cost of a building then, is not a clear-cut, easily distinguishable number to be estimated or defined—not unless the owner and contractor agree upon a specific price for work defined by a collection of professionally prepared documents. Many factors and variables may complicate the budget preparation process.

In an economy which is largely based on supply and demand, the time of year at which a building is to be constructed may cause considerable variation in the price for which a constructor is willing to undertake the task. For instance, in many sections of the country, the spring and the fall are the times of year when construction activity is at a peak. Depending upon the overall economy, most contractors and tradesmen are fully employed during these seasons—with as much as six months' backlog of work. Asked to bid new work during peak times, most companies tend to propose a much higher price for that work than they would at off seasons. Other factors of supply and demand also affect cost. Manufacturers who must keep up a consistent volume of production will be more willing to "bargain" during times of large inventories than when demand is high and inventories are low.

The traditional constructor, or general contractor, in the United States makes it his business to keep up with the market conditions of labor and materials throughout a given year. His "edge" against the competition in the construction industry depends upon skill in being able to purchase labor and material at prices that are not only favorable, but lower than those available to the competition. Such is the "game" of the construction business. Thus, the selection of the constructor to complete the triad of Owner-Professional-Contractor means finding someone who is not only competent, but who also has the best "edge" on cost.

Selection of the Contractor

When the owner is a private entity, the selection process may be conducted by either *competitive selection*, or *direct selection*. Where the owner is a public entity, the options are fewer. The expenditure of public funds is controlled as a matter of law. Therefore, in most instances, public sector owners are restricted to the process of competitive selection or, as it is usually known, *competitive bidding*.

There are two types of competitive selection. *Open competitive selection* is a process where an Advertisement for Bidders is made, and where no restriction or discrimination is made as to who the bidders may be, as long as they are qualified and responsible. *Closed competitive selection* is more discriminating. In this case, the owner may prepare a select list of qualified constructors to whom he issues an Invitation to Bid.

Open Competitive Selection

In *open competitive selection*, most often called *open bidding*, the opportunity to submit a proposal is not limited to specific bidders; instead, it is "open" to any qualified constructor who may wish to submit a proposal. In the open bidding process, the project is conspicuously advertised, and the Bidding Package is made available to any constructor who may wish to apply and conform to the Instructions to Bidders. In turn, this constructor must be prepared to subject himself to the scrutiny of the owner and/or architect and engineer. The owner and professional(s) will investigate the constructor's competency and ability to act responsibly in the event that the contract is awarded to him.

Although there are cases when a private owner may wish to utilize the process of open bidding, it is most often used in cases where the owner is a public agency, controlled by the law of a governing entity. Examples of typical public owners are a city, county, or state government. Various subdivisions of the federal government are other kinds of public entities. In the case of public owners, the law may include non-discriminatory legislation. This legislation requires that the award of a contract involving the expenditure of public funds must be available to any constructor who can meet the minimum requirements or test of competency and responsibility. Under such laws, the owner is prohibited from discriminating in the selection of a constructor, but may reasonably require evidence of competency and responsibility. Other legislation may specify the minimum wage rates for different trades.

To summarize open bidding, it may be said that any company (depending upon licensing requirements and other controls) may have the right to submit a proposal and compete with others for award of the contract on the basis of "the lowest proposed contract price submitted by a responsible bidder".

The Advertisement for Bids

In the case of open bidding, it is customary and usually a legal requirement that a formal Advertisement, or Legal Notice for Receipt of Bids be published in the local newspapers. Examples of such advertisements for bids are shown in Figures 5.1 and 5.2. A properly prepared advertisement contains minimum, but explicit data that enables a prospective bidder to determine the scope and exact location of the proposed work, the minimum requirements that a bidder must exhibit for award of contract, the extent of licensing that may be required, and the amount of time that is available to prepare an adequate proposal. The advertisement should be brief, simple, easy to read and understand, and free of the sort of detailed instructions and requirements that are more properly contained in a separate document entitled "Bidding Requirements", or "Instructions to Bidders".

Closed Competitive Selection

Closed competitive selection, most often called *Closed Bidding*, is a process whereby the owner invites certain constructors to compete for the construction contract. While open bidding requires an Advertisement to Bidders, published in a manner conspicuous to the business community, closed bidding involves only certain constructors, specially selected by the owner and perhaps issued an Invitation to Bid. Only those invited to participate are allowed to compete for the contract.

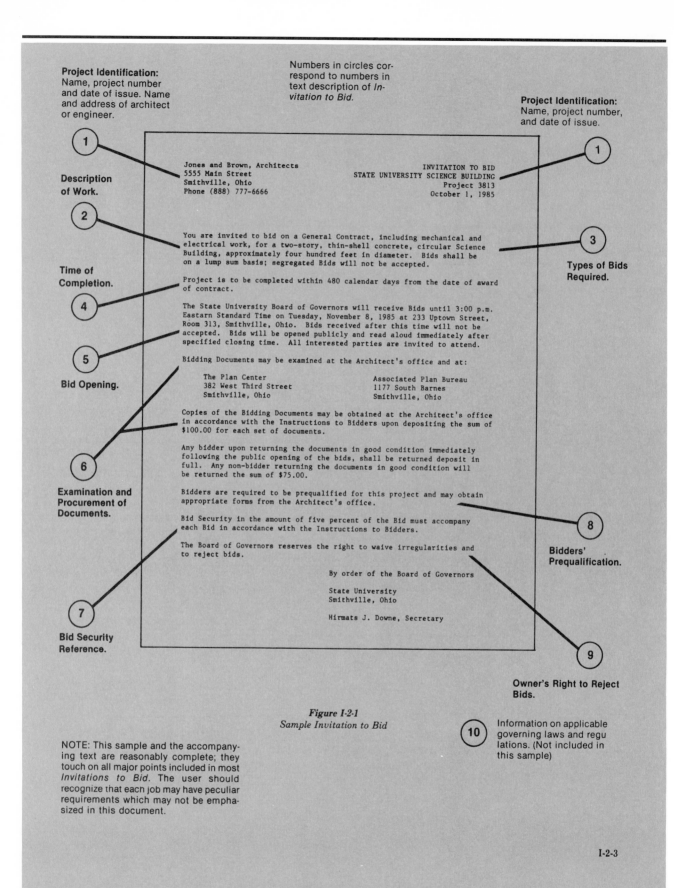

Project Identification: Name, project number and date of issue. Name and address of architect or engineer.

Numbers in circles correspond to numbers in text description of *Invitation to Bid.*

Project Identification: Name, project number, and date of issue.

(1)

Description of Work.

(2)

Time of Completion.

(4)

(5)

Bid Opening.

(6)

Examination and Procurement of Documents.

(7)

Bid Security Reference.

Jones and Brown, Architects
5555 Main Street
Smithville, Ohio
Phone (888) 777-6666

INVITATION TO BID
STATE UNIVERSITY SCIENCE BUILDING
Project 3813
October 1, 1985

(1)

(3)

Types of Bids Required.

You are invited to bid on a General Contract, including mechanical and electrical work, for a two-story, thin-shell concrete, circular Science Building, approximately four hundred feet in diameter. Bids shall be on a lump sum basis; segregated Bids will not be accepted.

Project is to be completed within 480 calendar days from the date of award of contract.

The State University Board of Governors will receive Bids until 3:00 p.m. Eastern Standard Time on Tuesday, November 8, 1985 at 233 Uptown Street, Room 313, Smithville, Ohio. Bids received after this time will not be accepted. Bids will be opened publicly and read aloud immediately after specified closing time. All interested parties are invited to attend.

Bidding Documents may be examined at the Architect's office and at:

The Plan Center
382 West Third Street
Smithville, Ohio

Associated Plan Bureau
1177 South Barnes
Smithville, Ohio

Copies of the Bidding Documents may be obtained at the Architect's office in accordance with the Instructions to Bidders upon depositing the sum of $100.00 for each set of documents.

Any bidder upon returning the documents in good condition immediately following the public opening of the bids, shall be returned deposit in full. Any non-bidder returning the documents in good condition will be returned the sum of $75.00.

Bidders are required to be prequalified for this project and may obtain appropriate forms from the Architect's office.

(8)

Bidders' Prequalification.

Bid Security in the amount of five percent of the Bid must accompany each Bid in accordance with the Instructions to Bidders.

The Board of Governors reserves the right to waive irregularities and to reject bids.

By order of the Board of Governors

State University
Smithville, Ohio

Hirmats J. Downe, Secretary

(9)

Owner's Right to Reject Bids.

Figure I-2-1
Sample Invitation to Bid

(10) Information on applicable governing laws and regulations. (Not included in this sample)

NOTE: This sample and the accompanying text are reasonably complete; they touch on all major points included in most *Invitations to Bid.* The user should recognize that each job may have peculiar requirements which may not be emphasized in this document.

I-2-3

Figure 5.1

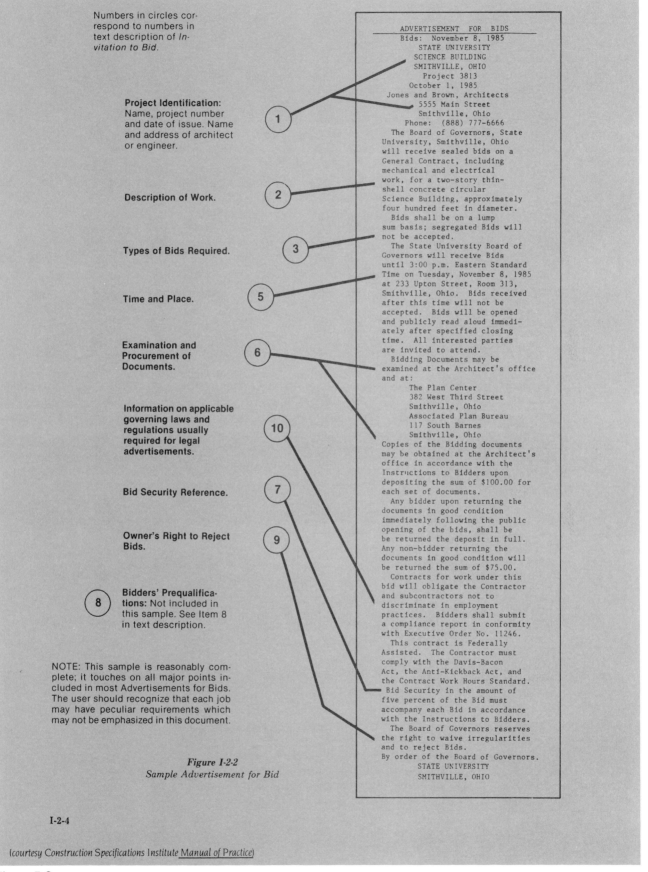

Numbers in circles correspond to numbers in text description of *Invitation to Bid*.

Project Identification: Name, project number and date of issue. Name and address of architect or engineer.
① ②

Description of Work.
②

Types of Bids Required.
③

Time and Place.
⑤

Examination and Procurement of Documents.
⑥

Information on applicable governing laws and regulations usually required for legal advertisements.
⑩

Bid Security Reference.
⑦

Owner's Right to Reject Bids.
⑨

⑧ **Bidders' Prequalifications:** Not included in this sample. See Item 8 in text description.

NOTE: This sample is reasonably complete; it touches on all major points included in most Advertisements for Bids. The user should recognize that each job may have peculiar requirements which may not be emphasized in this document.

Figure I-2-2
Sample Advertisement for Bid

ADVERTISEMENT FOR BIDS
Bids: November 8, 1985
STATE UNIVERSITY
SCIENCE BUILDING
SMITHVILLE, OHIO
Project 3813
October 1, 1985
Jones and Brown, Architects
5555 Main Street
Smithville, Ohio
Phone: (888) 777-6666
The Board of Governors, State University, Smithville, Ohio will receive sealed bids on a General Contract, including mechanical and electrical work, for a two-story thin-shell concrete circular Science Building, approximately four hundred feet in diameter.
Bids shall be on a lump sum basis; segregated Bids will not be accepted.
The State University Board of Governors will receive Bids until 3:00 p.m. Eastern Standard Time on Tuesday, November 8, 1985 at 233 Upton Street, Room 313, Smithville, Ohio. Bids received after this time will not be accepted. Bids will be opened and publicly read aloud immediately after specified closing time. All interested parties are invited to attend.
Bidding Documents may be examined at the Architect's office and at:
     The Plan Center
     382 West Third Street
     Smithville, Ohio
     Associated Plan Bureau
     117 South Barnes
     Smithville, Ohio
Copies of the Bidding documents may be obtained at the Architect's office in accordance with the Instructions to Bidders upon depositing the sum of $100.00 for each set of documents.
Any bidder upon returning the documents in good condition immediately following the public opening of the bids, shall be be returned the deposit in full. Any non-bidder returning the documents in good condition will be returned the sum of $75.00.
Contracts for work under this bid will obligate the Contractor and subcontractors not to discriminate in employment practices. Bidders shall submit a compliance report in conformity with Executive Order No. 11246.
This contract is Federally Assisted. The Contractor must comply with the Davis-Bacon Act, the Anti-Kickback Act, and the Contract Work Hours Standard.
Bid Security in the amount of five percent of the Bid must accompany each Bid in accordance with the Instructions to Bidders.
The Board of Governors reserves the right to waive irregularities and to reject Bids.
By order of the Board of Governors.
STATE UNIVERSITY
SMITHVILLE, OHIO

I-2-4

(*courtesy Construction Specifications Institute Manual of Practice*)

Figure 5.2

The private sector has much more latitude in the choice of constructor than does the public sector. While there are rare instances where public sector owners are permitted to be somewhat selective in the choice of bidders entering the competition, an increase of non-discriminatory practices has left the process of closed or selective bidding as the exclusive option of the private owner/entrepreneur.

The Invitation to Bid

In the case of closed, or selective, bidding a select list of constructors is prepared after careful investigation. A formal letter or notice of Invitation to Bid may be issued to those selected constructors. This notice is similar in content to the Advertisement for Bids, except that in this case, the invitation is limited to those who have been invited to make a proposal and is not "open" as in the case of open bidding. The Invitation is issued to two or more constructors, specially selected and pre-qualified by the owner and/or architect/engineer. A properly prepared Invitation to Bid will contain minimum, but explicit data that will enable an invited bidder to determine the scope and exact location of the proposed work, the extent of licensing that may be required, and the amount of time that is available to prepare an adequate proposal. Like the advertisement, the invitation to bid should also be brief, simple, easy to read and understand, and free of instructions and detailed requirements that are more appropriate in an accompanying document entitled, "Bidding Requirements", or "Instructions to Bidders".

Bidding Documents

In the case of either open or closed competitive selection, the Bidding Documents generally consist of the Advertisement or Invitation to Bidders, Instructions to Bidders, Form(s) of Proposal, Form(s) of Required Bonds, Supplemental Bidding Information, and Addenda. To these bidding documents are added the Contract Documents—generally consisting of the form(s) of the Agreement between Owner and Contractor, Conditions of the Contract, the Specifications, the Drawings, and any necessary Contract Modifications. The Bidding Documents, together with the contract documents, comprise the "package" generally known as the *Construction Documents*. Construction Documents are published and released to prospective contractors. They, in turn, study the documents, determine a proposed Contract Price, and according to the Instructions to Bidders, initiate a bid or proposal for the owner to consider in his objective of awarding the Contract for Construction.

Instructions to Bidders

The *bidding requirements*, more often called *Instructions to Bidders*, is a document which states the "ground rules" of the bidding procedure—both before and after the receipt of bids. When properly prepared, Instructions to Bidders will contain the following:

- Complete identification of owner, project, and architect/engineer.
- Description of the scope of the work.
- Time of completion: date and hour.
- Place where bids are to be received.
- Name of entity authorized to receive sealed bids.
- Availability and conditions whereby Bidding Documents can be studied or procured.

- Description of any Bid Security that may be required.
- Description of the basis (type) of bid that is desired.
- Pre-qualification standards whereby proposer or bidder will be judged to be competent and responsible.
- A statement whereby the owner may reserve the right to waive any formality and reject any and all proposals received without award of contract.

The Engineers Joint Documents Committee (EJDC), and the American Institute of Architects each publish Instructions to Bidders.

These formats have been recommended for use by certain professional organizations or societies and are generally accepted throughout the construction industry. It should also be noted that certain government agencies prefer to use Instructions to Bidders forms that have been compiled and published by the government. Where preprinted or published forms are used, it may be necessary to include a separate document entitled ''Supplemental Instructions to Bidders'', where minor modifications, alterations, and additions to the published document can be made.

Risks of the ''Low Bidder''

Recent statistics from data compiled by independent resources report that the business failure rate of companies engaged in general contracting is extremely high. Current figures indicate that a high percentage of general contracting companies in the United States declare bankruptcy or are forced into receivership by creditors. In recent history, it has not been unusual for the contractor to become insolvent during the process of building construction.

The process of competitive bidding requires the constructor to study the construction documents, estimate the total cost of building the project, factor in a profit, and be prepared to pay all costs foreseen and unforeseen that are included in the Contract Documents.

To ''win'' the award of the Contract for Construction, a bid must be the lowest number among all the other bids submitted by competitors. The bidder's work includes computing quantities, discerning exactly what is required by the documents, and anticipating changes in wage rates. Mistakes in any of these areas or the unforeseen failure of a subcontractor or material vendor to deliver as promised can result in losses to the constructor who wins the bid.

The failure rate of general contractors in the United States is the highest in the world. The industry may show better statistics elsewhere in the world because of different methods used to award the bid. In many European countries, such as England, the process of competitive bidding includes ''rules'' requiring the owner to disregard, or ''throw out'' the amount and name of both the highest and the lowest bidder. The amounts of the remaining bidders are then averaged, and the bidder whose bid amount comes closest to the average of all is selected and awarded the contract. This process has at least two distinct advantages. Since the final contract price is near the average of those proposed by all who have studied the project, the owner has some assurance that the work will be done properly, while the constructor is assured a reasonable profit. This approach may mean that the owner will pay several percentage points more for the work than he would under the low bidder system. Nevertheless, the quality of the building is apt to be better under a system where the constructor is not tempted to "cut corners", or cheapen the building in ways that may remain undetected for the first few years of its life.

Bid Bonds

Under the rules of formal, competitive bidding and those set forth in many Instructions to Bidders, each candidate prepares his bid in secret and submits it with other required information in a sealed envelope to be opened at the exact same time as are those of his competitors. In theory, no bidder can know the amount of any other bidder's proposal until all are informed at the Bid Opening.

Under the "low bidder wins" system of contract award, it is possible that a low bidder might bid an amount that is considerably lower than his next closest competitor. He may or may not have made an error in calculating his bid. In any event, it is a situation that is good for the owner and at least potentially bad for the constructor who bid low. Under these circumstances, the low bidder might wish to withdraw his bid once all of the bidding results are known.

To prevent a situation where the owner might lose his cost advantage in the competitive bidding process, or to give the owner some protection against the low bidder "backing out" on the promise tendered in the bid form, the owner can require that all bidders provide a bidder's bond. A bidder's bond, more often simply called the *Bid Bond*, is a guarantee in the form of a cashier's check or an agreement provided by a surety, that stipulates that the amount set forth on the face of the bond will be forfeited to the owner in the event that the proposer fails, for any reason, to enter a contract for construction with the owner for the amount of the proposer's bid.

Direct Selection of the Constructor

Direct Selection of the Constructor is a process whereby the time consuming bidding process is bypassed and the owner selects a constructor of his liking and confidence. An agreement is then negotiated between the parties. In direct selection, the Bidding Documents are usually not required; therefore the Advertisement or Invitation to Bidders, and Instructions to Bidders are not included in the "package" of documents.

Direct selection of the constructor is fast becoming the most popular method of contract award among owners in the private sector, and is receiving some success among public sector owners as well. By selecting the constructor before or during the process of developing the Contract Documents, the owner incurs an element of risk not inherent in Competitive Bidding, but also takes advantage of the element of time, and has the potential to save considerable sums of money. The architect will usually require between six months and a year to finalize the production of Bidding Documents. The competitive bidding process and award of contract may take three to four months longer. Since the architect or engineer is not in a position to guarantee the cost to an owner, budget overruns, when they occur, can cause even more delay in the start of construction. Because most private projects are highly leveraged by the borrowing of capital funds, the private sector owner begins to incur considerable cost the moment the project becomes committed. Since use and/or income from the project cannot begin until the building is occupied, the time required between the purchase of land and project completion can be critical to the achievement of a profit in highly competitive markets. Cutting out the time required for the competitive bidding process often results in greater savings than the difference between the highest and the lowest bid received. If the contractor is selected and committed before the completion of Contract Documents, the advice and guidance of the contractor in the selection of materials can be a definite advantage in assuring conformity to budget requirements.

Along with the direct selection process have come several innovative methods of contract award that greatly enhance the constructor's potential profit and provide an opportunity for the owner to save more as well. Chapter 6 deals with the Contract for Construction and methods of payment. It explores in some depth innovations in the OPC relationship—the results of contracting methods in the direct selection process.

Risk Factors Related to Direct Selection

In using the Direct Selection method, the owner takes certain calculated risks regarding the credibility and integrity of the constructor he chooses. To offset these risks, the architect, acting as the agent and representative of the owner, must thoroughly investigate the experience, financial resources, and capability of the candidates for contractor. The American Institute of Architects has developed AIA Document A305— *Contractor's Qualification Statement*. This form is designed to record detailed information about the prospective contractor, enabling the owner to make an informed decision whether or not to award the contract to that candidate.

"Fast Track" Method of Construction

In recent years, a construction method known as the "Fast Track" has evolved from the process of Direct Selection of the constructor. This technique allows the construction process to begin before the entire process of producing the Contract Documents is complete. As time is conserved, the owner's potential savings are increased. The methodology of construction contracting consists of a series of related but limited scope contracts which phase the construction, or a series of Multi-Prime Contracts, as discussed in subsequent paragraphs. Basically, the "fast track" method involves the start of certain portions of the work while subsequent phases are still "on the drawing board". The "fast track" method requires dynamic scheduling and coordination and may be organized in a series of phases as follows:

- **Phase 1** may involve site preparation and other related work which can be accomplished while the design professional is preparing contract documents for the substructure, foundation and superstructure construction.
- **Phase 2** may involve the construction of the building substructure and foundation while components of the superstructure are being shop-fabricated. Meanwhile, the design professional is preparing contract documents for the building envelope, special equipment, mechanical and electrical systems design.
- **Phase 3** may involve the construction of the building envelope, rough-in of special equipment, mechanical and electrical systems. Meanwhile, the design professional is preparing contract documents for interior construction, finish work and landscaping.
- **Phase 4** and subsequent phases of the work may involve the final work required to complete the building.

The Fast Track method involves a much higher risk factor for the owner than any of the other more conventional methods of contracting. However, when there is a high degree of professionalism, integrity experience, and skill, there is a potential for financial benefits that can be highly rewarding to all members of the OPC relationship.

In a highly charged and competitive economy, the selection of contractor is fundamental to the fortunes and objectives of the owner. The process of competitive bidding, although time consuming, has been the most universally accepted method, as it gives the owner reasonable assurance of the lowest possible cost. Because of restraints and the relationship of cost to time, the direct selection method is becoming popular among private owners and, to a lesser degree, public owners.

The risks in the OPC relationship are significant. The functions of each—owner, professional, and contractor—are based on the Agreement between Owner and Architect (or Engineer) and the Agreement between Owner and Contractor. The work of the professional is the creation and publication of professional documents that clearly describe the work to be done, the materials to be provided, the procedures to be used, and the areas left to the discretion of the contractor. Properly written, these documents go a long way in assuring that the project is constructed successfully and profitably.

The selection of the contractor completes the triad of Owner, professional and Contractor (OPC)—the essential relationship in the construction of any building project. Subsequent chapters of this text will deal with the various components of the Contract Documents.

Chapter 6
THE CONTRACT FOR CONSTRUCTION

Building construction has become a complex and often diverse undertaking requiring the coordinated efforts of many trades and professions. Today's building projects involve sums of money and a commitment of skills, material, and equipment that would have astonished our predecessors just two or three generations ago. The successful administration of both work and money calls for considerable management skills, planning, and documentation. An owner can no longer rely on verbal agreements, or leave work requirements, quality of construction, and matters of cost to trust or chance. A written, legally binding agreement or contract(s) has become a necessity, and should provide the following: maximum detail and disclosure of the work to be done, the extent of services required, the quality of materials to be employed, and other commitments that must be established in order to complete the project in an orderly manner.

Contracts Defined

A contract is an agreement between two or more parties. It represents a specified promise or series of promises to be performed, for which consideration is given. Common law recognizes performance under such an agreement to be an enforceable duty. A contract can be oral—made by spoken agreement, or it can be written—defined in writing and signed or sealed by the parties to the agreement. Oral contracts can be legally binding, but difficult to enforce because of the confusion that often occurs when the parties to the agreement must recall the exact specifications of the original agreement. Today's building owner requires documentation, not only to outline the specifications for completion of the building, but for legal and financial protection as well. In order to be a complete or valid agreement, any contract must contain the following:

Identification
The parties to the agreement must be named by the most appropriate legal identification. They can be individuals, partnerships, joint-ventures or corporations, or any combination thereof. Each party is represented by the name by which it is most commonly identified. The address of each party serves as further identification.

Covenants
A covenant is a clause in an agreement between two or more parties. It is a pledge to take, or refrain from taking, certain specified actions. The covenants form the "body" of the agreement for the work of construction.

Consideration

Consideration is a recompense or payment, as for work done. In the legal sense, consideration is the element that makes a promise legally binding, usually something of value given in exchange for the promise. In the contract for construction, the contract sum is the consideration paid by the owner to the constructor for the work of construction.

Acceptance

Acceptance is expressed with a seal, or representation of authenticity. A seal is a mark, symbol, impression, or signature attached to a legal document, representing the authority of the individual party to the agreement. By placing his signature (seal) on the agreement, each party indicates that he understands the content and terms of the agreement, and commits himself to them.

Figure 6.1 shows a view of the Contract for Construction in terms of a different set of requirements. This list shows the elements that should be included in a valid contract—from the standpoint of quality and preparation.

Qualities of a Valid Contract

Legal
- Content—Enforceable
- Form
- Language

I.D.
- Correct Names
- Addresses
- Signature
- (Seal)

Offer (Bid)
- Responsive
- Correct Sum
- Signature/Seal

Acceptance
- By Responsible Party
- Correct Signature/Seal
- Correct Sum
- Exhibits/Attachments

Technical Competence
- Professionally Prepared
- Complete
- Legally Reviewed
- Properly Issued/Bid

Figure 6.1

Agreement Between Owner and Contractor

The Contract for Construction is more correctly called the Agreement between Owner and Contractor. In order to be effective, the agreement must incorporate in the covenants, a complete definition of the work to be done. The materials, skills and other services to be employed in the construction must be described. The complex and interrelated responsibilities of the parties to the contract must be outlined. The agreement should also illustrate how the building is to be constructed. For the sake of convenience, the Contract for Construction is usually a single document which names and sets forth the basic covenants between the parties, states the method of payment, establishes the contract sum, states the date of expected completion, and sets forth the conditions under which final completion and acceptance will be accomplished. Figures 6.2a through 6.2d illustrate AIA Document A101—*Standard Form of Agreement Between Owner and Contractor*, 1977 Edition.

In order that the Contract for Construction be properly drawn up and the work defined, the prudent owner commissions a design professional (architect or engineer) and an attorney to advise him how best to achieve his needs. As a part of this service to the owner, the design professional will create documents to establish the design of the project and to create the contract documentation needed to carry out the requirements of the contract for construction. Once the project has been fully defined and documented, the design approved, and a budget committed for the anticipated cost, the owner is prepared to enter an agreement with a qualified constructor. Once chosen, the constructor is thereafter referred to as the "contractor".

In order for the work to be completely defined, the contract must be accompanied by a number of other documents which, for the sake of convenience and propriety, are prepared separately from the body of the contract. This collection of documents is generally known as the Contract Documents. Article 1 of the example contract form (illustrated in Figure 6.2b) lists these documents as the Agreement, the Conditions of the Contract, (General, Supplementary and other Conditions), the Drawings, the Specifications, and all Addenda issued prior to the execution of the Agreement. Figure 6.3a shows the relationship of the various unassembled Contract Document components. These components may be thought of as "building blocks", which are designed to fit together in a particular way. Figure 6.3b shows the process by which these basic "building blocks" are assembled. Together, they form the basis for the bidding or negotiating process. An additional "building block," the Addenda, may be added to the package prior to the execution of the agreement. Once a contract sum and other pertinent conditions (such as the number of days allowed for construction) have been agreed upon, the Agreement can be executed. Figure 6.3c illustrates the completed contract documents package. The Agreement between Owner and Contractor serves as the cord that ties all of the components together.

THE AMERICAN INSTITUTE OF ARCHITECTS

AIA Document A101

Standard Form of Agreement Between Owner and Contractor

where the basis of payment is a

STIPULATED SUM

1977 EDITION

THIS DOCUMENT HAS IMPORTANT LEGAL CONSEQUENCES; CONSULTATION WITH AN ATTORNEY IS ENCOURAGED WITH RESPECT TO ITS COMPLETION OR MODIFICATION

Use only with the 1976 Edition of AIA Document A201, General Conditions of the ~~~~~~~~~~~ Construction.

This document has been approved and endorsed by The Associated C~~~~~~~~~~~~~~~~~~ ca.

AGREEMENT

made as of the
Hundred and ~~~~~~ neteen

BETWEEN the Owner:

and the Contractor:

The Project:

The Architect:

The Owner and the Contractor agree as set forth below.

(courtesy American Institute of Architects)

Figure 6.2a

ARTICLE 1
THE CONTRACT DOCUMENTS

The Contract Documents consist of this Agreement, the Conditions of the Contract (General, Supplementary and other Conditions), the Drawings, the Specifications, all Addenda issued prior to and all Modifications issued after execution of this Agreement. These form the Contract, and all are as fully a part of the Contract as if attached to this Agreement or repeated herein. An enumeration of the Contract Documents appears in Article 7.

ARTICLE 2
THE WORK

The Contractor shall perform all the Work required by the Contract Documents for
(Here insert the caption descriptive of the Work as used on other Contract Documents.)

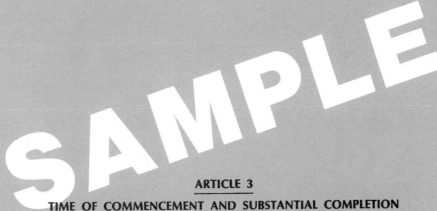

ARTICLE 3
TIME OF COMMENCEMENT AND SUBSTANTIAL COMPLETION

The Work to be performed under this Contract shall be commenced

and, subject to authorized adjustments, Substantial Completion shall be achieved not later than

(Here insert any special provisions for liquidated damages relating to failure to complete on time.)

AIA DOCUMENT A101 • OWNER-CONTRACTOR AGREEMENT • ELEVENTH EDITION • JUNE 1977 • AIA®
©1977 • THE AMERICAN INSTITUTE OF ARCHITECTS, 1735 NEW YORK AVE., N.W., WASHINGTON, D.C. 20006   **A101-1977**   **2**

(courtesy American Institute of Architects)

Figure 6.2b

ARTICLE 4

CONTRACT SUM

The Owner shall pay the Contractor in current funds for the performance of the Work, subject to additions and deductions by Change Order as provided in the Contract Documents, the Contract Sum of

The Contract Sum is determined as follows:
(State here the base bid or other lump sum amount, accepted alternates, and unit prices, as applicable.)

ARTICLE 5

PROGRESS PAYMENTS

Based upon Applications for Payment submitted to the Architect by the Contractor and Certificates for Payment issued by the Architect, the Owner shall make progress payments on account of the Contract Sum to the Contractor as provided in the Contract Documents for the period ending the   day of the month as follows:

Not later than   days following the end of the period covered by the Application for Payment   percent (%) of the portion of the Contract Sum properly allocable to labor, materials and equipment incorporated in the Work and   percent (%) of the portion of the Contract Sum properly allocable to materials and equipment suitably stored at the site or at some other location agreed upon in writing, for the period covered by the Application for Payment, less the aggregate of previous payments made by the Owner; and upon Substantial Completion of the entire Work, a sum sufficient to increase the total payments to   percent (%) of the Contract Sum, less such amounts as the Architect shall determine for all incomplete Work and unsettled claims as provided in the Contract Documents.

(If not covered elsewhere in the Contract Documents, here insert any provision for limiting or reducing the amount retained after the Work reaches a certain stage of completion.)

Payments due and unpaid under the Contract Documents shall bear interest from the date payment is due at the rate entered below, or in the absence thereof, at the legal rate prevailing at the place of the Project.
(Here insert any rate of interest agreed upon.)

(Usury laws and requirements under the Federal Truth in Lending Act, similar state and local consumer credit laws and other regulations at the Owner's and Contractor's principal places of business, the location of the Project and elsewhere may affect the validity of this provision. Specific legal advice should be obtained with respect to deletion, modification, or other requirements such as written disclosures or waivers.)

AIA DOCUMENT A101 • OWNER-CONTRACTOR AGREEMENT • ELEVENTH EDITION • JUNE 1977 • AIA®
©1977 • THE AMERICAN INSTITUTE OF ARCHITECTS, 1735 NEW YORK AVE., N.W., WASHINGTON, D. C. 20006   **A101-1977 3**

(courtesy American Institute of Architects)

Figure 6.2c

ARTICLE 6

FINAL PAYMENT

Final payment, constituting the entire unpaid balance of the Contract Sum, shall be paid by the Owner to the Contractor when the Work has been completed, the Contract fully performed, and a final Certificate for Payment has been issued by the Architect.

ARTICLE 7

MISCELLANEOUS PROVISIONS

7.1 Terms used in this Agreement which are defined in the Conditions of the Contract shall have the meanings designated in those Conditions.

7.2 The Contract Documents, which constitute the entire agreement between the Owner and the Contractor, are listed in Article 1 and, except for Modifications issued after execution of this Agreement, are enumerated as follows:

(List below the Agreement, the Conditions of the Contract (General, Supplementary, and other Conditions), the Drawings, the Specifications, and any Addenda and accepted alternates, showing page or sheet numbers in all cases and dates where applicable.)

This Agreement entered into as of the day and year first written above.

OWNER   CONTRACTOR

_____   _____

_____   _____

_____   _____

(courtesy American Institute of Architects)

Figure 6.2d

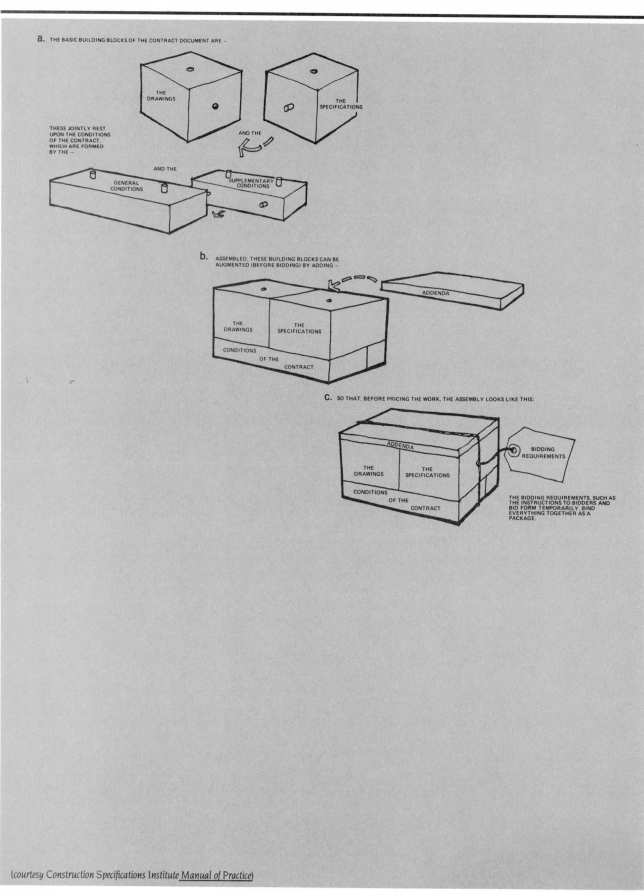

a. THE BASIC BUILDING BLOCKS OF THE CONTRACT DOCUMENT ARE –

THE DRAWINGS

THE SPECIFICATIONS

THESE JOINTLY REST UPON THE CONDITIONS OF THE CONTRACT, WHICH ARE FORMED BY THE –

AND THE

AND THE

GENERAL CONDITIONS

SUPPLEMENTARY CONDITIONS

b. ASSEMBLED, THESE BUILDING BLOCKS CAN BE AUGMENTED (BEFORE BIDDING) BY ADDING –

ADDENDA

THE DRAWINGS

THE SPECIFICATIONS

CONDITIONS OF THE CONTRACT

c. SO THAT, BEFORE PRICING THE WORK, THE ASSEMBLY LOOKS LIKE THIS:

ADDENDA

THE DRAWINGS

THE SPECIFICATIONS

CONDITIONS OF THE CONTRACT

BIDDING REQUIREMENTS

THE BIDDING REQUIREMENTS, SUCH AS THE INSTRUCTIONS TO BIDDERS AND BID FORM TEMPORARILY, BIND EVERYTHING TOGETHER AS A PACKAGE.

(courtesy Construction Specifications Institute Manual of Practice)

Figure 6.3

Components of the Contract Documents

Figure 6.3c shows that Bidding Requirements are not part of the contract documents, but rather, are supplemental. Information that is furnished to explain the constructor selection process, and if appropriate, to establish the rules for competitive bidding or negotiation for the award of the contract are the bidding, or negotiating, documents. The bidding documents generally consist of the advertisement or invitation to bid, instructions to bidders, bid forms and other information that may be made available to bidders or selected constructors with whom negotiations are being conducted. Once the contract is executed, the bidding documents are of no further value and are not a part of the main "package" of data.

It often becomes necessary or desirable to modify the Contract for Construction once the agreement has been executed and construction begun. Figure 6.4 shows the assembly of the Contract Documents together with additional modifications. In this illustration, the Agreement is represented by a "C" clamp which, when loosened, allows for the insertion of an additional "building block", the Modifications to the Contract for Construction. Notice that the bidding documents (represented by the tag) can now be removed as they are no longer needed.

Addenda

The Addenda are periodic publications issued by the professional on behalf of the owner during the bidding or negotiating process (see Chapter 5). Addenda are issued prior to execution of the Agreement between Owner and Contractor for the purpose of modifying or clarifying the intent of the Contract Documents. Addenda may contain changes or corrections to the work in addition to general information, answers to questions, and statements intended to clarify the general intent of the Contract Documents. Constructors bidding the work are usually encouraged to point out any errors or inconsistencies that they have discovered in the documents during the bidding or negotiating period. The design professional may use the bidding period to conduct a detailed "check" of the documents for his own benefit.

Conditions of the Contract

Because of the complexity of the OPC relationship (owner, professional and contractor—a complete explanation is provided in Chapter 1) and other contractual relationships, and the responsibilities of each party employed by the principals of the contract, it has become convenient to establish a definitive document accompanying and clarifying the Agreement. This document is called the General Conditions of the Contract (between Owner and Contractor) for Construction, or simply the General Conditions.

The General Conditions are discussed in detail in Chapter 7. Briefly, the General Conditions serve as the definitive or explanatory document among the contract documents. Therein, the parties are defined and their mutual responsibilities set forth. The general conditions outline the responsibilities of the owner, the design professional, the contractor and subcontractors. The work of the contract may also be defined. Work by the owner or separate contractors may also be defined. The General Conditions also contain miscellaneous provisions to define time, and include matters pertaining to payments and completion, protection of persons and property, insurance requirements, changes in the work, uncovering and correction of the unacceptable work, and termination of the contract.

4. WHEN BIDDING OR NEGOTIATING IS OVER,
   THE AGREEMENT IS EXECUTED.

   THIS BINDS THE DOCUMENTS TOGETHER FIRMLY AND PERMANENTLY

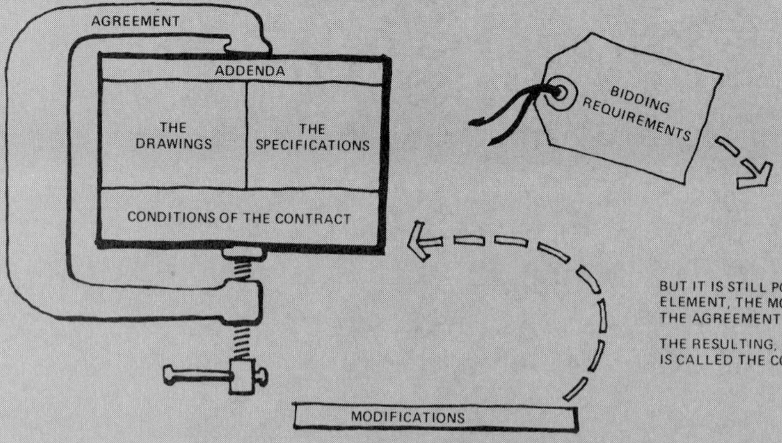

AGREEMENT

ADDENDA

THE DRAWINGS

THE SPECIFICATIONS

CONDITIONS OF THE CONTRACT

BIDDING REQUIREMENTS

MODIFICATIONS

BUT IT IS STILL POSSIBLE TO ADD ONE MORE
ELEMENT, THE MODIFICATIONS, BECAUSE
THE AGREEMENT IS EXPANDABLE.

THE RESULTING, TIGHTLY BOUND PACKAGE
IS CALLED THE CONTRACT DOCUMENT

FIGURE I-3-1
The Agreement

I-3-2

(courtesy Construction Specifications Institute Manual of Practice)

Figure 6.4

Supplemental Conditions of the Contract

Supplemental Conditions of the Contract are modifications of and additions to statements made in the General Conditions. In professional practice, the Supplemental Conditions are most often prepared as a separate document. This document details changes and additions to be made to the language of the General Conditions in order to meet the requirements of an individual project. Supplemental Conditions may address matters of local law, custom, and taxation. Equal Opportunity hiring requirements, minimum wage laws, and payment of local sales tax are examples of the kinds of laws and codes which may have jurisdiction over the project and the owner. The owner's own unique insurance requirements should also be spelled out in the Supplemental Conditions, as should the use of any tax exemption status, if applicable. Information should be included regarding record keeping and other administrative procedures that may be required by others outside of the OPC relationship. More specific administrative matters—the observation of certain project procedures, for example—will be discussed in subsequent chapters relating to Division 1 of the Specifications.

Specifications

Specifications are generally defined in the American Institute of Architects *Handbook of Professional Practice*. The following is a more specific definition from the Construction Specification Institute's *Manual of Practice*:

"Specifications define the qualitative requirements of products, materials, and workmanship upon which the contract (for construction) is based.

The full intent and content of the Contract for Construction cannot be fully expressed by words or drawings each acting independently of each other. Specifications and Drawings are complementary and for that reason must be created as parts of equivalent value to the whole."

Drawings

The *Manual of Practice* defines the Drawings as follows:

"The drawings are a graphic representation of the work to be done. They indicate the relationships between the components and materials and should show the following:

- Location of each material, assembly, component and accessory.
- Identification of all components and pieces of equipment.
- Dimensions of the construction and sizes of field assembled components.
- Details and diagrams of connections.

As with the writing of Specifications, well prepared drawings should be orchestrated to be in harmony and concert with the other Contract Documents, but designed with organization and logic in order to facilitate the time of the user in the field".

The contract for construction should be flexible enough to allow for changes, clarifications, additions, or deletions in the OPC relationship. Such alterations are often necessary, even desirable, and usually inevitable in such a complex undertaking as the construction of a modern building. The change order is the instrument by which modifications are made to the Contract for Construction. Figure 6.5 illustrates a Means Contract Change Order, a form which is often used for documenting such modifications.

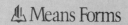 Means Forms

**CONTRACT
CHANGE ORDER**

FROM:

_____

_____

_____

TO:

_____

_____

_____

_____

		$					
CHANGE ORDER NO.							
DATE							
PROJECT							
LOCATION							
JOB NO.							
ORIGINAL CONTRACT AMOUNT	$						
TOTAL PREVIOUS CONTRACT CHANGES							
TOTAL BEFORE THIS CHANGE ORDER							
AMOUNT OF THIS CHANGE ORDER							
REVISED CONTRACT TO DATE							

Gentlemen:

This CHANGE ORDER includes all Material, Labor and Equipment necessary to complete the following work and to adjust the total contract as indicated;

☐ the work below to be paid for at actual cost of Labor, Materials and Equipment plus _____ percent (_____%)

☐ the work below to be completed for the sum of _____

_____ dollars ($_____)

_____

_____

_____

_____

_____

_____

_____

_____

_____

_____

_____

_____

_____

_____

_____

_____

_____

_____

CHANGES APPROVED

The work covered by this order shall be performed under the same Terms and Conditions as that included in the original contract unless stated otherwise above.

By_____

By_____

Signed_____

By_____

Figure 6.5

Types of Contracts

The forms of agreement that can be applied to the construction process are usually identified based on the method of payment to the contractor. The American Institute of Architects (AIA), the National Society of Professional Engineers (NSPE) and others have developed pre-printed forms. These forms are based on years of experience and considerable legal advice, and are commonly used and accepted throughout the construction industry. Some of the most widely used of these forms are described in the following text.

Single Prime Contracts

The majority of building projects in the United States today are organized under a single prime contract. A single prime contract is a contract or agreement between owner and contractor wherein the contractor, for consideration (which is named as the contract sum) agrees to become the prime party responsible for the construction of the project. (The project is defined by the Construction Documents prepared by the design professional.) The contractor is responsible for providing all materials, labor, tools, equipment and methods necessary for the completion of the work defined by the Contract Documents. The word ''prime'' is used to distinguish the contractor from other (sub)contractors whom the contractor might hire to perform portions of the work.

In the contract for construction, there is no direct contractual relationship between the owner and the subcontractor, nor between the contractor and the design professional. In most cases (by virtue of the agreement between owner and design professional), the design professional acts as the owner's representative during the construction process and performs a number of services known as the Administration of the Contract (see Chapter 4). The various consultants employed by the design professional may assist in the administration of the contract, but they are directly related only to the design professional who bears the total responsibility for professional services to the owner.

The subcontractor is related to the project by a separate agreement with the contractor. This agreement is known as the Subcontract. The subcontractor (defined in Chapter 1), usually a specialist in performing a particular portion of the building construction, serves the project at the discretion of the contractor. The contractor assumes total responsibility for the subcontractor's work and payment. Occasionally, the subcontractor requires a sub-subcontractor to perform portions of the subcontract work. In this case, the subcontractor is responsible for the sub-subcontractor's work and payment.

The supplier may be either a manufacturer or distributor of materials, assemblies or equipment. The supplier is directly related to the contractor either through a separate contract or a contract for the purchase of certain items, known as the Purchase Order. Figure 6.6 illustrates the contractual relationships that may occur under the single prime contract for construction.

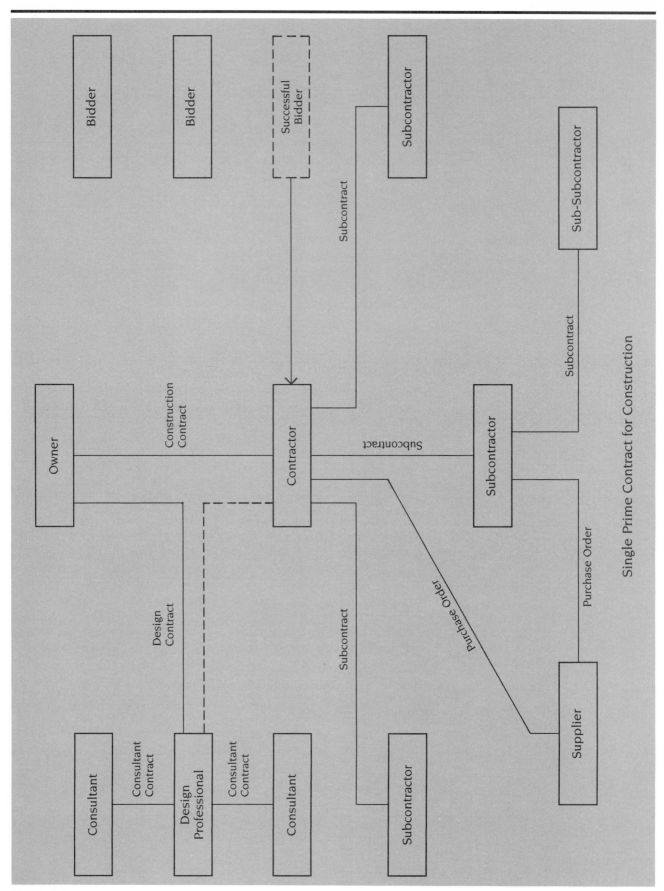

Single Prime Contract for Construction

Figure 6.6

(adapted from Construction Specifications Institute *Manual of Practice*)

Multiple Prime Contracts

Increasing numbers of construction projects involve several prime contractors doing work on the same project under related contracts. These contracts are usually referred to as "Multiple Prime Contracts".

The expression, "Time is Money," is certainly relevant in the construction industry. Regardless of whether an owner uses his own funds to construct a project or borrows the funds from a financial institution or similar source, the cost of money as a commodity is directly related to the time during which the money is used. The cost, or value of money used during the construction process is a primary factor in the total burden of cost that the owner must sustain to achieve the finished work.

In the traditional approach to project construction, the owner must first select the professional (architect or engineer) and finalize the acquisition of the building site. He then hires the professional to design the building, secures any required financing, arranges for the creation of contract documents, and selects the constructor (see Chapter 5). In the case of major projects, this process may require a year, or more, before any construction can begin. The expense sustained by the owner during this period is substantial. The outlay for land acquisition, professional fees, the cost of surveys, soil tests, zoning and planning reviews and approvals are all costs that must be borne prior to construction. These costs can amount to a significant percentage of the total project development cost. Occasionally, the owner must also sustain certain ancillary off site improvements such as construction of access roads, extension of utility lines, flood control structures, demolition of existing improvements and other preliminary work before any construction of the actual project can begin. If the owner borrows any funds to develop his project, interest must also be applied to the sums that are expended during both the pre-construction and the construction periods.

If the factors of time and expense are to become substantial (30 percent or more of the total project development cost) prior to the start of the actual project construction, the owner may wish to utilize an approach called the "fast track" method. Simply stated, the fast track method involves awarding a series of Multiple Prime Contracts, each of which accomplishes a subsequent phase or stage of the building construction. The basic principal of the "fast track" method is that time (and therefore, money) can be saved if the construction can begin before all of the traditional pre-construction functions are completed.

For example, consider the construction of a medium sized multi-story office building in a busy commercial neighborhood. The first three phases of the design professional's work are time related as follows:
- Phase 1—Schematic design
- Phase 2—Design development
- Phase 3—Contract documents

The construction of the building could be broken down into ten separate but time-related contracts as follows:
- Contract 1—Site Clearing and Demolition
- Contract 2—Site work
  — Phase 2A—Rough grading excavating
  — Phase 2B—Place structural base for foundations and structure
  — Phase 2C—Paving and site improvements

- Contract 3—Structural construction
  — Phase 3a—Foundation and substructure
  — Phase 3b—Superstructure
- Contract 4—Plumbing
  — Phase 4a—Underground plumbing
  — Phase 4b—Superstructure plumbing rough-in
  — Phase 4c—Placement of plumbing fixtures
- Contract 5—Construction of building envelope (shell)
- Contract 6—Heating, ventilating and air conditioning
  — Phase 6a—HVAC superstructure rough-in
  — Phase 6b—Place HVAC equipment and fixtures
- Contract 7—Electrical
  — Phase 7a—Underground electrical and site rough-in
  — Phase 7b—Superstructure electrical rough-in
  — Phase 7c—Place electrical equipment and fixtures
- Interior construction
- Interior finishing
- Landscaping

Once the design professional has established the design development phase of his work for the project, it may be possible for construction Contract 1—site clearing and preparation—to begin. This work could be done while the contract documents related to the building substructure, foundations, site improvements and similar work are being produced by the design professional. Shortly after the completion of Contract 1, the work of Phase 2A, Contract 2—excavation and construction of the substructure and foundations—can begin. This work is done in coordination with Phase 4A of Contract 4—the installation of underground plumbing utilities and Phase 7A of Contract 7—the installation of underground electrical services. Meanwhile, the design professional is preparing contract documents related to the superstructure of the project. At the completion of Contracts 2A, 4A and 7A, the work of Phase 3A—construction of foundation substructure—can begin while the design professional prepares contract documents for the envelope of the building. Phase 2B of Contract 2—the construction of the building superstructure—follows the work of Phase 2A. Contract 5—the construction of the building envelope—follows the construction of the superstructure. From this point on, the other contracts and their interrelated phases can proceed toward the orderly completion of the building. The end result is a time savings of, for example, four to five months. This is the time that would have been lost had the process waited until the design professional completed the contract documents and entered the competitive bidding for a single prime contract for construction. By utilizing the "fast track" method, the owner has realized considerable savings in interest expense and other costs. These savings may be worth the risk involved in starting the project early.

While this example of the "fast track" method has been simplified for purposes of explanation, the potential time savings are evident. Though subject to the perils of human error, misunderstanding and coordination, the fast track method can save time that would otherwise be spent by professionals in preparing fully implemented and complete Contract Documents and Bidding Requirements. This savings of time, and thereby money, as well as the accelerated date of owner occupancy, is often worth the risks. The chief risk is that of an error in contract document preparation. Such an error often results in the unforeseen cost of modifications to the various Prime Contracts as the project is being completed.

The "fast track" method of construction (by separate Multiple Prime Contracts) is becoming more and more common as a method of economical phased construction. In the fast track, each phase relates to others in a vertical type of progression with some parallel overlapping. "Parallel construction" is another construction method. It utilizes Multiple Prime Contracts, but is more horizontal in nature. "Parallel construction" applies to projects such as a Planned Unit Development (PUD)—a project with major components requiring specialized construction of various parts. Examples are a manufacturing plant, a medical research and treatment facility and a jail or prison. Each of these projects is apt to require specialized components and equipment. Therefore, they are appropriate projects for multiple prime contracts where a number of construction operations can take place at the same time.

Like the "fast track" approach which uses time-phased contracts in order to save time and money, the parallel method also provides certain economic advantages. The parallel method may save time and expense in terms of the contractor's overhead and profit factor. By utilizing parallel prime contracts, the owner does not depend on a single contractor to subcontract specialty items. The owner may save money by separately contracting and coordinating the work himself. Figure 6.7 illustrates the relationships that are created for multiple-prime contracts.

"Turn-Key" or Design/Build Contracts

A third method for project contract award, recently re-discovered in the United States, is the "turn-key" or, as it is sometimes called, the "design-build" contract. The term "turn-key" has commonly been applied to projects where the owner may accept (and pay for) the project at the time when he is able to turn his key in the lock of the main entrance and take possession of a completed project. It is at this time (and by previous agreement) that the owner accepts the design and construction of the building and make arrangements to purchase the building.

A common example of a "turn-key" contract approach is the business of a home-builder operating in any number of new residential subdivisions. Some builders find it economically advantageous to design several "prototype" homes, repeating these models over and over again with minor variations of exterior material, color and texture—an approach which seems to appeal to a "mass" market of American home buyers. Other builders contract with a prospective homeowner to build what is now commonly referred to as a "custom" home. In this case, the owner has considerable influence over the design. He may or may not employ a design professional, but arranges what is called a "stand-by" mortgage commitment for the long term financing of the project. The owner, together with the lender, accepts the building according to a contract of sale with the builder once the construction work is complete.

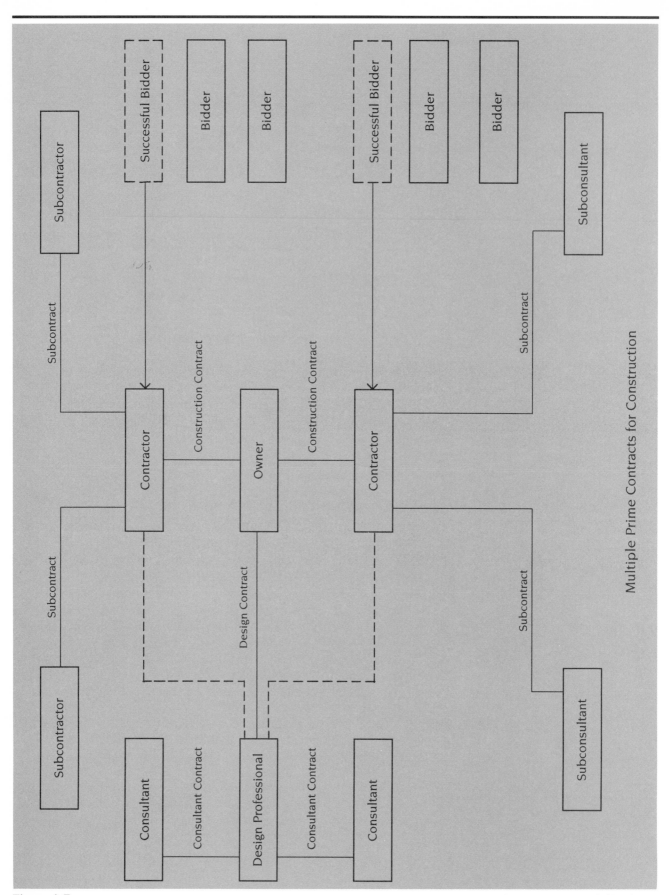

Multiple Prime Contracts for Construction

Figure 6.7

76

(adapted from Construction Specifications Institute Manual of Practice)

There is a growing element within the established construction industry—constructors who are looking to other contracting methods to overcome the many disadvantages of the competitive process. Although the traditional OPC relationship (described in Chapter 1) continues to serve the majority of projects constructed in the U.S., there is an increasing desire among owners, design professionals and particularly constructors, to find more profitable ways to carry out design and construction.

There is a growing demand to consolidate the functions of ownership, professional design and construction under a more predictable, if not controllable, atmosphere for survival and profit. The design-build method of organizing and implementing the construction process may be one of several answers to such a quest.

In the design-build approach to project completion, the owner presents his needs, program and budget. The constructor assembles a "team" of specialists. Among them may be the architects and engineers, together with traditional major subcontractors and others who will work together under the control of the contractor to satisfy the owner's needs according to a pre-established budget. In this process, a contract sum is negotiated, and the role and compensation of each team member is defined. This system often lends itself to the "fast-track" method of construction. In addition, each participant in the process may share in the final profit (or loss) that is achieved once the project is constructed. Figure 6.8 illustrates the relationships that may exist in the design/use/build process.

Owner as Contractor

It should be recognized that other variables may affect the design-build process. For instance, the owner may be a developer who acts as contractor and assembles the design-build team to produce a project. The project may be intended for his own use or for re-sale to a third party investor at completion (in the manner of "turn-key" contracting). In today's economy, there is a growing number of professional owner/developers. It is the business of the owner/developer to develop properties which will meet the market demand in the community. Such projects may include shopping centers, office buildings and other commercial uses. In many cases, experienced owner/developers act as contractor. In this way, their profitability may be increased as they bypass overhead and profit factors paid to someone else. Figure 6.9 illustrates the relationships that may exist with this kind of contracting.

Construction Management

An aggressive design professional may wish to expand his traditional role to include the responsibilities of the project or construction manager. As construction manager, he might use the fast track multiple contracts process, or the method of parallel contracting, thus eliminating the need to employ a general contractor. The design professional may be the owner, or he may perform such services under contract with an owner. Figure 6.10 shows the contractual relationships that may exist under the design professional/ construction manager type of contract arrangement.

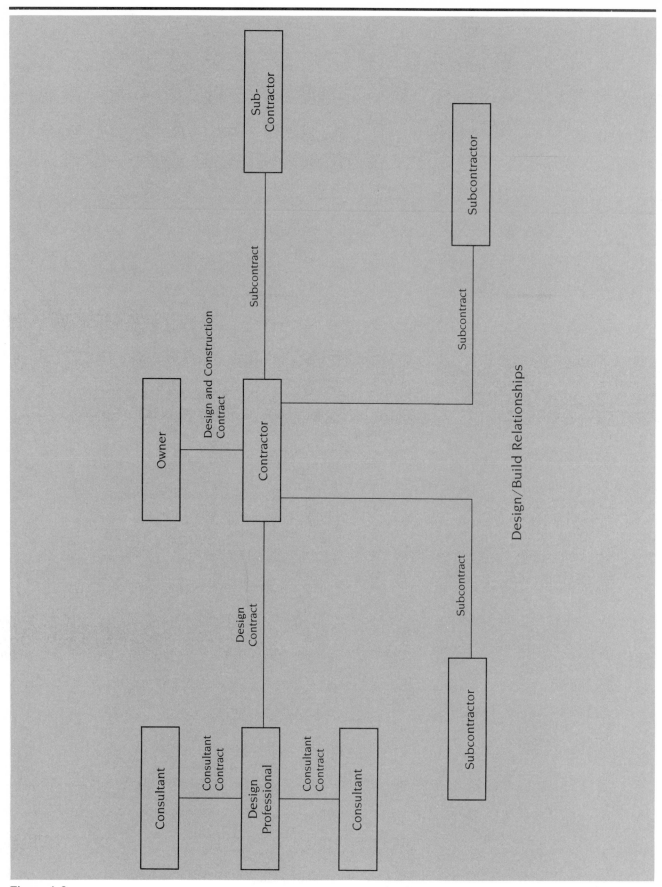

Design/Build Relationships

Figure 6.8

(adapted from Construction Specifications Institute Manual of Practice)

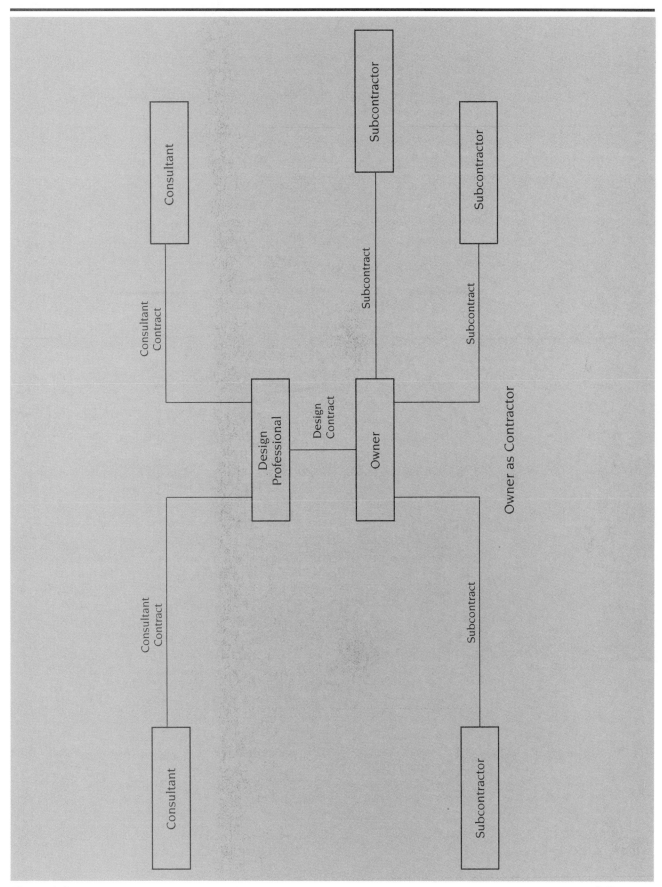

Figure 6.9

(adapted from Construction Specifications Institute Manual of Practice)

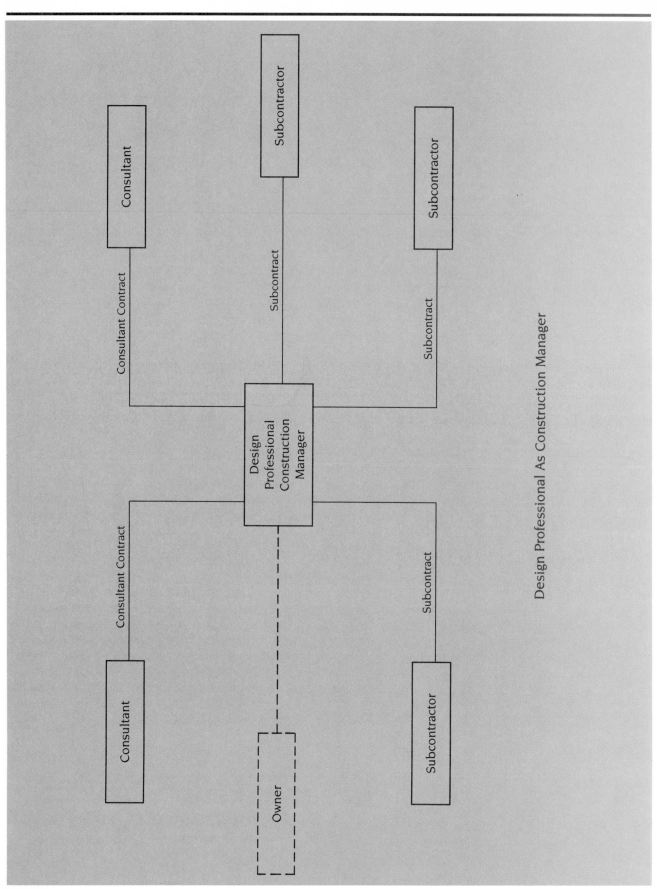

Design Professional As Construction Manager

Figure 6.10

Another possibility is the construction manager as a third party to the traditional OPC relationship. In this case, the construction manager assumes some of the responsibility traditionally held by both the design professional and the contractor before and during construction. In this situation, the contractor may be employed on a cost plus fee basis, or he may be limited to providing labor and construction equipment only with the owner purchasing materials directly. The construction manager provides continuous on site management of the project. He orders and receives items provided by the owner, oversees the activity of the contractor, schedules the work and approves the quality and workmanship of the work. The design professional consults with the construction manager to judge the intent of the contract documents and to determine conformance with the design intent. Figure 6.11 illustrates such an arrangement—whereby the services of a construction manager are retained by the owner.

Methods of Payment

Regardless of the contracting method, experience has proven that the preferred method of payment should employ a form of checks and balances in the best interest of both parties to the contract for construction. There are several terms that should be understood prior to a discussion of contract payment provisions.

The Contract Sum: the total value of the work, defined by the contract documents; the amount that is to be paid to the contractor according to the terms of the Agreement between Owner and Contractor.

The Schedule of Values: a listing or schedule of monetary values. Each item on the schedule represents a proportionate value for a definable portion of the work. The total amount is equal to the contract sum.

Retainage: a percentage (set forth in the agreement) which the owner retains or withholds from the total periodic payments according to the terms of the agreement. Retaining a portion of the contractor's earnings gives the owner some leverage in enforcing compliance with the requirements of the contract documents.

The Schedule of Values is usually determined by the contractor, reviewed and approved by the design professional and accepted by the owner at or very near the beginning of the construction process. Having been predetermined and agreed to by each party in the OPC relationship, the Schedule of Values is then used as a guide to determine amounts of incremental payments. These payments are made in proportion to the work completed on a monthly or other periodic basis. The contractor periodically prepares an Application and Certificate for Payment and makes adjustment to the contract sum for any Modifications or Change Orders that have been approved by each owner, contractor and design professional. Once approved by either the design professional or the construction manager, payment by the owner is made to the contractor. The mechanism of payment procedures and the use of various forms for application and approval are discussed more fully in subsequent chapters.

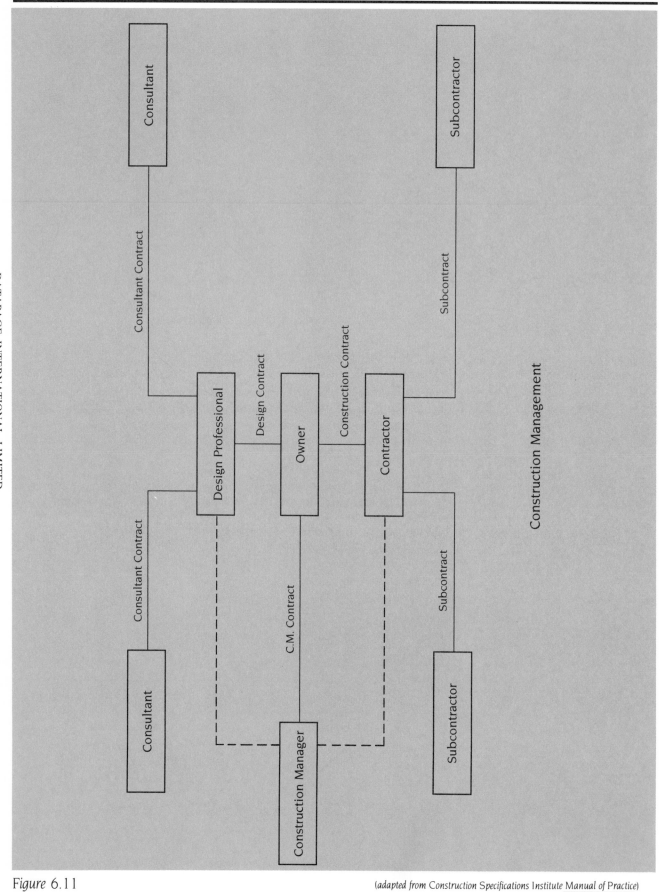

Construction Management

Figure 6.11

(*adapted from* Construction Specifications Institute Manual of Practice)

Definite or "Lump Sum" Contracts

The most common form of provision for payment is the "lump sum" or definite sum contract. The definite sum contract may be achieved by any of the various contracting methods described in this chapter. It may be derived by competitive bidding or by negotiation, and the contract(s) may be awarded to single or multiple prime contractors. Definite sum contracts may be applied to projects with a traditional OPC relationship, or to a variety of design-build projects which may or may not use the traditional relationships. Payment may be made periodically according to a percentage of work completed or in a single payment at completion of the entire project, as in the case of the turn-key type of contract.

Advantages of the definite sum contract are as follows:
- The owner can accept or reject the proposed contract sum according to his budget constraints.
- The contract sum is fixed thereby offering some protection to the owner from cost escalation due to outside economic factors.
- The cost of contract administration is included in the design professional's fee. Generally, there is no additional expenditure required to achieve project completion.

Disadvantages of the definite sum contract are listed below:
- The owner and/or design professional may be liable for extra cost because of errors and omissions in the contract documents.
- Modifications to the contract may cost more than if such changes had been incorporated originally.
- The contractor may sustain heavy losses due to error in estimating or cost changes due to economic factors.

Unit Cost Contracts

Unit cost contracts are most commonly used for projects involving heavy construction: highways, streets, roads, bridges, underground and above ground utilities, drainage structures and dams. The contract documents are similar to those of the definite cost contract, except that the value of each item of work is defined by an agreed unit price applicable to basic units or measurable quantities of work. Because the drawings for these types of contracts tend to be diagrammatic, and are not always measured drawings drawn to scale (as in the case of building construction drawings), the payments to the contractor must be determined by measuring the work completed in the field. The amount of work completed to date is established by actual measurement in terms of units of work, and the total value of work is determined by multiplying the units completed by the pre-agreed unit prices stated in the agreement.

Occasionally there is need to supplement a determined sum contract with provision for payment for certain portions of the work by unit prices. A typical example is a building that requires excavation for a basement, with the expectation that there will be considerable amounts of stone or rock strata. Leaving to guesswork the total cost of excavating solid rock could result in a higher cost to the owner, or a loss to the contractor because of unknown quantities. To avoid either of these repercussions, the contract for construction may provide a reasonable unit cost for rock removal based on units measured during the actual work. Payment is then made on the basis of actual work required, rather than a nebulous estimate that may prove to be incorrect. Other items that may vary from the anticipated quantities in building construction should be treated in a similar manner.

Another use of unit pricing is in determining the final length of structural piling that may be required for the substructure of a building where the upper strata of soil is not suitable to bear the weight of the structure. Soils data gathered before construction may not be sufficient to determine the actual depth to which structural piles must be constructed or driven in order to reach suitable bearing. In this case, unit prices can be established before any work is done. This is a suitable method for determining equitable payment due the contractor should the piles exceed the anticipated depth. This method is also useful for deciding the appropriate amount of credit to be given to the contract sum if pilings are not required to the depths originally anticipated.

The use of stipulated unit prices may be convenient for finish and other items if the owner wishes to postpone some design decisions. The owner may prefer to make these selections when the building has begun to take shape and he has a better perspective on budgetary adjustments.

Cost of Work Plus Fee

For various reasons, an owner may not be satisfied with a determined sum in a contract derived by the competitive bidding procedure. Since a contractor's contingency for unforeseen cost and profit margin is not usually disclosed by the competitive bidding process, there is always the lingering question that perhaps the contract price is more to the advantage of the contractor than it is to the owner. The negotiation process is sometimes more agreeable to both parties to the contract in that the actual cost of the work as well as the contractor's mark-up for overhead and profit are often disclosed. Contracting on the basis of cost of work plus fee helps to overcome any doubt that the owner may have as to "excessive" profits of the contractor. In the cost of the work plus a fee type of contract, a schedule of values is established representing the contractor's best estimate of the actual cost of each item of the work. The contract sum is derived either by adding a pre-established percentage mark-up to each item in the schedule, or by applying a fixed pre-determined fee for overhead and profit. This fee is added to the total cost. Periodic payment is made to the contractor when an accounting of the actual cost is submitted, along with proof that these costs have been paid for.

Advantages of the cost-plus-fee contract:
- Hidden contingencies that may otherwise be concealed in the contract sum may be avoided.
- Savings are possible through careful management and coordination.
- Many of the risks that the contractor takes in the fixed sum contract method may be eliminated in the cost-plus-fee contract.

Disadvantages of the cost-plus-fee contract:
- Some costs may escalate in the course of the project, causing the contract sum to be greater than if it were fixed in the beginning.
- The work of the design professional may be greatly increased, thus the professional fees would be larger.

Guaranteed Maximum Cost Contracts

It is to the owner's benefit that the contractor be given some substantial profit incentive in the contract. In this way, the contractor is more likely to make every effort to reduce the owner's expense—through good management of labor and supervision, competitive subcontractor award techniques, thrifty purchasing methods, and by maximum available discounts obtained from suppliers (e.g., for early payment during the construction process). The cost-of-work-plus-fee contract will often specify what is sometimes called the "up-set", or "not to exceed" price. The "up-set" price is an agreed maximum contract sum, not to be exceeded. This agreement is established as a condition of the contract. Should the final cost exceed such stated amount, the contractor pre-agrees to pay any such excess. This arrangement provides excellent protection for the owner against possible cost over-runs, but may be unreasonable to the contractor unless some reciprocal benefit or incentive is provided if he is able to complete the construction at a total cost plus fee which is less than the guaranteed maximum contract sum. This contingent amount may be set as a percentage, either fixed or on a "sliding" scale, based on the difference between actual cost plus fee and the guaranteed maximum sum. Or, it may be a percentage of the apparent savings with a fixed upper limit. In any event, this continuing method offers advantages to both parties.

Advantages of maximum cost contracts:
- The owner has a definite possibility of reducing costs, unlike the fixed sum method.
- The contractor's risk is reduced and he has a chance to increase his profit by exercising creative management of the project.

Disadvantages of maximum cost contracts:
- The design professional's work, and thereby his fee, may be increased.
- The contractor is vulnerable to loss if management techniques fail to produce the project for the guaranteed price.

Bonus Provisions

Many times the Instructions to Bidders will state that "..time is the essence of the contract..". That is to say, the bidder's pledge for the number of calendar days and a definite contract sum is of vital consideration to the owner's objectives. The time required for construction is often as valuable to the owner as is a determined price that is within the owner's budget. There was a time when it was not unusual for the conditions of the contract to set forth a penalty clause. This clause made provision for the owner to assess a charge to be deducted from the contract sum for each calendar day that the contractor was late, beyond the date for substantial completion established in the contract. By the late 1950's, the penalty provision was challenged in the courts as being arbitrary and grossly unfair to the contractor, particularly when delays were caused by events beyond his control. In several "test cases", the contractor challenged the owner's right to assess and enforce such a penalty. The courts held in favor of the contractor. As a result, legal opinions were handed down which prohibited the provision of penalty clauses in construction contracts unless there was an offsetting bonus provision providing an equal monetary reward to the contractor for each day that he was able to deliver the building ahead of the established schedule. Owners who once were eager to provide substantial penalty provisions in the contract were equally reluctant to agree to any bonus provisions. Nevertheless, there were and are instances where time is a critical factor and such bonus provisions are made as an incentive to the contractor to finish as soon as possible.

Liquidated Damages

While the matter of penalty and bonus provisions was being argued, the courts also held that the covenant of the contract which promised a certain date for substantial completion was not without certain binding legal consequences. Where the owner could prove the extent of actual damages resulting from the contractor's failure to deliver the building on time, damages could be assessed based on the contractor's failure to meet the terms of the covenant. Contract provisions for liquidated damages in the event a project is not completed on time may be enforced by the courts, if the amount of such liquidated damages is not so onerous as to constitute a penalty, and where the amount of actual damages cannot be precisely computed.

The legal rationale seems to be that if "real" damages are actually incurred, then a claim for compensation is valid, where an arbitrary amount assessed as a penalty was not. As a result of these determinations, it has become common practice for the matter of timely completion to be established in either of two ways:

- The owner may establish an amount per day in the form of liquidated damages to be assessed. This amount should represent a realistic estimate of his potential loss if completion is delayed. By agreeing to such an amount in the conditions of the contract, the parties may obviate the need to litigate the issue of damages for delay. The owner can be compensated by the terms of the agreement if the contractor cannot establish that the delay was caused by factors beyond his ability and control.
- In reasoning that time is truly the essence of the contract, and that the owner shall incur real damages if the project is delayed, it follows that the owner shall also benefit if the project is completed ahead of schedule. In projects where this is the case, there is a potential benefit to both owner and contractor if the contract provides a "bonus" to the contractor for each day he finishes early, and a "penalty" for each day he is late. The courts have consistently held that such provisions are fair, just and equitable.

Profit Sharing Provisions

Just as there are methods to give the contractor incentive to complete the work quickly and economically, it follows that savings can also be more readily achieved with similar incentives for those who work under the contractor. There is a growing tendency for general contractors to subcontract large portions of the work, leaving little or no work to be accomplished by the contractor's own forces. In these cases, it is unlikely that the contractor will earn bonus provisions for early completion or for "savings" unless maximum cooperation is achieved from the subcontractors. A prudent contractor, striving to earn bonus provisions under the contract will make a similar provision in the agreements with key subcontractors allowing the subcontractors to share in any bonus or extra profit that the contractor may realize. Even without a specific proposal for a bonus or share in the ''savings'', the contractor stands to gain substantial benefits from the maximum cooperation of subcontractors as well as his own employees. Thus, it is not unusual for the contractor to reward the superintendent and key employees with a bonus or a share of profits realized from a project that has been completed on time and at a profit.

Chapter 7
CONDITIONS OF THE CONTRACT

The Contract for Construction, described in Chapter 6, is the keystone of the series of legal instruments described as the Contract Documents. In order for any agreement to be complete, the following information must be recorded: the parties must be described completely and legally; the mutual responsibilities each to the other must be thoroughly described; the rights of each party must be explained or recognized; and other anticipated definitions, relationships, conditions, procedures, requirements and alternatives must be set forth in order to avoid disputes when misunderstandings are encountered. AIA Document A101, *Standard Form of Agreement Between Owner and Contractor*, 1977 edition, is only one of several different professionally prepared forms available to facilitate the arrangement between owner and contractor. AIA Document A101 (Figures 6.2a–6.2d) consists of seven articles that describe (1) The Contract Documents, (2) The Work, (3) Time of Commencement and Substantial Completion, (4) Contract Sum, (5) Progress Payments, (6) Final Payment, and (7) Miscellaneous Provisions.

The "fruit" of the Contract for Construction is the Work. The most convenient method by which the design professional can describe the Work is by preparing drawings and technical specifications. These drawings and specifications become part of the Contract for Construction by reference and attachment. In view of the countless disputes that have taken place over contract arrangements, the language of the Contract for Construction has become more and more explicit and detailed. It has become necessary for the design professional preparing the contract documents to anticipate situations that could lead to costly disputes. The most common approach to preventing such problems (in addition to seeking the advice of an attorney) has been the preparation of additional explanatory documents which, like the drawings and specifications, are referenced and attached to the Contract for Construction. One of these explanatory documents is the General Conditions of the Contract for Construction, the subject of this chapter.

Interrelated Contracts

The Contract for Construction is an agreement between the owner and the contractor. However, there are other issues and relationships that complicate this arrangement. There is usually a distinct and separate agreement relating the services of the design professional to the owner and his objectives. AIA Document B141—*Standard Form of Agreement Between Owner and Architect* is an example of such an agreement. In order to accomplish his services, the design professional, in this case, the architect will often contract with an engineer and other consultants to perform portions of the design. (see AIA Document C141—*Standard Form of Agreement between Architect and Engineer* and AIA Document C431—*Standard Form of Agreement Between Architect and Consultant*). The contractor, in turn, makes a series of contracts between himself and various subcontractors (see AIA Document A401—*Standard Form of Agreement between Contractor and Subcontractor*). Each subcontractor has the option of contracting portions of his work to others known as sub-subcontractors. Each of the contractors is also related to various suppliers and manufacturers, either by contract or by purchase order. The purchase order is, in effect, a contract wherein the contractor agrees to purchase materials or assemblies for use in executing the work.

Figure 7.1 shows typical contractual and implied relationships that enter the stream of activity required to construct a modern facility. In his responsibility to the owner, the design professional has an indirect and implied relationship to the contractor, as well as to the various subcontractors, sub-subcontractors, suppliers and manufacturers assigned by the contractors to portions of the work.

Because of the complexity of the relationships that exist in the construction process, disputes are possible when any of the involved parties do not agree on how specific work or materials are to be furnished and installed. Over the years, common solutions have been found for many problems, and certain language has been developed and accepted among most participants regularly involved in building construction. Much of this information, in written form, is commonly included in contract documents as the General Conditions. Figure 7.2 illustrates the title page of AIA Document A201—*General Conditions of the Contract for Construction*, 1976 edition. The remainder of this document is illustrated throughout this chapter.

The General Conditions are most often contained in a supplemental document to the Contract for Construction. This document uses detailed descriptive language, supportive of, and incidental to, the Agreement between Owner and Contractor, recognizing the related work of others acting under separate agreements toward a common goal. The General Conditions, if separate, are made a part of the Contract for Construction by reference and/or attachment.

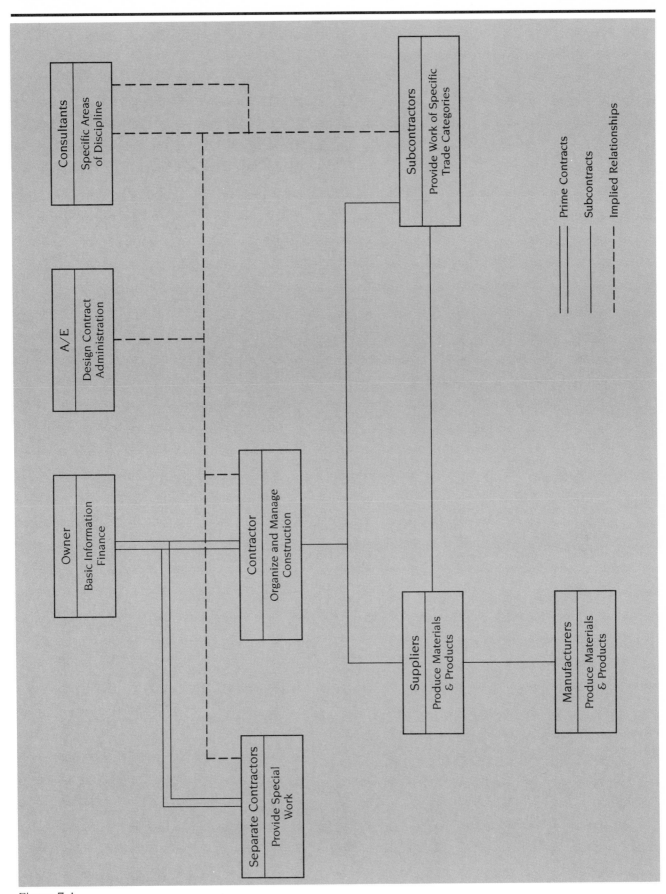

Figure 7.1

91

THE AMERICAN INSTITUTE OF ARCHITECTS

AIA Document A201

General Conditions of the Contract for Construction

THIS DOCUMENT HAS IMPORTANT LEGAL CONSEQUENCES; CONSULTATION WITH AN ATTORNEY IS ENCOURAGED WITH RESPECT TO ITS MODIFICATION

1976 EDITION
TABLE OF ARTICLES

1. CONTRACT DOCUMENTS

2. ARCHITECT

3. OWNER

4. CONTRACTOR

5. SUBCONTRACTORS

6. WORK BY OWNER OR SEPARATE CONTRACTO...

7. MISCELLANEOUS PROVIS...

14. TERMINATION OF THE CONTRACT

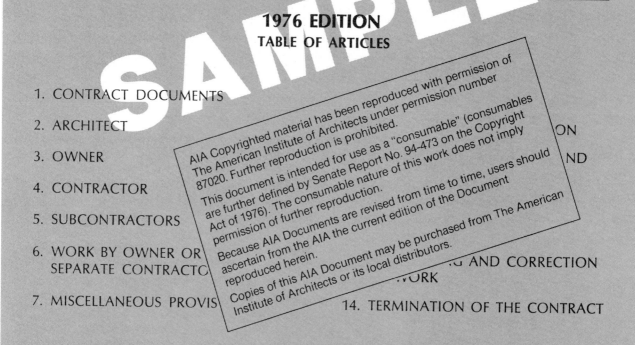

This document has been approved and endorsed by The Associated General Contractors of America.

AIA DOCUMENT A201 • GENERAL CONDITIONS OF THE CONTRACT FOR CONSTRUCTION • THIRTEENTH EDITION • AUGUST 1976
AIA® • © 1976 • THE AMERICAN INSTITUTE OF ARCHITECTS, 1735 NEW YORK AVENUE, N.W., WASHINGTON, D.C. 20006   A201-1976   1

(courtesy American Institute of Architects)

Figure 7.2

"Conditions" vs. "Requirements"

In a discussion of Conditions of the Contract, it is appropriate to contrast the difference between Conditions of the Contract, which are fundamental to the promissory relationship of the parties to the Contract for Construction, and General Requirements which are fundamental to the administrative relationship of the parties. Both elements are part of the Contract Documents. They are related, but serve very different functions. Conditions of the Contract describe and otherwise define the obligations that exist between the parties who have entered the agreement under which a project is constructed. General Requirements are specifications describing the methods by which the obligations of the agreement are to be administered.

The General Requirements are usually found in Division 1 of the technical specifications in accordance with the Construction Specification Institute's Masterformat. These requirements contain information describing the administrative provisions related to execution of the Contract for Construction. Because of the correlation that must exist among the Contract Documents, Division 1 has a direct bearing and relationship to information contained in the General Conditions and Supplemental General Conditions. Conditions of the Contract and General Requirements should be prepared carefully, and should be complementary, not redundant. Information related to contract obligation (as stated in the Conditions of the Contract) should be detailed according to administrative procedure in the General Requirements. Provisions described in Conditions of the Contract can and should be cross-referenced to the appropriate Division 1 Section which describes how the particular obligation is to be carried out. Information contained in the Conditions of the Contract should not be repeated in the General Requirements, and vice versa. The preparation of Division 1, and the content and preparation of the other 15 specifications divisions are discussed in Chapter 9—"Preparation of Specifications".

The General Conditions

There are a number of different versions of the Conditions of the Contract. Early in this century, joint committees comprised of architectural societies, ownership member groups, construction industry groups and others met and discussed mutual problems and objectives, made compromises, and jointly produced language in the form of written documents which suited many of the typical situations that were common to expensive disputes. Such a document, AIA Document A201—*General Conditions of the Contract for Construction*, is preferred for use by architects acting as the prime design professional. This document has been prepared for, and with the help of professional architects. Likewise, many engineers in the position of prime design professional prefer to use the *Standard General Conditions of the Construction Contract* which has been prepared by the Engineer's Joint Contract Documents Committee (EJCDC). The title page of this document is shown in Figure 7.3.

Many ownership agencies of state and federal government prefer to use proprietary forms of general conditions that have been specially written to suit particular types of public works projects. As published forms of contracts and general conditions have become more commonly used throughout the industry, courts of law and arbitrators have come to accept such forms as AIA Document A201 as evidence of accepted industry practice.

STANDARD
GENERAL CONDITIONS
OF THE
CONSTRUCTION CONTRACT

Prepared by

Engineers' Joint Contract Documents Committee

and

Issued and Published Jointly By

PROFESSIONAL ENGINEERS IN PRIVATE PRACTICE
A practice division of the
NATIONAL SOCIETY OF PROFESSIONAL ENGINEERS

———————————

AMERICAN CONSULTING ENGINEERS COUNCIL

———————————

AMERICAN SOCIETY OF CIVIL ENGINEERS

———————————

CONSTRUCTION SPECIFICATIONS INSTITUTE

This document has been approved and endorsed by

The Associated General Contractors of America

These General Conditions have been prepared for use with the Owner-Contractor Agreements (No. 1910-8-A-1 or 1910-8-A-2, 1983 editions). Their provisions are interrelated and a change in one may necessitate a change in the others. Comments concerning their usage are contained in the Commentary on Agreements for Engineering Services and Contract Documents, No. 1910-9, 1981 edition. For guidance in the preparation of Supplementary Conditions, see Guide to the Preparation of Supplementary Conditions (No. 1910-17, 1983 edition). When bidding is involved, the Standard Form of Instructions to Bidders (No. 1910-12, 1983 edition) may be used.

No. 1910-8 (1983 Edition)
Reprinted 8/85

Figure 7.3

It should be noted that the architect or engineer who prepares the contract documents is licensed to practice architecture or engineering, but not law, unless of course that person is a member of the bar as well. **Owners, design professionals and contractors alike should always retain competent legal counsel to review and give advice as to the form and language of the contract documents before agreements are consummated.** Design professionals must also exercise great care in preparing the contract documents, lest they inadvertently change a legal relationship or meaning. They should only do so following established legal guidelines and advice.

The Supplemental Conditions

The AIA documents have all been prepared by design and construction professionals with careful coordination of language and content under experienced legal counsel. These documents have been generally accepted by the design professions, the construction industry and the courts. **The General Conditions or any other prepared documents which are either directly or indirectly related to all of the other published contract forms and contract documents, should never be modified except by creation of a supplementary document, which is written to make any necessary alterations in the language and intent of the General Conditions. This supplementary document, common to most projects, is called the *Supplemental General Conditions*. In no case should any alteration or addenda be made to prepared documents without competent legal advice.**

Figure 7.4 illustrates a *Special Notice*, a suggested instruction placed at the beginning of the Supplemental General Conditions. This statement should clearly describe the document that it supplements as well as the intention of the supplementary document. It is helpful if the statement contains language reinforcing the fact that the document is not intended to change the general provisions of the document being modified.

Articles of the General Conditions

The following paragraphs will address the general content, objectives, and use of the General Conditions as a separate document related to the contract, and the Supplementary Conditions as a document modifying the General Conditions. AIA Documents A201 and A101 will be used as models. For demonstration purposes, the contract documents shall assume the construction of a new public building, owned by a typical municipality in the United States. For convenience in illustrating the relationships of local and state law, the author will use legislation common to the state of Texas as part of the example. Other states may have similar legislation that may vary in content and intent from state to state. It will be assumed that the Contract Documents have been prepared by a design professional who is an architect (with the benefit of legal counsel), working with engineering consultants including a civil engineer, a structural engineer, a mechanical engineer and an electrical engineer. Figures illustrating AIA Document A201 articles are shown, together with corresponding language of the Supplemental General Conditions that could accompany that document in the public building illustration. The example shall also assume that the project has been competitively bid, and the contractor with the lowest responsible bid has been awarded the contract. It is assumed that the contractor has made agreements with various subcontractors, material suppliers and manufacturers for purchase of the materials.

SPECIAL NOTICE:

The following Supplementary General Conditions amend and/or supplement the "General Conditions of the contract for Construction," hereinafter called the "General Conditions". Where any Article of the General Conditions is supplemented hereby, the provisions of the General Conditions Article shall remain in effect, and the supplemental provisions shall be considered as added thereto. Where any such article is amended, voided or superseded hereby, the provisions of the General Conditions Article not so specifically amended, voided or superseded shall remain in effect.

ARTICLE 1 - CONTRACT DOCUMENTS:

A. ADD the following new Paragraph 1.1.5:

1.1.5 MISCELLANEOUS DEFINITIONS

1.1.5.1   The term "Architect's Representative" shall mean any individual authorized to act for the Architect. Architect is defined in Article 2 of AIA Document A201 "General Conditions of the Contract for Construction" 1976 edition, as supplemented herein.

1.1.5.2   The term "Owner's Representative shall mean any individual authorized to act for the Owner. Owner is defined in Article 3 of AIA Document A201 "General Conditions of the Contract for Construction" 1976 edition.

1.1.5.3 The term "Project Manual" as used in the "Bidding Requirements", and the "Contract Documents means the bound volume containing the Table of Contents, the Bidding Requirements, the Conditions of the Contract (General and Supplemental), the Form of Performance Bond, the Form of Payment Bond, the Form of Agreement Between Owner and Contractor, the approved Forms for Use During Construction, the Sixteen Divisions of the Specifications, Contract Modifications and (by reference) the Drawings as set forth in the Schedule of Drawings.

1.1.5.4   The term "Bidding Requirements" as used in the Project Manual refers to the Invitation to Bid, the Instructions to Bidders, the Form of Proposal and the Addenda.

1.1.5.5 The term "Addenda", as used in the Project Manual, are additions or modifications made to the Contract Documents during the bidding (or negotiation) period. They are used to revise, delete, or add to any of the Bidding Requirements or Contract Documents. Addenda are a part of the Bidding Requirements as well as the Contract Documents.

1.1.5.6 The term "Specifications", as used in the Project Manual, means the technical specifications, organized in the Project Manual into sixteen (16) Divisions, that define the qualitative requirements for products, materials, and workmanship upon which the contract is based.

1.1.5.7   The term "Drawings," as used in the Project Manual, refer to graphic representations of the work to be done. They are intended to show the relationship of the materials to each other, including sizes, shapes, locations, and connections. The Drawings may include schematic diagrams showing such things as mechanical and electrical systems. They may also include schedules of structural elements, equipment, finishes and other similar items.

1.1.5.8   The term "general" as used in the Project Manual means information related to administration of the work or information of a general nature.

1.1.5.9   The title PART 1 - GENERAL is that part of a specification Section that defines the specific administrative and procedural requirements unique to that Section.

1.1.5.10   The term "product" as generally used in the Project Manual includes materials, systems and equipment.

1.1.5.11   The title PART 2 - PRODUCT is that part of a specification Section that describes in detail, the quality of items that are required for incorporation into the project under the provisions of that Section.

1.1.5.12   The term "execution" as used in the Project Manual refers to completion of incorporating an item of work into the project.

1.1.5.13   The title PART 3 - EXECUTION is that part of a specification Section that describes, in detail, preparatory actions and how the products are to be incorporated into the project.

1.1.5.14   The word "provide" is defined to mean "Furnish and install, complete, in place and ready for operation and use".

Figure 7.4

The architect includes AIA Document A201 in its entirety as part of the contract documents for the example project. AIA Document A201—*General Conditions of the Contract for Construction*, has been written and published by the American Institute of Architects as a companion document for use with a variety of other documents (such as AIA Documents A101—*Standard Form of Agreement between Owner and Contractor* and B141—*Standard Form of Agreement between Owner and Architect*). In order to adjust the conditions of the contract to better suit the client's needs, the architect correctly elects to include a separate supplemental document entitled "Supplemental General Conditions of the Contract." By creating a parallel document that refers to specific items requiring adjustment, and by using language intended to expand or modify the General Conditions for the unique purposes of his project, the design professional accomplishes such modifications without risking an interruption of the legal "harmony", of the related AIA documents forming the basis of the OPC relationship (see Chapter 1).

The remainder of this Chapter is devoted to the subject matter contained in the Conditions of the Contract for Construction. The provisions of the various articles of AIA Document A201 will be discussed along with how those provisions can be modified or expanded by the Supplemental General Conditions—to suit the example public building project and the unique requirements and mandates of the owner municipality. Related information that should be reserved for inclusion in Division 1—General Requirements of the specifications will be mentioned.

Article 1— Contract Documents

Paragraph 1.1 Definitions is shown in Figure 7.5. In the General Conditions, the Bidding Documents are clearly noted as being separate from the contract documents (subparagraph 1.1.1). Also excluded are any portions of the Addenda that may refer to the Bidding Documents. However, any portions of the Addenda which modify other contract documents do carry over to become part of the Contract Documents.

Often, either the owner, the design professional or the contractor will require a special representative or organization to represent his interests and objectives. In the case of the example municipal building project, both owner and architect require special representatives. Figure 7.4 illustrates definitions that are appropriate for inclusion in the Supplemental General Conditions to describe those representatives. In other types of projects, the Supplemental General Conditions might describe "Contracting Officer", "Project Manager", "Construction Manager" and/or other applicable titles that might be appropriate.

In the case of multiple-prime contracts, the same general and supplemental general conditions should be used. The supplemental general conditions should offer a description of each contract and briefly state the scope of that contract.

Optional supplemental definitions, such as those shown in Figure 7.4, should be included in the supplemental general conditions in order to define special terms such as "Project Manual", "Bidding Requirements" and "Addenda". It should never be assumed that because a particular term is commonly used in construction, it will be completely understood by all those involved in a construction agreement. It can be shown that terms used in the professional office can be quite different from the "jargon" of the job site. For instance, architects and engineers are familiar with the meaning and use of the "Project Manual". Those on

ARTICLE 1

CONTRACT DOCUMENTS

1.1 DEFINITIONS

1.1.1 THE CONTRACT DOCUMENTS

The Contract Documents consist of the Owner-Contractor Agreement, the Conditions of the Contract (General, Supplementary and other Conditions), the Drawings, the Specifications, and all Addenda issued prior to and all Modifications issued after execution of the Contract. A Modification is (1) a written amendment to the Contract signed by both parties, (2) a Change Order, (3) a written interpretation issued by the Architect pursuant to Subparagraph 2.2.8, or (4) a written order for a minor change in the Work issued by the Architect pursuant to Paragraph 12.4. The Contract Documents do not include Bidding Documents such as the Advertisement or Invitation to Bid, the Instructions to Bidders, sample forms, the Contractor's Bid or portions of Addenda relating to any of these, or any other documents, unless specifically enumerated in the Owner-Contractor Agreement.

1.1.2 THE CONTRACT

The Contract Documents form the Contract for Construction. This Contract represents the entire and integrated agreement between the parties hereto and supersedes all prior negotiations, representations, or agreements, either written or oral. The Contract may be amended or modified only by a Modification as defined in Subparagraph 1.1.1. The Contract Documents shall not be construed to create any contractual relationship of any kind between the Architect and the Contractor, but the Architect shall be entitled to performance of obligations intended for his benefit, and to enforcement thereof. Nothing contained in the Contract Documents shall create any contractual relationship between the Owner or the Architect and any Subcontractor or Sub-subcontractor.

1.1.3 THE WORK

The Work comprises the completed construction required by the Contract Documents and includes all labor necessary to produce such construction, and all materials and equipment incorporated or to be incorporated in such construction.

1.1.4 THE PROJECT

The Project is the total construction of which the Work performed under the Contract Documents may be the whole or a part.

1.2 EXECUTION, CORRELATION AND INTENT

1.2.1 The Contract Documents shall be signed in not less than triplicate by the Owner and Contractor. If either the Owner or the Contractor or both do not sign the Conditions of the Contract, Drawings, Specifications, or any of the other Contract Documents, the Architect shall identify such Documents.

1.2.2 By executing the Contract, the Contractor represents that he has visited the site, familiarized himself with the local conditions under which the Work is to be performed, and correlated his observations with the requirements of the Contract Documents.

1.2.3 The intent of the Contract Documents is to include all items necessary for the proper execution and completion of the Work. The Contract Documents are complementary, and what is required by any one shall be as binding as if required by all. Work not covered in the Contract Documents will not be required unless it is consistent therewith and is reasonably inferable therefrom as being necessary to produce the intended results. Words and abbreviations which have well-known technical or trade meanings are used in the Contract Documents in accordance with such recognized meanings.

1.2.4 The organization of the Specifications into divisions, sections and articles, and the arrangement of Drawings shall not control the Contractor in dividing the Work among Subcontractors or in establishing the extent of Work to be performed by any trade.

1.3 OWNERSHIP AND USE OF DOCUMENTS

1.3.1 All Drawings, Specifications and copies thereof furnished by the Architect are and shall remain his property. They are to be used only with respect to this Project and are not to be used on any other project. With the exception of one contract set for each party to the Contract, such documents are to be returned or suitably accounted for to the Architect on request at the completion of the Work. Submission or distribution to meet official regulatory requirements or for other purposes in connection with the Project is not to be construed as publication in derogation of the Architect's common law copyright or other reserved rights.

ARTICLE 2

ARCHITECT

2.1 DEFINITION

2.1.1 The Architect is the person lawfully licensed to practice architecture, or an entity lawfully practicing architecture identified as such in the Owner-Contractor Agreement, and is referred to throughout the Contract Documents as if singular in number and masculine in gender. The term Architect means the Architect or his authorized representative.

2.2 ADMINISTRATION OF THE CONTRACT

2.2.1 The Architect will provide administration of the Contract as hereinafter described.

2.2.2 The Architect will be the Owner's representative during construction and until final payment is due. The Architect will advise and consult with the Owner. The Owner's instructions to the Contractor shall be forwarded

(courtesy American Institute of Architects)

Figure 7.5

the job site may refer to the same bound volume containing the Bid Requirements, the Conditions of the Contract, and the Technical Specifications as the "Specs". The design professional should define the subdivisions of information to be found in the three part format of each section of the specifications. Again, it should not be assumed that the contractor or those among his work force will be familiar with the design professional's method for organizing the Contract Documents.

Subparagraph 1.1.1—The Contract Documents is shown in Figure 7.5. There are occasions when owners, particularly those in the public sector, will want the Bidding Requirements included in the Contract Documents. The reason for this seems to be the need to establish the contractor's bid and the conditions under which the bid was tendered as part of the Contract Documents for the public record. As competitive bidding is a requirement of law for many public sector owners, the inclusion of the bidding documents serves as a defense should a rejected bidder choose to challenge the selection of the contractor.

Subparagraph 1.1.2—The Contract shown in Figure 7.5, binds together the named Contract Documents specifically, excluding any other information by stating that the Contract supersedes all prior negotiations, representations, or agreements—either written or oral. If a claim should later be made by one of the parties to the contract (based on the negotiation phase or some other event prior to contractual acceptance by both parties) and it is not specifically written in or otherwise included in the agreement, that claim would be unfounded.

The statement regarding the Contract is very specific in stating that there is no contractual relationship or obligation between the contractor and the architect (or engineer), and that the owner has no contractual relationship or other obligation to subcontractors or sub-subcontractors.

Subparagraph 1.1.3—The Work is also shown in Figure 7.5. This rather brief description of the Work is sufficient because of the key words "completed" and "all" used in relation to labor and material. Any further description of the work would be redundant as the content and various descriptions are contained in other contract documents.

Subparagraph 1.1.4—The Project is shown in Figure 7.5. The word "project" is often used to describe the Work. The Contract for Construction may not always be related to the total project. For example, in the case of "fast-track" projects, only certain portions of the Project may be contracted at one time. In the case of separate prime contracts, described portions of the project may be assigned to separate contractors working in a parallel or coordinated manner. If this method was used for the example public building, the Supplementary General Conditions would contain a statement referring to a Division 1 section, such as Section 01010—*Summary of the Work*. The individual duties and procedures of each contractor can be found in this section for purposes of coordination.

The Supplemental General Conditions could also support this paragraph, giving a more detailed description of the project such as name of project, address, county and state. Such a statement may include a legal description of the owner's property, stating the volume and page number of recorded deeds and other legal descriptions. Subparagraph 3.2.2 (see Figure 7.8) establishes certain owner-furnished information including surveys and property descriptions. The design professional should decide upon the most appropriate location for descriptive property information, and not attempt to duplicate that information in more that one location in the documents.

Paragraph 1.2—Execution, Correlation and Intent is shown in Figure 7.5. Some legal counsellors believe that, unless all of the Contract Documents are initialled and dated by each of the parties to the contract on each page, it may be difficult to prove in a court of law the exact understanding of each provision of the agreement. In the case of major projects, where the pages of the contract documents could number into the hundreds, this requirement is impractical. Subparagraph 1.2.1 shown in Figure 7.5 intends that identification of the appropriate documents be left to the architect (or engineer).

Subparagraph 1.2.2 does not allow the contractor any legitimate defense based on a plead of ignorance of site conditions. On the other hand, it would be unfair to hold the contractor responsible for conditions that become known only after work begins. If either the owner or the design professional anticipates the possibility that these kinds of unknown conditions may affect the projects, the Supplemental General Conditions should modify this paragraph and should refer to the Division 1 section of the specifications, Section 01025— *Measurement and Payment*, to provide for the measurement and payment of such conditions as excess rock found in excavations, or for extra length of foundation piles that may be recommended by the architect's structural consultant. By anticipating such events, and providing unit prices in the Form of Proposal as well as the Contract for Construction, work that may vary from the requirements of the Contract Documents can be paid for under pre-arranged terms. In this way, both the owner and the contractor are protected from disputes that may arise over unspecified work discovered after the Contract for Construction is executed. Unit prices included in the body of the Contract for Construction establish pre-agreed prices for labor and materials; these prices may be applied to any contingent work not covered by the Contract Documents or included in the bid price.

It is important that the constructors who bid the work be completely familiar with the site and its conditions. The design professional may wish to reinforce this requirement with supplemental language such as that illustrated in Subparagraph 1.2.2 in Figure 7.6.

Subparagraph 1.2.3, shown in Figure 7.5 stresses the complementary nature of the contract documents in relation to each other. It also eliminates any misconception that there is an "unwritten" precedence among the Contract Documents as to which document will govern in the case of error or inconsistency. Subparagraph 4.2.1, in Figure 7.6 includes supplemental language requiring that the design professional be the judge of precedence in the case of error or inconsistency in the documents. It is not necessary to modify the language of Subparagraph 1.2.3 (Figure 7.5) by supplement unless there are some unusual conditions in the description of the work. In such cases, a description in Division 1, Section 01010—*Summary of the Work* may suffice.

A great many disputes occur because of the contractor's failure to fully describe the extent of work that he may expect of a subcontractor. In such cases, a subcontractor may wish to use the organization of the specifications or drawings as a defense of the extent of his responsibility. Subparagraph 1.2.4, shown in Figure 7.5, clearly states that the organization of the specification sections or arrangement of the drawings has no bearing on jurisdictional matters related to the work of

1.2.2 - EXECUTION, CORRELATION AND INTENT

C.   ADD to Subparagraph 1.2.2 the following:

No allowance shall subsequently be made on behalf of the Contractor on account of an error on his part or his negligence or failure to acquaint himself with the conditions of the site.

D.   ADD to Subparagraph 1.2.4 the following:

Such separations shall not make the Architect an arbiter to establish subcontract limits. No responsibility, either lindirect or implied, is assumed by the Architect for omissions or duplications by the Contractor or by his Subcontractors due to real or alleged error in the arrangement of the Specifications.

1.3 - OWNERSHIP AND USE OF DOCUMENTS:

E.   ADD to Subparagraph 1.3.1 the following:

All copies of drawings and specifications shall be returned to the Architect as a part of the Contractor's application for final payment. The Contractor shall make an accounting satisfactory to the Architect for sets lost or destroyed during construction.

ARTICLE 2 - ARCHITECT:

A.   ADD to Subparagraph 2.1.1 the following:

The term "Architect" shall refer to (Name of Architect) (Address of Architect), (Telephone number of Architect).

   (Add Names and Addresses of Architect's Consultants)

2.2 - ADMINISTRATION OF THE CONTRACT:

A.   ADD to Subparagraph 2.2.1 the following:

The Contractor shall, in writing, call to the attention of the Architect any discrepancies between Specifications, Plans, details or schedules. The Architect will then inform the Contractor, in writing, which document takes precedence.

B.   ADD to Subparagraph 2.2.13 the following:

Certain portions of the work will be tested and/or observed at various stages, sometimes off the site, between their observation and final positioning in the completed work. Nothing in any prior approval or satisfactory test result shall govern if at any subsequent time the work or portion thereof, is found not to conform to requirements of the Contract Documents.

ARTICLE 3 - OWNER

3.2 - INFORMATION AND SERVICES REQUIRED OF THE OWNER.

E.   ADD to Subparagraph 3.2.5 the following:

At the time of award of Contract, the Contractor will be furnished free of charge, eighteen (18) complete sets of Drawings and Specifications for use as instruments of the Contract. At the request of the General Contractor, additional sets of Drawings and/or Specifications will be furnished at actual reproduction costs, to be paid by the General Contractor. All save two, sets of Drawings and Specifications issued to the Contractor shall be returned, or a strict accounting of the disposition of any sets not returned, to the Architect within 10 days of the issuance of a Certificate of Completion by the Architect.

ARTICLE 4 - CONTRACTOR

4.2 - REVIEW OF CONTRACT DOCUMENTS

A: DELETE Paragraph 4.2.1 in its entirety and SUBSTITUTE the following:

4.2.1   Contractor shall carefully study and compare all of the Contract Documents and shall at once report to the Architect, in writing, any error, inconsistency or omission he may discover. The Architect will then inform the contractor, in writing, which document takes precedence. Contractor shall be liable for any damage to Owner for failure to so report any error, inconsistency or omission he may discover or should have discovered, but he shall not be liable to Owner or Architect for any damage resulting from any such error, inconsistency or omission which he should not have discovered or which he did discover and at once so reported. Contractor shall perform no portion of the work at any time without Contract Documents or, where required, approved Shop Drawings, Product Data or Samples for such portions of the Work.

Figure 7.6

various trades. To reinforce this statement, the design professional may wish to add by supplement, a statement to the effect that the design professional will not be an arbiter in such disputes. A typical supplemental statement is shown in Figure 7.6.

In coordinating the contract documents, the design professional should always bear in mind that the language of the documents is directed to the relationship between owner and contractor. No matter how tempting it may be to address certain notes or language to a traditional trade or subcontractor or to arbitrarily set the boundaries of sub-trades either directly or indirectly, such practices are incorrect. The contractor alone is the party responsible for establishing the limits of those parties related to him by separate contract or other agreement.

Paragraph 1.3 Ownership and Use of Documents is shown in Figure 7.5. The statement in the General Conditions relative to ownership of the drawings and specifications serves a number of useful purposes. First of all, it clearly establishes that the contract documents belong to the design professional (architect), and that their purpose is to serve as Instruments of Service for this contract only. The effect of this ownership and use statement is to prevent the owner or contractor from any re-use of the documents for any other purpose without compensating the design professional for the value of their re-use. The statement also implies that the documents, firmly in the possession of the design professional, will remain as permanent documentation of the work, available for use in the future when additions or alterations may be desirable.

The owner (federal, state or town government) may in the future wish to construct several other public buildings identical or similar to that described in the Contract Documents. Certain language may be inserted into the agreement between owner and design professional regarding compensation for reuse of the Documents for similar or multiple projects.

Article 2— Architect

Article 2 of the General Conditions (Figures 7.5, 7.7, and 7.8) shows the language of the General Conditions used to identify the design professional, in this case, the Architect. Also included is the role of the design professional in the OPC relationship and the indirect relationship to the Contract for Construction. Many design professionals and owners prefer to supplement Article 2 by adding language in the Supplemental General Conditions, as shown in Figure 7.6, that identifies the design professional by name and naming the consultants serving the design professional as well.

The duties of the design professional are set forth in detail in the General Conditions. The design professional may wish to supplement sub-paragraph 2.2.1, shown in Figure 7.5 by the corresponding supplemental statement shown in Figure 7.6. This statement, directing the contractor to report errors and inconsistencies to the design professional has a bearing on sub-paragraph 1.2.3 of the General Conditions (Figure 7.5).

To reinforce the judgment of the design professional in determining and approving work, Subparagraph 2.2.13 (shown in Figure 7.7) states the authority of the design professional, as interpreter of the Contract Documents. (See Subparagraph 2.2.7, Figure 7.7). In order to prove whether or not work meets specified Quality Standards, the design through the Architect. The Architect will have authority to act on behalf of the Owner only to the extent provided in the Contract Documents, unless otherwise modified by written instrument in accordance with Subparagraph 2.2.18.

2.2.3 The Architect will visit the site at intervals appropriate to the stage of construction to familiarize himself generally with the progress and quality of the Work and to determine in general if the Work is proceeding in accordance with the Contract Documents. However, the Architect will not be required to make exhaustive or continuous on-site inspections to check the quality or quantity of the Work. On the basis of his on-site observations as an architect, he will keep the Owner informed of the progress of the Work, and will endeavor to guard the Owner against defects and deficiencies in the Work of the Contractor.

2.2.4 The Architect will not be responsible for and will not have control or charge of construction means, methods, techniques, sequences or procedures, or for safety precautions and programs in connection with the Work, and he will not be responsible for the Contractor's failure to carry out the Work in accordance with the Contract Documents. The Architect will not be responsible for or have control or charge over the acts or omissions of the Contractor, Subcontractors, or any of their agents or employees, or any other persons performing any of the Work.

2.2.5 The Architect shall at all times have access to the Work wherever it is in preparation and progress. The Contractor shall provide facilities for such access so the Architect may perform his functions under the Contract Documents.

2.2.6 Based on the Architect's observations and an evaluation of the Contractor's Applications for Payment, the Architect will determine the amounts owing to the Contractor and will issue Certificates for Payment in such amounts, as provided in Paragraph 9.4.

2.2.7 The Architect will be the interpreter of the requirements of the Contract Documents and the judge of the performance thereunder by both the Owner and Contractor.

2.2.8 The Architect will render interpretations necessary for the proper execution or progress of the Work, with reasonable promptness and in accordance with any time limit agreed upon. Either party to the Contract may make written request to the Architect for such interpretations.

2.2.9 Claims, disputes and other matters in question between the Contractor and the Owner relating to the execution or progress of the Work or the interpretation of the Contract Documents shall be referred initially to the Architect for decision which he will render in writing within a reasonable time.

2.2.10 All interpretations and decisions of the Architect shall be consistent with the intent of and reasonably inferable from the Contract Documents and will be in writing or in the form of drawings. In his capacity as interpreter and judge, he will endeavor to secure faithful performance by both the Owner and the Contractor, will not

show partiality to either, and will not be liable for the result of any interpretation or decision rendered in good faith in such capacity.

2.2.11 The Architect's decisions in matters relating to artistic effect will be final if consistent with the intent of the Contract Documents.

2.2.12 Any claim, dispute or other matter in question between the Contractor and the Owner referred to the Architect, except those relating to artistic effect as provided in Subparagraph 2.2.11 and except those which have been waived by the making or acceptance of final payment as provided in Subparagraphs 9.9.4 and 9.9.5, shall be subject to arbitration upon the written demand of either party. However, no demand for arbitration of any such claim, dispute or other matter may be made until the earlier of (1) the date on which the Architect has rendered a written decision, or (2) the tenth day after the parties have presented their evidence to the Architect or have been given a reasonable opportunity to do so, if the Architect has not rendered his written decision by that date. When such a written decision of the Architect states (1) that the decision is final but subject to appeal, and (2) that any demand for arbitration of a claim, dispute or other matter covered by such decision must be made within thirty days after the date on which the party making the demand receives the written decision, failure to demand arbitration within said thirty days' period will result in the Architect's decision becoming final and binding upon the Owner and the Contractor. If the Architect renders a decision after arbitration proceedings have been initiated, such decision may be entered as evidence but will not supersede any arbitration proceedings unless the decision is acceptable to all parties concerned.

2.2.13 The Architect will have authority to reject Work which does not conform to the Contract Documents. Whenever, in his opinion, he considers it necessary or advisable for the implementation of the intent of the Contract Documents, he will have authority to require special inspection or testing of the Work in accordance with Subparagraph 7.7.2 whether or not such Work be then fabricated, installed or completed. However, neither the Architect's authority to act under this Subparagraph 2.2.13, nor any decision made by him in good faith either to exercise or not to exercise such authority, shall give rise to any duty or responsibility of the Architect to the Contractor, any Subcontractor, any of their agents or employees, or any other person performing any of the Work.

2.2.14 The Architect will review and approve or take other appropriate action upon Contractor's submittals such as Shop Drawings, Product Data and Samples, but only for conformance with the design concept of the Work and with the information given in the Contract Documents. Such action shall be taken with reasonable promptness so as to cause no delay. The Architect's approval of a specific item shall not indicate approval of an assembly of which the item is a component.

2.2.15 The Architect will prepare Change Orders in accordance with Article 12, and will have authority to order minor changes in the Work as provided in Subparagraph 12.4.1.

AIA DOCUMENT A201 • GENERAL CONDITIONS OF THE CONTRACT FOR CONSTRUCTION • THIRTEENTH EDITION • AUGUST 1976
AIA® • © 1976 • THE AMERICAN INSTITUTE OF ARCHITECTS, 1735 NEW YORK AVENUE, N.W., WASHINGTON, D.C. 20006

(courtesy American Institute of Architects)

Figure 7.7

2.2.16 The Architect will conduct inspections to determine the dates of Substantial Completion and final completion, will receive and forward to the Owner for the Owner's review written warranties and related documents required by the Contract and assembled by the Contractor, and will issue a final Certificate for Payment upon compliance with the requirements of Paragraph 9.9.

2.2.17 If the Owner and Architect agree, the Architect will provide one or more Project Representatives to assist the Architect in carrying out his responsibilities at the site. The duties, responsibilities and limitations of authority of any such Project Representative shall be as set forth in an exhibit to be incorporated in the Contract Documents.

2.2.18 The duties, responsibilities and limitations of authority of the Architect as the Owner's representative during construction as set forth in the Contract Documents will not be modified or extended without written consent of the Owner, the Contractor and the Architect.

2.2.19 In case of the termination of the employment of the Architect, the Owner shall appoint an architect against whom the Contractor makes no reasonable objection whose status under the Contract Documents shall be that of the former architect. Any dispute in connection with such appointment shall be subject to arbitration.

ARTICLE 3

OWNER

3.1   DEFINITION

3.1.1 The Owner is the person or entity identified as such in the Owner-Contractor Agreement and is referred to throughout the Contract Documents as if singular in number and masculine in gender. The term Owner means the Owner or his authorized representative.

3.2   INFORMATION AND SERVICES REQUIRED OF THE OWNER

3.2.1 The Owner shall, at the request of the Contractor, at the time of execution of the Owner-Contractor Agreement, furnish to the Contractor reasonable evidence that he has made financial arrangements to fulfill his obligations under the Contract. Unless such reasonable evidence is furnished, the Contractor is not required to execute the Owner-Contractor Agreement or to commence the Work.

3.2.2 The Owner shall furnish all surveys describing the physical characteristics, legal limitations and utility locations for the site of the Project, and a legal description of the site.

3.2.3 Except as provided in Subparagraph 4.7.1, the Owner shall secure and pay for necessary approvals, easements, assessments and charges required for the construction, use or occupancy of permanent structures or for permanent changes in existing facilities.

3.2.4 Information or services under the Owner's control shall be furnished by the Owner with reasonable promptness to avoid delay in the orderly progress of the Work.

3.2.5 Unless otherwise provided in the Contract Documents, the Contractor will be furnished, free of charge, all copies of Drawings and Specifications reasonably necessary for the execution of the Work.

3.2.6 The Owner shall forward all instructions to the Contractor through the Architect.

3.2.7 The foregoing are in addition to other duties and responsibilities of the Owner enumerated herein and especially those in respect to Work by Owner or by Separate Contractors, Payments and Completion, and Insurance in Articles 6, 9 and 11 respectively.

3.3   OWNER'S RIGHT TO STOP THE WORK

3.3.1 If the Contractor fails to correct defective Work as required by Paragraph 13.2 or persistently fails to carry out the Work in accordance with the Contract Documents, the Owner, by a written order signed personally or by an agent specifically so empowered by the Owner in writing, may order the Contractor to stop the Work, or any portion thereof, until the cause for such order has been eliminated; however, this right of the Owner to stop the Work shall not give rise to any duty on the part of the Owner to exercise this right for the benefit of the Contractor or any other person or entity, except to the extent required by Subparagraph 6.1.3.

3.4   OWNER'S RIGHT TO CARRY OUT THE WORK

3.4.1 If the Contractor defaults or neglects to carry out the Work in accordance with the Contract Documents and fails within seven days after receipt of written notice from the Owner to commence and continue correction of such default or neglect with diligence and promptness, the Owner may, after seven days following receipt by the Contractor of an additional written notice and without prejudice to any other remedy he may have, make good such deficiencies. In such case an appropriate Change Order shall be issued deducting from the payments then or thereafter due the Contractor the cost of correcting such deficiencies, including compensation for the Architect's additional services made necessary by such default, neglect or failure. Such action by the Owner and the amount charged to the Contractor are both subject to the prior approval of the Architect. If the payments then or thereafter due the Contractor are not sufficient to cover such amount, the Contractor shall pay the difference to the Owner.

ARTICLE 4

CONTRACTOR

4.1   DEFINITION

4.1.1 The Contractor is the person or entity identified as such in the Owner-Contractor Agreement and is referred to throughout the Contract Documents as if singular in number and masculine in gender. The term Contractor means the Contractor or his authorized representative.

4.2   REVIEW OF CONTRACT DOCUMENTS

4.2.1 The Contractor shall carefully study and compare the Contract Documents and shall at once report to the Architect any error, inconsistency or omission he may discover. The Contractor shall not be liable to the Owner or

(courtesy American Institute of Architects)

Figure 7.8

professional will often rely on the results of specified testing to confirm his judgment. However, it is possible for a material or an assembly to meet the test while failing to meet other specified criteria. To establish the relative significance of test results, the design professional may wish to include a corresponding supplementary statement (Figure 7.6). This statement may indicate that testing of materials, systems and other items may be conducted from time to time and from place to place, and that the test results, relative to specified quality, etc., take precedence over the design professional's judgment in approving the completed work.

Article 3—Owner

Paragraph 3.1, shown in Figure 7.8 identifies the owner, a prime party to the Contract for Construction. Since the owner has already been identified by name in the Contract for Construction, it is not necessary to add a supplemental statement with the owner's name identification in the Supplemental General Conditions.

Paragraph 3.2 Information and Services required of the Owner (Figure 7.8) set forth duties, obligations, information and services that the owner is normally obligated to perform. If the owner's ability to make payment is for any reason dependent upon the award of contract or budget limitations that could be exceeded by the bid proposals or if additional financial arrangements or commitments must be made, the owner's legal counsel may wish to add supplemental language to this paragraph. The purpose of such a supplemental statement is to protect the owner from claims of non-performance or damages should the Contract Sum exceed the owner's ability to make 100% of payments under the agreement. The statements of Subparagraph 3.2.2 (Figure 7.8) may be sufficient to generally describe the information furnished by the owner about the property. In the discussion of Subparagraph 1.1.4, it was mentioned that the design professional should choose the best and most appropriate location for supplemental information regarding property descriptions. If this kind of legal description of the owner's property has not been supplemented to Subparagraph 1.1.4, the design professional may wish to do so in relation to Subparagraph 3.2.2. Subparagraph 3.2.4 requires the owner's services to be timely in order not to delay the work. No supplemental language is usually needed to enforce that obligation.

The Supplemental General Conditions may add language (as shown in Figure 7.6) to supplement Subparagraph 3.2.5 (Figure 7.8). Such a statement may address the issue of the owner's responsibility to furnish copies of the Contract Documents. This matter otherwise involves an anticipated expense on the part of the contractor. If the project has been through the competitive bidding process, additional copies of the Contract Documents may already be available for the contractor's purposes without much, or any, additional expense on the part of the owner. Anticipating the need for bidding documents to be returned after or during the competitive bidding process, the design professional may be prompted to add specific language to the Invitation (or Advertisement) for Bids which would establish the conditions for return of documents used by the bidders as a condition of Proposal consideration. The design professional may have included a statement in the Instructions to Bidders regarding payment of deposits for the issuance and use of sets of the Contract Documents.

Paragraph 3.3 Owner's Right to Stop the Work is shown in Figure 7.8. The owner has the right to stop the work and terminate the Contract for Construction if the contractor persistently fails to correct portions of the work, or in the case of consistent failure to perform the work in accordance with the Contract Documents. This statement usually needs no supplemental language.

Paragraph 3.4 Owner's Right to Carry Out the Work is shown in Figure 7.8. Although the design professional has the right to reject work as illustrated in Figure 7.7, he does not have the right to stop the continuity of work if and when he may discover that the work does not conform to the requirements of the Contract Documents. The design professional is responsible for making full written disclosure of his findings and opinion on such matters to the owner. The owner, in turn, as a party to the Contract for Construction, must take the required action to stop the work, should that action become necessary. Subparagraph 3.4.1, shown in Figure 7.8, defines the owner's right to carry out the work in case of default and provides for the collection of any expense that may exceed the Contract Sum expressed in the agreement. In other words, this provision acknowledges the owner's right to collect his actual damages incurred as a result of the contractor's default.

Article 4— Contractor

Paragraph 4.1, (Figure 7.8) is a brief definition and identification of the contractor—the second party to the Contract for Construction. Since the contractor, like the owner, is a party to (and is identified in) the Contract for Construction, it is not usually necessary to add supplemental language for the purpose of further identification.

Subparagraphs 4.2.1 through 4.17.3 expand the responsibilities of the contractor, setting forth duties and procedures common to and necessary for most construction projects.

Paragraph 4.2 deals with the contractor's responsibility to review the contract documents. The contractor is charged with the responsibility of thoroughly studying the Contract Documents and reporting any inconsistencies to the design professional. This subparagraph further states that the contractor is not to be held liable for any damage resulting from errors and omissions on the part of the design professional. There is an intended spirit of trust and mutual cooperation among all parties in the OPC relationship. Many practicing design professionals believe that the spirit of cooperation is not sufficiently reinforced by the wording of this statement. It would be grossly unfair if the contractor were required to pay for the consequences of an error on the part of the design professional. Nevertheless, it is also intended that should any such error exist, it be discovered and disclosed at the earliest possible time. In most cases, early discovery and remedy of such inconsistencies will prevent possible litigation along with legal and court fees and payment of damages.

Intending to discover any inconsistencies in the Contract Documents at the earliest possible moment, many design professionals prefer to supplement or replace the language of Paragraph 4.2.1 with a supplemental subparagraph such as that shown in Figure 7.6. Subparagraph 4.2.1 further states that under no conditions shall the contractor attempt to accomplish any work without the Contract Documents as his guide. Here again we see the vital importance of the Contract Documents in defining, controlling and illustrating the work.

the Architect for any damage resulting from any such errors, inconsistencies or omissions in the Contract Documents. The Contractor shall perform no portion of the Work at any time without Contract Documents or, where required, approved Shop Drawings, Product Data or Samples for such portion of the Work.

4.3 SUPERVISION AND CONSTRUCTION PROCEDURES

4.3.1 The Contractor shall supervise and direct the Work, using his best skill and attention. He shall be solely responsible for all construction means, methods, techniques, sequences and procedures and for coordinating all portions of the Work under the Contract.

4.3.2 The Contractor shall be responsible to the Owner for the acts and omissions of his employees, Subcontractors and their agents and employees, and other persons performing any of the Work under a contract with the Contractor.

4.3.3 The Contractor shall not be relieved from his obligations to perform the Work in accordance with the Contract Documents either by the activities or duties of the Architect in his administration of the Contract, or by inspections, tests or approvals required or performed under Paragraph 7.7 by persons other than the Contractor.

4.4 LABOR AND MATERIALS

4.4.1 Unless otherwise provided in the Contract Documents, the Contractor shall provide and pay for all labor, materials, equipment, tools, construction equipment and machinery, water, heat, utilities, transportation, and other facilities and services necessary for the proper execution and completion of the Work, whether temporary or permanent and whether or not incorporated or to be incorporated in the Work.

4.4.2 The Contractor shall at all times enforce strict discipline and good order among his employees and shall not employ on the Work any unfit person or anyone not skilled in the task assigned to him.

4.5 WARRANTY

4.5.1 The Contractor warrants to the Owner and the Architect that all materials and equipment furnished under this Contract will be new unless otherwise specified, and that all Work will be of good quality, free from faults and defects and in conformance with the Contract Documents. All Work not conforming to these requirements, including substitutions not properly approved and authorized, may be considered defective. If required by the Architect, the Contractor shall furnish satisfactory evidence as to the kind and quality of materials and equipment. This warranty is not limited by the provisions of Paragraph 13.2.

4.6 TAXES

4.6.1 The Contractor shall pay all sales, consumer, use and other similar taxes for the Work or portions thereof provided by the Contractor which are legally enacted at the time bids are received, whether or not yet effective.

4.7 PERMITS, FEES AND NOTICES

4.7.1 Unless otherwise provided in the Contract Documents, the Contractor shall secure and pay for the building permit and for all other permits and governmental fees, licenses and inspections necessary for the proper execution and completion of the Work which are customarily secured after execution of the Contract and which are legally required at the time the bids are received.

4.7.2 The Contractor shall give all notices and comply with all laws, ordinances, rules, regulations and lawful orders of any public authority bearing on the performance of the Work.

4.7.3 It is not the responsibility of the Contractor to make certain that the Contract Documents are in accordance with applicable laws, statutes, building codes and regulations. If the Contractor observes that any of the Contract Documents are at variance therewith in any respect, he shall promptly notify the Architect in writing, and any necessary changes shall be accomplished by appropriate Modification.

4.7.4 If the Contractor performs any Work knowing it to be contrary to such laws, ordinances, rules and regulations, and without such notice to the Architect, he shall assume full responsibility therefor and shall bear all costs attributable thereto.

4.8 ALLOWANCES

4.8.1 The Contractor shall include in the Contract Sum all allowances stated in the Contract Documents. Items covered by these allowances shall be supplied for such amounts and by such persons as the Owner may direct, but the Contractor will not be required to employ persons against whom he makes a reasonable objection.

4.8.2 Unless otherwise provided in the Contract Documents:

 .1 these allowances shall cover the cost to the Contractor, less any applicable trade discount, of the materials and equipment required by the allowance delivered at the site, and all applicable taxes;

 .2 the Contractor's costs for unloading and handling on the site, labor, installation costs, overhead, profit and other expenses contemplated for the original allowance shall be included in the Contract Sum and not in the allowance;

 .3 whenever the cost is more than or less than the allowance, the Contract Sum shall be adjusted accordingly by Change Order, the amount of which will recognize changes, if any, in handling costs on the site, labor, installation costs, overhead, profit and other expenses.

4.9 SUPERINTENDENT

4.9.1 The Contractor shall employ a competent superintendent and necessary assistants who shall be in attendance at the Project site during the progress of the Work. The superintendent shall represent the Contractor and all communications given to the superintendent shall be as binding as if given to the Contractor. Important communications shall be confirmed in writing. Other communications shall be so confirmed on written request in each case.

4.10 PROGRESS SCHEDULE

4.10.1 The Contractor, immediately after being awarded the Contract, shall prepare and submit for the Owner's and Architect's information an estimated progress sched-

(courtesy American Institute of Architects)

Figure 7.9

ule for the Work. The progress schedule shall be related to the entire Project to the extent required by the Contract Documents, and shall provide for expeditious and practicable execution of the Work.

4.11 DOCUMENTS AND SAMPLES AT THE SITE

4.11.1 The Contractor shall maintain at the site for the Owner one record copy of all Drawings, Specifications, Addenda, Change Orders and other Modifications, in good order and marked currently to record all changes made during construction, and approved Shop Drawings, Product Data and Samples. These shall be available to the Architect and shall be delivered to him for the Owner upon completion of the Work.

4.12 SHOP DRAWINGS, PRODUCT DATA AND SAMPLES

4.12.1 Shop Drawings are drawings, diagrams, schedules and other data specially prepared for the Work by the Contractor or any Subcontractor, manufacturer, supplier or distributor to illustrate some portion of the Work.

4.12.2 Product Data are illustrations, standard schedules, performance charts, instructions, brochures, diagrams and other information furnished by the Contractor to illustrate a material, product or system for some portion of the Work.

4.12.3 Samples are physical examples which illustrate materials, equipment or workmanship and establish standards by which the Work will be judged.

4.12.4 The Contractor shall review, approve and submit, with reasonable promptness and in such sequence as to cause no delay in the Work or in the work of the Owner or any separate contractor, all Shop Drawings, Product Data and Samples required by the Contract Documents.

4.12.5 By approving and submitting Shop Drawings, Product Data and Samples, the Contractor represents that he has determined and verified all materials, field measurements, and field construction criteria related thereto, or will do so, and that he has checked and coordinated the information contained within such submittals with the requirements of the Work and of the Contract Documents.

4.12.6 The Contractor shall not be relieved of responsibility for any deviation from the requirements of the Contract Documents by the Architect's approval of Shop Drawings, Product Data or Samples under Subparagraph 2.2.14 unless the Contractor has specifically informed the Architect in writing of such deviation at the time of submission and the Architect has given written approval to the specific deviation. The Contractor shall not be relieved from responsibility for errors or omissions in the Shop Drawings, Product Data or Samples by the Architect's approval thereof.

4.12.7 The Contractor shall direct specific attention, in writing or on resubmitted Shop Drawings, Product Data or Samples, to revisions other than those requested by the Architect on previous submittals.

4.12.8 No portion of the Work requiring submission of a Shop Drawing, Product Data or Sample shall be commenced until the submittal has been approved by the Architect as provided in Subparagraph 2.2.14. All such

portions of the Work shall be in accordance with approved submittals.

4.13 USE OF SITE

4.13.1 The Contractor shall confine operations at the site to areas permitted by law, ordinances, permits and the Contract Documents and shall not unreasonably encumber the site with any materials or equipment.

4.14 CUTTING AND PATCHING OF WORK

4.14.1 The Contractor shall be responsible for all cutting, fitting or patching that may be required to complete the Work or to make its several parts fit together properly.

4.14.2 The Contractor shall not damage or endanger any portion of the Work or the work of the Owner or any separate contractors by cutting, patching or otherwise altering any work, or by excavation. The Contractor shall not cut or otherwise alter the work of the Owner or any separate contractor except with the written consent of the Owner and of such separate contractor. The Contractor shall not unreasonably withhold from the Owner or any separate contractor his consent to cutting or otherwise altering the Work.

4.15 CLEANING UP

4.15.1 The Contractor at all times shall keep the premises free from accumulation of waste materials or rubbish caused by his operations. At the completion of the Work he shall remove all his waste materials and rubbish from and about the Project as well as all his tools, construction equipment, machinery and surplus materials.

4.15.2 If the Contractor fails to clean up at the completion of the Work, the Owner may do so as provided in Paragraph 3.4 and the cost thereof shall be charged to the Contractor.

4.16 COMMUNICATIONS

4.16.1 The Contractor shall forward all communications to the Owner through the Architect.

4.17 ROYALTIES AND PATENTS

4.17.1 The Contractor shall pay all royalties and license fees. He shall defend all suits or claims for infringement of any patent rights and shall save the Owner harmless from loss on account thereof, except that the Owner shall be responsible for all such loss when a particular design, process or the product of a particular manufacturer or manufacturers is specified, but if the Contractor has reason to believe that the design, process or product specified is an infringement of a patent, he shall be responsible for such loss unless he promptly gives such information to the Architect.

4.18 INDEMNIFICATION

4.18.1 To the fullest extent permitted by law, the Contractor shall indemnify and hold harmless the Owner and the Architect and their agents and employees from and against all claims, damages, losses and expenses, including but not limited to attorneys' fees, arising out of or resulting from the performance of the Work, provided that any such claim, damage, loss or expense (1) is attributable to bodily injury, sickness, disease or death, or to injury to or destruction of tangible property (other than the Work itself) including the loss of use resulting therefrom,

(courtesy American Institute of Architects)

Figure 7.10

The contractor incurs significant liability if he deviates from the Contract Documents. The design professional also bears significant liability based on his responsibility to be thorough, competent and diligent in creating the Contract Documents.

Paragraph 4.3—Supervision and Construction Procedures sets forth detailed responsibilities of the contractor in dispatching the work. Subparagraph 4.3.3, illustrated in Figure 7.9, provides no relief for the contractor because of any alleged interference with the work by the design professional who represents the owner.

Paragraph 4.4 Labor and Materials, shown in Figure 7.9, presents the general requirement that the contractor provide all labor and materials necessary for the construction of the project. It is appropriate that supplemental statements be made to paragraph 4.4 stipulating disclosure of materials and manufacturers that the contractor intends to use for the project. Figure 7.11 shows several additional statements that may be used to supplement Sub-paragraph 4.4 regarding disclosure and approval of materials. It is important that the design professional and the owner be able to approve the materials to be incorporated in the work. The design professional may specify materials and methods of construction in several different ways. Competition for lowest possible price is primarily required for public works projects, and this might tend to leave the final choice of materials to the contractor. If the design professional uses the **proprietary** method of specifying (Chapter 9), he must name two or more products by name brand or by manufacturer that he is willing to approve for use. However, because of the "open" bidding requirement, the contractor should be afforded some discretion in the material selection for an advantage in the competitive bidding process. If a bidder wishes to use a material not named in the Specifications, he may apply to the design professional to approve such a substitute during the bidding process. The design professional may set certain guidelines and requirements in the Instructions to Bidders wherein he allows enough time for this process to take place. If such a substitute is approved, he may inform other bidders by Addendum of his approval of a substitute material in order to be fair. It is appropriate that a supplemental statement (such as that illustrated in Figure 7.11) be added in the Supplemental General Conditions, setting forth substitution criteria and procedures for seeking substitution approval. Substitutions after the Contract for Construction has been executed can be handled similarly except that the contractor is, in this case, expected to give the owner credit or other benefit, if warranted, for approving a substitution after all terms of the Contract Documents have been agreed upon. Division 1, Section 01600—*Material and Equipment*—should specify the methods whereby the contractor may propose substitutions for specified materials.

Paragraph 4.5 Warranty is shown in Figure 7.9. The warranty promises that the work shall conform to the requirements of the Contract Documents. The warranty provisions provided by the General Conditions in Subparagraph 4.5.1 (Figure 7.9) are generally acceptable for their intended purpose and may not require supplemental amendment.

Paragraph 4.6 Taxes. In the case of the example, public ownership may exempt the contractor from the payment of certain taxes. Figure 7.11 illustrates supplemental statements to the provisions of Subparagraph 4.6.2 (see Figure 7.9) that must be included in the Supplementary General Conditions for a public project located in a

4.3 - SUPERVISION & CONSTRUCTION PROCEDURES

B.   ADD the following new Paragraph 4.3.4:

4.3.4 In laying out the work, Contractor shall verify all measurements and dimensions and shall immediately report any errors to Architect.

4.4 - LABOR AND MATERIALS

A.   ADD the following new Subparagraph 4.4.3:

4.4.3 Not later than ten (10) days from the Contract Date, the Contractor shall provide a list showing the name of the manufacturer proposed to be used for each of the products identified in the General Requirements of the Specifications (Division 1 - Section 01600) and, where applicable, the name of the installing Subcontractor.

B.   ADD the following new Subparagraph 4.4.4:

4.4.4   The Architect will promptly reply in writing to the Contractor stating whether the Owner or the Architect, after due investigation, has reasonable objection to any such proposal. If adequate data on any proposed manufacturer or installer is not available, the Architect may state that action will be deferred until the Contractor provides further data. Failure of the Owner or the Architect to reply promptly shall constitute notice of no reasonable objection. Failure to object to a manufacturer shall not constitute a waiver of any of the requirements of the Contract Documents, and all products furnished by the listed manufacturer must conform to such requirements.

C.   ADD the following new Subparagraph 4.4.5:

4.4.5   After the Contract has been executed, the Owner and the Architect will consider a formal request for the substitution of products in place of those specified only under the conditions set forth in the General Requirements of the Specifications (Division 1).

D.   ADD the following new Subparagraph 4.4.6:

4.4.6   By making requests for substitutions based on Subparagraph 4.4.5, the Contractor:

        (a) represents that the Contractor has personally investigated the proposed substitute product and determined that it is equal or superior in all respects to that specified; and...

        (b) represents that the Contractor will provide the same warranty for the substitution that the Contractor would for that specified; and...

        (c) certifies that no additional cost will be incurred as a result of approving the substitution and includes any credit or savings which might result from approval and waives all claims for additional costs related to the substitution which subsequently become apparent; and...

        (d) will coordinate the installation of the accepted substitute, making such change as may be required for the Work to be complete in all respects; and

        (e) agrees to reimburse the Owner for any costs of re-design required of the Architect as a result of the substitution being incorporated into the work.

4.6 - TAXES

A.   ADD the following new Subparagraph 4.6.2:

4.6.2 - STATE (or Municipal) SALES TAX EXEMPTION:

The Owner, as an exempt organization, is not required to pay the State Sales Tax. The materials provided for this project will be exempt from the Limited Sales, Excise and Use Tax imposed by (Name the legislation that provides the tax requirement and location of published form of tax law). The Contractor shall obtain instructions for the issuance of an Exemption Certificate from the local representative of the Texas State Comptroller of Public Accounts.

4.7 - PERMITS, FEES AND NOTICES

A.   OMIT Subparagraph 4.7.1 in it's entirety and substitute the following:

The Project Manual and the Drawings will be submitted to the Building Official of (Name of Municipality) the Owner, who will bear all costs of the Building Permit required by (name of municipality). Unless otherwise provided in the Contract Documents, the Contractor shall secure and pay for any other permits and government fees, licenses and inspections necessary for the proper execution and completion of the Work which may be required.

Figure 7.11

state which exempts public projects from payment of sales tax. Upon presentation of a Certified Exemption Permit, vendors can waive the requirement of collecting (and paying) sales tax. In the case of private ownership where the owner has no tax exempt status, Subparagraph 4.6.1 may not need to be supplemented in any way.

Paragraph 4.7 Permits, Fees and Notices is shown in Figure 7.9. In the example project, the owner, a municipality, may wish to waive the requirement for the contractor to pay for building permits, since the city is the authority for such charge and collection. In public works projects such as this, a supplemental statement (Figure 7.11) may be used as a substitute for General Conditions statements 4.7.1. In the case of a privately owned project, no modification of the provisions of Subparagraphs 4.7.1 through 4.7.4 is usually required.

Paragraph 4.8 Allowances defines a device whereby certain material, assembly appliances or other equipment may be included in the contract sum without a final decision on the exact item to be provided. Division 1 Section 01020—Allowances specifies those items that are to be included in the contract sum by the inclusion of certain specified prices or unit prices for that purpose. Since the provision of these items is an obligation of the Contract as well as a specification, the General Conditions (in Paragraph 4.8) set forth the means by which the specified allowances are to be applied to the contract sum. It is important that the contract documents be clear as to exactly what is to be included in the allowance and how the excess or deficit monies are to be handled should the item be more or less expensive than the amount set forth in the allowance. The provisions of Subparagraphs 4.8.1 and 4.8.2 (shown in Figure 7.9) are the usual procedures to be followed regarding allowances. Generally, no supplemental information is needed in the Supplemental General Conditions. The design professional may include additional criteria together with a listing of the various allowances in an appropriate section of Division 1.

Paragraph 4.9 Superintendent contains statements regarding the contractor's superintendent. The superintendent is the contractor's key employee at the jobsite. Not only is his competence and experience crucial to the proper administration of the project, but his constant presence at the jobsite is to the advantage of owner, design professional and contractor. The design professional may wish to add a supplemental statement (Figure 7.12) to provide assurance that the superintendent would not be moved or substituted without good reason, and even then, only with the design professional's approval. The design professional may also wish to include statements in the Supplemental General Conditions regarding the qualifications of the contractor's general superintendent and the superintendents of major subcontractors. Commensurate with controls that assure the timely and efficient accomplishment of the construction work, it is not unusual for such additional requirements to be placed in the Supplemental General Conditions.

Paragraph 4.10 Progress Schedule is shown in Figures 7.9 and 7.10. Division 1 Section 01310—Progress Schedules—is the proper specification section to detail the scheduling and documenting requirements as the work progresses. No supplemental statements are usually required for Progress Scheduling in the Supplemental General Conditions.

4.9 - SUPERINTENDENT

A.   ADD the following new Subparagraph 4.9.2:

4.9.2 SUPERINTENDENT:

At beginning of Project, Contractor shall transmit, in writing, to Architect for his information, the name of his superintendent and the names of the superintendents of his prime subcontractors, this to include a list of past projects on which each superintendent has worked or been in charge of. Once approved by the Architect and established on the job site, the Contractor shall not remove the Superintendent, or cause his services to be employed elsewhere, with out the express written consent of the Architect.

4.11 - DOCUMENTS AND SAMPLES AT THE SITE

A. ADD to Subparagraph 4.11.1 the following sentence:

The Contractor, immediately upon receiving each document, shall mark it clearly "PROJECT RECORD COPY". The Project Record Document shall be kept separated from, and shall not be used as, working documents for construction purposes. Comply with the provisions of Section 01720 - PROJECT RECORD DOCUMENTS of the Specifications.

4.13 - USE OF THE SITE

A.   ADD the following new Subparagraph 4.13.2:

4.13.2 Contractor shall conduct his operations so as not to close or interfere in any way with traffic on public thoroughfares without written permission of the Owner and under strict coordination with the Owner's Representative..

ARTICLE 5 - SUBCONTRACTORS

5.1 DEFINITION

A.   Add the following new Subparagraph 5.1.3

5.1.3 The Electrical Subcontractor shall be licensed as a Master Electrician by the (Name of Municipality).

B. Add the following new paragraph 5.1.4

5.1.4 The Mechanical Subcontractor and the Plumbing Subcontractor shall hold licenses approved by the State of (Name of State).

ARTICLE 7 - MISCELLANEOUS PROVISIONS

7.1 - GOVERNING LAW

A.   ADD the following new Subparagraphs 7.1.2:

7.1.2 The Contractor shall at all times observe and comply with all Federal, State and local laws, ordinances and regulations which in any manner affect the Contract or the work, and shall indemnify and save harmless the Owner and the Architect against any claim arising from the violation of any such laws or ordinances, whether by the Contractor, his employees, any Subcontractor or his employees, any Sub-Subcontractor or his employees or any Vendor, Materialman, or Service Company serving or employed by the Contractor. The Owner is a body politic and corporate. The law from which it derives its powers, insofar as the same regulates the objects for which, or the manner in which, or the conditions under which the Owner may enter into contract, shall be controlling and shall be considered as part of the Agreement Between Owner and Contractor to the same effect as though embodied herein.

7.5 - PERFORMANCE BOND AND LABOR AND MATERIAL PAYMENT BOND

A.   ADD the following new subparagraph 7.5.2:

7.5.2 Prior to signing the Owner-Contractor Agreement the successful Bidder shall furnish Performance Bond and Labor and Material Payment Bond in the amount of 100% of the Contract Sum, in such form as the Owner may prescribe and with such sureties as he approves. These bonds shall meet the requirements of (Name of applicable legislation governing labor rates in the State). If the Work is commenced prior to execution of the Agreement, the Bidder shall, prior to commencement of the Work, submit evidence satisfactory to the Owner that such bonds will be issued.

B.   ADD the following new subparagraph 7.5.3:

7.5.3   The Bidder shall require the Attorney-In-Fact who executes the required bonds on behalf of the surety to affix thereto a certified and current copy of his Power of Attorney indicating the monetary limit of such power.

Figure 7.12

Paragraph 4.11 documents and Samples at the Site. Submittal procedures made from time to time during the construction process are important to the administration of (1) documentation of the quality of the work, (2) adherence to the requirements of the Contract Documents, (3) conformity to the design, (4) preservation of Project Record Documents and (5) the general coordination, dispatch, conduct and scheduling of the work. Documents and samples often referred to in Division 1 of the Specifications, Section 01300—Submittals, are key to the quality and performance of materials and other systems that are to be part of the building. The experience of most design professionals is that unless stringent record-keeping requirements are established and undertaken, much valuable information necessary for the owner's use during the life of the building will be forever lost. It is recommended that the design professional include a supplemental statement similar to that shown in Figure 7.12. This statement sets forth a discipline for marking, filing and otherwise preserving project record documents at the jobsite, which will, at Substantial Completion, be turned over to the owner. Additional requirements should be specified in Division 1 Section 01720—Project Record Documents. Other submittals including shop drawings, product data and samples are equally important to the conduct and approval of the work progress as are project record documents.

Paragraph 4.12 Shop Drawings, Product Data, and Samples are defined as supplemental construction drawings, prepared by manufacturers or fabricators, to illustrate the materials, details, dimensions, connections, finishes, and other pertinent data regarding the numerous systems and subsystems that must be manufactured or fabricated either at the job site or in the factory or fabrication shop, to be included as part of the building construction. One example of shop drawings is an illustration of the fabrication details for cabinetry and casework. Such drawings are prepared by the fabricator from the design professional's drawings. The provisions of Subparagraph 4.12.1 (shown in Figure 7.10) are usually adequate for the purposes of the General Conditions. The design professional may include other more detailed information and requirements regarding Shop Drawings in Division 1 Section 01300—*Submittals*, and in Part 1—*General* of those sections of the specifications for work that requires shop drawings.

Product data, described in Subparagraph 4.12.2 is technical information commonly supplied by the manufacturers of various products to be incorporated in the work. Product data may consist of specifications describing the character of various ingredients incorporated into the product, limitations and recommendations as to use and application, and instructions for installation as well as the manufacturer's recommendations for maintenance of the material once installed. Product data required by the contract documents is generally specified in Division 1, Section 01300—*Submittals*, and is further described in each section of the specifications in terms of particular units of work. No additional statements are usually made in the Supplemental General Conditions regarding the contractor's product data obligations.

Samples, described in Subparagraph 4.12.3, are actual "pieces" of materials to be incorporated into the work. These samples should represent the actual physical properties of a material typical of composition, texture, color, finish and other attributes that the design professional may approve before installation or application. Again, the matter of samples, as with other Submittal Data, should be specified in Division 1 Section 01300—*Submittals*, and in the individual sections of the specifications describing units of work. No additional statements are usually required in the Supplemental General Conditions.

Paragraphs 4.13 through 4.17 describe: (4.13) Use of Site by the contractor, (4.14) Cutting and Patching of work, (4.15) Cleaning Up after construction procedures, (4.16) Communications, and (4.17) Responsibilities regarding royalties and patents. Figure 7.12 shows a supplemental statement that might be required by a public owner as part of the Supplemental General Conditions regarding use of site (with cautions against any interference with traffic on adjacent public thoroughfares). Additional and more specific requirements regarding cutting and patching of work and cleaning up the construction debris are usually handled in Division 1 of the specifications and the individual sections of the specifications, rather than requiring additional supplemental conditions of the contract.

Paragraph 4.17 Royalties and Patents shown in Figure 7.10, is generally sufficient for the conditions surrounding most products. The design professional may need to elaborate on these requirements when preparing documents for special use structures and devices, as in the case of special manufacturing facilities, research laboratories, and utility plants.

Paragraph 4.18 Indemnification shown in Figures 7.10 and 7.13, is a statement regarding indemnification of the owner and the architect from liability in connection with the construction process. In some jurisdictions, there may be statutory restrictions or other conditions imposed on the contractor indemnifying the owner and, in some cases, the design professional. The design professional should suggest that the owner seek legal counsel regarding any required supplementary information for identification of the parties in the OPC relationship.

Article 5— Subcontractors

The subcontractor is related to the Contract for Construction in an indirect way. The contractor is solely responsible for the selection of the subcontractor, for the quality and timeliness of the subcontractor's work, and for his compensation and scheduling. However, since a very high percentage of a modern building may be constructed by subcontractors and sub-subcontractors, the General Conditions of the Contract are obliged to define and identify the subcontractor, set guidelines and approval mechanisms for the owner's protection and make provision for the exclusion of a proposed subcontractor to whom the owner or design professional may have objection. **Paragraph 5.3** in Figure 7.13 requires that the agreement between contractor and subcontractor, as well as the agreement between subcontractor and sub-subcontractor, be written in such manner as to bind the subcontractor to the intent and terms of the Contract Documents that form the basis of the Contract for Construction.

Most jurisdictions in the United States now require that electricians, plumbers, and heating ventilating and air conditioning (HVAC) mechanics be qualified by licensing. Licensing at the journeyman's level usually involves the following: certain educational requirements, a specific number of years of experience or apprenticeship served under a principal holding a master's license, and successful completion of the journeyman's examination. The holder of a master's license is required to have certain educational requirements in addition to those at the

and (2) is caused in whole or in part by any negligent act or omission of the Contractor, any Subcontractor, anyone directly or indirectly employed by any of them or anyone for whose acts any of them may be liable, regardless of whether or not it is caused in part by a party indemnified hereunder. Such obligation shall not be construed to negate, abridge, or otherwise reduce any other right or obligation of indemnity which would otherwise exist as to any party or person described in this Paragraph 4.18.

4.18.2 In any and all claims against the Owner or the Architect or any of their agents or employees by any employee of the Contractor, any Subcontractor, anyone directly or indirectly employed by any of them or anyone for whose acts any of them may be liable, the indemnification obligation under this Paragraph 4.18 shall not be limited in any way by any limitation on the amount or type of damages, compensation or benefits payable by or for the Contractor or any Subcontractor under workers' or workmen's compensation acts, disability benefit acts or other employee benefit acts.

4.18.3 The obligations of the Contractor under this Paragraph 4.18 shall not extend to the liability of the Architect, his agents or employees, arising out of (1) the preparation or approval of maps, drawings, opinions, reports, surveys, change orders, designs or specifications, or (2) the giving of or the failure to give directions or instructions by the Architect, his agents or employees provided such giving or failure to give is the primary cause of the injury or damage.

ARTICLE 5

SUBCONTRACTORS

5.1 DEFINITION

5.1.1 A Subcontractor is a person or entity who has a direct contract with the Contractor to perform any of the Work at the site. The term Subcontractor is referred to throughout the Contract Documents as if singular in number and masculine in gender and means a Subcontractor or his authorized representative. The term Subcontractor does not include any separate contractor or his subcontractors.

5.1.2 A Sub-subcontractor is a person or entity who has a direct or indirect contract with a Subcontractor to perform any of the Work at the site. The term Sub-subcontractor is referred to throughout the Contract Documents as if singular in number and masculine in gender and means a Sub-subcontractor or an authorized representative thereof.

5.2 AWARD OF SUBCONTRACTS AND OTHER CONTRACTS FOR PORTIONS OF THE WORK

5.2.1 Unless otherwise required by the Contract Documents or the Bidding Documents, the Contractor, as soon as practicable after the award of the Contract, shall furnish to the Owner and the Architect in writing the names of the persons or entities (including those who are to furnish materials or equipment fabricated to a special design) proposed for each of the principal portions of the Work. The Architect will promptly reply to the Contractor in writing stating whether or not the Owner or the Architect, after due investigation, has reasonable objection to any

such proposed person or entity. Failure of the Owner or Architect to reply promptly shall constitute notice of no reasonable objection.

5.2.2 The Contractor shall not contract with any such proposed person or entity to whom the Owner or the Architect has made reasonable objection under the provisions of Subparagraph 5.2.1. The Contractor shall not be required to contract with anyone to whom he has a reasonable objection.

5.2.3 If the Owner or the Architect has reasonable objection to any such proposed person or entity, the Contractor shall submit a substitute to whom the Owner or the Architect has no reasonable objection, and the Contract Sum shall be increased or decreased by the difference in cost occasioned by such substitution and an appropriate Change Order shall be issued; however, no increase in the Contract Sum shall be allowed for any such substitution unless the Contractor has acted promptly and responsively in submitting names as required by Subparagraph 5.2.1.

5.2.4 The Contractor shall make no substitution for any Subcontractor, person or entity previously selected if the Owner or Architect makes reasonable objection to such substitution.

5.3 SUBCONTRACTUAL RELATIONS

5.3.1 By an appropriate agreement, written where legally required for validity, the Contractor shall require each Subcontractor, to the extent of the Work to be performed by the Subcontractor, to be bound to the Contractor by the terms of the Contract Documents, and to assume toward the Contractor all the obligations and responsibilities which the Contractor, by these Documents, assumes toward the Owner and the Architect. Said agreement shall preserve and protect the rights of the Owner and the Architect under the Contract Documents with respect to the Work to be performed by the Subcontractor so that the subcontracting thereof will not prejudice such rights, and shall allow to the Subcontractor, unless specifically provided otherwise in the Contractor-Subcontractor agreement, the benefit of all rights, remedies and redress against the Contractor that the Contractor, by these Documents, has against the Owner. Where appropriate, the Contractor shall require each Subcontractor to enter into similar agreements with his Sub-subcontractors. The Contractor shall make available to each proposed Subcontractor, prior to the execution of the Subcontract, copies of the Contract Documents to which the Subcontractor will be bound by this Paragraph 5.3, and identify to the Subcontractor any terms and conditions of the proposed Subcontract which may be at variance with the Contract Documents. Each Subcontractor shall similarly make copies of such Documents available to his Sub-subcontractors.

ARTICLE 6

WORK BY OWNER OR BY SEPARATE CONTRACTORS

6.1 OWNER'S RIGHT TO PERFORM WORK AND TO AWARD SEPARATE CONTRACTS

6.1.1 The Owner reserves the right to perform work related to the Project with his own forces, and to award

AIA DOCUMENT A201 • GENERAL CONDITIONS OF THE CONTRACT FOR CONSTRUCTION • THIRTEENTH EDITION • AUGUST 1976
AIA® • © 1976 • THE AMERICAN INSTITUTE OF ARCHITECTS, 1735 NEW YORK AVENUE, N.W., WASHINGTON, D.C. 20006

(courtesy American Institute of Architects)

Figure 7.13

journeyman's level and to have served a specific number of years as a journeyman as well as passing the master's examination. These requirements, as with the professional licensing requirements, are established to protect the public health and welfare.

Figure 7.12 illustrates a supplemental statement that the municipal owner, in the example project may require that subcontractors and sub-subcontractors hold a master's license, issued by the city, or in some jurisdictions, the state, where the work is to be accomplished. This provision assures that the contractor will have selected qualified subcontractors under the licensing requirement for the example project.

Article 6— Work by Owner or by Separate Contractors

Figures 7.13 and 7.14 illustrate Article 6 of the General Conditions concerning the owner's right to accomplish separate work, or to contract work by separate contractors. This provision allows the owner to accomplish work, outside of the subject Contract for Construction and also allows him to seek and award other such contracts. Subparagraph 6.2.1 requires that the owner be responsible to coordinate separate work and pledges the contractor's cooperation. The paragraphs associated with Article 6.2 address mutual responsibility and set forth procedural requirements intended to establish harmony among disassociated contractors. The statement also provides for reimbursement, one contractor to the other, for any damage to the other's work. In the event of a dispute, at which time separate contractors are the least likely to be cooperative with each other, subparagraph 6.3.1 makes provision allowing the owner to accomplish the necessary clean up, charging either or both contractors for his expense in so doing. Unless the example municipal project requires separate contractors for some reason, there is no need to supplement the statements of Article 6 of the General Conditions. If separate contracts are anticipated, then Subparagraph 6.3.1 should be supplemented to recognize and name such contracts. Division 1—Section 01010—*Summary of the Work* might include the limits of each contract and the procedures required by each separate contractor in order to properly coordinate the work of each contract.

Article 7— Miscellaneous Provisions

Figure 7.14 illustrates Subparagraph 7.1.1 of the General Conditions establishing the place of the project as the jurisdiction which governs the Contract for Construction. This statement is designed to prevent any litigation associated with disputes during construction from being further complicated by lawsuits filed in jurisdictions outside that of the project. The global nature of material and manpower supply in the late twentieth century makes widely separated jurisdictional disputes a legitimate concern. Such actions can be lengthy and expensive. Figure 7.12 illustrates a possible supplemental statement to General Conditions Subparagraph 7.1.1. This example might be appropriate for public sector projects. This statement requires the contractor to conform to all applicable laws, codes and regulations whether they be local, state or federal, and requires the contractor to hold the owner harmless from any violation of any such regulation that may occur. In addition, the statement adds to the Contract Documents (by reference), the statutes by which the example municipality derives its authority.

Figure 7.14 shows a statement from the General Conditions regarding successors and assigns, **Paragraph 7.2.** This statement is common to most forms of agreement made between two or more parties. The separate contracts in connection with other portions of the Project or other work on the site under these or similar Conditions of the Contract. If the Contractor claims that delay or additional cost is involved because of such action by the Owner, he shall make such claim as provided elsewhere in the Contract Documents.

6.1.2 When separate contracts are awarded for different portions of the Project or other work on the site, the term Contractor in the Contract Documents in each case shall mean the Contractor who executes each separate Owner-Contractor Agreement.

6.1.3 The Owner will provide for the coordination of the work of his own forces and of each separate contractor with the Work of the Contractor, who shall cooperate therewith as provided in Paragraph 6.2.

6.2 MUTUAL RESPONSIBILITY

6.2.1 The Contractor shall afford the Owner and separate contractors reasonable opportunity for the introduction and storage of their materials and equipment and the execution of their work, and shall connect and coordinate his Work with theirs as required by the Contract Documents.

6.2.2 If any part of the Contractor's Work depends for proper execution or results upon the work of the Owner or any separate contractor, the Contractor shall, prior to proceeding with the Work, promptly report to the Architect any apparent discrepancies or defects in such other work that render it unsuitable for such proper execution and results. Failure of the Contractor so to report shall constitute an acceptance of the Owner's or separate contractors' work as fit and proper to receive his Work, except as to defects which may subsequently become apparent in such work by others.

6.2.3 Any costs caused by defective or ill-timed work shall be borne by the party responsible therefor.

6.2.4 Should the Contractor wrongfully cause damage to the work or property of the Owner, or to other work on the site, the Contractor shall promptly remedy such damage as provided in Subparagraph 10.2.5.

6.2.5 Should the Contractor wrongfully cause damage to the work or property of any separate contractor, the Contractor shall upon due notice promptly attempt to settle with such other contractor by agreement, or otherwise to resolve the dispute. If such separate contractor sues or initiates an arbitration proceeding against the Owner on account of any damage alleged to have been caused by the Contractor, the Owner shall notify the Contractor who shall defend such proceedings at the Owner's expense, and if any judgment or award against the Owner arises therefrom the Contractor shall pay or satisfy it and shall reimburse the Owner for all attorneys' fees and court or arbitration costs which the Owner has incurred.

6.3 OWNER'S RIGHT TO CLEAN UP

6.3.1 If a dispute arises between the Contractor and separate contractors as to their responsibility for cleaning up as required by Paragraph 4.15, the Owner may clean up

and charge the cost thereof to the contractors responsible therefor as the Architect shall determine to be just.

ARTICLE 7

MISCELLANEOUS PROVISIONS

7.1 GOVERNING LAW

7.1.1 The Contract shall be governed by the law of the place where the Project is located.

7.2 SUCCESSORS AND ASSIGNS

7.2.1 The Owner and the Contractor each binds himself, his partners, successors, assigns and legal representatives to the other party hereto and to the partners, successors, assigns and legal representatives of such other party with respect to all covenants, agreements and obligations contained in the Contract Documents. Neither party to the Contract shall assign the Contract or sublet it as a whole without the written consent of the other, nor shall the Contractor assign any moneys due or to become due to him hereunder, without the previous written consent of the Owner.

7.3 WRITTEN NOTICE

7.3.1 Written notice shall be deemed to have been duly served if delivered in person to the individual or member of the firm or entity or to an officer of the corporation for whom it was intended, or if delivered at or sent by registered or certified mail to the last business address known to him who gives the notice.

7.4 CLAIMS FOR DAMAGES

7.4.1 Should either party to the Contract suffer injury or damage to person or property because of any act or omission of the other party or of any of his employees, agents or others for whose acts he is legally liable, claim shall be made in writing to such other party within a reasonable time after the first observance of such injury or damage.

7.5 PERFORMANCE BOND AND LABOR AND MATERIAL PAYMENT BOND

7.5.1 The Owner shall have the right to require the Contractor to furnish bonds covering the faithful performance of the Contract and the payment of all obligations arising thereunder if and as required in the Bidding Documents or in the Contract Documents.

7.6 RIGHTS AND REMEDIES

7.6.1 The duties and obligations imposed by the Contract Documents and the rights and remedies available thereunder shall be in addition to and not a limitation of any duties, obligations, rights and remedies otherwise imposed or available by law.

7.6.2 No action or failure to act by the Owner, Architect or Contractor shall constitute a waiver of any right or duty afforded any of them under the Contract, nor shall any such action or failure to act constitute an approval of or acquiescence in any breach thereunder, except as may be specifically agreed in writing.

AIA DOCUMENT A201 • GENERAL CONDITIONS OF THE CONTRACT FOR CONSTRUCTION • THIRTEENTH EDITION • AUGUST 1976
AIA® • © 1976 • THE AMERICAN INSTITUTE OF ARCHITECTS, 1735 NEW YORK AVENUE, N.W., WASHINGTON, D.C. 20006   **A201-1976 11**

(courtesy American Institute of Architects)

Figure 7.14

statement makes provision for the unforeseen demise or incapacity of either party to continue performance under the Contract for Construction and binds any partners, successors, assigns and legal representatives of each of the parties to all provisions of the agreement. By this provision, each party offers the other reasonable assurance of completion of the covenant between themselves, regardless of any circumstance that may otherwise prevent performance by one or the other. Unless counselled to do so, no amendment of this statement is usually required by the Supplemental General Conditions.

Figure 7.14 illustrates provisions in the General Conditions related to procedures of written notice (Paragraph 7.3), claims for damages (Paragraph 7.4), owner's right to require performance and payment bonds (Paragraph 7.5), and the rights and remedies (Paragraph 7.6), that the parties to the Contract for Construction have under the law. With the exception of the bond provision (Paragraph 7.5), the purpose of these provisions is to pre-establish procedure (under the requirements generally established by law) for any legal remedies that one party may require of the other during the course of contract fulfillment. Paragraph 7.3 describes the accepted procedure for service of any notice by one party to the other. **Paragraph 7.4** describes the requirement of written notice, one party to the other, in case of any damage that one party may allege has been caused by the other.

Paragraph 7.5 of the General Conditions, shown in Figure 7.14, establishes the owner's right to require the contractor to provide Performance and Labor and Material Payment bonds. In the case of the example municipal project, the design professional may be advised to elaborate upon any requirements of local law related to bonding. Figure 7.12 shows a supplemental statement regarding possible public works bond requirements under statutes that may be required by a particular state. If the project had been one of private rather than public ownership, the design professional may have chosen a similar statement, but one which indicates the law regarding performance, labor and material payment bonds, if any, as they apply to private work.

Paragraph 7.6 of the General Conditions deals with the legal rights and remedies that the parties may have under the law. The language is structured so as to preserve the duties of both parties with rights and remedies under the law in addition to any provision of the agreement. This paragraph has important legal implications.

Paragraph 7.7 of the General Conditions, shown in Figure 7.15, establishes the responsibilities of the parties to the contract regarding Tests. The right of the design professional or owner to require testing should be as broad as possible. Therefore, the design professional may include additional language in this paragraph in the Supplemental General Conditions as is shown in Figure 7.16. Division 1 sections of the specifications related to testing should describe in detail the procedures for testing, state the required qualifications of the testing laboratory and describe other matters of procedure. The various sections of the specifications should indicate what products and assemblies should be tested and the types of tests to be administered. The matter of who should pay for testing is a subject of debate among participants in the OPC relationship. Paragraph 7.7.1, shown in Figure 7.15, suggests that the contractor should pay for tests required by the governing authorities and that the owner should pay for other testing and approvals. Some owners and design professionals may require the

7.7 TESTS

7.7.1 If the Contract Documents, laws, ordinances, rules, regulations or orders of any public authority having jurisdiction require any portion of the Work to be inspected, tested or approved, the Contractor shall give the Architect timely notice of its readiness so the Architect may observe such inspection, testing or approval. The Contractor shall bear all costs of such inspections, tests or approvals conducted by public authorities. Unless otherwise provided, the Owner shall bear all costs of other inspections, tests or approvals.

7.7.2 If the Architect determines that any Work requires special inspection, testing, or approval which Subparagraph 7.7.1 does not include, he will, upon written authorization from the Owner, instruct the Contractor to order such special inspection, testing or approval, and the Contractor shall give notice as provided in Subparagraph 7.7.1. If such special inspection or testing reveals a failure of the Work to comply with the requirements of the Contract Documents, the Contractor shall bear all costs thereof, including compensation for the Architect's additional services made necessary by such failure; otherwise the Owner shall bear such costs, and an appropriate Change Order shall be issued.

7.7.3 Required certificates of inspection, testing or approval shall be secured by the Contractor and promptly delivered by him to the Architect.

7.7.4 If the Architect is to observe the inspections, tests or approvals required by the Contract Documents, he will do so promptly and, where practicable, at the source of supply.

7.8 INTEREST

7.8.1 Payments due and unpaid under the Contract Documents shall bear interest from the date payment is due at such rate as the parties may agree upon in writing or, in the absence thereof, at the legal rate prevailing at the place of the Project.

7.9 ARBITRATION

7.9.1 All claims, disputes and other matters in question between the Contractor and the Owner arising out of, or relating to, the Contract Documents or the breach thereof, except as provided in Subparagraph 2.2.11 with respect to the Architect's decisions on matters relating to artistic effect, and except for claims which have been waived by the making or acceptance of final payment as provided by Subparagraphs 9.9.4 and 9.9.5, shall be decided by arbitration in accordance with the Construction Industry Arbitration Rules of the American Arbitration Association then obtaining unless the parties mutually agree otherwise. No arbitration arising out of or relating to the Contract Documents shall include, by consolidation, joinder or in any other manner, the Architect, his employees or consultants except by written consent containing a specific reference to the Owner-Contractor Agreement and signed by the Architect, the Owner, the Contractor and any other person sought to be joined. No arbitration shall include by consolidation, joinder or in any other manner, parties other than the Owner, the Contractor and any other persons substantially involved in a common question of fact or law, whose presence is required if complete relief is to be accorded in the arbitration. No person other than the Owner or Contractor shall be included as an original third party or additional third party to an arbitration whose interest or responsibility is insubstantial. Any consent to arbitration involving an additional person or persons shall not constitute consent to arbitration of any dispute not described therein or with any person not named or described therein. The foregoing agreement to arbitrate and any other agreement to arbitrate with an additional person or persons duly consented to by the parties to the Owner-Contractor Agreement shall be specifically enforceable under the prevailing arbitration law. The award rendered by the arbitrators shall be final, and judgment may be entered upon it in accordance with applicable law in any court having jurisdiction thereof.

7.9.2 Notice of the demand for arbitration shall be filed in writing with the other party to the Owner-Contractor Agreement and with the American Arbitration Association, and a copy shall be filed with the Architect. The demand for arbitration shall be made within the time limits specified in Subparagraph 2.2.12 where applicable, and in all other cases within a reasonable time after the claim, dispute or other matter in question has arisen, and in no event shall it be made after the date when institution of legal or equitable proceedings based on such claim, dispute or other matter in question would be barred by the applicable statute of limitations.

7.9.3 Unless otherwise agreed in writing, the Contractor shall carry on the Work and maintain its progress during any arbitration proceedings, and the Owner shall continue to make payments to the Contractor in accordance with the Contract Documents.

ARTICLE 8

TIME

8.1 DEFINITIONS

8.1.1 Unless otherwise provided, the Contract Time is the period of time allotted in the Contract Documents for Substantial Completion of the Work as defined in Subparagraph 8.1.3, including authorized adjustments thereto.

8.1.2 The date of commencement of the Work is the date established in a notice to proceed. If there is no notice to proceed, it shall be the date of the Owner-Contractor Agreement or such other date as may be established therein.

8.1.3 The Date of Substantial Completion of the Work or designated portion thereof is the Date certified by the Architect when construction is sufficiently complete, in accordance with the Contract Documents, so the Owner can occupy or utilize the Work or designated portion thereof for the use for which it is intended.

8.1.4 The term day as used in the Contract Documents shall mean calendar day unless otherwise specifically designated.

8.2 PROGRESS AND COMPLETION

8.2.1 All time limits stated in the Contract Documents are of the essence of the Contract.

(courtesy American Institute of Architects)

Figure 7.15

7.7 - TESTS

A.   ADD the following sentence to Subparagraph 7.7.2:

The requirements of this Paragraph apply to inspections, testing, or approvals which Subparagraph 7.7.1 does not include or the Specifications do not otherwise require.

ADD THE FOLLOWING NEW PARAGRAPH 7.10:

7.10 REFERENCE CODES, STANDARDS

7.10.1 References in the Specifications to codes, reference standards product association grading standards or manufacturers' instructions shall mean the latest printed edition of each in effect at the Bid Date, unless specifically referenced by date or other identification of edition in the Specifications.

7.10.2 Any language contained in reference codes, standards, product association standards or other documents that may be included in the Contract Documents by reference or otherwise shall not alter the relationships between Owner and Architect or Owner and Contractor, set forth in other articles and provisions of the General Conditions of the Contract for Construction or a Supplemented in these Supplemental General Conditions, nor shall any such language alter or diminish the mutual responsibilities of Owner, Contractor or Architect.

ADD THE FOLLOWING NEW PARAGRAPH 7.11:

7.11 EQUAL OPPORTUNITY

7.11.1 The Contractor shall maintain lawful policies of employment.

7.11.2   The Contractor and all Subcontractors shall not discriminate against any employee or applicant for employment because of race, religion, color, sex, national origin or age. The Contractor shall take affirmative action to insure that applicants are employed, and that employees are treated during employment without regard to their race, religion, color, sex, national original or age.

ARTICLE 8 - TIME

8.3 - DELAYS & EXTENSIONS OF TIME

A.   ADD the following new Paragraph 8.3.5:

8.3.5   Contractor shall have all materials delivered at the site in such quantities as required for the uninterrupted progress of the work and the least obstruction of the premises and the adjoining property. No extension of time or extra cost will be allowed for failure by Contractor to order the material on time or in insufficient quantities.

ARTICLE 9 - PAYMENTS AND COMPLETION

9.1 - CONTRACT SUM

A.   ADD the following new Paragraph 9.1.2:

9.1.2   All costs of overtime work required by the nature of this work, except emergencies as covered in Article 10.3.1 shall be included in the Contract Sum.

9.3 - APPLICATIONS FOR PAYMENT

A.   ADD the following sentences to Subparagraph 9.3.1:

Along with Progress Schedule Contractor shall submit to Architect a schedule of the anticipated amount of each monthly payment that will become due the Contractor in accordance with the Progress Schedule. Upon the Contractor's application for same, the Owner will make payment on account of the Contract as follows:

9.3.1.1.   On or about the tenth day of each month, 90 percent of the value, based on the Contract prices of labor and materials incorporated in the work and of materials suitably stored at the site thereof up to the first day of that month, as estimated by the Architect, less the aggregate of previous payments; and upon substantial completion of the entire work, a sum sufficient to increase the total payments to 95 percent of the Contract price. After 9.3.1.1 add the following.

9.3.1.2. The Owner (Municipality) shall establish, in the name of the Owner and the Contractor, an interest bearing, money market account, placed with the official depository named by the (Name of Municipality), and shall within seven (7) days of the date of each payment, based on the Contractor's Application for payment, duly certified by the Architect, place in that account amount sufficient to bring the total equal to the total amount of RETAINAGE shown on the Application for Payment. All interest earned on the account shall accumulate to the benefit of the Contractor, and amounts in this account shall be released by the Owner to the Contractor in accordance with Sub-paragraph 9.3.1.1.

Figure 7.16

contractor to pay for all specified testing. In this way, the costs should be included in the contract sum. Other owners and design professionals prefer to control the testing as well as select the laboratory that will accomplish the testing. In either case, it would be unfair and inappropriate to expect the contractor to pay for testing unless testing requirements are described by the contract documents. Listed below are three alternatives to requiring and/or specifying testing during construction.

(1) The design professional can specify, in the Contract Documents, the exact number and character of tests that will be required and list two or more testing laboratories that are acceptable to the owner. Under this provision, the contractor is expected to have provided for the cost of testing in the contract sum. In this case, a modification is required in the language of Subparagraph 7.7.1 of the Supplemental General Conditions. This change omits the owner requirement and substitute language, making the contractor responsible for all testing costs.

(2) The design professional can specify, in Division 1 of the Project Manual, an allowance to cover the cost of testing. In this event, the contractor will pay for testing under the provisions of the allowance, but the owner can select and the design professional can confirm or waive testing requirements as the work progresses. If this alternative is chosen, a supplementary statement is required omitting the last sentence of Subparagraph 7.7.1. In this case, the design professional must carefully coordinate the allowance provisions in appropriate sections of Division 1 of the Specifications.

(3) The Contract Documents can also require that the owner select the testing laboratory and pay for all required tests, with the contractor pledged to cooperate with the needs of the testing laboratory at no additional cost to the owner. This alternative gives the owner complete control of the testing. Most of the required testing should be specified so that the contractor can properly anticipate when and where testing will take place. Under this arrangement, the design professional may, with the owner's permission, require additional testing at any time if, in his professional judgment, a system or material may not meet specified standards. This alternative does not require a modification by the Supplemental General Conditions.

Paragraph 7.8 of the General Conditions in Figure 7.15 concerns the required payment of interest on amounts due under the Contract for Construction that remain unpaid according to the terms of the Agreement. There is usually no need to modify or supplement this statement unless the owner is counselled to do so. Accumulation of interest is a standard provision of law found in most contracts.

Paragraph 7.9, shown in Figure 7.15, describes procedures of settling disputes by arbitration. There are some jurisdictions where a public entity is prohibited by law from submitting to arbitration. The design professional should seek competent legal advice in modifying or omitting this requirement if the owner wishes or is required to avoid arbitration.

Other miscellaneous provisions and obligations may be added by the Supplemental General Conditions that relate to the individual project circumstances. Figure 7.16 illustrates a possible supplemental paragraph related to Reference Standards. There are a number of organizations that dedicate themselves to determining, defining, specifying and publishing standards of quality and performance for generic materials and assemblies commonly used in building construction. Other organizations establish model codes for building which are then adopted by governing bodies and made into law. In most cases, published standards and model codes are dated when published, and frequently up-dated. Design professionals often make use of such standards when specifying. Supplemental subparagraph 7.10.1 (shown in Figure 7.15) provides that such reference standards and codes (which are in effect on the date that bids are received) will govern. This provision helps to avoid disputes during construction should a particular standard be revised after the bid date and thereby change the contractor's anticipated cost of construction. In the case of negotiated contract, the supplemental provision could change the words ''bid date'' to ''date of agreement between owner and contractor''.

Supplemental Paragraph 7.11 (Figure 7.16) may be applied (and required) in the case of a public owner. Public owners are legally obligated to demand certain employment practices by the contractor and his subcontractors. These employment practices must be lawful and must observe equal opportunity employment guidelines.

Article 8—Time

Figure 7.15 illustrates provisions of the General Conditions concerning time and the Contract for Construction. As stated in Subparagraph 8.2.1, the time limits specified in the Contract Documents (namely the agreement between owner and contractor) are the essence of the contract. The legal implications of time, compensation by contractor to owner for failure to complete in a timely manner, and other related contract considerations are discussed in Chapter 4—Legal Concerns. The General Conditions do not define *Statutes of Limitations*, a subject which should be of major concern to all participants in the OPC relationship. Most jurisdictions place a time limitation on legal claims. This limit is based on the amount of time that passes from the occurrence to the time the claim is made. The statutes that prescribe such time limits are called *Statutes of Limitations*. With the incidence of major liability claims being filed against owners, contractors and design professionals alike, all should be advised by both legal and insurance counsel.

Because the time required for the construction process has great impact on the fortunes of both owner and contractor, the matter of agreeing on a completion time, as well as timely completion are of great importance. The contractor is normally granted extra time to complete the Contract when the work has encountered delays that are clearly beyond his control. These ''legitimate'' delays may include inclement weather in the early months of construction or labor and transportation strikes that could delay both labor and material reaching the job site. The design professional, in the best interest of his client may wish to expand or make more specific the matter of how the contractor can and cannot receive credit for delays in the work. Figure 7.16 illustrates a supplemental statement that may be included in the Supplementary General Conditions. This statement deals with the contractor's marshaling of materials on and to the job site.

Unless the number of days allowed for completion are set by the owner as a condition of the Contract, the more prudent design professional may see the advantage of publishing in the Contract Documents, a schedule of historical weather information. Such a schedule gives bidders some idea of how many days (during certain months of the year) the site of the project has been subjected to inclement weather that would prohibit work continuing in similar circumstances. Having furnished this information (in order that bidders take these facts into consideration when preparing their bids) the owner may be less forgiving to requests for additional time due to weather delay.

Article 9–Payments and Completion

Paragraph 9.1 of the General Conditions (Figure 7.17) defines the term Contract Sum as the total consideration to be paid to the contractor for the work. Under certain federal and state wage guidelines, it is a legal requirement for employers (such as municipalities) to pay a premium over the normal hourly wage for the time beyond 40 hours per week that a worker is required to work. The owner may be counselled to include a statement in the Supplemental General Conditions (shown in Figure 7.16) requiring the contractor to anticipate any overtime cost in the contract sum, and to be responsible for payment of any overtime rates that may be required during the course of the work. In this way, the owner is more completely protected from any claims that may arise concerning overtime pay.

Paragraph 9.2 (shown in Figure 7.17) of the General Conditions requires that the contractor prepare a Schedule of Values. This document becomes the basis for periodic payments to the contractor throughout the project. There is usually no need to supplement the General Conditions regarding the Schedule of Values. However, there are certain implications in approving the Schedule of Values that owners and design professionals should understand. The design professional should be knowledgeable of the construction costs, and able to recognize unreasonable amounts for any component in the project. The design professional should be prepared to object to the value of any line item in the contractor's proposed Schedule of Values if necessary. The design professional is liable for any possible overpayment to the contractor during the construction process. In the event that the contractor should default in the completion of the project, the bonding company would then be responsible for completion the work. If the design professional had allowed the owner to overpay the contractor for any work completed up to that date, the bonding company would have the right to refuse to give the owner the credit for the amount of the overage. The owner, in turn, could claim that the design professional had certified the applications of payment and therefore should be responsible to pay for any deficit.

Paragraph 9.3 of the General Conditions (Figure 7.17) addresses the Application for Payment and describes how it is prepared, processed, and paid. The contractor should prepare the application, and submit it to the design professional for approval. The design professional then reviews the application in light of his own observations and records, and certifies an amount that he believes to be appropriate.

The owner may want a definitive estimate of the contractor's anticipated monthly payment requests in order to budget his own cash reserves. In addition, he may wish to more closely define the payment and retainage procedure. Figure 7.16 shows supplemental statements to Paragraph 9.3 (Figure 7.17) applicable to the example public project for the purpose of requiring a schedule of anticipated monthly draws against the contract sum. This supplementary language further defines the

8.2.2 The Contractor shall begin the Work on the date of commencement as defined in Subparagraph 8.1.2. He shall carry the Work forward expeditiously with adequate forces and shall achieve Substantial Completion within the Contract Time.

8.3 DELAYS AND EXTENSIONS OF TIME

8.3.1 If the Contractor is delayed at any time in the progress of the Work by any act or neglect of the Owner or the Architect, or by any employee of either, or by any separate contractor employed by the Owner, or by changes ordered in the Work, or by labor disputes, fire, unusual delay in transportation, adverse weather conditions not reasonably anticipatable, unavoidable casualties, or any causes beyond the Contractor's control, or by delay authorized by the Owner pending arbitration, or by any other cause which the Architect determines may justify the delay, then the Contract Time shall be extended by Change Order for such reasonable time as the Architect may determine.

8.3.2 Any claim for extension of time shall be made in writing to the Architect not more than twenty days after the commencement of the delay; otherwise it shall be waived. In the case of a continuing delay only one claim is necessary. The Contractor shall provide an estimate of the probable effect of such delay on the progress of the Work.

8.3.3 If no agreement is made stating the dates upon which interpretations as provided in Subparagraph 2.2.8 shall be furnished, then no claim for delay shall be allowed on account of failure to furnish such interpretations until fifteen days after written request is made for them, and not then unless such claim is reasonable.

8.3.4 This Paragraph 8.3 does not exclude the recovery of damages for delay by either party under other provisions of the Contract Documents.

ARTICLE 9

PAYMENTS AND COMPLETION

9.1 CONTRACT SUM

9.1.1 The Contract Sum is stated in the Owner-Contractor Agreement and, including authorized adjustments thereto, is the total amount payable by the Owner to the Contractor for the performance of the Work under the Contract Documents.

9.2 SCHEDULE OF VALUES

9.2.1 Before the first Application for Payment, the Contractor shall submit to the Architect a schedule of values allocated to the various portions of the Work, prepared in such form and supported by such data to substantiate its accuracy as the Architect may require. This schedule, unless objected to by the Architect, shall be used only as a basis for the Contractor's Applications for Payment.

9.3 APPLICATIONS FOR PAYMENT

9.3.1 At least ten days before the date for each progress payment established in the Owner-Contractor Agreement, the Contractor shall submit to the Architect an itemized Application for Payment, notarized if required, supported by such data substantiating the Contractor's right to payment as the Owner or the Architect may require, and reflecting retainage, if any, as provided elsewhere in the Contract Documents.

9.3.2 Unless otherwise provided in the Contract Documents, payments will be made on account of materials or equipment not incorporated in the Work but delivered and suitably stored at the site and, if approved in advance by the Owner, payments may similarly be made for materials or equipment suitably stored at some other location agreed upon in writing. Payments for materials or equipment stored on or off the site shall be conditioned upon submission by the Contractor of bills of sale or such other procedures satisfactory to the Owner to establish the Owner's title to such materials or equipment or otherwise protect the Owner's interest, including applicable insurance and transportation to the site for those materials and equipment stored off the site.

9.3.3 The Contractor warrants that title to all Work, materials and equipment covered by an Application for Payment will pass to the Owner either by incorporation in the construction or upon the receipt of payment by the Contractor, whichever occurs first, free and clear of all liens, claims, security interests or encumbrances, hereinafter referred to in this Article 9 as "liens"; and that no Work, materials or equipment covered by an Application for Payment will have been acquired by the Contractor, or by any other person performing Work at the site or furnishing materials and equipment for the Project, subject to an agreement under which an interest therein or an encumbrance thereon is retained by the seller or otherwise imposed by the Contractor or such other person.

9.4 CERTIFICATES FOR PAYMENT

9.4.1 The Architect will, within seven days after the receipt of the Contractor's Application for Payment, either issue a Certificate for Payment to the Owner, with a copy to the Contractor, for such amount as the Architect determines is properly due, or notify the Contractor in writing his reasons for withholding a Certificate as provided in Subparagraph 9.6.1.

9.4.2 The issuance of a Certificate for Payment will constitute a representation by the Architect to the Owner, based on his observations at the site as provided in Subparagraph 2.2.3 and the data comprising the Application for Payment, that the Work has progressed to the point indicated; that, to the best of his knowledge, information and belief, the quality of the Work is in accordance with the Contract Documents (subject to an evaluation of the Work for conformance with the Contract Documents upon Substantial Completion, to the results of any subsequent tests required by or performed under the Contract Documents, to minor deviations from the Contract Documents correctable prior to completion, and to any specific qualifications stated in his Certificate); and that the Contractor is entitled to payment in the amount certified. However, by issuing a Certificate for Payment, the Architect shall not thereby be deemed to represent that he has made exhaustive or continuous on-site inspections to check the quality or quantity of the Work or that he has reviewed the construction means, methods, techniques,

(courtesy American Institute of Architects)

Figure 7.17

retainage percentage held by the owner and stipulates the increase of payment expected upon Substantial Completion.

It should also be noted that some states have enacted legislation, for public works projects that governs the percentage of the contract sum that may be withheld from a contractor's periodic payment without compensation. The design professional would be well advised to rely upon legal counsel in determining amounts and/or percentages to be applied to such retainage.

Paragraph 9.4 (Figures 7.17 and 7.18) contains statements from the General Conditions concerning Certificates for Payment normally issued by the design professional. No supplemental statement is usually necessary to these provisions. However, a word of caution is in order for the design professional who prepares the Certificate for Payment. There have been cases where the contractor has become insolvent prior to completing the work and where the bonding company has become obligated to see that the work is completed and all labor and materials paid. Again, the amounts paid to the contractor relative to the value of the work completed and properly stored is of critical importance. If the bonding company could show that the design professional had miscalculated the actual amount of work completed, and as a result, the owner had paid the contractor amounts exceeding the value of work completed, it is likely that the bonding company would seek the legal collection of damages for any overage from the design professional.

Paragraph 9.5 of the General Conditions (Figure 7.18) contains statements from the General Conditions regarding Progress Payments. These provisions are quite clear and appropriate and unless advised otherwise by counsel, no supplemental language is usually required.

Paragraph 9.6 Payments Withheld is shown in Figure 7.18. Here the administrative duties and responsibilities of the design professional come into full focus. If, in the opinion of the design professional, the work is lagging behind and the provisions of the contract documents are not being properly met, he can refuse to certify all or part of any current application for payment. The General Conditions speak to the submission of a Schedule of Values. Division 1, Section 01300, *Submissions*, requires a *Progress Schedule*, the contractor's best estimate of the time and sequencing requirements for completion of the work. The design professional is advised to require such a progress schedule. This information, together with the schedule of values, gives the design professional a pre-agreed frame of reference. In this way, an opinion as to the timeliness of the work during any monthly period can be substantiated. Figure 7.19 shows a possible supplemental statement to Paragraph 9.6 to enforce the design professional's control over payments to the contractor.

Paragraph 9.7 of the General Conditions (Figure 7.18) establishes a pre-agreed course of action for the contractor in the event that the design professional should fail to expedite processing of the application for payment, or should the owner fail to pay the contractor in accordance with the agreement. No supplemental statements are usually necessary.

The term *Substantial Completion* is defined by Subparagraph 8.1.3 of the General Conditions shown in Figure 7.15. Figure 7.18 illustrates **Paragraph 9.8**, which sets forth the conditions under which substantial completion is achieved, and the actions that are necessary for final completion and final payment. In the normal project, there is usually no sequences or procedures, or that he has made any examination to ascertain how or for what purpose the Contractor has used the moneys previously paid on account of the Contract Sum.

9.5 PROGRESS PAYMENTS

9.5.1 After the Architect has issued a Certificate for Payment, the Owner shall make payment in the manner and within the time provided in the Contract Documents.

9.5.2 The Contractor shall promptly pay each Subcontractor, upon receipt of payment from the Owner, out of the amount paid to the Contractor on account of such Subcontractor's Work, the amount to which said Subcontractor is entitled, reflecting the percentage actually retained, if any, from payments to the Contractor on account of such Subcontractor's Work. The Contractor shall, by an appropriate agreement with each Subcontractor, require each Subcontractor to make payments to his Subsubcontractors in similar manner.

9.5.3 The Architect may, on request and at his discretion, furnish to any Subcontractor, if practicable, information regarding the percentages of completion or the amounts applied for by the Contractor and the action taken thereon by the Architect on account of Work done by such Subcontractor.

9.5.4 Neither the Owner nor the Architect shall have any obligation to pay or to see to the payment of any moneys to any Subcontractor except as may otherwise be required by law.

9.5.5 No Certificate for a progress payment, nor any progress payment, nor any partial or entire use or occupancy of the Project by the Owner, shall constitute an acceptance of any Work not in accordance with the Contract Documents.

9.6 PAYMENTS WITHHELD

9.6.1 The Architect may decline to certify payment and may withhold his Certificate in whole or in part, to the extent necessary reasonably to protect the Owner, if in his opinion he is unable to make representations to the Owner as provided in Subparagraph 9.4.2. If the Architect is unable to make representations to the Owner as provided in Subparagraph 9.4.2 and to certify payment in the amount of the Application, he will notify the Contractor as provided in Subparagraph 9.4.1. If the Contractor and the Architect cannot agree on a revised amount, the Architect will promptly issue a Certificate for Payment for the amount for which he is able to make such representations to the Owner. The Architect may also decline to certify payment or, because of subsequently discovered evidence or subsequent observations, he may nullify the whole or any part of any Certificate for Payment previously issued, to such extent as may be necessary in his opinion to protect the Owner from loss because of:

.1 defective Work not remedied,

.2 third party claims filed or reasonable evidence indicating probable filing of such claims,

.3 failure of the Contractor to make payments properly to Subcontractors or for labor, materials or equipment,

.4 reasonable evidence that the Work cannot be completed for the unpaid balance of the Contract Sum,

.5 damage to the Owner or another contractor,

.6 reasonable evidence that the Work will not be completed within the Contract Time, or

.7 persistent failure to carry out the Work in accordance with the Contract Documents.

9.6.2 When the above grounds in Subparagraph 9.6.1 are removed, payment shall be made for amounts withheld because of them.

9.7 FAILURE OF PAYMENT

9.7.1 If the Architect does not issue a Certificate for Payment, through no fault of the Contractor, within seven days after receipt of the Contractor's Application for Payment, or if the Owner does not pay the Contractor within seven days after the date established in the Contract Documents any amount certified by the Architect or awarded by arbitration, then the Contractor may, upon seven additional days' written notice to the Owner and the Architect, stop the Work until payment of the amount owing has been received. The Contract Sum shall be increased by the amount of the Contractor's reasonable costs of shut-down, delay and start-up, which shall be effected by appropriate Change Order in accordance with Paragraph 12.3.

9.8 SUBSTANTIAL COMPLETION

9.8.1 When the Contractor considers that the Work, or a designated portion thereof which is acceptable to the Owner, is substantially complete as defined in Subparagraph 8.1.3, the Contractor shall prepare for submission to the Architect a list of items to be completed or corrected. The failure to include any items on such list does not alter the responsibility of the Contractor to complete all Work in accordance with the Contract Documents. When the Architect on the basis of an inspection determines that the Work or designated portion thereof is substantially complete, he will then prepare a Certificate of Substantial Completion which shall establish the Date of Substantial Completion, shall state the responsibilities of the Owner and the Contractor for security, maintenance, heat, utilities, damage to the Work, and insurance, and shall fix the time within which the Contractor shall complete the items listed therein. Warranties required by the Contract Documents shall commence on the Date of Substantial Completion of the Work or designated portion thereof unless otherwise provided in the Certificate of Substantial Completion. The Certificate of Substantial Completion shall be submitted to the Owner and the Contractor for their written acceptance of the responsibilities assigned to them in such Certificate.

9.8.2 Upon Substantial Completion of the Work or designated portion thereof and upon application by the Contractor and certification by the Architect, the Owner shall make payment, reflecting adjustment in retainage, if any, for such Work or portion thereof, as provided in the Contract Documents.

9.9 FINAL COMPLETION AND FINAL PAYMENT

9.9.1 Upon receipt of written notice that the Work is ready for final inspection and acceptance and upon receipt of a final Application for Payment, the Architect will

AIA DOCUMENT A201 • GENERAL CONDITIONS OF THE CONTRACT FOR CONSTRUCTION • THIRTEENTH EDITION • AUGUST 1976
AIA® • © 1976 • THE AMERICAN INSTITUTE OF ARCHITECTS, 1735 NEW YORK AVENUE, N.W., WASHINGTON, D.C. 20006

(courtesy American Institute of Architects)

Figure 7.18

9.3.1.3.   The Contractor shall submit with each application for payment which concludes the work of a subcontractor or materials from a supplier, a certificate of release and waiver of lien from the subcontractor or supplier. Failure of the Contractor to supply these certificates of release and waiver of liens will be due cause for the Owner to withhold the payment otherwise due until they are presented.

9.6 - PAYMENTS WITHHELD

A. ADD the following Subsubparagraph 9.6.1.6:

9.6.1.6   The progress of construction must not lag behind the Construction Progress Schedule. If, in the opinion of the Architect, the construction or any portion or phase thereof falls behind schedule, all further payments due on account of the Contract will be withheld until the pace of construction in accelerated sufficiently, in the opinion of the Architect, to meet the completion date.

9.9 - FINAL COMPLETION AND FINAL PAYMENT

A.   ADD the following sentence to Paragraph 9.9.1:

Final payment shall be due thirty-one days after acceptance or Substantial Completion of the work, provided the work be then fully completed and the Contract fully performed.

ARTICLE 11 - INSURANCE:

11.1 - CONTRACTOR'S INSURANCE

A.   Omit Paragraph 11.1.4 entirely - substitute the following:

11.1.4   Contractor shall provide Owner with duplicate copy of required Insurance Policies, together with endorsements to the effect that Insurance Carrier shall give the Owner thirty (30) days notice of cancellation or any reduction of coverage under the policy or change in scope of limits there under.

11.1.4.1   All insurance shall be maintained in a company or companies licensed to do business in the State (Name of State).

B.   ADD the following subparagraph 11.1.5:

11.1.5.   Liability Insurance coverage specified to be provided by the Contractor under Article 11 of the General Conditions and other insurance described below shall be furnished by the Contractor with the following minimum limits.

C.   ADD the following new Paragraph 11.1.5:

11.1.5 - WORKMEN'S COMPENSATION INSURANCE

        Applicable Federal, State.....................Texas
        Employers' Liability..........................($ By Owner)

D.   ADD the following new Paragraph 11.1.6:

11.1.6 - CONTRACTOR'S LIABILITY INSURANCE AND CONTRACTUAL LIABILITY INSURANCE

Form of insurance shall be:

Comprehensive General Liability, plus Contractual Liability coverage. Comprehensive Automobile Liability

a.   BODILY INJURY

        Each Occurrence...........................($ By Owner)
        Aggregate.................................($ By Owner)

b.   PROPERTY DAMAGE
     Including Completed Operations Broad Form

        Each Occurrence...........................($ By Owner)
        Aggregate.................................($ By Owner)

c.   PERSONAL INJURY

        Each Person Aggregate....................($ By Owner)
        General Aggregate........................($ By Owner)

Figure 7.19

need to add supplementary statements regarding substantial completion. Any administrative procedures regarding inspections, preparation of a final "punch list" of items to be completed, transition to owner occupancy, terminating contractor's responsibility for insurance, utilities and similar concerns can be specified in an appropriate Division 1 Section.

Figures 7.18 and 7.20 show **Paragraph 9.9** of the General Conditions. This statement sets forth conditions which establish final completion and final payment. Written notice is required of the contractor to the owner together with the final application for payment. At the time of final payment, the design professional should have made previous inspection of the project to confirm substantial completion. These are administrative rather than obligatory requirements and should therefore be appropriately written into Division 1, Section 01700, *Project Closeout*, and Section 01710, *Project Record Documents* of the specifications. Chapter 9 addresses Division 1 specifications in more detail.

Article 10— Protection of Persons and Property

Article 10 of the General Conditions, shown in Figures 7.20 and 7.21 sets forth the contractor's duties and responsibilities regarding safety and protection of property. Generally, whether the project is publicly or privately owned, (and in the case of the example municipally owned project) no supplemental language is necessary to that contained in Article 10. The design professional or the owner may require that certain specific steps be taken regarding protection of persons and property. Nevertheless, these items are generally specified in Division 1 of the specifications.

Article 11— Insurance

Chapter 5 of this book addresses the role of insurance companies in the construction industry. Each of the United States and many districts have different conditions, regulations and requirements for insurance. Article 11 of the General Conditions (Figure 7.21 and 7.22) sets forth general insurance requirements, types of insurance, and conditions related to insurance coverage. The design professional is generally not qualified to be an insurance counsellor. Professional liability coverage does not cover the design practitioner who (incorrectly) attempts to provide insurance advice. It is, therefore, in the best interest of owner, professional and contractor alike that the owner retain an insurance counsellor to discover both the minimum and maximum amounts of insurance coverage that should be made a condition of the contract, and the types of insurance that should be carried for the project.

Paragraph 11.1 of the General Conditions (Figure 7.21) states the general requirements for liability coverage that the contractor is required to provide. Because of the licensing regulations maintained by each of the United States, the Supplemental Conditions should substitute language to the provisions of Subparagraph 11.1.1 that would require the insurance companies to be licensed by the state having jurisdiction over the project. Figures 7.19 and 7.23 show possible supplemental language to define such licensing requirements as well as other possible insurance requirements.

promptly make such inspection and, when he finds the Work acceptable under the Contract Documents and the Contract fully performed, he will promptly issue a final Certificate for Payment stating that to the best of his knowledge, information and belief, and on the basis of his observations and inspections, the Work has been completed in accordance with the terms and conditions of the Contract Documents and that the entire balance found to be due the Contractor, and noted in said final Certificate, is due and payable. The Architect's final Certificate for Payment will constitute a further representation that the conditions precedent to the Contractor's being entitled to final payment as set forth in Subparagraph 9.9.2 have been fulfilled.

9.9.2 Neither the final payment nor the remaining retained percentage shall become due until the Contractor submits to the Architect (1) an affidavit that all payrolls, bills for materials and equipment, and other indebtedness connected with the Work for which the Owner or his property might in any way be responsible, have been paid or otherwise satisfied, (2) consent of surety, if any, to final payment and (3), if required by the Owner, other data establishing payment or satisfaction of all such obligations, such as receipts, releases and waivers of liens arising out of the Contract, to the extent and in such form as may be designated by the Owner. If any Subcontractor refuses to furnish a release or waiver required by the Owner, the Contractor may furnish a bond satisfactory to the Owner to indemnify him against any such lien. If any such lien remains unsatisfied after all payments are made, the Contractor shall refund to the Owner all moneys that the latter may be compelled to pay in discharging such lien, including all costs and reasonable attorneys' fees.

9.9.3 If, after Substantial Completion of the Work, final completion thereof is materially delayed through no fault of the Contractor or by the issuance of Change Orders affecting final completion, and the Architect so confirms, the Owner shall, upon application by the Contractor and certification by the Architect, and without terminating the Contract, make payment of the balance due for that portion of the Work fully completed and accepted. If the remaining balance for Work not fully completed or corrected is less than the retainage stipulated in the Contract Documents, and if bonds have been furnished as provided in Paragraph 7.5, the written consent of the surety to the payment of the balance due for that portion of the Work fully completed and accepted shall be submitted by the Contractor to the Architect prior to certification of such payment. Such payment shall be made under the terms and conditions governing final payment, except that it shall not constitute a waiver of claims.

9.9.4 The making of final payment shall constitute a waiver of all claims by the Owner except those arising from:

.1 unsettled liens,
.2 faulty or defective Work appearing after Substantial Completion,
.3 failure of the Work to comply with the requirements of the Contract Documents, or
.4 terms of any special warranties required by the Contract Documents.

9.9.5 The acceptance of final payment shall constitute a waiver of all claims by the Contractor except those previously made in writing and identified by the Contractor as unsettled at the time of the final Application for Payment.

ARTICLE 10

PROTECTION OF PERSONS AND PROPERTY

10.1   SAFETY PRECAUTIONS AND PROGRAMS

10.1.1 The Contractor shall be responsible for initiating, maintaining and supervising all safety precautions and programs in connection with the Work.

10.2   SAFETY OF PERSONS AND PROPERTY

10.2.1 The Contractor shall take all reasonable precautions for the safety of, and shall provide all reasonable protection to prevent damage, injury or loss to:

.1 all employees on the Work and all other persons who may be affected thereby;
.2 all the Work and all materials and equipment to be incorporated therein, whether in storage on or off the site, under the care, custody or control of the Contractor or any of his Subcontractors or Sub-subcontractors; and
.3 other property at the site or adjacent thereto, including trees, shrubs, lawns, walks, pavements, roadways, structures and utilities not designated for removal, relocation or replacement in the course of construction.

10.2.2 The Contractor shall give all notices and comply with all applicable laws, ordinances, rules, regulations and lawful orders of any public authority bearing on the safety of persons or property or their protection from damage, injury or loss.

10.2.3 The Contractor shall erect and maintain, as required by existing conditions and progress of the Work, all reasonable safeguards for safety and protection, including posting danger signs and other warnings against hazards, promulgating safety regulations and notifying owners and users of adjacent utilities.

10.2.4 When the use or storage of explosives or other hazardous materials or equipment is necessary for the execution of the Work, the Contractor shall exercise the utmost care and shall carry on such activities under the supervision of properly qualified personnel.

10.2.5 The Contractor shall promptly remedy all damage or loss (other than damage or loss insured under Paragraph 11.3) to any property referred to in Clauses 10.2.1.2 and 10.2.1.3 caused in whole or in part by the Contractor, any Subcontractor, any Sub-subcontractor, or anyone directly or indirectly employed by any of them, or by anyone for whose acts any of them may be liable and for which the Contractor is responsible under Clauses 10.2.1.2 and 10.2.1.3, except damage or loss attributable to the acts or omissions of the Owner or Architect or anyone directly or indirectly employed by either of them, or by anyone for whose acts either of them may be liable, and not attributable to the fault or negligence of the Contractor. The foregoing obligations of the Contractor are in addition to his obligations under Paragraph 4.18.

AIA DOCUMENT A201 • GENERAL CONDITIONS OF THE CONTRACT FOR CONSTRUCTION • THIRTEENTH EDITION • AUGUST 1976
AIA® • © 1976 • THE AMERICAN INSTITUTE OF ARCHITECTS, 1735 NEW YORK AVENUE, N.W., WASHINGTON, D.C. 20006   **A201-1976   15**

(courtesy American Institute of Architects)

Figure 7.20

10.2.6 The Contractor shall designate a responsible member of his organization at the site whose duty shall be the prevention of accidents. This person shall be the Contractor's superintendent unless otherwise designated by the Contractor in writing to the Owner and the Architect.

10.2.7 The Contractor shall not load or permit any part of the Work to be loaded so as to endanger its safety.

10.3 EMERGENCIES

10.3.1 In any emergency affecting the safety of persons or property, the Contractor shall act, at his discretion, to prevent threatened damage, injury or loss. Any additional compensation or extension of time claimed by the Contractor on account of emergency work shall be determined as provided in Article 12 for Changes in the Work.

ARTICLE 11

INSURANCE

11.1 CONTRACTOR'S LIABILITY INSURANCE

11.1.1 The Contractor shall purchase and maintain such insurance as will protect him from claims set forth below which may arise out of or result from the Contractor's operations under the Contract, whether such operations be by himself or by any Subcontractor or by anyone directly or indirectly employed by any of them, or by anyone for whose acts any of them may be liable:

.1 claims under workers' or workmen's compensation, disability benefit and other similar employee benefit acts;

.2 claims for damages because of bodily injury, occupational sickness or disease, or death of his employees;

.3 claims for damages because of bodily injury, sickness or disease, or death of any person other than his employees;

.4 claims for damages insured by usual personal injury liability coverage which are sustained (1) by any person as a result of an offense directly or indirectly related to the employment of such person by the Contractor, or (2) by any other person;

.5 claims for damages, other than to the Work itself, because of injury to or destruction of tangible property, including loss of use resulting therefrom; and

.6 claims for damages because of bodily injury or death of any person or property damage arising out of the ownership, maintenance or use of any motor vehicle.

11.1.2 The insurance required by Subparagraph 11.1.1 shall be written for not less than any limits of liability specified in the Contract Documents, or required by law, whichever is greater.

11.1.3 The insurance required by Subparagraph 11.1.1 shall include contractual liability insurance applicable to the Contractor's obligations under Paragraph 4.18.

11.1.4 Certificates of Insurance acceptable to the Owner shall be filed with the Owner prior to commencement of the Work. These Certificates shall contain a provision that coverages afforded under the policies will not be cancelled until at least thirty days' prior written notice has been given to the Owner.

11.2 OWNER'S LIABILITY INSURANCE

11.2.1 The Owner shall be responsible for purchasing and maintaining his own liability insurance and, at his option, may purchase and maintain such insurance as will protect him against claims which may arise from operations under the Contract.

11.3 PROPERTY INSURANCE

11.3.1 Unless otherwise provided, the Owner shall purchase and maintain property insurance upon the entire Work at the site to the full insurable value thereof. This insurance shall include the interests of the Owner, the Contractor, Subcontractors and Sub-subcontractors in the Work and shall insure against the perils of fire and extended coverage and shall include "all risk" insurance for physical loss or damage including, without duplication of coverage, theft, vandalism and malicious mischief. If the Owner does not intend to purchase such insurance for the full insurable value of the entire Work, he shall inform the Contractor in writing prior to commencement of the Work. The Contractor may then effect insurance which will protect the interests of himself, his Subcontractors and the Sub-subcontractors in the Work, and by appropriate Change Order the cost thereof shall be charged to the Owner. If the Contractor is damaged by failure of the Owner to purchase or maintain such insurance and to so notify the Contractor, then the Owner shall bear all reasonable costs properly attributable thereto. If not covered under the all risk insurance or otherwise provided in the Contract Documents, the Contractor shall effect and maintain similar property insurance on portions of the Work stored off the site or in transit when such portions of the Work are to be included in an Application for Payment under Subparagraph 9.3.2.

11.3.2 The Owner shall purchase and maintain such boiler and machinery insurance as may be required by the Contract Documents or by law. This insurance shall include the interests of the Owner, the Contractor, Subcontractors and Sub-subcontractors in the Work.

11.3.3 Any loss insured under Subparagraph 11.3.1 is to be adjusted with the Owner and made payable to the Owner as trustee for the insureds, as their interests may appear, subject to the requirements of any applicable mortgagee clause and of Subparagraph 11.3.8. The Contractor shall pay each Subcontractor a just share of any insurance moneys received by the Contractor, and by appropriate agreement, written where legally required for validity, shall require each Subcontractor to make payments to his Sub-subcontractors in similar manner.

11.3.4 The Owner shall file a copy of all policies with the Contractor before an exposure to loss may occur.

11.3.5 If the Contractor requests in writing that insurance for risks other than those described in Subparagraphs 11.3.1 and 11.3.2 or other special hazards be included in the property insurance policy, the Owner shall, if possible, include such insurance, and the cost thereof shall be charged to the Contractor by appropriate Change Order.

(courtesy American Institute of Architects)

Figure 7.21

11.3.6 The Owner and Contractor waive all rights against (1) each other and the Subcontractors, Sub-subcontractors, agents and employees each of the other, and (2) the Architect and separate contractors, if any, and their subcontractors, sub-subcontractors, agents and employees, for damages caused by fire or other perils to the extent covered by insurance obtained pursuant to this Paragraph 11.3 or any other property insurance applicable to the Work, except such rights as they may have to the proceeds of such insurance held by the Owner as trustee. The foregoing waiver afforded the Architect, his agents and employees shall not extend to the liability imposed by Subparagraph 4.18.3. The Owner or the Contractor, as appropriate, shall require of the Architect, separate contractors, Subcontractors and Sub-subcontractors by appropriate agreements, written where legally required for validity, similar waivers each in favor of all other parties enumerated in this Subparagraph 11.3.6.

11.3.7 If required in writing by any party in interest, the Owner as trustee shall, upon the occurrence of an insured loss, give bond for the proper performance of his duties. He shall deposit in a separate account any money so received, and he shall distribute it in accordance with such agreement as the parties in interest may reach, or in accordance with an award by arbitration in which case the procedure shall be as provided in Paragraph 7.9. If after such loss no other special agreement is made, replacement of damaged work shall be covered by an appropriate Change Order.

11.3.8 The Owner as trustee shall have power to adjust and settle any loss with the insurers unless one of the parties in interest shall object in writing within five days after the occurrence of loss to the Owner's exercise of this power, and if such objection be made, arbitrators shall be chosen as provided in Paragraph 7.9. The Owner as trustee shall, in that case, make settlement with the insurers in accordance with the directions of such arbitrators. If distribution of the insurance proceeds by arbitration is required, the arbitrators will direct such distribution.

11.3.9 If the Owner finds it necessary to occupy or use a portion or portions of the Work prior to Substantial Completion thereof, such occupancy or use shall not commence prior to a time mutually agreed to by the Owner and Contractor and to which the insurance company or companies providing the property insurance have consented by endorsement to the policy or policies. This insurance shall not be cancelled or lapsed on account of such partial occupancy or use. Consent of the Contractor and of the insurance company or companies to such occupancy or use shall not be unreasonably withheld.

11.4   LOSS OF USE INSURANCE

11.4.1 The Owner, at his option, may purchase and maintain such insurance as will insure him against loss of use of his property due to fire or other hazards, however caused. The Owner waives all rights of action against the Contractor for loss of use of his property, including consequential losses due to fire or other hazards however caused, to the extent covered by insurance under this Paragraph 11.4.

ARTICLE 12

CHANGES IN THE WORK

12.1   CHANGE ORDERS

12.1.1 A Change Order is a written order to the Contractor signed by the Owner and the Architect, issued after execution of the Contract, authorizing a change in the Work or an adjustment in the Contract Sum or the Contract Time. The Contract Sum and the Contract Time may be changed only by Change Order. A Change Order signed by the Contractor indicates his agreement therewith, including the adjustment in the Contract Sum or the Contract Time.

12.1.2 The Owner, without invalidating the Contract, may order changes in the Work within the general scope of the Contract consisting of additions, deletions or other revisions, the Contract Sum and the Contract Time being adjusted accordingly. All such changes in the Work shall be authorized by Change Order, and shall be performed under the applicable conditions of the Contract Documents.

12.1.3 The cost or credit to the Owner resulting from a change in the Work shall be determined in one or more of the following ways:

  .1 by mutual acceptance of a lump sum properly itemized and supported by sufficient substantiating data to permit evaluation;

  .2 by unit prices stated in the Contract Documents or subsequently agreed upon;

  .3 by cost to be determined in a manner agreed upon by the parties and a mutually acceptable fixed or percentage fee; or

  .4 by the method provided in Subparagraph 12.1.4.

12.1.4 If none of the methods set forth in Clauses 12.1.3.1, 12.1.3.2 or 12.1.3.3 is agreed upon, the Contractor, provided he receives a written order signed by the Owner, shall promptly proceed with the Work involved. The cost of such Work shall then be determined by the Architect on the basis of the reasonable expenditures and savings of those performing the Work attributable to the change, including, in the case of an increase in the Contract Sum, a reasonable allowance for overhead and profit. In such case, and also under Clauses 12.1.3.3 and 12.1.3.4 above, the Contractor shall keep and present, in such form as the Architect may prescribe, an itemized accounting together with appropriate supporting data for inclusion in a Change Order. Unless otherwise provided in the Contract Documents, cost shall be limited to the following: cost of materials, including sales tax and cost of delivery; cost of labor, including social security, old age and unemployment insurance, and fringe benefits required by agreement or custom; workers' or workmen's compensation insurance; bond premiums; rental value of equipment and machinery; and the additional costs of supervision and field office personnel directly attributable to the change. Pending final determination of cost to the Owner, payments on account shall be made on the Architect's Certificate for Payment. The amount of credit to be allowed by the Contractor to the Owner for any deletion

(courtesy American Institute of Architects)

Figure 7.22

d. AUTOMOBILE LIABILITY - Owner, Non-Owned and Hired

    Bodily Injury Each Person...............($ By Owner)
    Bodily Injury Each Occurrence..........($ By Owner)
    Property Damage Each Occurrence.........($ By Owner)

D. ADD the following new Paragraph 11.1.6:

11.1.6 The CONTRACTOR shall carry liability insurance in addition to that specifically named by the General Conditions as follows:

    .1 COMPLETED OPERATIONS AND PRODUCTS LIABILITY.

    .2 OTHER INSURANCE AMOUNT:

        Excess Liability..........................($ By Owner)

    .3 OWNERS PROTECTIVE LIABILITY INSURANCE and PROPERTY

F. SUB-PARAGRAPH 11.1.4:

    ADD the following sentence to the end of Paragraph 11.1.4 :

    Furnish one copy of each certificate for each copy of The Agreement; specifically set forth evidence of all coverage required under Article 11 and these supplements thereto:

G. SUB-ARTICLE 11.2 - OWNER'S LIABILITY INSURANCE:

    AMEND title of Article 11.2 to read as follows:

11.2 OWNERS PROTECTIVE LIABILITY INSURANCE AND PROPERTY INSURANCE:

A. Omit paragraph 11.2.1 in it's entirely. Substitute the following.

11.2.1 Contractor's Liability coverage shall name as "Insureds" the (Name of Owner), it's elected and appointed officials (officers), employees and volunteers.

11.2.2 BUILDER'S RISK: Contractor shall purchase and maintain property insurance upon entire work at site to full insurable value thereof. Such insurance shall be in the company or companies against which Owner has no reasonable objection. This insurance shall include the interests of Owner, and Contractor, Subcontractors and Sub-Subcontractors in the work and shall insure against perils of fire and extended coverage and shall "All Risk" insurance for physical loss or damage including flood. If not covered under "All Risk" insurance or otherwise provided in Contract Documents, Contractor shall effect and maintain similar property insurance on portions of the work stored off of site or in transit when such portion of the work is to be included in an application for payment. The policies must be endorsed to permit occupancy by Owner prior to final acceptable of the Project.

11.2.3 In the event of loss or damage under the Builder's Risk Insurance, the building, improvements and premises shall be rebuilt and restored be the Contractor promptly at his own expense.

11.2.4 The amount of insurance carried from time to time shall be sufficient to cover the total amount of materials fabricated and installed, or in storage and work completed, subject to loss or damage to the date of each payment, until the work is completed, when insurance coverage shall be carried by the Contractors until the Owner places permanent insurance on the finished work.

11.2.5 Waiver of Subrogation: The Owner and Contractor waive all rights and the rights of their respective insurance companies against each other for damage caused by fire of other perils to the extent such damages are covered by property insurance purchased by either party.

11.2.6 Contractor shall maintain "All Risk" Insurance in full and effective force throughout the entire period of construction and for a period, after the date of SUBSTANTIAL COMPLETION not to exceed sixty (60) days, or until such time as the Owner has obtained PROPERTY INSURANCE satisfactory to his needs and has so notified the Contractor in Writing.

Figure 7.23

The insurance counsellor may advise additional language in the Supplementary General Conditions that would provide other comprehensive coverage in other major divisions of insurance depending upon the nature of the project. These coverages may include but are not limited to:

(1) Premises Operations, including extended or universal coverage.
(2) Independent contractors' Protective.
(3) Products and Completed Operations.
(4) Personal Injury Liability with Employment exclusion deleted.
(5) Owned, non-owned and hired motor vehicles.
(6) Broad Form Property Damage including Completed operations.
(7) Umbrella excess liability.

Item 1 includes risks that could occur from any operation on the job site, including extended or universal coverage (explosion, collapse or underground mishap). These coverages, normally excluded from "Premises Operations" would be included by endorsement if required. Item 2 provides coverage from claims from other (independent) contractors. This coverage would be applicable in the case of separate contracts or owner employed separate contractor(s). Items 3 through 6 can be written individually but are generally named in a combined "All Risk" policy, custom written to meet the excess or unique insurance requirements of the project. Item 3 would cover loss to completed work due to a hazard not usually covered by other forms of insurance. Item 4 provides for personal injury above and beyond the statutory limits of workman's compensation. Item 5 should include liability and damage to motor vehicles of all types related to the work during the construction process. Item 6 usually refers to coverage against the perils of fire and includes other natural hazards such as windstorm, lighting damage and hazards of a natural nature, as well as malicious mischief and vandalism. Item 7 adds general liability coverage in the broadest form and serves as an "umbrella" loss from liability over and above the limits of other liability insurance. Supplemental language might be provided to the provisions of Paragraph 11.1 that would be appropriate for a particular project, based on advice of counsel.

Paragraph 11.2 of the General Conditions (Figure 7.21) provides for the owner to purchase or maintain separate liability insurance and such coverage as he may wish to maintain in order to cover claims arising from the construction. It is not unusual for the Supplemental General Conditions to require that the contractor pay for certain insurance to cover the owner and the design professional in the contract sum. Figures 7.19 and 7.23 illustrate supplemental language that might be appropriate for the example public project.

Paragraph 11.4 of the General Conditions provides the owner's right to carry separate loss of use insurance. This coverage would provide relief, over and above any coverage carried by the contractor. Supplemental language is not usually required to amend these provisions.

Article 12— Changes in the Work

Paragraph 12.1.1 (Figure 7.22) defines the term Change Order. The Contract for Construction provides for changes to be made in the work based on a variety of needs or conditions. Any such change or modification must be signed, indicating acceptance by the owner and the contractor, with the approval of the design professional. Little if any supplemental language is usually necessary to the provisions of Article

12. Figure 7.24 illustrates supplemental statements contained in the Supplemental General Conditions that might be appropriate for the example municipal project.

Article 13— Uncovering and Correction of Work

Article 13 of the General Conditions, shown in Figures 7.25 and 7.26, provide procedures for uncovering work that has been completed (for reasons and requirements that may become evident during construction) and for correcting work for a variety of other reasons. Most of the provisions of the article are procedural but nevertheless represent an obligation that must be placed as a condition, not a specification, of the contract documents. It may be appropriate for the Supplemental General Conditions to contain some supplemental language (Figure 7.24) to establish any desired change to the time limits established in General Conditions Subparagraph 13.2.2. Paragraph 13.3 (Figure 7.26) provides for financial settlement and acceptance of defective work in cases where it may be completely impractical for the defective work to be removed and/or replaced. Figure 7.24 contains supplemental language to further stipulate conditions under which, at the owner's option, non-conforming work would be accepted.

Article 14— Termination of the Contract

The terms set forth in Article 14 of the General Conditions (Figure 7.26) allow the Contract for Construction to be terminated by either party for certain stipulated causes, and with notice of such action each to the other. Generally, supplemental language is not required in addition to the provisions of Article 14.

ARTICLE 12 - CHANGES IN THE WORK

A. SUB-ARTICLE 12.1 - Change Orders:

AMEND Paragraph 12.1.4 as follows:

In the second sentence, delete the words "a reasonable allowance for overhead and profit" and substitute "an allowance for overhead and profit in accordance with the schedule set forth in Subparagraph 12.1.6".

ADD the following Subparagraph 12.1.6:

12.1.6 In Subparagraph 12.1.3 and 12.1.4 the allowances for overhead and profit combined, included in the total cost to the Owner, shall be based on the following schedule:

1. For the Contractor, for any Work performed by the Contractor's own forces, fifteen percent (15%) of the cost. (Not allowed for Contingency Allowance change orders.)

2. For the Contractor, for Work performed by the Contractor's Subcontractor, five percent (5%) of the amount due the Subcontractor. (Not allowed for Contingency Allowance change orders.)

3. For each Subcontractor or Subcontractor involved, for any Work performed by that Subcontractor's own forces, fifteen percent (15%) of the cost.

4. Cost to which overhead and profit is to be applied shall be determined in accordance with Subparagraph 12.1.4.

5. In order to facilitate checking of quotations for extras or credits, all proposals, except those so minor that their propriety can be seen by inspection, shall be accompanied by a complete itemization of costs including labor, materials and Subcontracts. Labor and materials shall be itemized in the manner prescribed above. Where major cost items are Subcontracts, they shall be itemized also. In no case will a change involving over $250.00 be approved without such itemization.

ARTICLE 13 - UNCOVERING AND CORRECTION OF WORK

A. SUB-ARTICLE 13.2 - CORRECTION OF THE WORK:

AMEND Sub-Paragraph 13.2.2 as follows:

DELETE the words " One year after the date of Substantial Completion of the Work" and substitute the words " One year after date of Final Acceptance of the Work by the Owner"

At the end of the sub-paragraph ADD the following sentence:

Where Guarantees are specified in any Section of the Specifications for periods exceeding one year, the longer of the periods shall apply fully to the intent of this sub-paragraph.

B. SUB-ARTICLE 13.3 - ACCEPTANCE OF DEFECTIVE OR NON-CONFORMING WORK:

ADD the following sentence to sub-article 13.3:

When any such work is found, the entire area of work involved shall be corrected unless the Contractor can completely define the limits to the Architect's satisfaction. Additional testing, sampling or inspecting needed to define the non-conforming work shall be done at the Contractor's expense. The Contractor shall employ a testing laboratory selected by the Owner if such services are required or recommended by the Architect. All corrected work shall be retested at the Contractor's expense. Any extra Architectural or Engineering work required to analyze or establish conformity of the work shall be paid for by the Contractor at no additional expense to the Owner.

END OF SUPPLEMENTAL GENERAL CONDITIONS

Figure 7.24

or change which results in a net decrease in the Contract Sum will be the amount of the actual net cost as confirmed by the Architect. When both additions and credits covering related Work or substitutions are involved in any one change, the allowance for overhead and profit shall be figured on the basis of the net increase, if any, with respect to that change.

12.1.5 If unit prices are stated in the Contract Documents or subsequently agreed upon, and if the quantities originally contemplated are so changed in a proposed Change Order that application of the agreed unit prices to the quantities of Work proposed will cause substantial inequity to the Owner or the Contractor, the applicable unit prices shall be equitably adjusted.

12.2 CONCEALED CONDITIONS

12.2.1 Should concealed conditions encountered in the performance of the Work below the surface of the ground or should concealed or unknown conditions in an existing structure be at variance with the conditions indicated by the Contract Documents, or should unknown physical conditions below the surface of the ground or should concealed or unknown conditions in an existing structure of an unusual nature, differing materially from those ordinarily encountered and generally recognized as inherent in work of the character provided for in this Contract, be encountered, the Contract Sum shall be equitably adjusted by Change Order upon claim by either party made within twenty days after the first observance of the conditions.

12.3 CLAIMS FOR ADDITIONAL COST

12.3.1 If the Contractor wishes to make a claim for an increase in the Contract Sum, he shall give the Architect written notice thereof within twenty days after the occurrence of the event giving rise to such claim. This notice shall be given by the Contractor before proceeding to execute the Work, except in an emergency endangering life or property in which case the Contractor shall proceed in accordance with Paragraph 10.3. No such claim shall be valid unless so made. If the Owner and the Contractor cannot agree on the amount of the adjustment in the Contract Sum, it shall be determined by the Architect. Any change in the Contract Sum resulting from such claim shall be authorized by Change Order.

12.3.2 If the Contractor claims that additional cost is involved because of, but not limited to, (1) any written interpretation pursuant to Subparagraph 2.2.8, (2) any order by the Owner to stop the Work pursuant to Paragraph 3.3 where the Contractor was not at fault, (3) any written order for a minor change in the Work issued pursuant to Paragraph 12.4, or (4) failure of payment by the Owner pursuant to Paragraph 9.7, the Contractor shall make such claim as provided in Subparagraph 12.3.1.

12.4 MINOR CHANGES IN THE WORK

12.4.1 The Architect will have authority to order minor changes in the Work not involving an adjustment in the Contract Sum or an extension of the Contract Time and not inconsistent with the intent of the Contract Documents. Such changes shall be effected by written order, and shall be binding on the Owner and the Contractor.

The Contractor shall carry out such written orders promptly.

ARTICLE 13

UNCOVERING AND CORRECTION OF WORK

13.1 UNCOVERING OF WORK

13.1.1 If any portion of the Work should be covered contrary to the request of the Architect or to requirements specifically expressed in the Contract Documents, it must, if required in writing by the Architect, be uncovered for his observation and shall be replaced at the Contractor's expense.

13.1.2 If any other portion of the Work has been covered which the Architect has not specifically requested to observe prior to being covered, the Architect may request to see such Work and it shall be uncovered by the Contractor. If such Work be found in accordance with the Contract Documents, the cost of uncovering and replacement shall, by appropriate Change Order, be charged to the Owner. If such Work be found not in accordance with the Contract Documents, the Contractor shall pay such costs unless it be found that this condition was caused by the Owner or a separate contractor as provided in Article 6, in which event the Owner shall be responsible for the payment of such costs.

13.2 CORRECTION OF WORK

13.2.1 The Contractor shall promptly correct all Work rejected by the Architect as defective or as failing to conform to the Contract Documents whether observed before or after Substantial Completion and whether or not fabricated, installed or completed. The Contractor shall bear all costs of correcting such rejected Work, including compensation for the Architect's additional services made necessary thereby.

13.2.2 If, within one year after the Date of Substantial Completion of the Work or designated portion thereof or within one year after acceptance by the Owner of designated equipment or within such longer period of time as may be prescribed by law or by the terms of any applicable special warranty required by the Contract Documents, any of the Work is found to be defective or not in accordance with the Contract Documents, the Contractor shall correct it promptly after receipt of a written notice from the Owner to do so unless the Owner has previously given the Contractor a written acceptance of such condition. This obligation shall survive termination of the Contract. The Owner shall give such notice promptly after discovery of the condition.

13.2.3 The Contractor shall remove from the site all portions of the Work which are defective or non-conforming and which have not been corrected under Subparagraphs 4.5.1, 13.2.1 and 13.2.2, unless removal is waived by the Owner.

13.2.4 If the Contractor fails to correct defective or nonconforming Work as provided in Subparagraphs 4.5.1, 13.2.1 and 13.2.2, the Owner may correct it in accordance with Paragraph 3.4.

18 A201-1976 AIA DOCUMENT A201 • GENERAL CONDITIONS OF THE CONTRACT FOR CONSTRUCTION • THIRTEENTH EDITION • AUGUST 1976
AIA® • © 1976 • THE AMERICAN INSTITUTE OF ARCHITECTS, 1735 NEW YORK AVENUE, N.W., WASHINGTON, D.C. 20006

(courtesy American Institute of Architects)

Figure 7.25

13.2.5 If the Contractor does not proceed with the correction of such defective or non-conforming Work within a reasonable time fixed by written notice from the Architect, the Owner may remove it and may store the materials or equipment at the expense of the Contractor. If the Contractor does not pay the cost of such removal and storage within ten days thereafter, the Owner may upon ten additional days' written notice sell such Work at auction or at private sale and shall account for the net proceeds thereof, after deducting all the costs that should have been borne by the Contractor, including compensation for the Architect's additional services made necessary thereby. If such proceeds of sale do not cover all costs which the Contractor should have borne, the difference shall be charged to the Contractor and an appropriate Change Order shall be issued. If the payments then or thereafter due the Contractor are not sufficient to cover such amount, the Contractor shall pay the difference to the Owner.

13.2.6 The Contractor shall bear the cost of making good all work of the Owner or separate contractors destroyed or damaged by such correction or removal.

13.2.7 Nothing contained in this Paragraph 13.2 shall be construed to establish a period of limitation with respect to any other obligation which the Contractor might have under the Contract Documents, including Paragraph 4.5 hereof. The establishment of the time period of one year after the Date of Substantial Completion or such longer period of time as may be prescribed by law or by the terms of any warranty required by the Contract Documents relates only to the specific obligation of the Contractor to correct the Work, and has no relationship to the time within which his obligation to comply with the Contract Documents may be sought to be enforced, nor to the time within which proceedings may be commenced to establish the Contractor's liability with respect to his obligations other than specifically to correct the Work.

13.3 ACCEPTANCE OF DEFECTIVE OR NON-CONFORMING WORK

13.3.1 If the Owner prefers to accept defective or non-conforming Work, he may do so instead of requiring its removal and correction, in which case a Change Order will be issued to reflect a reduction in the Contract Sum where appropriate and equitable. Such adjustment shall be effected whether or not final payment has been made.

ARTICLE 14

TERMINATION OF THE CONTRACT

14.1 TERMINATION BY THE CONTRACTOR

14.1.1 If the Work is stopped for a period of thirty days under an order of any court or other public authority having jurisdiction, or as a result of an act of government, such as a declaration of a national emergency making materials unavailable, through no act or fault of the Contractor or a Subcontractor or their agents or employees or any other persons performing any of the Work under a contract with the Contractor, or if the Work should be stopped for a period of thirty days by the Contractor because the Architect has not issued a Certificate for Payment as provided in Paragraph 9.7 or because the Owner has not made payment thereon as provided in Paragraph 9.7, then the Contractor may, upon seven additional days' written notice to the Owner and the Architect, terminate the Contract and recover from the Owner payment for all Work executed and for any proven loss sustained upon any materials, equipment, tools, construction equipment and machinery, including reasonable profit and damages.

14.2 TERMINATION BY THE OWNER

14.2.1 If the Contractor is adjudged a bankrupt, or if he makes a general assignment for the benefit of his creditors, or if a receiver is appointed on account of his insolvency, or if he persistently or repeatedly refuses or fails, except in cases for which extension of time is provided, to supply enough properly skilled workmen or proper materials, or if he fails to make prompt payment to Subcontractors or for materials or labor, or persistently disregards laws, ordinances, rules, regulations or orders of any public authority having jurisdiction, or otherwise is guilty of a substantial violation of a provision of the Contract Documents, then the Owner, upon certification by the Architect that sufficient cause exists to justify such action, may, without prejudice to any right or remedy and after giving the Contractor and his surety, if any, seven days' written notice, terminate the employment of the Contractor and take possession of the site and of all materials, equipment, tools, construction equipment and machinery thereon owned by the Contractor and may finish the Work by whatever method he may deem expedient. In such case the Contractor shall not be entitled to receive any further payment until the Work is finished.

14.2.2 If the unpaid balance of the Contract Sum exceeds the costs of finishing the Work, including compensation for the Architect's additional services made necessary thereby, such excess shall be paid to the Contractor. If such costs exceed the unpaid balance, the Contractor shall pay the difference to the Owner. The amount to be paid to the Contractor or to the Owner, as the case may be, shall be certified by the Architect, upon application, in the manner provided in Paragraph 9.4, and this obligation for payment shall survive the termination of the Contract.

(*courtesy American Institute of Architects*)

Figure 7.26

Chapter 8
THE PROJECT MANUAL

Construction specifications have traditionally been written and bound separately from the contract drawings as a matter of convenience. As the various trades became familiar with the "Book of Specifications" during the boom years at the turn of the century, this bound document became known as the "Specs". Over the years, practitioners included bidding information, conditions of the contract, and other necessary data in order to facilitate bidding or negotiating for the award of contract. The legal significance, competence, coordination and content of the contract documents are more important today than ever before. As more and more legal, technical and qualitative information has been demanded by the OPC (Owner-Professional-Contractor) relationship, the contract documents (in addition to the specifications) have commonly been written, reproduced and bound into a booklet intended to accompany the drawings. This bound volume, containing much more than just the specifications, has come to be called the Project Manual.

The American Institute of Architects is credited with having coined the term "Project Manual". The early 1960's represented a period of professional re-evaluation, during which design professionals made an effort to "streamline" the language of specifications. The AIA improved and expanded the uniform published forms used to supplement the contract documents for common building projects. At this time, the bidding requirements, conditions of the contract, and other forms related to the contract, were being reproduced and bound into the "Specifications Book". Upon reflection, many design professionals recognized that much of the information contained in the "Specs", while related to the work, was not technical specification data. The Bidding Requirements, for instance, commonly bound into the "specs" were neither contract documents nor specifications, but were included as a matter of convenience to facilitate the award of the contract. To this day, many practitioners within the construction industry continue to refer to the bound documents used during bidding and construction as "Specs". The term "Project Manual" more clearly and correctly expresses the use and intention of this collection of information, while at the same time, implying that something other than the technical specifications reside there. Indeed, such is the intent. This chapter is dedicated to the organization, content and use of the Project Manual.

Today's Project Manual contains, but is not limited to the following documents by category of information:

Bidding Requirements
- Invitation to Bid
- Instructions to Bidders
- Information Available to Bidders
    - —Property Survey
    - —Soil Analysis
    - —Related Construction Documents
- Bid Forms
- Form of Bid Bond

Supplemental Forms
- Form of Agreement
- Form of Performance Bond
- Form of Payment Bond
- Certificate of Insurance
- Certificate of Compliance

Conditions of the Contract
- General Conditions
- Supplementary General Conditions
- Regulatory Conditions
    - —Wage Rates
    - —Equal Opportunity Requirements
    - —Domestic Materials Requirements
- Index of Drawings

Technical Specifications
- Division 1—General Requirements
- Division 2—Sitework
- Division 3—Concrete
- Division 4—Masonry
- Division 5—Metals
- Division 6—Wood and Plastics
- Division 7—Thermal and Moisture Protection
- Division 8—Doors and Windows
- Division 9—Finishes
- Division 10—Specialties
- Division 11—Equipment
- Division 12—Furnishings
- Division 13—Special Construction
- Division 14—Conveying Systems
- Division 15—Mechanical
- Division 16—Electrical

Modifications to the Contract

Invitation for and Advertisment to Bidders

It is customary that the owner advertise in some way his intention to receive competitive bids. In the case of public work, open competitive bidding is usually mandated by law, and the advertisement for bids is published in the local media by statutory requirement. Some statutes require that the advertisement appear for a specific length of time in one or more local newspapers. Figure 8.1 is an example of a typical public project advertisement to be found in the classified section of a local newspaper. (Chapter 5 discusses the procedures and issues related to competitive bidding and negotiation for the award of the contract for construction.)

In the case of private projects, it is more common to offer an Invitation to Bid to selected firms. The private owner may advertise if he so desires. However, he may also privately invite whomever he pleases to enter the bidding competition, or he may pre-select the constructor and negotiate the contract for construction. Figure 8.2 is a common form of an Invitation to Bid. The Invitation to Bid and the Advertisement for Bids accomplish the same basic function, that is to attract bids from constructors in order to award the contract.

Both the Advertisement for Bids and the Invitation to Bid should incorporate certain information. As a minimum requirement these documents should include the following:

Project Identification
- Name of project
- Address of project
- Name of owner
- Contract authority (if required)
- Name of design professional
- Address of design professional
- Telephone number of design professional
- Name of design professional's project manager

The body of these documents should include: a brief description of the project, the owner's requirements for time of completion, the types of bids required, the date of the bid opening, the availability and procurement of bidding documents, any pre-qualification required of bidders, bid security requirements, and a statement regarding the owner's right to reject any or all bids. In the case of public work, statements applicable to governing laws should be included.

Instructions to Bidders

The key document to the bidding process is the Instructions to Bidders. Figure 8.3a is the title sheet to AIA Document A701—*Instructions to Bidders*. This document is commonly used in conjunction with AIA Document A201—*General Conditions of the Contract for Construction* (described in Chapter 7).

The text of AIA Document A701 document appears in Figures 8.3b through 8.3e. Following the basic "rule" that information should not be repeated unnecessarily throughout the documents, the Instructions to Bidders should first refer the reader to pertinent definitions contained in other documents. Definitions that are included should set forth specific explanations to make clear the terms used in the bidding process. Some of the terms which should be defined are: addenda, bid, base bid, alternate bid, unit price, bidder and sub-bidder. (See Article 1 of AIA Document A701, Figure 8.3b).

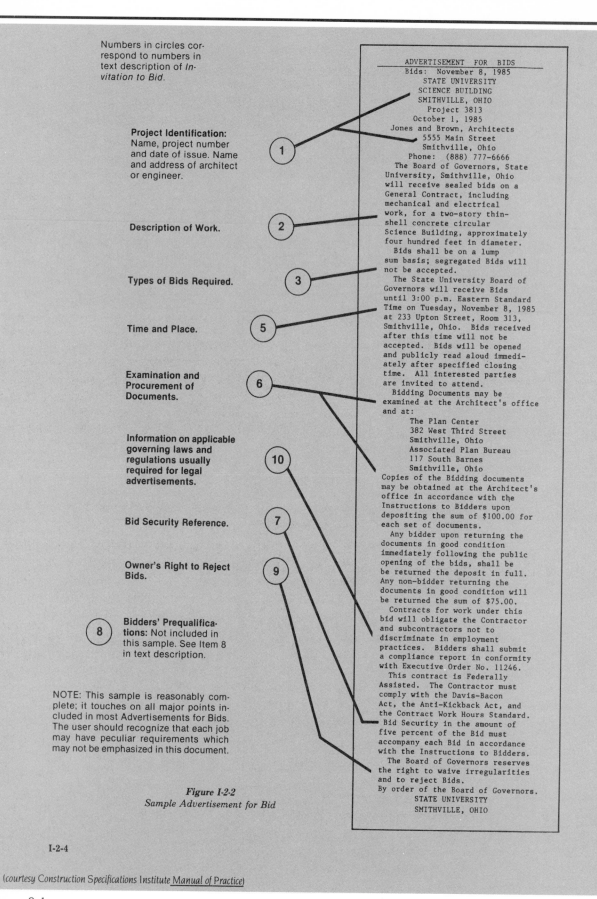

Numbers in circles correspond to numbers in text description of *Invitation to Bid.*

Project Identification: Name, project number and date of issue. Name and address of architect or engineer.

(1)

Description of Work.

(2)

Types of Bids Required.

(3)

Time and Place.

(5)

Examination and Procurement of Documents.

(6)

Information on applicable governing laws and regulations usually required for legal advertisements.

(10)

Bid Security Reference.

(7)

Owner's Right to Reject Bids.

(9)

(8) **Bidders' Prequalifications:** Not included in this sample. See Item 8 in text description.

NOTE: This sample is reasonably complete; it touches on all major points included in most Advertisements for Bids. The user should recognize that each job may have peculiar requirements which may not be emphasized in this document.

Figure I-2-2
Sample Advertisement for Bid

```
       ADVERTISEMENT  FOR  BIDS
     Bids:  November 8, 1985
        STATE UNIVERSITY
        SCIENCE BUILDING
       SMITHVILLE, OHIO
         Project 3813
        October 1, 1985
    Jones and Brown, Architects
        5555 Main Street
        Smithville, Ohio
     Phone:  (888) 777-6666
    The Board of Governors, State
University, Smithville, Ohio
will receive sealed bids on a
General Contract, including
mechanical and electrical
work, for a two-story thin-
shell concrete circular
Science Building, approximately
four hundred feet in diameter.
    Bids shall be on a lump
sum basis; segregated Bids will
not be accepted.
    The State University Board of
Governors will receive Bids
until 3:00 p.m. Eastern Standard
Time on Tuesday, November 8, 1985
at 233 Upton Street, Room 313,
Smithville, Ohio.  Bids received
after this time will not be
accepted.  Bids will be opened
and publicly read aloud immedi-
ately after specified closing
time.  All interested parties
are invited to attend.
    Bidding Documents may be
examined at the Architect's office
and at:
        The Plan Center
        382 West Third Street
        Smithville, Ohio
        Associated Plan Bureau
        117 South Barnes
        Smithville, Ohio
Copies of the Bidding documents
may be obtained at the Architect's
office in accordance with the
Instructions to Bidders upon
depositing the sum of $100.00 for
each set of documents.
    Any bidder upon returning the
documents in good condition
immediately following the public
opening of the bids, shall be
be returned the deposit in full.
Any non-bidder returning the
documents in good condition will
be returned the sum of $75.00.
    Contracts for work under this
bid will obligate the Contractor
and subcontractors not to
discriminate in employment
practices.  Bidders shall submit
a compliance report in conformity
with Executive Order No. 11246.
    This contract is Federally
Assisted.  The Contractor must
comply with the Davis-Bacon
Act, the Anti-Kickback Act, and
the Contract Work Hours Standard.
    Bid Security in the amount of
five percent of the Bid must
accompany each Bid in accordance
with the Instructions to Bidders.
    The Board of Governors reserves
the right to waive irregularities
and to reject Bids.
By order of the Board of Governors.
        STATE UNIVERSITY
        SMITHVILLE, OHIO
```

I-2-4

(courtesy Construction Specifications Institute *Manual of Practice*)

Figure 8.1

142

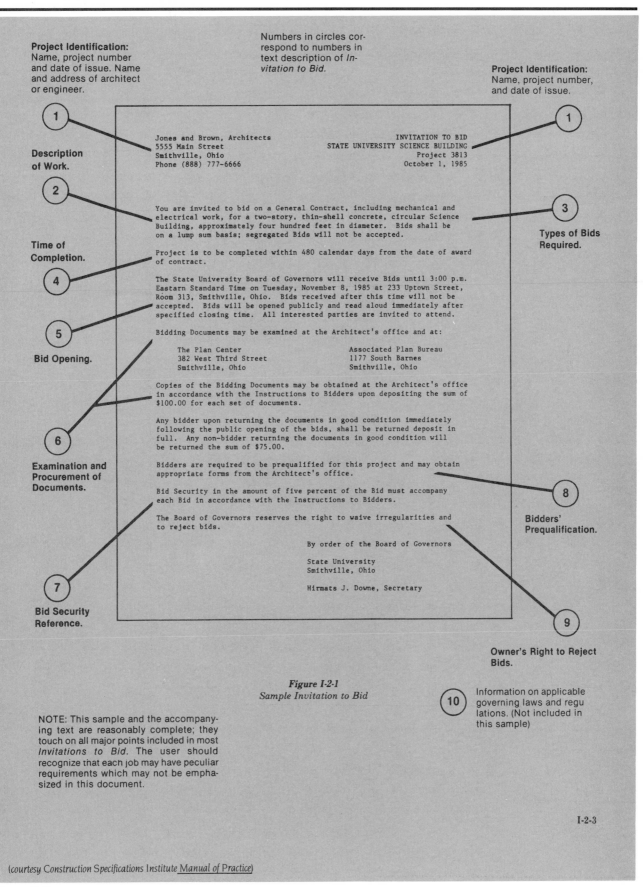

Project Identification:
Name, project number
and date of issue. Name
and address of architect
or engineer.

Numbers in circles cor-
respond to numbers in
text description of *In-
vitation to Bid.*

Project Identification:
Name, project number,
and date of issue.

(1)

**Description
of Work.**

(2)

**Time of
Completion.**

(4)

Bid Opening.

(5)

**Examination and
Procurement of
Documents.**

(6)

**Bid Security
Reference.**

(7)

(1)

(3)

**Types of Bids
Required.**

(8)

**Bidders'
Prequalification.**

(9)

**Owner's Right to Reject
Bids.**

Jones and Brown, Architects
5555 Main Street
Smithville, Ohio
Phone (888) 777-6666

INVITATION TO BID
STATE UNIVERSITY SCIENCE BUILDING
Project 3813
October 1, 1985

You are invited to bid on a General Contract, including mechanical and
electrical work, for a two-story, thin-shell concrete, circular Science
Building, approximately four hundred feet in diameter. Bids shall be
on a lump sum basis; segregated Bids will not be accepted.

Project is to be completed within 480 calendar days from the date of award
of contract.

The State University Board of Governors will receive Bids until 3:00 p.m.
Eastern Standard Time on Tuesday, November 8, 1985 at 233 Uptown Street,
Room 313, Smithville, Ohio. Bids received after this time will not be
accepted. Bids will be opened publicly and read aloud immediately after
specified closing time. All interested parties are invited to attend.

Bidding Documents may be examined at the Architect's office and at:

The Plan Center   Associated Plan Bureau
382 West Third Street   1177 South Barnes
Smithville, Ohio   Smithville, Ohio

Copies of the Bidding Documents may be obtained at the Architect's office
in accordance with the Instructions to Bidders upon depositing the sum of
$100.00 for each set of documents.

Any bidder upon returning the documents in good condition immediately
following the public opening of the bids, shall be returned deposit in
full. Any non-bidder returning the documents in good condition will
be returned the sum of $75.00.

Bidders are required to be prequalified for this project and may obtain
appropriate forms from the Architect's office.

Bid Security in the amount of five percent of the Bid must accompany
each Bid in accordance with the Instructions to Bidders.

The Board of Governors reserves the right to waive irregularities and
to reject bids.

By order of the Board of Governors

State University
Smithville, Ohio

Hirmats J. Downe, Secretary

Figure I-2-1
Sample Invitation to Bid

(10) Information on applicable
governing laws and regu-
lations. (Not included in
this sample)

NOTE: This sample and the accompanying text are reasonably complete; they
touch on all major points included in most
Invitations to Bid. The user should
recognize that each job may have peculiar
requirements which may not be emphasized in this document.

I-2-3

(courtesy Construction Specifications Institute <u>Manual of Practice</u>)

Figure 8.2

THE AMERICAN INSTITUTE OF ARCHITECTS

AIA Document A701

Instructions to Bidders

1978 EDITION

Use only with the 1976 Edition of AIA Document A201, General Conditions of the Contract for Construction

TABLE OF ARTICLES

1. DEFINITIONS

2. BIDDER'S REPRESENTATIONS

3. BIDDING DOCUME

4. BIDDING PROCEDU

5. CONSIDERATION OF

6. POS

BOND

NER

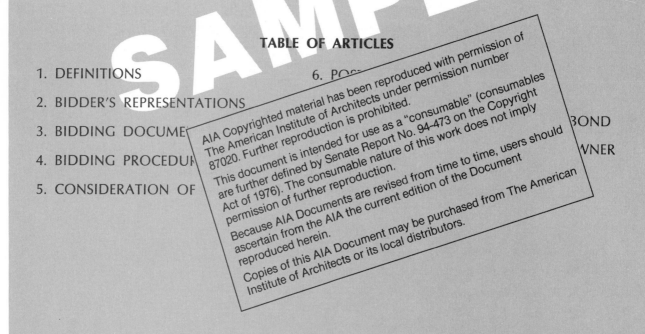

AIA DOCUMENT A701 • INSTRUCTIONS TO BIDDERS • THIRD EDITION • MAY 1978 • AIA® • ©1978
THE AMERICAN INSTITUTE OF ARCHITECTS, 1735 NEW YORK AVE., N.W., WASHINGTON, D. C. 20006   **A701-1978 1**

(courtesy American Institute of Architects)

Figure 8.3a

ARTICLE 1

DEFINITIONS

1.1 Bidding Documents include the Advertisement or Invitation to Bid, Instructions to Bidders, the bid form, other sample bidding and contract forms and the proposed Contract Documents including any Addenda issued prior to receipt of bids. The Contract Documents proposed for the Work consist of the Owner-Contractor Agreement, the Conditions of the Contract (General, Supplementary and other Conditions), the Drawings, the Specifications and all Addenda issued prior to and all Modifications issued after execution of the Contract.

1.2 All definitions set forth in the General Conditions of the Contract for Construction, AIA Document A201, or in other Contract Documents are applicable to the Bidding Documents.

1.3 Addenda are written or graphic instruments issued by the Architect prior to the execution of the Contract which modify or interpret the Bidding Documents by additions, deletions, clarifications or corrections.

1.4 A Bid is a complete and properly signed proposal to do the Work or designated portion thereof for the sums stipulated therein, submitted in accordance with the Bidding Documents.

1.5 The Base Bid is the sum stated in the Bid for which the Bidder offers to perform the Work described in the Bidding Documents as the base, to which work may be added or from which work may be deleted for sums stated in Alternate Bids.

1.6 An Alternate Bid (or Alternate) is an amount stated in the Bid to be added to or deducted from the amount of the Base Bid if the corresponding change in the Work, as described in the Bidding Documents, is accepted.

1.7 A Unit Price is an amount stated in the Bid as a price per unit of measurement for materials or services as described in the Bidding Documents or in the proposed Contract Documents.

1.8 A Bidder is a person or entity who submits a Bid.

1.9 A Sub-bidder is a person or entity who submits a bid to a Bidder for materials or labor for a portion of the Work.

ARTICLE 2

BIDDER'S REPRESENTATIONS

2.1 Each Bidder by making his Bid represents that:

2.1.1 He has read and understands the Bidding Documents and his Bid is made in accordance therewith.

2.1.2 He has visited the site, has familiarized himself with the local conditions under which the Work is to be performed and has correlated his observations with the requirements of the proposed Contract Documents.

2.1.3 His Bid is based upon the materials, systems and equipment required by the Bidding Documents without exception.

ARTICLE 3

BIDDING DOCUMENTS

3.1 COPIES

3.1.1 Bidders may obtain complete sets of the Bidding Documents from the issuing office designated in the Advertisement or Invitation to Bid in the number and for the deposit sum, if any, stated therein. The deposit will be refunded to Bidders who submit a bona fide Bid and return the Bidding Documents in good condition within ten days after receipt of Bids. The cost of replacement of any missing or damaged documents will be deducted from the deposit. A Bidder receiving a Contract award may retain the Bidding Documents and his deposit will be refunded.

3.1.2 Bidding Documents will not be issued directly to Sub-bidders or others unless specifically offered in the Advertisement or Invitation to Bid.

3.1.3 Bidders shall use complete sets of Bidding Documents in preparing Bids; neither the Owner nor the Architect assume any responsibility for errors or misinterpretations resulting from the use of incomplete sets of Bidding Documents.

3.1.4 The Owner or the Architect in making copies of the Bidding Documents available on the above terms do so only for the purpose of obtaining Bids on the Work and do not confer a license or grant for any other use.

3.2 INTERPRETATION OR CORRECTION OF BIDDING DOCUMENTS

3.2.1 Bidders and Sub-bidders shall promptly notify the Architect of any ambiguity, inconsistency or error which they may discover upon examination of the Bidding Documents or of the site and local conditions.

3.2.2 Bidders and Sub-bidders requiring clarification or interpretation of the Bidding Documents shall make a written request which shall reach the Architect at least seven days prior to the date for receipt of Bids.

3.2.3 Any interpretation, correction or change of the Bidding Documents will be made by Addendum. Interpretations, corrections or changes of the Bidding Documents made in any other manner will not be binding, and Bidders shall not rely upon such interpretations, corrections and changes.

3.3 SUBSTITUTIONS

3.3.1 The materials, products and equipment described in the Bidding Documents establish a standard of required function, dimension, appearance and quality to be met by any proposed substitution.

3.3.2 No substitution will be considered prior to receipt of Bids unless written request for approval has been re-

(courtesy American Institute of Architects)

Figure 8.3b

ceived by the Architect at least ten days prior to the date for receipt of Bids. Each such request shall include the name of the material or equipment for which it is to be substituted and a complete description of the proposed substitute including drawings, cuts, performance and test data and any other information necessary for an evaluation. A statement setting forth any changes in other materials, equipment or other Work that incorporation of the substitute would require shall be included. The burden of proof of the merit of the proposed substitute is upon the proposer. The Architect's decision of approval or disapproval of a proposed substitution shall be final.

3.3.3 If the Architect approves any proposed substitution prior to receipt of Bids, such approval will be set forth in an Addendum. Bidders shall not rely upon approvals made in any other manner.

3.3.4 No substitutions will be considered after the Contract award unless specifically provided in the Contract Documents.

3.4 ADDENDA

3.4.1 Addenda will be mailed or delivered to all who are known by the Architect to have received a complete set of Bidding Documents.

3.4.2 Copies of Addenda will be made available for inspection wherever Bidding Documents are on file for that purpose.

3.4.3 No Addenda will be issued later than four days prior to the date for receipt of Bids except an Addendum withdrawing the request for Bids or one which includes postponement of the date for receipt of Bids.

3.4.4 Each Bidder shall ascertain prior to submitting his bid that he has received all Addenda issued, and he shall acknowledge their receipt in his Bid.

ARTICLE 4

BIDDING PROCEDURE

4.1 FORM AND STYLE OF BIDS

4.1.1 Bids shall be submitted on forms identical to the form included with the Bidding Documents, in the quantity required by Article 9.

4.1.2 All blanks on the bid form shall be filled in by typewriter or manually in ink.

4.1.3 Where so indicated by the makeup of the bid form, sums shall be expressed in both words and figures, and in case of discrepancy between the two, the amount written in words shall govern.

4.1.4 Any interlineation, alteration or erasure must be initialed by the signer of the Bid.

4.1.5 All requested Alternates shall be bid. If no change in the Base Bid is required, enter "No Change."

4.1.6 Where two or more Bids for designated portions of the Work have been requested, the Bidder may, without forfeiture of his bid security, state his refusal to accept award of less than the combination of Bids he so stipulates. The Bidder shall make no additional stipulations on the bid form nor qualify his Bid in any other manner.

4.1.7 Each copy of the Bid shall include the legal name of the Bidder and a statement that the Bidder is a sole proprietor, a partnership, a corporation, or some other legal entity. Each copy shall be signed by the person or persons legally authorized to bind the Bidder to a contract. A Bid by a corporation shall further give the state of incorporation and have the corporate seal affixed. A Bid submitted by an agent shall have a current power of attorney attached certifying the agent's authority to bind the Bidder.

4.2 BID SECURITY

4.2.1 If so stipulated in the Advertisement or Invitation to Bid, each Bid shall be accompanied by a bid security in the form and amount required by Article 9 pledging that the Bidder will enter into a Contract with the Owner on the terms stated in his Bid and will, if required, furnish bonds as described hereunder in Article 7 covering the faithful performance of the Contract and the payment of all obligations arising thereunder. Should the Bidder refuse to enter into such Contract or fail to furnish such bonds if required, the amount of the bid security shall be forfeited to the Owner as liquidated damages, not as a penalty. The amount of the bid security shall not be forfeited to the Owner in the event the Owner fails to comply with Subparagraph 6.2.1.

4.2.2 If a surety bond is required it shall be written on AIA Document A310, Bid Bond, and the attorney-in-fact who executes the bond on behalf of the surety shall affix to the bond a certified and current copy of his power of attorney.

4.2.3 The Owner will have the right to retain the bid security of Bidders to whom an award is being considered until either (a) the Contract has been executed and bonds, if required, have been furnished, or (b) the specified time has elapsed so that Bids may be withdrawn, or (c) all Bids have been rejected.

4.3 SUBMISSION OF BIDS

4.3.1 All copies of the Bid, the bid security, if any, and any other documents required to be submitted with the Bid shall be enclosed in a sealed opaque envelope. The envelope shall be addressed to the party receiving the Bids and shall be identified with the Project name, the Bidder's name and address and, if applicable, the designated portion of the Work for which the Bid is submitted. If the Bid is sent by mail the sealed envelope shall be enclosed in a separate mailing envelope with the notation "SEALED BID ENCLOSED" on the face thereof.

4.3.2 Bids shall be deposited at the designated location prior to the time and date for receipt of Bids indicated in the Advertisement or Invitation to Bid, or any extension thereof made by Addendum. Bids received after the time and date for receipt of Bids will be returned unopened.

4.3.3 The Bidder shall assume full responsibility for timely delivery at the location designated for receipt of Bids.

4.3.4 Oral, telephonic or telegraphic Bids are invalid and will not receive consideration.

4.4 MODIFICATION OR WITHDRAWAL OF BID

4.4.1 A Bid may not be modified, withdrawn or canceled by the Bidder during the stipulated time period following the time and date designated for the receipt of Bids, and each Bidder so agrees in submitting his Bid.

AIA DOCUMENT A701 • INSTRUCTIONS TO BIDDERS • THIRD EDITION • MAY 1978 • AIA® • ©1978
THE AMERICAN INSTITUTE OF ARCHITECTS, 1735 NEW YORK AVE., N.W., WASHINGTON, D. C. 20006

(courtesy American Institute of Architects)

Figure 8.3c

4.4.2 Prior to the time and date designated for receipt of Bids, any Bid submitted may be modified or withdrawn by notice to the party receiving Bids at the place designated for receipt of Bids. Such notice shall be in writing over the signature of the Bidder or by telegram; if by telegram, written confirmation over the signature of the Bidder shall be mailed and postmarked on or before the date and time set for receipt of Bids, and it shall be so worded as not to reveal the amount of the original Bid.

4.4.3 Withdrawn Bids may be resubmitted up to the time designated for the receipt of Bids provided that they are then fully in conformance with these Instructions to Bidders.

4.4.4 Bid security, if any is required, shall be in an amount sufficient for the Bid as modified or resubmitted.

ARTICLE 5
CONSIDERATION OF BIDS

5.1 OPENING OF BIDS

5.1.1 Unless stated otherwise in the Advertisement or Invitation to Bid, the properly identified Bids received on time will be opened publicly and will be read aloud. An abstract of the Base Bids and Alternate Bids, if any, will be made available to Bidders. When it has been stated that Bids will be opened privately, an abstract of the same information may, at the discretion of the Owner, be made available to the Bidders within a reasonable time.

5.2 REJECTION OF BIDS

5.2.1 The Owner shall have the right to reject any or all Bids and to reject a Bid not accompanied by any required bid security or by other data required by the Bidding Documents, or to reject a Bid which is in any way incomplete or irregular.

5.3 ACCEPTANCE OF BID (AWARD)

5.3.1 It is the intent of the Owner to award a Contract to the lowest responsible Bidder provided the Bid has been submitted in accordance with the requirements of the Bidding Documents and does not exceed the funds available. The Owner shall have the right to waive any informality or irregularity in any Bid or Bids received and to accept the Bid or Bids which, in his judgment, is in his own best interests.

5.3.2 The Owner shall have the right to accept Alternates in any order or combination, unless otherwise specifically provided in Article 9, and to determine the low Bidder on the basis of the sum of the Base Bid and the Alternates accepted.

ARTICLE 6
POST BID INFORMATION

6.1 CONTRACTOR'S QUALIFICATION STATEMENT

6.1.1 Bidders to whom award of a Contract is under consideration shall submit to the Architect, upon request, a properly executed AIA Document A305, Contractor's Qualification Statement, unless such a Statement has been previously required and submitted as a prerequisite to the issuance of Bidding Documents.

6.2 OWNER'S FINANCIAL CAPABILITY

6.2.1 The Owner shall, at the request of the Bidder to whom award of a Contract is under consideration and no later than seven days prior to the expiration of the time for withdrawal of Bids, furnish to the Bidder reasonable evidence that the Owner has made financial arrangements to fulfill the Contract obligations. Unless such reasonable evidence is furnished, the Bidder will not be required to execute the Owner-Contractor Agreement.

6.3 SUBMITTALS

6.3.1 The Bidder shall, within seven days of notification of selection for the award of a Contract for the Work, submit the following information to the Architect:

.1 a designation of the Work to be performed by the Bidder with his own forces;

.2 the proprietary names and the suppliers of principal items or systems of materials and equipment proposed for the Work;

.3 a list of names of the Subcontractors or other persons or entities (including those who are to furnish materials or equipment fabricated to a special design) proposed for the principal portions of the Work.

6.3.2 The Bidder will be required to establish to the satisfaction of the Architect and the Owner the reliability and responsibility of the persons or entities proposed to furnish and perform the Work described in the Bidding Documents.

6.3.3 Prior to the award of the Contract, the Architect will notify the Bidder in writing if either the Owner or the Architect, after due investigation, has reasonable objection to any such proposed person or entity. If the Owner or Architect has reasonable objection to any such proposed person or entity, the Bidder may, at his option, (1) withdraw his Bid, or (2) submit an acceptable substitute person or entity with an adjustment in his bid price to cover the difference in cost occasioned by such substitution. The Owner may, at his discretion, accept the adjusted bid price or he may disqualify the Bidder. In the event of either withdrawal or disqualification under this Subparagraph, bid security will not be forfeited, notwithstanding the provisions of Paragraph 4.4.1.

6.3.4 Persons and entities proposed by the Bidder and to whom the Owner and the Architect have made no reasonable objection under the provisions of Subparagraph 6.3.3 must be used on the Work for which they were proposed and shall not be changed except with the written consent of the Owner and the Architect.

ARTICLE 7
PERFORMANCE BOND AND LABOR AND MATERIAL PAYMENT BOND

7.1 BOND REQUIREMENTS

7.1.1 Prior to execution of the Contract, if required in Article 9 hereinafter, the Bidder shall furnish bonds covering the faithful performance of the Contract and the payment of all obligations arising thereunder in such form and amount as the Owner may prescribe. Bonds may be secured through the Bidder's usual sources. If the furnish-

---

(courtesy American Institute of Architects)

Figure 8.3d

ing of such bonds is stipulated hereinafter in Article 9, the cost shall be included in the Bid.

7.1.2 If the Owner has reserved the right to require that bonds be furnished subsequent to the execution of the Contract, the cost shall be adjusted as provided in the Contract Documents.

7.1.3 If the Owner requires that bonds be obtained from other than the Bidder's usual source, any change in cost will be adjusted as provided in the Contract Documents.

7.2 TIME OF DELIVERY AND FORM OF BONDS

7.2.1 The Bidder shall deliver the required bonds to the Owner not later than the date of execution of the Contract, or if the Work is to be commenced prior thereto in response to a letter of intent, the Bidder shall, prior to commencement of the Work, submit evidence satisfactory to the Owner that such bonds will be furnished.

7.2.2 Unless otherwise required in Article 9, the bonds shall be written on AIA Document A311, Performance Bond and Labor and Material Payment Bond.

7.2.3 The Bidder shall require the attorney-in-fact who executes the required bonds on behalf of the surety to affix thereto a certified and current copy of his power of attorney.

ARTICLE 8

FORM OF AGREEMENT BETWEEN OWNER AND CONTRACTOR

8.1 FORM TO BE USED

8.1.1 Unless otherwise required in the Bidding Documents, the Agreement for the Work will be written on AIA Document A101, Standard Form of Agreement Between Owner and Contractor, where the basis of payment is a Stipulated Sum.

ARTICLE 9
SUPPLEMENTARY INSTRUCTIONS

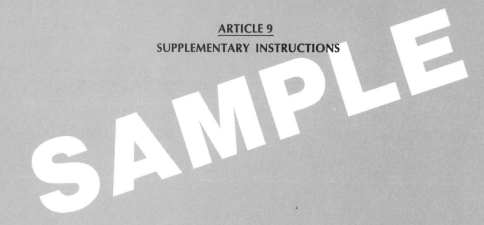

AIA DOCUMENT A701 • INSTRUCTIONS TO BIDDERS • THIRD EDITION • MAY 1978 • AIA® • ©1978
THE AMERICAN INSTITUTE OF ARCHITECTS, 1735 NEW YORK AVE., N.W., WASHINGTON, D. C. 20006

(courtesy American Institute of Architects)

Figure 8.3e

There are many practical, moral and legal implications attached to the content of a proposal submitted as a result of the bidding process. It is important that these implications be fully set forth and detailed in the Instructions to Bidders. (See Article 2 of AIA Document A701—Figure 8.3b). The acceptance of a bid implies that the proposal is based on the site as it exists, the bidding documents as they are written, and the materials and systems as specified. The validity of the entire competitive bidding process is based upon the principle that each competitor is working with identical criteria.

Establishing proper bidding procedures is crucial when instructing bidders. (See Figure 8.3c—Article 4 of AIA Document A701). The bid forms used should be carefully designed and the forms submitted by each bidder should be identical. A legal problem could occur if there were any variation in the form or the wording of the proposal provisions, or any deviation in its content. It is the preferred practice that the design professional furnish the bidders with forms that require only the filling in of blanks for responses. Figures 8.4a through 8.4c illustrate a typical three-page Form of Proposal for a public works project. This form asks the bidders to respond with a proposed contract sum (base bid), a proposed number of calendar days within which the bidder pledges to complete the project, and the bidder's proposal for any Alternates that may be included for consideration by the owner. The proposal of alternates suggests that certain portions of the work may be desirable to the owner, but not essential to his basic needs. When the owner's budget requirements are restrictive, he is able to get estimates for variations of project requirements. These alternates allow the owner the option to either accept the proposed price for the alternate item, or to reject it altogether. If the item is accepted, the proposed amount is added to the base bid price. If rejected, the proposed amount in the base bid is unaffected. By designing the bidding documents to allow for additive rather than subtractive alternates, the contractor is able to include a sufficient amount for overhead and profit related to the base bid that is unaffected if the price for alternates is added to the base bid amount. If, on the other hand, the alternates were to be subtracted, the owner might question whether or not a corresponding deduction for overhead and profit had been included.

The protocol for receiving, accepting, opening and considering bids, and the amount of time that the owner requires for considering the bids are all important criteria that should be covered by the Instructions to Bidders. (See Figure 8.3d—Article 5 of AIA Document A701.)

In the case of public work, the owner may be mandated to accept the lowest responsible bid. "Contractor responsibility" is key to the owner's vulnerability under this requirement. Whether a project is public or private, it is a serious situation when and if the chosen bidder proves unable to complete the work. Experience reveals that while a contractor may be bonded, this alone is no guarantee that the bidder will be able to fulfill the requirements of the contract for construction. It is good policy to require a "screening" process whereby bidders are required to file certain credentials. These credentials should reveal their current financial condition, the extent of their current work load, and examples of completed work, with names of owners and design professionals who can furnish references. Figure 8.5a through 8.5f show paragraphs from AIA Document A305—*Contractor's Qualification Statement* (CQS). Article 6 of

PROPOSAL FORM - GENERAL CONSTRUCTION

PROPOSAL OF: ____

(Name of Bidder)

TO: City of (Name of City, State)
(Name of party to receive bids)
(Street address where bids are to be delivered)
(Name of City, State, Zip Code)

FOR: Prime Contract for General Construction
(Address of project site)
(Name of city, State, Zip Code)

Gentlemen:

The Undersigned has received the Bidding Documents (Project Manual and Drawings) for the referenced project including Addenda numbered _________________. The provisions of these Addenda have been included in this Proposal. The undersigned has examined both the site and the documents, and is fully informed on the scope and conditions of the work.

The Undersigned hereby proposes to furnish all labor and materials and perform all work related to the Prime Contract for General Construction for the new (Name of Project as it appears on all contract documents) located at (Address of site), in strict accordance with the Contract Documents included or listed in the Project Manual, for the consideration of the following:

BASE BID: For all labor and materials and all work related to the General Construction of the proposed project, including the Plumbing, Mechanical and Electrical work, in full consideration of all that is required by the Contract Documents for the sum of:

____ DOLLARS

($___________________________)

City Hall Building Proposal Page 1

Figure 8.4a

Furthermore:

1. If awarded the Prime Contract for General Construction, the undersigned agrees to complete the Work on or before the expiration of _____ calendar days from date of written Notice to Proceed.

2. In accordance with Additive Alternate Item No. 1, understood to be (name of item to be bid as an additive alternate) as described in Section (Provide appropriate specification section number) of the specifications, and as shown on the drawings, the undersigned offers to include, at the owner's option, this additive alternate for a total consideration, to be added to the amount shown above as the "Base Bid", the sum of:

_____ Dollars.

($ _____.__)

    Furthermore, if the Owner elects to accept our offer for Additive Alternate Item No. 1 to be added to the Base Bid, the undersigned would require _____ days to be added to the number of calendar days required for completion of the work first stated in Paragraph 2 above.

The undersigned hereby certifies to have complied with all conditions stated in the Instructions to Bidders.

Bid Security in the form of a certified check or bid bond in the sum of five percent (5%) of the greatest possible amount of the Contract Sum as bid is attached hereto, as a guarantee of the execution of a satisfactory contract and furnishing of bonds as required by the Contract Documents.

It is understood and agreed that the Owner has the right to reject any and all bids and to waive any technicalities. Furthermore, it is understood that the Owner, at his option, may accept or reject any offer stated in Paragraphs 2 through 5 above for possible inclusion in the Prime Contract for General Construction.

City Hall Building Proposal Page 2

Figure 8.4b

If written notice of the acceptance of Bid is mailed, telegraphed or delivered to the undersigned within ninety (90) days after the date of opening bids, or at any time thereafter before this bid is withdrawn by writing, the undersigned agrees that he will execute and deliver a contract, in accordance with the bid as accepted, all within ten (10) days (unless a longer period of time is allowed) after the prescribed forms are presented to him for signature.

Notice of acceptance should be mailed, telegraphed or delivered to the undersigned at the following address:

Signed_____

For_____
                    Legal Name of Bidder

Address_____

_____

SEAL
(If Bid is by a Corporation)

NOTE: Amounts shall be shown in both written form and figures. In case of discrepancy between the written amount and the figures, the written amount will govern.

If Bidder is a Corporation, write State of Incorporation under signature and if a Partnership, give full names of all partners.

CAUTION: This Bid may be rejected if not accompanied by a Guarantee in the amount specified. Any Certified Checks may be held uncollected at the risk of the Bidder submitting them.

END OF PROPOSAL FORM

City Hall Building Proposal Page 3

Figure 8.4c

the *Instructions to Bidders* (AIA Document A701) suggests that the *Contractor's Qualification Statement* be offered after bids are received. It is, however, becoming a frequent practice for the Instructions to Bidders to require the filing of a current Contractor's Qualification Statement with the owner prior to the opening of bids. This practice tends to discourage overextended or under-qualified constructors from submitting a bid, and gives the owner (usually acting through the design professional) valuable time to conduct the screening process. When the contractor's qualification statement is a pre-bid requirement, the owner, particularly a public owner, has more control over the apparent competency and capability of those who respond to the "open" invitation to bid. For instance, the Contractor's Qualification Statement had not been prepared and filed as instructed, the owner would be justified in returning the sealed bid to the bidder unopened and unconsidered.

If for any reason a bidder becomes unwilling to commit to a contract for construction based upon the proposal he has submitted, the owner may have the right to collect the amount of the bid security included in the bid package as liquidated damages for such refusal. It should be stressed that compliance with the requirements of the Instructions to Bidders should be followed in all respects and with no exceptions. Receipt of bids ends at the exact hour on the date stated in the Advertisement or Invitation. Any bid received after the stipulated time can be returned to the bidder unopened. Any bid that is found incomplete in any way can be set aside, not read aloud, and returned to the bidder with an explanation of the rejection. Telephone or other communication not in accordance with the Instructions should not be accepted. Bidders are not allowed to add any kind of unique statements of qualification to the Form of Proposal. Finally, no commitment should be made as to award of the contract until both owner and design professional have had sufficient time to study each proposal, reflect upon the bidders' qualifications, review the proposed list of subcontractors and verify the availability of the specified performance and payment bonds.

Information Available to Bidders

The *General Conditions of the Contract for Construction*, AIA Document A201, Article 3, Paragraph 3.2 lists the information normally furnished to bidders. Other information which would further the bidder's understanding of the project may include:

(1) Soils investigation and recommendations.

(2) Local weather information.

(3) Owner's financial qualifications, financial statement or authority to commit construction funds.

(4) Property survey and existing conditions.
- Existing improvements
- "As built" drawings
- Existing utilities

THE AMERICAN INSTITUTE OF ARCHITECTS

AIA Document A305

Contractor's Qualification Statement
1979 EDITION

This form is approved and recommended by The American Institute of Architects (AIA) and The Associated General Contractors of America (AGC) for use in evaluating the qualifications of contractors. No endorsement of the submitting party or verification of the information is made by the AIA or AGC.

The Undersigned certifies under oath the truth and correctness of all statements and of all answers to questions made hereinafter.

SUBMITTED TO:

ADDRESS:

SUBMITTED BY:
NAME:
ADDRESS:
PRINCIPAL OFFICE:

1.0 How many years has your or

2.0 How many years has your organ
    2.1 Under what other or former

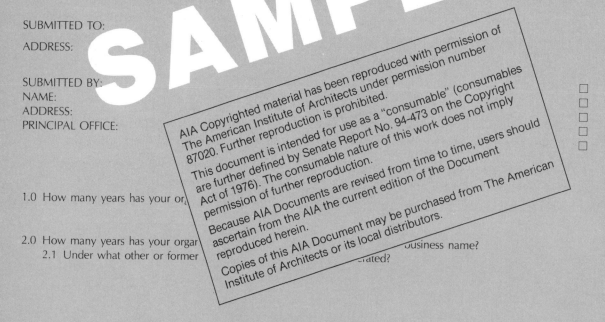

(courtesy American Institute of Architects)

Figure 8.5a

3.0 If a corporation answer the following:
    3.1 Date of incorporation:
    3.2 State of incorporation:
    3.3 President's name:
    3.4 Vice-president's name(s):

    3.5 Secretary's name:
    3.6 Treasurer's name:

4.0 If an individual or a partnership answer the following:
    4.1 Date of organization:
    4.2 Name and address of all partners (State whether general or limited partnership):

5.0 If other than a corporation or partnership, describe organization and name principals:

6.0 List states and categories in which your organization is legally qualified to do business. Indicate registration or license numbers, if applicable. List states in which partnership or trade name is filed.

(courtesy American Institute of Architects)

Figure 8.5b

7.0 We normally perform the following work with our own forces:

8.0 Have you ever failed to complete any work awarded to you? If so, note when, where, and why:

9.0 Within the last five years, has any officer or partner of your organization ever been an officer or partner of another organization when it failed to complete a construction contract? If so, attach a separate sheet of explanation.

SAMPLE

10.0 On a separate sheet, list major construction projects your organization has in process, giving the name of project, owner, architect, contract amount, percent complete, and scheduled completion date.

11.0 On a separate sheet, list the major projects your organization has completed in the past five years, giving the name of project, owner, architect, contract amount, date of completion, and percentage of the cost of the work performed with your own forces.

12.0 On a separate sheet, list the construction experience of the key individuals of your organization.

AIA DOCUMENT A305 • CONTRACTOR'S QUALIFICATION STATEMENT • MARCH 1979 EDITION • AIA®
©1979 • THE AMERICAN INSTITUTE OF ARCHITECTS, 1735 NEW YORK AVENUE, N.W., WASHINGTON, D.C. 20006   A305-1979 3

(courtesy American Institute of Architects)

Figure 8.5c

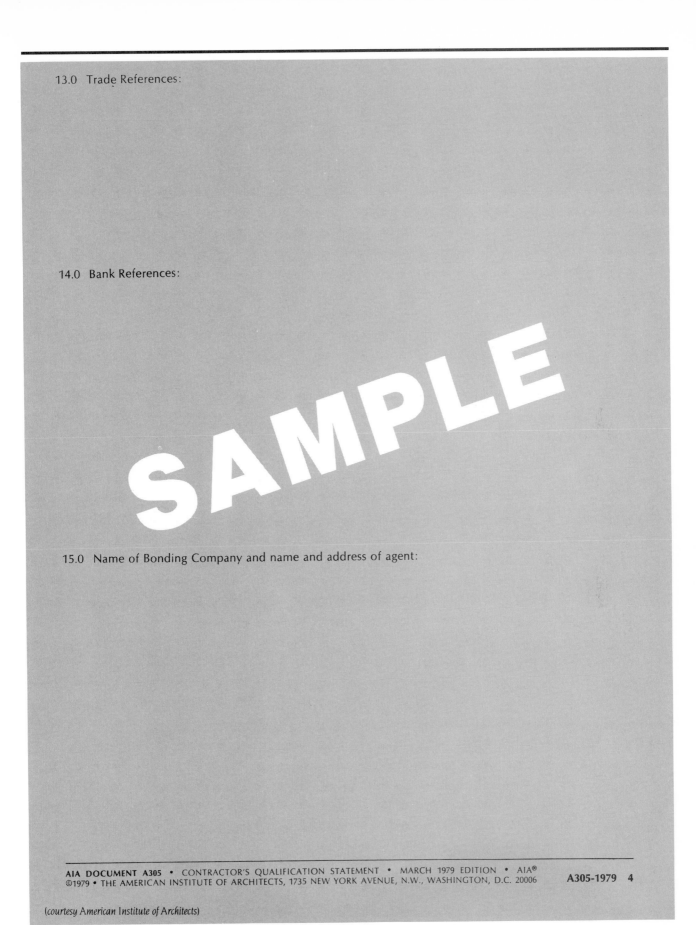

13.0 Trade References:

14.0 Bank References:

SAMPLE

15.0 Name of Bonding Company and name and address of agent:

(courtesy American Institute of Architects)

Figure 8.5d

16.0 Attach a financial statement, audited if available, including Contractor's latest balance sheet and income statement showing the following items:

A. Current Assets (e.g., cash, joint venture accounts, accounts receivable, notes receivable, accrued income, deposits, materials inventory and prepaid expenses):

B. Net Fixed Assets:

C. Other Assets:

D. Current Liabilities (e.g., accounts payable, notes payable, accrued expenses, provision for income taxes, advances, accrued salaries, and accrued payroll taxes):

E. Other Liabilities (e.g., capital, capital stock, authorized and outstanding shares par values, earned surplus, and retained earnings):

Name of firm preparing financial statement and date thereof:

Is this financial statement for the identical organization named on page one?

If not, explain the relationship and financial responsibility of the organization whose financial statement is provided (e.g., parent-subsidiary).

Will this organization act as guarantor of the contract for construction?

AIA DOCUMENT A305 • CONTRACTOR'S QUALIFICATION STATEMENT • MARCH 1979 EDITION • AIA®
©1979 • THE AMERICAN INSTITUTE OF ARCHITECTS, 1735 NEW YORK AVENUE, N.W., WASHINGTON, D.C. 20006   **A305-1979 5**

(courtesy American Institute of Architects)

Figure 8.5e

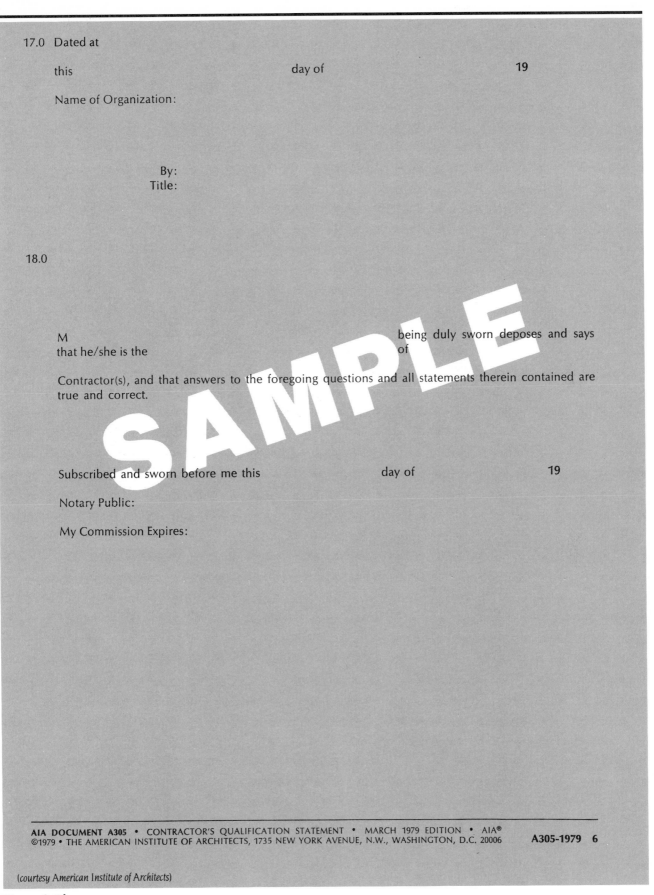

17.0 Dated at

this   day of   19

Name of Organization:

By:
Title:

18.0

M   being duly sworn deposes and says
that he/she is the   of

Contractor(s), and that answers to the foregoing questions and all statements therein contained are
true and correct.

SAMPLE

Subscribed and sworn before me this   day of   19

Notary Public:

My Commission Expires:

(courtesy American Institute of Architects)

Figure 8.5f

Conditions of the Contract

Conditions of the Contract are documents which complement the contract for construction. Conditions of the contract define the basic rights, responsibilities and relationships of the parties involved in the construction process, namely the owner, the design professional, the contractor, the subcontractor and the sub-subcontractor. Conditions of the contract normally appear in the two related documents described below.

The General Conditions of the Contract contain general statements defining the responsibilities of the parties during the construction process. In most instances, the forms prepared by national professional organizations (e.g., American Institute of Architects) are used. These kinds of forms represent a consensus of agreement among various groups within the building industry.

The Supplemental General Conditions are used to modify and expand the General Conditions as needed in order to provide for requirements unique to the individual project.

The General Conditions of the Contract along with its companion document, the Supplemental General Conditions, are discussed, paragraph by paragraph, in Chapter 7.

Specifications

Techniques of specification writing and organization are discussed in Chapter 9. The word "specify" is defined as the action required to name or to state in detail. Construction specifications have been defined as the qualitative requirements for products, materials and workmanship upon which the Contract for Construction is based.

During the period following World War II, many design professionals became concerned with specification writing practices. It was at this time that the Construction Specifications Institute came into being for the express purpose of improving the quality, uniformity and usefulness of construction specifications. Many design professionals began to speak out and publicly discuss the many concerns that the industry shared regarding the creation and use of contract documents. One such article which appeared in the March 1949 edition of the *National Architect*, a publication of the American Institute of Architects and a forerunner of today's *Architecture* magazine, discussed the discovery of a set of specifications written for a residential project in New England about 1835. The "Carpenter's Specification" section is reported to have included the following description:

"... Base 12 inches including moldings not inferior to Dan'l Smith's house on fifth street...."

While this statement was probably specific enough for 1835, today, a more appropriate specification would probably include the following language:

"... Hardwood base: plain sliced, clear red oak (Quercus Rubra), meeting the requirements of PS 20 and ASTM D 2555, shaped to traditional base No. WM 6186, 4 inches by 9/16 inches, prepared for transparent finish as specified in Section 09900."

In modern specifications, stating the latin name for red oak is intended to establish the certainty of the species desired, rather than relying upon a common name that could be misunderstood if the nomenclature for certain wood species varied from one locale to another. "Standard PS-20" refers to a voluntary standard for wood products, developed and published by the National Bureau of Standards. These designations establish dimensional requirements for standard sizes of wood, and technical requirements for uniform manufacture and grading of wood products. ASTM D 2555, commonly called "the clear wood standard", is a standard specification published by the American Society for Testing Materials (ASTM). "Traditional Base WM 6185" refers to a certain shape of molding, established as a standard by the Wood Molding and Millwork Producers Association.

The techniques of specification writing have clearly changed since 1835. In today's highly competitive, litigation-prone technological world, construction specifiers must keep pace with the times in language and technical proficiency.

The Function of Project Manual Components

In order to understand the organization and content of the Project Manual, the following basic factors should be clearly understood and observed:

Bidding Requirements:
- Are not specifications.
- Are procedures that apply to the competition for award of the contract for construction.
- Are in effect only until the signing of the contract for construction or during the construction process.

Conditions of the Contract:
- Include both the General and Supplemental Conditions.
- Are not specifications.
- Are an integral part of the Contract
- With the Contract, govern the content of the entire contract.
- Contain contractual principals applicable to most projects with supplemental provisions for individual projects.

General Conditions:
- Are broad contractual conditions.
- Contain requirements, establish relationships, and define obligations.

Supplemental General Conditions:
- Modify the General Conditions.
- Modify the constraints for a specific region or project.
- Take precedence over General Conditions.
- Must be written separately for each project.

General Requirements:
- Are specifications.
- Establish procedural and administrative requirements.
- Are enforceable under the Contract for Construction.
- Must be written separately for each project.

Finally, in conceiving the organization and application of the Project Manual, the design professional should consider the overall relationship of the various components of the Bidding and Contract Documents to the Project Manual as these documents are prepared and issued to prospective bidders.

Figure 8.6 illustrates the relationship of the various documents that make up the "Bidding Package", which becomes the basis for the contract for construction.

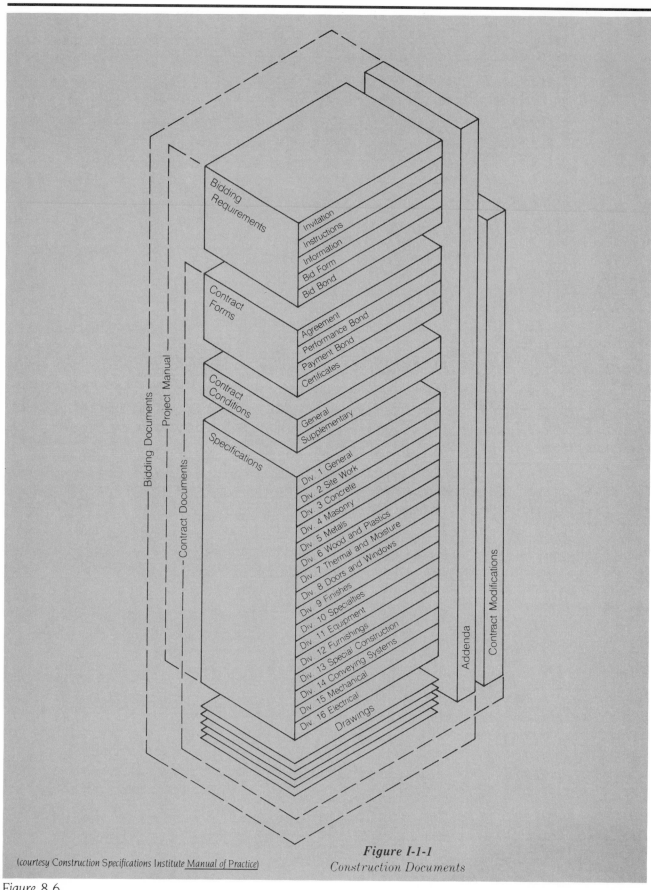

Bidding Requirements
- Invitation
- Instructions
- Information
- Bid Form
- Bid Bond

Contract Forms
- Agreement
- Performance Bond
- Payment Bond
- Certificates

Contract Conditions
- General
- Supplementary

Specifications
- Div. 1 General
- Div. 2 Site Work
- Div. 3 Concrete
- Div. 4 Masonry
- Div. 5 Metals
- Div. 6 Wood and Plastics
- Div. 7 Thermal and Moisture
- Div. 8 Doors and Windows
- Div. 9 Finishes
- Div. 10 Specialties
- Div. 11 Equipment
- Div. 12 Furnishings
- Div. 13 Special Construction
- Div. 14 Conveying Systems
- Div. 15 Mechanical
- Div. 16 Electrical

Drawings

Addenda

Contract Modifications

Bidding Documents

Project Manual

Contract Documents

(courtesy Construction Specifications Institute *Manual of Practice*)

Figure I-1-1
Construction Documents

Figure 8.6

Creating the Project Manual

Clear, concise and complete communications throughout the contract documents is the key to effective economy and success in building construction. Effective communication of the design information depends largely upon effective coordination and the content of the components of the Project Manual. Information must be presented in such manner as to be readily accessible, logically and obviously placed, clearly written, simply stated, and systematically coordinated. Everyone involved in the process of building construction benefits from a well conceived, properly written Project Manual.

The responsibility for preparing the Project Manual clearly falls to the prime design professional. However, in today's highly complex and technically oriented economy, it is usually the Specification Writer who is ultimately responsible for preparing and coordinating the Project Manual. This task usually involves a "team effort" coordinated by the specification writer. This is true regardless of whether the design professional is a single practitioner, acting as the specification writer, or a multi-disciplined office within which the specification writer is but one of a team of experienced specialists. Figure 8.7 illustrates the process by which the Project Manual is developed.

The Specification Writer

The specification writer may be an independent practitioner who performs his specialty as a consultant to the design professional. Just as the language and content of the Contract Documents has become more important to the success of the finished project, so also have the qualities and attributes of the specification writer become more critical to his role in the construction process. Because his responsibility involves a specific use of language, the specification writer must be knowledgeable regarding grammar, punctuation, and word definition. Statements must be precisely written and presented in sentences and paragraphs that will provide a clear understanding to a great number and diversity of people. Many readers of the Project Manual will not be sophisticated in technical reading or writing.

The specification writer must also be able to deal skillfully with a profusion of details and technical elements. A great deal of reading and in-depth research are essential attributes because of the voluminous quantities of technical data that must be handled, stored, retrieved, and appropriately applied to a wide variety of project types with differing requirements.

There is no single educational program that is specifically designed to train the construction specifier. An academic background must be supplemented with experience that can be gained only in professional practice before one can become a qualified specifier. The academic credentials for an aspiring construction specifier would include, in order of preference:

(1) A Bachelor's degree in architecture and engineering.

(2) A vocational associate degree in architecture or engineering.

(3) A high school diploma supplemented with on-the-job training in architecture or engineering.

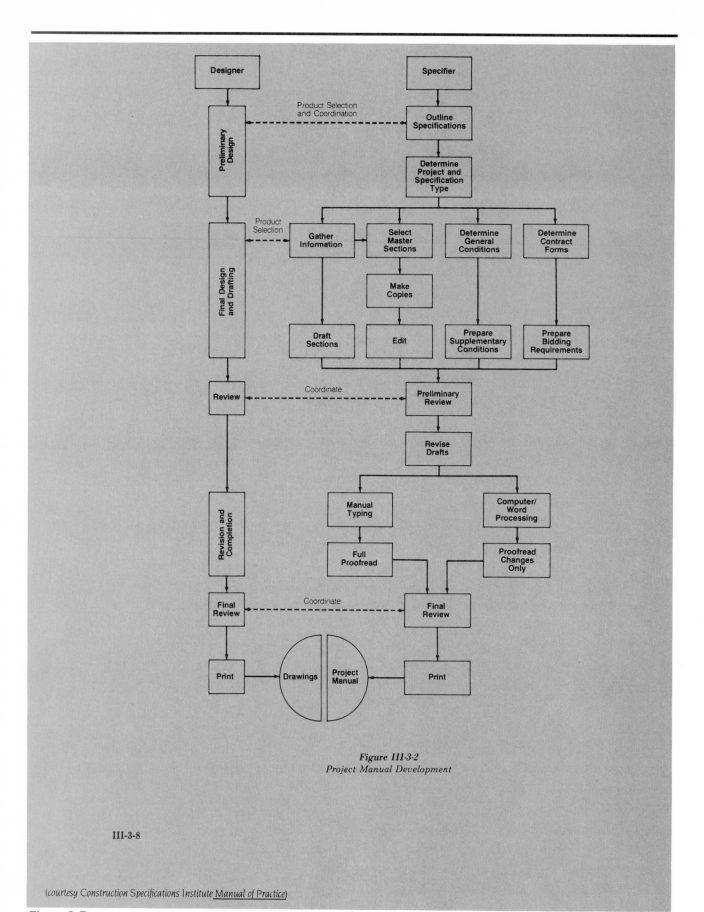

Figure III-3-2
Project Manual Development

III-3-8

Figure 8.7

The following are among the personality traits that are desirable in a construction specifier:

- Keen observation and attention to detail.
- Ability to visualize three dimensional objects.
- Ability to organize thoughts into orderly statements.
- Ability to isolate essential elements of a problem.
- Ability to listen and accurately understand other people.
- Ability to reach equitable agreements without compromising important principles.
- Ability to accurately express ideas and concepts.

The accomplished specifier should be able to use the above listed personality traits to develop specific skills that should include:

- A thorough understanding of construction materials and construction methods.
- Well developed written communications skills.
- Ability to understand graphic information presented in drawings, tables and charts.
- Ability to negotiate successfully.
- Ability to coordinate the activities of others.
- Ability to manage time in order to meet critical production schedules.
- Ability to know resources in order to effectively perform in-depth research.
- Possess a thorough knowledge of construction law.
- Possess a thorough knowledge of building codes and ordinances.
- Possess a thorough knowledge of insurance and bonds as they apply to the construction industry.
- Possess a thorough knowledge of construction trade jurisdictions and customary divisions of work.

In the mid-1970's, the board of directors of the Construction Specifications Institute authorized the Institute to create and maintain a system for examining qualified professionals engaged in the writing or developing of construction specifications. The goal has been to recognize and certify the qualified specifier as a Certified Construction Specifier (CCS).

Documents Related to the Project Manual

Various documents included in the Bidding Package (Figure 8.6) are interrelated with the documents in the Project Manual. The project documentation is not complete without all of its parts.

The Drawings

A layman is most likely to associate an architect with tee squares, drawing boards and rolls of drawings. When thinking of the engineer, he adds to that picture a transit and a slide rule. For many generations, the drawings produced by architects and engineers were thought to be, and most probably were, the most important of the documents produced by the design professional. Because of the need to diagram building assemblies to scale with dimensions, material symbols, cross sections, details and schedules in order to clearly create a "picture" of the project, the drawings continue to perform a critical function in complementing the other contract documents. Nevertheless, the drawings, even with sophisticated photography, computer aided drafting (CAD) and other visual aids, are still not of a convenient size to be "read", or bound into the Project Manual book. An index of the drawings is usually included as a separate document, or as a section of Division 1—General Requirements of the specifications. In this way, the drawings are a part of the manual, and by reference, a part of the contract documents. Drawings are discussed in more detail in Chapter 10.

Modification Documents

Addenda: The Project Manual is designed to assist in the bidding or negotiating activities which lead to the contract for construction, but it also continues to serve the project during construction. At the time that the project is being bid, modifications to the contract documents are often made by published Addenda. The Addendum plays a special role in the link between the bidding process and the contract documents. It informs the bidders of modifications that may affect project requirements and therefore the contract sum during the bidding process. It then becomes one of the contract documents after the contract is signed. It should be attached to or become part of the Project Manual. Figure 8.8 is a typical addendum published during the bidding period. Each addendum should contain the following information:

- Addendum number and date of issue.
- Reference to the project by title and project number if applicable.
- Name and address of party issuing the addendum, usually the design professional.
- Identification of parties to whom the addenda is directed or addressed.
- A brief explanation of the purpose of the addendum, the documents that it intends to modify and a reminder to bidders that acknowledgment of receipt of addenda is required on the bid form.

Addenda can be designed to modify any of the following:

- Changes to prior addenda.
- Changes to bidding requirements.
- Changes to information available to bidders.
- Changes to conditions to the contract.
- Changes to the specifications.
- Changes to the drawings.

Field Orders: Once the contract for construction has been executed and construction has begun, the design professional may need to issue, from time to time, supplemental instructions that (1) clarify a specific intent of the contract documents, (2) approve a minor change in the work, or (3) instruct the contractor on a matter pertaining to the execution of the work. This communication is accomplished by use of the Field Order or Supplemental Instructions issued by the design professional. Figure 8.9 illustrates AIA Document G710—*Architect's Supplemental Instructions*. The form is useful for making minor modifications to the contract for construction so long as these changes do not in any way increase or decrease the contract sum, or change the scheduled date of completion. Modifications that would in any way alter the contract sum or require additional time for completion must be prepared in the form of a Change Order.

Change Orders: The Change Order is an instrument that provides for significant changes in the contract for construction. These kinds of changes affect the contract sum or the number of calendar days required for completion of the contract. The Change Order requires the agreement of the parties to the Contract for Construction (owner and

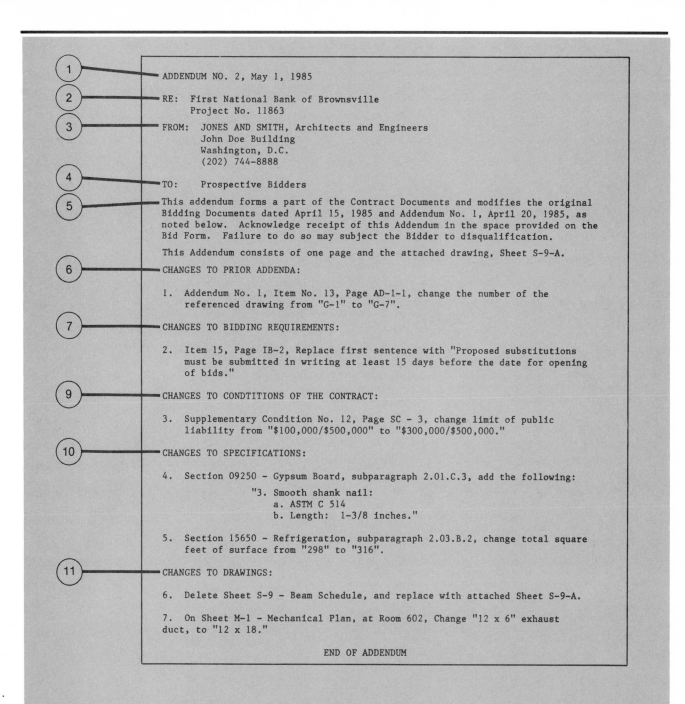

① ADDENDUM NO. 2, May 1, 1985

② RE: First National Bank of Brownsville
      Project No. 11863

③ FROM: JONES AND SMITH, Architects and Engineers
        John Doe Building
        Washington, D.C.
        (202) 744-8888

④ TO: Prospective Bidders

⑤ This addendum forms a part of the Contract Documents and modifies the original Bidding Documents dated April 15, 1985 and Addendum No. 1, April 20, 1985, as noted below. Acknowledge receipt of this Addendum in the space provided on the Bid Form. Failure to do so may subject the Bidder to disqualification.

This Addendum consists of one page and the attached drawing, Sheet S-9-A.

⑥ CHANGES TO PRIOR ADDENDA:

1. Addendum No. 1, Item No. 13, Page AD-1-1, change the number of the referenced drawing from "G-1" to "G-7".

⑦ CHANGES TO BIDDING REQUIREMENTS:

2. Item 15, Page IB-2, Replace first sentence with "Proposed substitutions must be submitted in writing at least 15 days before the date for opening of bids."

⑨ CHANGES TO CONDTITIONS OF THE CONTRACT:

3. Supplementary Condition No. 12, Page SC - 3, change limit of public liability from "$100,000/$500,000" to "$300,000/$500,000."

⑩ CHANGES TO SPECIFICATIONS:

4. Section 09250 - Gypsum Board, subparagraph 2.01.C.3, add the following:

        "3. Smooth shank nail:
            a. ASTM C 514
            b. Length: 1-3/8 inches."

5. Section 15650 - Refrigeration, subparagraph 2.03.B.2, change total square feet of surface from "298" to "316".

⑪ CHANGES TO DRAWINGS:

6. Delete Sheet S-9 - Beam Schedule, and replace with attached Sheet S-9-A.

7. On Sheet M-1 - Mechanical Plan, at Room 602, Change "12 x 6" exhaust duct, to "12 x 18."

                    END OF ADDENDUM

Figure 1-6-2
Sample Addendum

I-6-5

(*courtesy* Construction Specifications Institute Manual of Practice)

Figure 8.8

167

ARCHITECT'S SUPPLEMENTAL INSTRUCTIONS

Owner	☐
Architect	☐
Consultant	☐
Contractor	☐
Field	☐
Other	☐

AIA DOCUMENT G710 (Instructions on reverse side)

PROJECT:
(name, address)

ARCHITECT'S SUPPLEMENTAL
INSTRUCTION NO:

OWNER:

DATE OF ISSUANCE:

TO:
(Contractor)

ARCHITECT:

CONTRACT FOR:

ARCHITECT'S PROJECT NO:

The Work shall be carried out in accordance with the following supplemental instructions issued in accordance with the Contract Documents without change in Contract Sum or Contract Time. Prior to proceeding in accordance with these instructions, indicate your acceptance of these instructions for minor change to the Work as consistent with the Contract Documents and return a copy to the Architect.

Description:

Attachments: *(Here insert listing of doc*

ISSUED:

ACCEPTED:

BY

BY

Architect

Contractor

Date

AIA DOCUMENT G710 • ARCHITECT'S SUPPLEMENTAL INSTRUCTIONS • MARCH 1979 EDITION • AIA®
©1979 • THE AMERICAN INSTITUTE OF ARCHITECTS, 1735 NEW YORK AVE., N.W., WASHINGTON, D.C. 20006   **G710 — 1979**

(courtesy American Institute of Architects)

Figure 8.9

Means Forms

**CONTRACT
CHANGE ORDER**

FROM:

_____

_____

_____

_____

TO:

_____

_____

_____

_____

CHANGE ORDER NO.		
DATE		
PROJECT		
LOCATION		
JOB NO		
ORIGINAL CONTRACT AMOUNT	$	
TOTAL PREVIOUS CONTRACT CHANGES		
TOTAL BEFORE THIS CHANGE ORDER		
AMOUNT OF THIS CHANGE ORDER		
REVISED CONTRACT TO DATE		

Gentlemen:

This CHANGE ORDER includes all Material, Labor and Equipment necessary to complete the following work and to adjust the total contract as indicated;

☐ the work below to be paid for at actual cost of Labor, Materials and Equipment plus _____ percent (_____%)

☐ the work below to be completed for the sum of _____

_____ dollars ($_____)

_____

_____

_____

_____

_____

_____

_____

_____

_____

_____

_____

_____

_____

_____

_____

_____

_____

_____

_____

_____

_____

CHANGES APPROVED

The work covered by this order shall be performed under the same Terms and Conditions as that included in the original contract unless stated otherwise above.

By_____

By_____

Signed_____

By_____

Figure 8.10

contractor) as well as the design professional. Figure 8.10 illustrates a Means Contract Change Order.

Industry Resources

Previous chapters have noted the unique and invaluable role of the Construction Specifications Institute (CSI) in the development of uniform language, format, content and approach to the contract documents— particularly specifications— for modern construction. CSI developed the 16 Division Format for the primary purpose of organizing the technical specifications. The "16 Division Format" approach to classifying technical construction data has been applied to accounting, cost estimating, filing and other functions related to information handling and classification in construction. In 1978, the Construction Specifications Institute and its Canadian counterpart, Construction Specifications Canada (CSC) developed an organizational system called the *Masterformat*. The Masterformat, provides a numeric identity, or "address", and numerical order for each of the major components of the contract documents. Figure 8.11a and 8.11b illustrate the basic organization and numbering system recommended by Masterformat for the contents of the Project Manual.

Reference Standards and Technical Information

Reference Standards are requirements, set by authority, custom or general consensus. Composition, quality and workmanship can be measured based on these standards of the industry. Typical reference standards are authored by those who represent manufacturers, producers, and installers, and others who are extremely knowledgeable on the subject. Various standards, currently accepted in the industry, are published by trade associations, government and institutional organizations. As technology and experience expand, standards are frequently re-written and new standards emerge, creating a vital, self improving, ever expanding support for new methods and new ideas in the construction industry.

In order to save time, specifiers frequently reference certain standards in specification sections. The following is a concrete specification with a reference to certain industry standards:

"Cement: Shall be standard brand Portland Cement, conforming to ASTM Specification C-150, the latest edition."

At first reading, it may seem as if the specifier has covered the subject sufficiently. However, a review of the referenced document shows that ASTM C150-83a specifies eight types of cement, and refers to several other published reference standards. Thus, the type of Portland Cement to be used has not been clearly stated. While reference standard specifying is a valid method for writing specifications, it requires a thorough and careful approach to avoid the kinds of errors shown above. Reference standard specifying is discussed in more detail in Chapter 9.

A number of trade unions, industry organizations, and government agencies produce published standards that are recognized and used throughout the construction industry. In order that the source of a reference standard can be identified, the various organizations are recognized by initials, and the standard by number and date. In the above example, "ASTM" refers to the American Society for Testing Materials, and "C150" is the number identifying the particular specification established by ASTM. "83a" represents the year and

BIDDING REQUIREMENTS, CONTRACT FORMS, AND CONDITIONS OF THE CONTRACT

00010	PRE-BID INFORMATION
00100	INSTRUCTIONS TO BIDDERS
00200	INFORMATION AVAILABLE TO BIDDERS
00300	BID FORMS
00400	SUPPLEMENTS TO BID FORMS
00500	AGREEMENT FORMS
00600	BONDS AND CERTIFICATES
00700	GENERAL CONDITIONS
00800	SUPPLEMENTARY CONDITIONS
00850	DRAWINGS AND SCHEDULES
00900	ADDENDA AND MODIFICATIONS

Note: Since the items listed above are not specification sections, they are referred to as "Documents" in lieu of "Sections" in the Master List of Section Titles, Numbers, and Broadscope Explanations.

SPECIFICATIONS

DIVISION 1—GENERAL REQUIREMENTS

01010	SUMMARY OF WORK
01020	ALLOWANCES
01025	MEASUREMENT AND PAYMENT
01030	ALTERNATES/ALTERNATIVES
01040	COORDINATION
01050	FIELD ENGINEERING
01060	REGULATORY REQUIREMENTS
01070	ABBREVIATIONS AND SYMBOLS
01080	IDENTIFICATION SYSTEMS
01090	REFERENCE STANDARDS
01100	SPECIAL PROJECT PROCEDURES
01200	PROJECT MEETINGS
01300	SUBMITTALS
01400	QUALITY CONTROL
01500	CONSTRUCTION FACILITIES AND TEMPORARY CONTROLS
01600	MATERIAL AND EQUIPMENT
01650	STARTING OF SYSTEMS/COMMISSIONING
01700	CONTRACT CLOSEOUT
01800	MAINTENANCE

DIVISION 2—SITEWORK

02010	SUBSURFACE INVESTIGATION
02050	DEMOLITION
02100	SITE PREPARATION
02140	DEWATERING
02150	SHORING AND UNDERPINNING
02160	EXCAVATION SUPPORT SYSTEMS
02170	COFFERDAMS
02200	EARTHWORK
02300	TUNNELING
02350	PILES AND CAISSONS
02450	RAILROAD WORK
02480	MARINE WORK
02500	PAVING AND SURFACING
02600	PIPED UTILITY MATERIALS
02660	WATER DISTRIBUTION
02680	FUEL DISTRIBUTION
02700	SEWERAGE AND DRAINAGE
02760	RESTORATION OF UNDERGROUND PIPELINES
02770	PONDS AND RESERVOIRS
02780	POWER AND COMMUNICATIONS
02800	SITE IMPROVEMENTS
02900	LANDSCAPING

DIVISION 3—CONCRETE

03100	CONCRETE FORMWORK
03200	CONCRETE REINFORCEMENT
03250	CONCRETE ACCESSORIES
03300	CAST-IN-PLACE CONCRETE
03370	CONCRETE CURING
03400	PRECAST CONCRETE
03500	CEMENTITIOUS DECKS
03600	GROUT
03700	CONCRETE RESTORATION AND CLEANING
03800	MASS CONCRETE

DIVISION 4—MASONRY

04100	MORTAR
04150	MASONRY ACCESSORIES
04200	UNIT MASONRY
04400	STONE
04500	MASONRY RESTORATION AND CLEANING
04550	REFRACTORIES
04600	CORROSION RESISTANT MASONRY

DIVISION 5—METALS

05010	METAL MATERIALS
05030	METAL FINISHES
05050	METAL FASTENING
05100	STRUCTURAL METAL FRAMING
05200	METAL JOISTS
05300	METAL DECKING
05400	COLD-FORMED METAL FRAMING
05500	METAL FABRICATIONS
05580	SHEET METAL FABRICATIONS
05700	ORNAMENTAL METAL
05800	EXPANSION CONTROL
05900	HYDRAULIC STRUCTURES

DIVISION 6—WOOD AND PLASTICS

06050	FASTENERS AND ADHESIVES
06100	ROUGH CARPENTRY
06130	HEAVY TIMBER CONSTRUCTION
06150	WOOD-METAL SYSTEMS
06170	PREFABRICATED STRUCTURAL WOOD
06200	FINISH CARPENTRY
06300	WOOD TREATMENT
06400	ARCHITECTURAL WOODWORK
06500	PREFABRICATED STRUCTURAL PLASTICS
06600	PLASTIC FABRICATIONS

DIVISION 7—THERMAL AND MOISTURE PROTECTION

07100	WATERPROOFING
07150	DAMPPROOFING
07190	VAPOR AND AIR RETARDERS
07200	INSULATION
07250	FIREPROOFING
07300	SHINGLES AND ROOFING TILES
07400	PREFORMED ROOFING AND CLADDING/SIDING
07500	MEMBRANE ROOFING
07570	TRAFFIC TOPPING
07600	FLASHING AND SHEET METAL
07700	ROOF SPECIALTIES AND ACCESSORIES
07800	SKYLIGHTS
07900	JOINT SEALERS

DIVISION 8—DOORS AND WINDOWS

08100	METAL DOORS AND FRAMES
08200	WOOD AND PLASTIC DOORS
08250	DOOR OPENING ASSEMBLIES
08300	SPECIAL DOORS
08400	ENTRANCES AND STOREFRONTS
08500	METAL WINDOWS
08600	WOOD AND PLASTIC WINDOWS
08650	SPECIAL WINDOWS
08700	HARDWARE
08800	GLAZING
08900	GLAZED CURTAIN WALLS

DIVISION 9—FINISHES

09100	METAL SUPPORT SYSTEMS
09200	LATH AND PLASTER
09230	AGGREGATE COATINGS
09250	GYPSUM BOARD
09300	TILE
09400	TERRAZZO
09500	ACOUSTICAL TREATMENT
09540	SPECIAL SURFACES
09550	WOOD FLOORING
09600	STONE FLOORING
09630	UNIT MASONRY FLOORING
09650	RESILIENT FLOORING
09680	CARPET
09700	SPECIAL FLOORING
09780	FLOOR TREATMENT
09800	SPECIAL COATINGS
09900	PAINTING
09950	WALL COVERINGS

12

(courtesy Construction Specifications Institute)

Figure 8.11a

DIVISION 10—SPECIALTIES

10100	CHALKBOARDS AND TACKBOARDS
10150	COMPARTMENTS AND CUBICLES
10200	LOUVERS AND VENTS
10240	GRILLES AND SCREENS
10250	SERVICE WALL SYSTEMS
10260	WALL AND CORNER GUARDS
10270	ACCESS FLOORING
10280	SPECIALTY MODULES
10290	PEST CONTROL
10300	FIREPLACES AND STOVES
10340	PREFABRICATED EXTERIOR SPECIALTIES
10350	FLAGPOLES
10400	IDENTIFYING DEVICES
10450	PEDESTRIAN CONTROL DEVICES
10500	LOCKERS
10520	FIRE PROTECTION SPECIALTIES
10530	PROTECTIVE COVERS
10550	POSTAL SPECIALTIES
10600	PARTITIONS
10650	OPERABLE PARTITIONS
10670	STORAGE SHELVING
10700	EXTERIOR SUN CONTROL DEVICES
10750	TELEPHONE SPECIALTIES
10800	TOILET AND BATH ACCESSORIES
10880	SCALES
10900	WARDROBE AND CLOSET SPECIALTIES

DIVISION 11—EQUIPMENT

11010	MAINTENANCE EQUIPMENT
11020	SECURITY AND VAULT EQUIPMENT
11030	TELLER AND SERVICE EQUIPMENT
11040	ECCLESIASTICAL EQUIPMENT
11050	LIBRARY EQUIPMENT
11060	THEATER AND STAGE EQUIPMENT
11070	INSTRUMENTAL EQUIPMENT
11080	REGISTRATION EQUIPMENT
11090	CHECKROOM EQUIPMENT
11100	MERCANTILE EQUIPMENT
11110	COMMERCIAL LAUNDRY AND DRY CLEANING EQUIPMENT
11120	VENDING EQUIPMENT
11130	AUDIO-VISUAL EQUIPMENT
11140	SERVICE STATION EQUIPMENT
11150	PARKING CONTROL EQUIPMENT
11160	LOADING DOCK EQUIPMENT
11170	SOLID WASTE HANDLING EQUIPMENT
11190	DETENTION EQUIPMENT
11200	WATER SUPPLY AND TREATMENT EQUIPMENT
11280	HYDRAULIC GATES AND VALVES
11300	FLUID WASTE TREATMENT AND DISPOSAL EQUIPMENT
11400	FOOD SERVICE EQUIPMENT
11450	RESIDENTIAL EQUIPMENT
11460	UNIT KITCHENS
11470	DARKROOM EQUIPMENT
11480	ATHLETIC, RECREATIONAL AND THERAPEUTIC EQUIPMENT
11500	INDUSTRIAL AND PROCESS EQUIPMENT
11600	LABORATORY EQUIPMENT
11650	PLANETARIUM EQUIPMENT
11660	OBSERVATORY EQUIPMENT
11700	MEDICAL EQUIPMENT
11780	MORTUARY EQUIPMENT
11850	NAVIGATION EQUIPMENT

DIVISION 12—FURNISHINGS

12050	FABRICS
12100	ARTWORK
12300	MANUFACTURED CASEWORK
12500	WINDOW TREATMENT
12600	FURNITURE AND ACCESSORIES
12670	RUGS AND MATS
12700	MULTIPLE SEATING
12800	INTERIOR PLANTS AND PLANTERS

DIVISION 13—SPECIAL CONSTRUCTION

13010	AIR SUPPORTED STRUCTURES
13020	INTEGRATED ASSEMBLIES
13030	SPECIAL PURPOSE ROOMS
13080	SOUND, VIBRATION, AND SEISMIC CONTROL
13090	RADIATION PROTECTION
13100	NUCLEAR REACTORS
13120	PRE-ENGINEERED STRUCTURES
13150	POOLS
13160	ICE RINKS
13170	KENNELS AND ANIMAL SHELTERS
13180	SITE CONSTRUCTED INCINERATORS
13200	LIQUID AND GAS STORAGE TANKS
13220	FILTER UNDERDRAINS AND MEDIA
13230	DIGESTION TANK COVERS AND APPURTENANCES
13240	OXYGENATION SYSTEMS
13260	SLUDGE CONDITIONING SYSTEMS
13300	UTILITY CONTROL SYSTEMS
13400	INDUSTRIAL AND PROCESS CONTROL SYSTEMS
13500	RECORDING INSTRUMENTATION
13550	TRANSPORTATION CONTROL INSTRUMENTATION
13600	SOLAR ENERGY SYSTEMS
13700	WIND ENERGY SYSTEMS
13800	BUILDING AUTOMATION SYSTEMS
13900	FIRE SUPPRESSION AND SUPERVISORY SYSTEMS

DIVISION 14—CONVEYING SYSTEMS

14100	DUMBWAITERS
14200	ELEVATORS
14300	MOVING STAIRS AND WALKS
14400	LIFTS
14500	MATERIAL HANDLING SYSTEMS
14600	HOISTS AND CRANES
14700	TURNTABLES
14800	SCAFFOLDING
14900	TRANSPORTATION SYSTEMS

DIVISION 15—MECHANICAL

15050	BASIC MECHANICAL MATERIALS AND METHODS
15250	MECHANICAL INSULATION
15300	FIRE PROTECTION
15400	PLUMBING
15500	HEATING, VENTILATING, AND AIR CONDITIONING (HVAC)
15550	HEAT GENERATION
15650	REFRIGERATION
15750	HEAT TRANSFER
15850	AIR HANDLING
15880	AIR DISTRIBUTION
15950	CONTROLS
15990	TESTING, ADJUSTING, AND BALANCING

DIVISION 16—ELECTRICAL

16050	BASIC ELECTRICAL MATERIALS AND METHODS
16200	POWER GENERATION
16300	HIGH VOLTAGE DISTRIBUTION (Above 600-Volt)
16400	SERVICE AND DISTRIBUTION (600-Volt and Below)
16500	LIGHTING
16600	SPECIAL SYSTEMS
16700	COMMUNICATIONS
16850	ELECTRIC RESISTANCE HEATING
16900	CONTROLS
16950	TESTING

(courtesy Construction Specifications Institute)

Figure 8.11b

sequence of order during the year that the standard was written. A listing of industry and professional organizations is included in the Appendix.

Manufacturers' Literature

The most reliable information resource for both the design professional and the specification writer is the literature produced by manufacturers of building materials, products, and assemblies. Many construction industry services provide annual catalogues as a service to design professionals. In fact, most licensed practitioners receive a profusion of manufacturers' literature by mail. This literature can serve as a library of general product data.

Most manufacturers of major building products provide the services of a Manufacturer's Representative. The manufacturer's representative usually keeps the company's literature up to date, makes himself available to answer questions about his company's products, and makes suggestions as to proper use, cost considerations, availability, restrictions and similar data.

To promote uniformity in commercial product literature, the Construction Specifications Institute provides a suggested format. This system is used by manufacturers for the presentation of data to design professionals. It uses the *Spec-Data Sheet*. The standard Spec-Data Sheet, as designed by the Construction Specifications Institute, organizes product data into ten groups (headings) of related information. This is an excellent format for the specifier for classifying any product. These Spec-Data headings are as follows:

1. Product name
2. Manufacturer
3. Product description
4. Technical data
5. Installation
6. Availability and cost
7. Warranty
8. Maintenance
9. Technical services
10. Filing systems

Professional and Industry Publications

Most professional institutes and societies publish journals featuring articles, research studies, and editorials on subjects of interest to their membership. Membership in such organizations provides many benefits to the construction specifier, including the journals which become a permanent part of his professional library.

A number of construction industries produce their own trade magazines and publications. These publications feature articles on projects, legal matters, new product development and evaluations, and the work and practice of outstanding practitioners. To catalogue and store great numbers of magazines may not be practical. However, several indexes are published that cross reference industry publications by year and month with listings by author, subject and general content. Most publications are available at the local library or through vendors who can supply periodicals on microfilm. A good construction index of products and methods is essential to the library of today's construction professional.

The Professional Library

A complete and well implemented library is essential to the needs of today's design professional and the specifier. Such a library shall contain as a minimum the following items:

- Current catalogues of building products, equipment and furnishings.
- Current volumes of applicable published building codes.
- Industry reference standards and specifications.
- Professional journals.
- Current texts on construction industry subjects and innovations.
- Graphic and construction standards.
- Dictionary of construction terms and usage.
- Current guides to estimates of cost.
- Project manuals for previous projects.

Continuing Education

Regardless of his education, experience and success, today's construction professional must pursue a course of continuing education throughout the course of his professional life. Just as ignorance of the law is no defense in legal matters, ignorance of the ever changing technology of building construction is no excuse for the modern construction professional.

Chapter 9
PREPARATION OF SPECIFICATIONS

To specify is to name or to describe in detail a material or a process. Construction Specifications are the qualitative requirements for products, materials and workmanship upon which the Contract for Construction is based. As part of the Contract Documents, the Construction Specifications have a definite legal implication, as well as a more common practical purpose.

Specification Language

Claude Fayette Bragdon, writing for the American Architect and Building News in 1893 discovered a specification for the "Salem Witch House" dating from 1674 which states:

"To lath and plaister the partitions of the house with clay and lime and to fill, lath and plaister, the porch and porch chambers and to plaister them with lime and haire besides; and to siele and lath them over with lime and to fill, lath and plaister the kitchen up the wall plate on every side. . . ."

From early times, most building projects were constructed from materials which were of local origin and well known by practitioners of the trades. In 1674 there was little need to describe in detail the source or the technical and performance properties of materials to be used for plastering. The plasterer was expected to know the source of his raw material and, by his expertise, to be responsible for the quality of his materials. This included a knowledge of: (1) how to mix and apply the material, (2) which tools and accessories to use, and, (3) how to attend the curing and "set" of the material once applied. As manufacturing processes have improved, and transportation and advertising have evolved, the designers' options for choosing and specifying materials and methods has broadened. As a result, the language and content of construction specifications have become more exact in establishing the designers' choice of materials and methods. At the same time, the designer has come to depend less upon the knowledge and skill of the tradesman in properly selecting and applying the material. Growing competition among materials manufacturers as well as contractors requires the specifier to spell out the performance requirements of materials and assemblies in great detail. The materials and processes selected by the designer must be described in a way that the designer's full intention, as well as the reliability of the product or system can be upheld in case of dispute or litigation. Ben John Small AIA, in his book *Streamlined Specifications Standards*, describes the specification writer's responsibility. He writes, "We are not lawyers, yet by indirection we are compelled to compete with them in the sense that should there exist any shortcomings in our specifications, the lawyers unearth them, waving claims in our face. We are not seers, yet in the event of a dispute, should we have had the good fortune to have written the right thing in the right place we become a 'good man'. If not, we are labeled a you know what".

In an effort to enforce equal opportunity in publicly funded building construction, as well as to insure the lowest possible cost by maximizing competition in bidding, the government has entered the process of construction specifying. The use of generic language is required to describe materials and processes used in the contract documentation for public work. The term "generic" is defined as (1) of, in, or referring to a genus, or family of similar origin, (2) applicable to a family, class or group of similar kind, or (3) not protected by a trademark. As new materials and methods have evolved over the years, manufacturers have tended to protect their products from use or duplication by competitors by obtaining patents, registering trademarks and trade names under copyright laws. Such trade names for popular products have tended to become the common description or identification of the product. As a result, the term "generic" has a critical impact on the language used by the specifier.

In the "common" language of construction, there have been, over the years, many inconsistencies in the meaning and application of terms and in the organization of data. The Construction Specifications Institute together with many other professional and industry organizations have responded to this problem, improving, and making universal the language, coordination, content, format and usefulness of contract documents. Special emphasis has been placed on construction specifications. Because of these efforts and the contributions of committee work by dedicated professionals, an understanding now exists whereby the specifier can describe requirements to inform the various segments of the construction industry.

The Three Part Section Format

Competition in the marketplace and constant technological developments have forced design professionals to use a more and more detailed approach. In 1674 when the Salem Witch House was built, the specifier had to do little more than generically name the product, describe the application, and indicate the surfaces to which it would be applied. Today, it is necessary to specify procedures, state administrative requirements, and establish quality standards, as well as to describe the product and its accessories, methods of application and workmanship requirements. Specifications have always been intended to serve the following functions: to equalize the competitive bidding process, to act as a reference guide to the constructor in the field, and to provide assurance of acceptable quality standards. In order to successfully carry out these functions, specifications must be highly structured and stated as briefly as possible in an outline format. As time becomes increasingly valuable, it is even more important that the specifications are as organized and consistent as possible. As more uniformity is achieved in the format, outline, placement and sequence of specification data, the response to that data becomes more efficient—both in estimating and in accomplishing the work. These goals have come of age in the techniques and standards that have been developed under the leadership of the Construction Specifications Institute. The

CSI 16 division organization of data, coupled with a standardized three-part section format for specifying segments of work has greatly improved the economy and utility of information in the work place.

The three-part format as discussed below, is an industry accepted standard for listing specification information. This format aids both writer and user in locating information quickly and efficiently. Since the location of information is consistent and pre-defined, it serves as a checklist for verifying compliance with written requirements. Both the coordination of design decisions, and the work of professional staff and consultants are enhanced and facilitated. Use of this format minimizes duplication, errors, and omissions.

Part 1—General

Part 1 is intended to contain specific administrative and procedural requirements unique to the item or items of work. As a minimum, Part 1—General should introduce the subject matter, relate the subject to other sections and describe any coordination with other work specified elsewhere. Part 1 can also refer the reader to applicable general requirements found in Division 1, state any reference information that would be helpful in establishing quality and performance standards, and list any requirements for shop drawings, manufacturer's literature, samples and other data that must be submitted for the approval of the design professional. Finally, Part 1 should also include any project, site, or environmental restraints as well as scheduling and sequencing requirements, guarantees, warranties, and maintenance requirements.

Part 2—Products

Part 2 deals exclusively with the material or product, or related products, including (if applicable) the manufacturer or manufacturing process. The design professional's requirements for composition of the materials and fabrication should also be described along with quality control standards acceptable to the design professional and regulatory authorities.

Part 3—Execution

Part 3 addresses issues involving the incorporation of the products into the work. The requirements of the Execution direct the contractor to verify conditions that must be properly accomplished prior to installing or applying the product. The requirements for erection, installation or application are specified in terms of special techniques, tolerances, interface with other products, tests, and inspections related to quality control in the field. Part 3 should also deal with final adjustments, cleaning, and protection during construction, as well as any other requirements leading to final acceptance at substantial completion.

Definitions

Included in the three-part section format are certain definitions. These definitions are part of the concept and define the use, location and outline of specification information. Examples of such definitions are listed below.

Division: A standard category of information organized as a general topic. There are 16 divisions which together cover the scope of information required to describe the work.

Section: A basic unit of the specification. Each section concentrates on an item or category of items that constitute an element of work. Sections are grouped under any one of the 16 divisions.

Part: A further subdivision of a Section. A part divides a section into three related groupings of information.

Article: A subdivision of a Part. An article consists of a few paragraphs covering a major subject.

Paragraph: One or more sentences that deal with a particular item or point of information within an Article.

Part 1— General

1.01 Requirements Included

A. What items of work are described by the section? B. What generic types of work, products or requirements are to be included in this section?

Note: The intention of this paragraph is to allow the reader to quickly assess the section content and should not intend to "scope" the overall work requirement in a way that would imply trade jurisdiction. The specifier should bear in mind that the entire specification is addressed to the (general) contractor, who is a principle party to the contract for construction. Although the actual work may be part of divisions that are commonly assigned to a subcontractor, it is the contractor who bears the responsibility for accomplishing the work specified in any section, and it is to the contractor and the contractor alone that the information is addressed.

1.02 Related Requirements

A. What is the relationship of this work to work specified in other sections?

B. Where is the other related work specified?

C. Are any requirements specified elsewhere to be erected, installed or applied under provisions of this section?

D. Are any products specified in this section but installed under the provisions of other sections?

Note: Related requirements should include sections that deal with work related to this section and requiring coordination, previous preparation, adjacency or interface. Question C may refer to owner furnished items which are normally specified in an appropriate Division 1 section. Question D may refer to a material such as glazing that is specified under Section 08800—Glass and Glazing, but installed by the manufacturer under the provisions of Section 08500—Metal Windows.

1.03 Allowances and Unit Prices

A. Are any items of work to be furnished under cash allowances specified in Section 01020—Allowances? If so, is the allowance limited to purchase of material only, or does it include labor and accessories specified in this and related sections also?

B. Are unit prices specified in Division 1 applicable to overages or underages of materials or labor provided? If so what system or authority for measuring is to be used?

1.04 References

A. Are there any published, industry accepted standard specifications, testing requirements or other written standards that should be listed for reference purposes—to complement the requirements of the section or to anticipate challenges involving quality or performance considerations?

B. Does the design professional or the specifier own or have access to a copy of the standard listed?

C. Does the standard state any provisions that contradict, obviate or otherwise confuse the requirements of this section?

Note: The specifier is cautioned that available and commonly used reference standards (such as those provided by organizations listed in Chapter 8) should be readily available and well known to the specifier. It is not unusual for such standards to list multiple types of materials, some of which may not be acceptable for the use intended. Moreover, some standards may contain statements that could change the relationships established either in the Conditions of the Contract or the General Requirements (Division 1). Such misleading or incorrect provisions must be omitted or made inapplicable in this paragraph when appropriate. Specifiers should never list a reference standard unless absolutely certain of its content and possible impact on the intentions established by the Contract Documents.

1.05 Definitions

A. Are there any terms, trade names or processes specified in this section that may be unfamiliar to the reader and which have not been defined elsewhere?

B. Is there any coordination with other sections or requirements specified elsewhere that could be clarified by a definition placed in this particular section? Does the owner's option to contract portions of the work separately have any bearing on the work of this section?

1.07 System Description

Note: This article should be restricted to statements describing the performance or design requirements and tolerances of a complete system. Descriptions should be limited to composite and operational properties needed to link multiple components of a system or to interface with other systems.

1.08 Submittals

A. Does the design professional require that manufacturer's literature, installation instructions, disclaimers, guarantees, warranties or other statements be submitted for information or approval purposes?

B. Are shop drawings of the scope of work, method of erection, assembly, or application required for submittal and approval?

C. Are samples of materials required? If so specify number and size if appropriate.

D. Are design data, quality control standards, test reports, certificates, or manufacturers' field reports required?

E. Are contract closeout submittals, project record documents, operational instructions, maintenance data, and warranty submittals required? If so, this information must be coordinated with provisions of Section 01700 -Contract Closeout and Section 01710— Project Record Documents.

Note: Section 01300—Submittals—deals with the detailed requirements of submissions that are called for in individual sections. Careful coordination is required between submittal requirements and this section.

1.09 Quality Assurance

A. What standards of quality are expected?

B. What credentials, and how many years of experience, if any, must manufacturers and mechanics exhibit?

C. What regulatory and code requirements is the work expected to meet? It is not necessary to name local building code ordinances which are generally known, but it is necessary to name codes and regulations that may not be known.

D. Are there any certifications of quality and compliance required?

E. Is a material or assembly mock-up required for approval and/or to serve as the model for quality and workmanship? If so, specify the size required, the location, and the length of time during which protection and maintenance is expected. State whether or not the sample can be incorporated into the work once approved.

F. Are pre-installation meetings required in order to coordinate and insure the quality of the work?

1.10 Delivery, Storage and Handling

A. How should the product be protected, packaged, and shipped?

B. Are there any unusual site conditions that may require special attention to methods of storage and protection during construction?

Note: Statements should supplement the general requirements of product protection stated in Section 01600—Material and Equipment (Division 1).

1.11 Project/Site Conditions

A. What environmental considerations apply to storage and application of the product?

B. Does adverse temperature affect the storage or application of the product? If so state limits of temperature.

C. Are there any existing conditions at the site that must be considered?

Note: This information may require coordination with "Information Available to Bidders" stated in the Bidding Requirements.

1.12 Sequencing and Scheduling

Do the requirements of this section require special sequencing and coordination with work of another section, or contract, or with work done by the owner?

Note: Section 01010—Summary of the Work, in Division 1, normally contains statements concerning overall sequencing and scheduling. Any statement made here must be coordinated with Division 1 requirements.

1.13 Guarantee and Warranty

A. Are there any guarantee and/or warranty provisions required of the manufacturer or contractor?

B. Are there any provisions required that would exceed the provisions of guarantees or warranties as established in the Conditions of the Contract?

Note: It is important that the specifier coordinate the requirements specified in this section with the provisions of the Conditions of the Contract so as not to void one or the other because of conflict. Guarantees and Warranties are difficult to enforce at best, and any conflict between the provisions of a particular section and the Conditions of the Contract is almost sure to give the purveyor an "out" thereby making the owner vulnerable and the design professional liable.

1.14 Maintenance

A. Does the nature of the work specified in this section require special maintenance during and after construction?

B. Should the contractor be required to maintain a paid-up service policy during the construction period?

C. Has consideration been given to requiring the contractor to provide extra stock for the owner's initial maintenance and replacement purposes?

Note: The requirements of C should be coordinated with Section 01700 —Contract Closeout

Part 2— Products

This part is governed in large degree by the type of specification that is intended. Recognized specification types are:
- Descriptive Specifications
- Performance Specifications
- Specifications based on Reference Standards
- Proprietary Specifications
    —Closed Proprietary Specifications
    —Open Proprietary Specifications

Specification applications include:
- Restrictive Specifications
- Non-Restrictive Specifications

The type and application of specifications determines the approach and application of the various articles of Part 2.

2.01 Products and Manufacture

This article is applicable to the proprietary type of specification. It can be used for either open or closed application where the product can be described by naming one or more manufacturers and the acceptable products. The Instructions to Bidders should deal with procedures that enable bidders to propose substitutions and seek approval prior to the receipt of bids. Section 01600— Materials and Equipment should provide a procedure whereby the contractor can propose substitutions after the execution of the contract for construction. Reference to these provisions should be made if the non-restrictive application is to be upheld.

A. Has the design professional selected a particular product produced by a manufacturer to fulfill the requirements and intent of this section?

Note: If the Closed Proprietary method is used, no further information is necessary. If the Open Proprietary method is used, the following questions are applicable.

B. Can two or more similar products produced by other manufacturers also meet the requirements of this section so as to be equally acceptable to the design professional?

C. Have the products named above been recently researched to determine if they are currently available as specified?

2.02 Materials

This article is used where the Descriptive, Performance or Reference Standard type specification is applicable. The specifier should name each material and describe its attributes according to the type of specification. In the case of the descriptive specification, the specifier should state in detail the minimum acceptable features of the material. In the case of performance specifying, the specifier should describe the end results to be achieved by the use of the product. In the case of reference standard specifying, the specifier should name the standard specification to be followed.

2.03 Accessories

This article is intended to provide requirements for subordinate or secondary items which aid, assist, or are required to complete, prepare, or install the primary products or materials that are the subject of the section. The article is not intended to specify basic options available for manufactured units and equipment. Accessory options should be named together with the product or material.

2.04 Mixes

This article should provide proportions and procedures for mixing materials, and is unique to descriptive specifying of such materials as asphalt paving, concrete, mortar and plaster.

2.05 Fabrication

This article is intended to describe items that must be shop-manufactured, fabricated, or assembled before they are delivered to the job site. The specifier should specify any required factory-applied finishing and should specify acceptable tolerances or variations from specified requirements.

2.06 Source Quality Control

A. Are any tests and/or inspections required of the product or material before it leaves the source of manufacture or assembly?

B. Is verification of performance required before the product or material is shipped to the job site?

Note: Any testing or inspection that is required at the source of the product or material should be coordinated with Section 01400— Quality Control.

Part 3— Execution

3.01 Examination

A. Does the installation of the product or material depend upon the work of another section? Must an existing condition be properly prepared before erection, installation, or application can take place?

B. Are any preparations required under this section involving the surface area, surrounding materials, or the site? Are such preparations needed in order to properly incorporate the primary products or materials specified in this section?

3.02 Preparation

A. Does the nature of the work require any special protective measures to insure that adjacent surfaces, equipment, or installations are not damaged?

B. Does the work require any special preparation at adjacent locations before it can be incorporated into the project?

3.03 Erection, Installation, or Application

Note: Only one of the titles listed above is applicable.

A. What actions are required to accomplish the specified unit of work?

B. Are products specified in other sections installed under this section?

C. Can or does the manufacturer provide complete instructions as to the proper erection, installation, or application of the unit of work?

Note: In instances where a guarantee or warranty is required, erection, installation, or application of the unit of work must be specified in strict accordance with the manufacturer's instructions in order to assure compliance with guarantee and/or warranty provisions.

D. Does the unit of work require any special procedures prior to incorporation into the project?

E. Does the interface of the unit of work with other elements require any process, accessory, anchorage, special separation, or bonding?

F. What are the acceptable tolerances, and variations from plumb or form allowed when the unit of work is erected or installed?

G. What is the required wet or cured thickness of a unit of applied work?

3.04 Field Quality Control

A. Are any tests or inspections required during or after the specified unit of work is erected, installed or applied?

Note: Coordination with Section 01400—Quality Control, or Section 01410—Testing may be required.

B. Does the nature of the unit of work require the manufacturer to provide any service in the field such as instruction or supervision?

3.05 Adjusting and Cleaning

A. Does the erection of the unit of work require adjustments and/or cleaning prior to acceptance?

B. If temporary protective coatings or coverings have been specified in Part 1, when is it acceptable to remove such protective coatings or coverings?

Note: The requirements of this article may involve coordination with one or more Division 1 sections such as Section 01500—Construction Facilities and Temporary Controls and/or Section 01700—Contract Closeout.

3.06 Demonstration

Does the nature of the unit of work require that the manufacturer or contractor perform demonstration of the operation and maintenance for the owner's benefit?

3.07 Protection

Are any special procedures required to protect the unit of work subsequent to erection, installation or application?

3.08 Schedules

Note: The specifier may find it convenient to create a schedule to be included in the specification at this point.

Page Format

Figure 9.1 shows the recommended page outline format now commonly used by specifiers who choose to follow the guidelines of the CSI "Manual of Practice". There are a number of advantages in using this format to organize the specification material; some are listed below:

- Parallel documents such as other specification sections, addenda, and other contract documents can easily refer to specific items that have an "address" in the outline. Example: ". . . as provided in Article 2.04, paragraph A, item 2 of Section 07900—Joint Sealants. . .''.
- The specification is more easily "scan" read when the user is searching for an item of interest, etc.
- The document is effective in outline form as the provisions stand out for the user rather than being buried in a mass of verbage difficult to spot.

The 16 Divisions

The *Masterformat* is the outgrowth of the 16 Division Format created by the Construction Specifications Institute (CSI) and Construction Specifications Canada (CSC). It is a logical, complete, and uniform system for organizing building construction information. This system has professional and industry acceptance and has been adopted by most professional organizations as well as most manufacturers and information services associated with the construction industry. Under this system, Division 1—General Requirements deals with the procedural and administrative requirements specified for the individual project. Divisions 2 through 16 contain technical specifications each section of which may contain provisions dependent in some way on Division 1.

Masterformat has allocated descriptions and five digit numbers to elements of the Project Manual including the 16 divisions of the technical specifications. Figures 9.2a and 9.2b offer a summary of those section numbers and subject descriptions. The *Masterformat* system of information description and numbering has received almost universal acceptance by the construction industry. This acceptance can be seen in manufacturers' literature, information systems libraries, and government specifications. Specifiers are encouraged to follow this system for the sake of uniformity and coordination— when writing the individual specification as well as when creating, organizing, and publishing the Project Manual.

Division 1—General Requirements

The General Requirements of the project (allocated by the 16 Division Format to be contained in Division 1 of the specifications) is one of the key components of the contract documents. Division 1 specifications establish the administrative requirements, procedural requirements, restrictions, and other pertinent requirements that define the parameters under which the contractor shall conduct the work. The General Requirements have a fundamental relationship to all of the other contract documents including Divisions 2 through 16 of the specifications. Figure 9.3 illustrates the relationships between Division 1 and the other contract documents. Figures 9.4a through 9.4c illustrate a list of sections typical of Division 1 topics with descriptions of information that should be contained in each section.

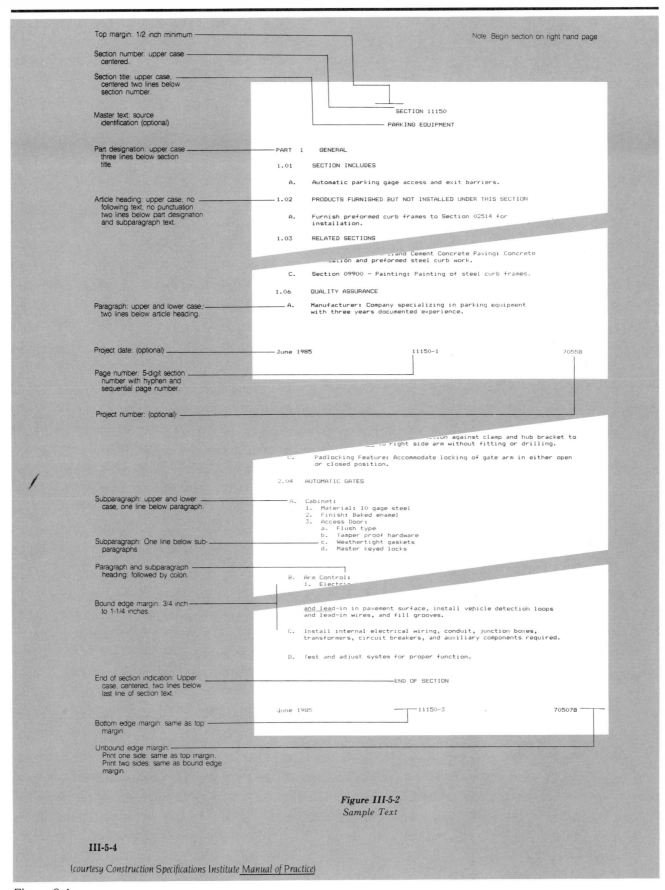

Top margin: 1/2 inch minimum

Note: Begin section on right hand page

Section number: upper case centered.

Section title: upper case, centered two lines below section number.

Master text: source identification (optional)

Part designation: upper case three lines below section title.

Article heading: upper case, no following text, no punctuation two lines below part designation and subparagraph text.

Paragraph: upper and lower case; two lines below article heading.

Project date: (optional)

Page number: 5-digit section number with hyphen and sequential page number.

Project number: (optional)

Subparagraph: upper and lower case, one line below paragraph.

Subparagraph: One line below subparagraphs

Paragraph and subparagraph heading: followed by colon.

Bound edge margin: 3/4 inch to 1-1/4 inches.

End of section indication: Upper case, centered, two lines below last line of section text.

Bottom edge margin: same as top margin.

Unbound edge margin:
Print one side: same as top margin.
Print two sides: same as bound edge margin.

SECTION 11150
PARKING EQUIPMENT

PART 1   GENERAL

1.01   SECTION INCLUDES

A.   Automatic parking gage access and exit barriers.

1.02   PRODUCTS FURNISHED BUT NOT INSTALLED UNDER THIS SECTION

A.   Furnish preformed curb frames to Section 02514 for installation.

1.03   RELATED SECTIONS

        ....land Cement Concrete Paving: Concrete
        ....ation and preformed steel curb work.

C.   Section 09900 — Painting: Painting of steel curb frames.

1.06   QUALITY ASSURANCE

A.   Manufacturer: Company specializing in parking equipment with three years documented experience.

June 1985   11150-1   70558

        ....ion against clamp and hub bracket to
        ...o right side arm without fitting or drilling.

C.   Padlocking Feature: Accommodate locking of gate arm in either open or closed position.

2.04   AUTOMATIC GATES

A.   Cabinet:
      1. Material: 10 gage steel
      2. Finish: Baked enamel
      3. Access Door:
          a. Flush type
          b. Tamper proof hardware
          c. Weathertight gaskets
          d. Master keyed locks

B.   Arm Control:
      1. Electri...

      and lead-in in pavement surface, install vehicle detection loops and lead-in wires, and fill grooves.

C.   Install internal electrical wiring, conduit, junction boxes, transformers, circuit breakers, and auxiliary components required.

D.   Test and adjust system for proper function.

                    END OF SECTION

June 1985   11150-3   705078

Figure III-5-2
Sample Text

III-5-4

(courtesy Construction Specifications Institute Manual of Practice)

Figure 9.1

185

BIDDING REQUIREMENTS, CONTRACT FORMS, AND CONDITIONS OF THE CONTRACT

00010	PRE-BID INFORMATION
00100	INSTRUCTIONS TO BIDDERS
00200	INFORMATION AVAILABLE TO BIDDERS
00300	BID FORMS
00400	SUPPLEMENTS TO BID FORMS
00500	AGREEMENT FORMS
00600	BONDS AND CERTIFICATES
00700	GENERAL CONDITIONS
00800	SUPPLEMENTARY CONDITIONS
00850	DRAWINGS AND SCHEDULES
00900	ADDENDA AND MODIFICATIONS

Note: Since the items listed above are not specification sections, they are referred to as "Documents" in lieu of "Sections" in the Master List of Section Titles, Numbers, and Broadscope Explanations.

SPECIFICATIONS

DIVISION 1—GENERAL REQUIREMENTS

01010	SUMMARY OF WORK
01020	ALLOWANCES
01025	MEASUREMENT AND PAYMENT
01030	ALTERNATES/ALTERNATIVES
01040	COORDINATION
01050	FIELD ENGINEERING
01060	REGULATORY REQUIREMENTS
01070	ABBREVIATIONS AND SYMBOLS
01080	IDENTIFICATION SYSTEMS
01090	REFERENCE STANDARDS
01100	SPECIAL PROJECT PROCEDURES
01200	PROJECT MEETINGS
01300	SUBMITTALS
01400	QUALITY CONTROL
01500	CONSTRUCTION FACILITIES AND TEMPORARY CONTROLS
01600	MATERIAL AND EQUIPMENT
01650	STARTING OF SYSTEMS/COMMISSIONING
01700	CONTRACT CLOSEOUT
01800	MAINTENANCE

DIVISION 2—SITEWORK

02010	SUBSURFACE INVESTIGATION
02050	DEMOLITION
02100	SITE PREPARATION
02140	DEWATERING
02150	SHORING AND UNDERPINNING
02160	EXCAVATION SUPPORT SYSTEMS
02170	COFFERDAMS
02200	EARTHWORK
02300	TUNNELING
02350	PILES AND CAISSONS
02450	RAILROAD WORK
02480	MARINE WORK
02500	PAVING AND SURFACING
02600	PIPED UTILITY MATERIALS
02660	WATER DISTRIBUTION
02680	FUEL DISTRIBUTION
02700	SEWERAGE AND DRAINAGE
02760	RESTORATION OF UNDERGROUND PIPELINES
02770	PONDS AND RESERVOIRS
02780	POWER AND COMMUNICATIONS
02800	SITE IMPROVEMENTS
02900	LANDSCAPING

DIVISION 3—CONCRETE

03100	CONCRETE FORMWORK
03200	CONCRETE REINFORCEMENT
03250	CONCRETE ACCESSORIES
03300	CAST-IN-PLACE CONCRETE
03370	CONCRETE CURING
03400	PRECAST CONCRETE
03500	CEMENTITIOUS DECKS
03600	GROUT
03700	CONCRETE RESTORATION AND CLEANING
03800	MASS CONCRETE

DIVISION 4—MASONRY

04100	MORTAR
04150	MASONRY ACCESSORIES
04200	UNIT MASONRY
04400	STONE
04500	MASONRY RESTORATION AND CLEANING
04550	REFRACTORIES
04600	CORROSION RESISTANT MASONRY

DIVISION 5—METALS

05010	METAL MATERIALS
05030	METAL FINISHES
05050	METAL FASTENING
05100	STRUCTURAL METAL FRAMING
05200	METAL JOISTS
05300	METAL DECKING
05400	COLD-FORMED METAL FRAMING
05500	METAL FABRICATIONS
05580	SHEET METAL FABRICATIONS
05700	ORNAMENTAL METAL
05800	EXPANSION CONTROL
05900	HYDRAULIC STRUCTURES

DIVISION 6—WOOD AND PLASTICS

06050	FASTENERS AND ADHESIVES
06100	ROUGH CARPENTRY
06130	HEAVY TIMBER CONSTRUCTION
06150	WOOD-METAL SYSTEMS
06170	PREFABRICATED STRUCTURAL WOOD
06200	FINISH CARPENTRY
06300	WOOD TREATMENT
06400	ARCHITECTURAL WOODWORK
06500	PREFABRICATED STRUCTURAL PLASTICS
06600	PLASTIC FABRICATIONS

DIVISION 7—THERMAL AND MOISTURE PROTECTION

07100	WATERPROOFING
07150	DAMPPROOFING
07190	VAPOR AND AIR RETARDERS
07200	INSULATION
07250	FIREPROOFING
07300	SHINGLES AND ROOFING TILES
07400	PREFORMED ROOFING AND CLADDING/SIDING
07500	MEMBRANE ROOFING
07570	TRAFFIC TOPPING
07600	FLASHING AND SHEET METAL
07700	ROOF SPECIALTIES AND ACCESSORIES
07800	SKYLIGHTS
07900	JOINT SEALERS

DIVISION 8—DOORS AND WINDOWS

08100	METAL DOORS AND FRAMES
08200	WOOD AND PLASTIC DOORS
08250	DOOR OPENING ASSEMBLIES
08300	SPECIAL DOORS
08400	ENTRANCES AND STOREFRONTS
08500	METAL WINDOWS
08600	WOOD AND PLASTIC WINDOWS
08650	SPECIAL WINDOWS
08700	HARDWARE
08800	GLAZING
08900	GLAZED CURTAIN WALLS

DIVISION 9—FINISHES

09100	METAL SUPPORT SYSTEMS
09200	LATH AND PLASTER
09230	AGGREGATE COATINGS
09250	GYPSUM BOARD
09300	TILE
09400	TERRAZZO
09500	ACOUSTICAL TREATMENT
09540	SPECIAL SURFACES
09550	WOOD FLOORING
09600	STONE FLOORING
09630	UNIT MASONRY FLOORING
09650	RESILIENT FLOORING
09680	CARPET
09700	SPECIAL FLOORING
09780	FLOOR TREATMENT
09800	SPECIAL COATINGS
09900	PAINTING
09950	WALL COVERINGS

(courtesy Construction Specifications Institute)

Figure 9.2a

DIVISION 10—SPECIALTIES

10100	CHALKBOARDS AND TACKBOARDS
10150	COMPARTMENTS AND CUBICLES
10200	LOUVERS AND VENTS
10240	GRILLES AND SCREENS
10250	SERVICE WALL SYSTEMS
10260	WALL AND CORNER GUARDS
10270	ACCESS FLOORING
10280	SPECIALTY MODULES
10290	PEST CONTROL
10300	FIREPLACES AND STOVES
10340	PREFABRICATED EXTERIOR SPECIALTIES
10350	FLAGPOLES
10400	IDENTIFYING DEVICES
10450	PEDESTRIAN CONTROL DEVICES
10500	LOCKERS
10520	FIRE PROTECTION SPECIALTIES
10530	PROTECTIVE COVERS
10550	POSTAL SPECIALTIES
10600	PARTITIONS
10650	OPERABLE PARTITIONS
10670	STORAGE SHELVING
10700	EXTERIOR SUN CONTROL DEVICES
10750	TELEPHONE SPECIALTIES
10800	TOILET AND BATH ACCESSORIES
10880	SCALES
10900	WARDROBE AND CLOSET SPECIALTIES

DIVISION 11—EQUIPMENT

11010	MAINTENANCE EQUIPMENT
11020	SECURITY AND VAULT EQUIPMENT
11030	TELLER AND SERVICE EQUIPMENT
11040	ECCLESIASTICAL EQUIPMENT
11050	LIBRARY EQUIPMENT
11060	THEATER AND STAGE EQUIPMENT
11070	INSTRUMENTAL EQUIPMENT
11080	REGISTRATION EQUIPMENT
11090	CHECKROOM EQUIPMENT
11100	MERCANTILE EQUIPMENT
11110	COMMERCIAL LAUNDRY AND DRY CLEANING EQUIPMENT
11120	VENDING EQUIPMENT
11130	AUDIO-VISUAL EQUIPMENT
11140	SERVICE STATION EQUIPMENT
11150	PARKING CONTROL EQUIPMENT
11160	LOADING DOCK EQUIPMENT
11170	SOLID WASTE HANDLING EQUIPMENT
11190	DETENTION EQUIPMENT
11200	WATER SUPPLY AND TREATMENT EQUIPMENT
11280	HYDRAULIC GATES AND VALVES
11300	FLUID WASTE TREATMENT AND DISPOSAL EQUIPMENT
11400	FOOD SERVICE EQUIPMENT
11450	RESIDENTIAL EQUIPMENT
11460	UNIT KITCHENS
11470	DARKROOM EQUIPMENT
11480	ATHLETIC, RECREATIONAL AND THERAPEUTIC EQUIPMENT
11500	INDUSTRIAL AND PROCESS EQUIPMENT
11600	LABORATORY EQUIPMENT
11650	PLANETARIUM EQUIPMENT
11660	OBSERVATORY EQUIPMENT
11700	MEDICAL EQUIPMENT
11780	MORTUARY EQUIPMENT
11850	NAVIGATION EQUIPMENT

DIVISION 12—FURNISHINGS

12050	FABRICS
12100	ARTWORK
12300	MANUFACTURED CASEWORK
12500	WINDOW TREATMENT
12600	FURNITURE AND ACCESSORIES
12670	RUGS AND MATS
12700	MULTIPLE SEATING
12800	INTERIOR PLANTS AND PLANTERS

DIVISION 13—SPECIAL CONSTRUCTION

13010	AIR SUPPORTED STRUCTURES
13020	INTEGRATED ASSEMBLIES
13030	SPECIAL PURPOSE ROOMS
13080	SOUND, VIBRATION. AND SEISMIC CONTROL
13090	RADIATION PROTECTION
13100	NUCLEAR REACTORS
13120	PRE-ENGINEERED STRUCTURES
13150	POOLS
13160	ICE RINKS
13170	KENNELS AND ANIMAL SHELTERS
13180	SITE CONSTRUCTED INCINERATORS
13200	LIQUID AND GAS STORAGE TANKS
13220	FILTER UNDERDRAINS AND MEDIA
13230	DIGESTION TANK COVERS AND APPURTENANCES
13240	OXYGENATION SYSTEMS
13260	SLUDGE CONDITIONING SYSTEMS
13300	UTILITY CONTROL SYSTEMS
13400	INDUSTRIAL AND PROCESS CONTROL SYSTEMS
13500	RECORDING INSTRUMENTATION
13550	TRANSPORTATION CONTROL INSTRUMENTATION
13600	SOLAR ENERGY SYSTEMS
13700	WIND ENERGY SYSTEMS
13800	BUILDING AUTOMATION SYSTEMS
13900	FIRE SUPPRESSION AND SUPERVISORY SYSTEMS

DIVISION 14—CONVEYING SYSTEMS

14100	DUMBWAITERS
14200	ELEVATORS
14300	MOVING STAIRS AND WALKS
14400	LIFTS
14500	MATERIAL HANDLING SYSTEMS
14600	HOISTS AND CRANES
14700	TURNTABLES
14800	SCAFFOLDING
14900	TRANSPORTATION SYSTEMS

DIVISION 15—MECHANICAL

15050	BASIC MECHANICAL MATERIALS AND METHODS
15250	MECHANICAL INSULATION
15300	FIRE PROTECTION
15400	PLUMBING
15500	HEATING, VENTILATING, AND AIR CONDITIONING (HVAC)
15550	HEAT GENERATION
15650	REFRIGERATION
15750	HEAT TRANSFER
15850	AIR HANDLING
15880	AIR DISTRIBUTION
15950	CONTROLS
15990	TESTING, ADJUSTING, AND BALANCING

DIVISION 16—ELECTRICAL

16050	BASIC ELECTRICAL MATERIALS AND METHODS
16200	POWER GENERATION
16300	HIGH VOLTAGE DISTRIBUTION (Above 600-Volt)
16400	SERVICE AND DISTRIBUTION (600-Volt and Below)
16500	LIGHTING
16600	SPECIAL SYSTEMS
16700	COMMUNICATIONS
16850	ELECTRIC RESISTANCE HEATING
16900	CONTROLS
16950	TESTING

(courtesy Construction Specifications Institute)

Figure 9.2b

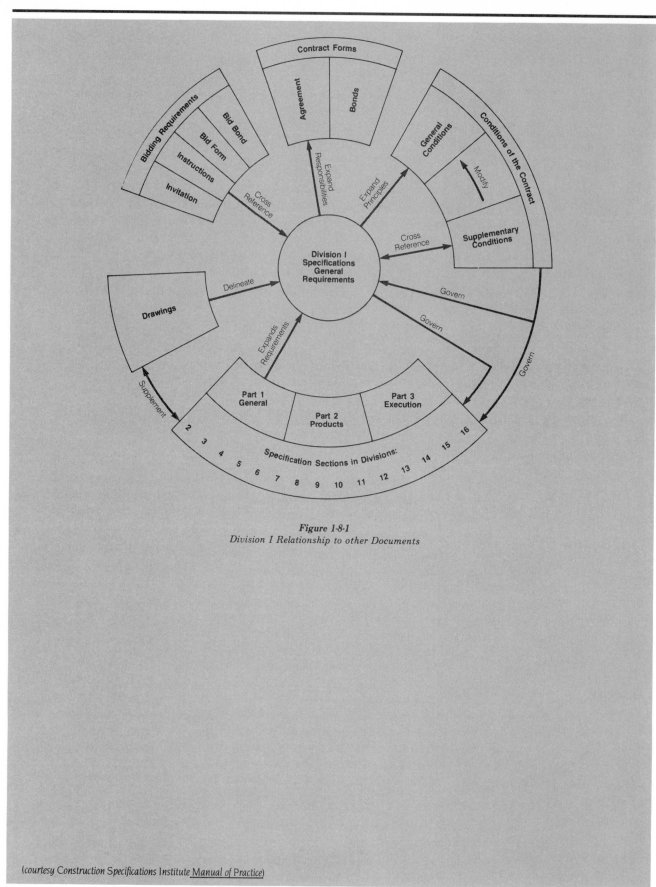

Figure 1-8-1
Division I Relationship to other Documents

(courtesy Construction Specifications Institute Manual of Practice)

Figure 9.3

SECTION 01010 - SUMMARY OF THE WORK

This section describes the scope and extent of the work covered by the Contract Documents, denotes work to be accomplished by others, the sequence of the work, restrictions on use of site, coordination of the work, regulatory requirements and similar items related to the conduct of the work.

SECTION 01020 - CASH ALLOWANCES

This section itemizes and describes allowances in terms of lump sum cash amounts that are specified to be included in the Contract Sum for providing items of materials and/or work that shall be selected by the owner.

SECTION 01028 - CHANGE ORDER PROCEDURES

This section describes procedures to be followed in the probable event that changes in the contract will occur.

SECTION 01030 - ALTERNATES

This section describes bidding procedures required to propose itemized alternates to be added or subtracted from the Contract Sum at the Owner's option.

SECTION 01031 - ALTERATION PROCEDURES

This section describes special procedures that are required for projects which involve the work of additions and/or alterations to existing facilities.

SECTION 01040 - CONTRACT COORDINATION

This section describes the procedures required for coordination of the work, including separate contracts, work or items furnished by the owner as well as coordination of work under this contract.

SECTION 01045 - CUTTING AND PATCHING

This section describes the restrictions and procedures required for cutting and patching of existing work, correction of contract work, or for accommodation of related work.

SECTION 01050 - FIELD ENGINEERING

This section describes requirements of contractor furnished engineering for building location and layout, verification of site controls and other professional engineering confirmation and certification related to the execution of the work.

(courtesy Construction Specifications Institute)

Figure 9.4a

SECTION 01090 - REFERENCE STANDARDS

This section describes and lists the organizations capable of providing published reference standards offered or required by the various specification sections.

SECTION 01100 - SPECIAL PROJECT PROCEDURES

This section describes any specialized or unusual procedures, out of the ordinary, that must be observed by the contractor in the conduct of the work. This section is used rarely in cases of sensitive or unusual owner requirements.

SECTION 01152 - APPLICATIONS FOR PAYMENT

This section describes procedures, specifies forms to be used and information to be contained in contractor's applications for payment.

SECTION 01200 - PROJECT MEETINGS

This section describes procedures in conducting meetings during the process of construction for purposes of coordinating the activities of those related to the work and others.

SECTION 01300 - SUBMITTALS

This section describes the requirements related to submittals of various kinds that require design professional approval.

SECTION 01400 - QUALITY CONTROL

This section describes the procedures to be followed in achieving, determining and verifying specified quality of materials and methods during construction.

SECTION 01410 - TESTING LABORATORY SERVICES

This section describes the standards, procedures and conditions related to testing of materials and applications. Normally specified in Section 01400, this section is commonly used if testing is to be paid for or conducted in some manner other than as required by Paragraph 7.7 of AIA Document A201 - General Conditions of the Contract for Construction.

SECTION 01500 - CONSTRUCTION FACILITIES TEMPORARY CONTROLS

This section describes the requirements and restrictions placed on the use of equipment, site, utilities, temporary facilities, safety measures and other procedures related to the conduct of the work.

(courtesy Construction Specifications Institute)

Figure 9.4b

SECTION 01600 - MATERIAL AND EQUIPMENT

This section describes the requirements of product quality control, transportation to the site, storage and protection, product options, procedures related to substitutions and required certifications.

SECTION 01700 - CONTRACT CLOSE OUT

This section describes the procedures and requirements, final submittals and other information related to the completion and close out of the project leading to final payment and transition of contractor control to owner control.

SECTION 01720 - PROJECT RECORD DOCUMENTS

This section describes the requirements of records and documentation of the construction process for the owner's benefit that is required of the contractor.

(courtesy Construction Specifications Institute)

Figure 9.4c

AIA Document A201 - General Conditions of the Contract for Construction, August 1976

4.12 SHOP DRAWINGS, PRODUCT DATA AND SAMPLES

4.12.1 Shop Drawings are drawings, diagrams, schedules and other data specially prepared for the Work by the Contractor or any Subcontractor, manufacturer, supplier or distributor to illustrate some portion of the Work.

4.12.2 Product Data are illustrations, standard schedules, performance charts, instructions, brochures, diagrams and other information furnished by the Contractor to illustrate a material, product or system for some portion of the Work.

4.12.3 Samples are physical examples which illustrate materials, equipment or workmanship and establish standards by which the Work will be judged.

4.12.4 The Contractor shall review, approve and submit, with reasonable promptness and in such sequence as to cause no delay in the Work or in the work of the Owner or any separate contractor, all Shop Drawings, Product Data and Samples required by the Contract Documents.

4.12.5 By approving and submitting Shop Drawings, Product Data and Samples, the Contractor represents that he has determined and verified all materials, field measurements, and field construction criteria related thereto, or will do so, and that he has checked and coordinated the information contained within such submittals with the requirements of the Work and of the Contract Documents.

4.12.6 The Contractor shall not be relieved of responsibility for any deviation from the requirements of the Contract Documents by the Architect's approval of Shop Drawings, Product Data or Samples under Subparagraph 2.2.14 unless the Contractor has specifically informed the Architect in writing of such deviation at the time of submission and the Architect has given written approval to the specific deviation. The Contractor shall not be relieved from responsibility for errors or omissions in the Shop Drawings, Product Data or Samples by the Architect's approval thereof.

4.12.7 The Contractor shall direct specific attention, in writing or on resubmitted Shop Drawings, Product Data or Samples, to revisions other than those requested by the Architect on previous submittals.

4.12.8 No portion of the Work requiring submission of a Shop Drawing, Product Data or Sample shall be commenced until the submittal has been approved by the Architect as provided in Subparagraph 2.2.14. All such portions of the Work shall be in accordance with approved submittals.

Supplementary Conditions

> 3. In Paragraph 4.12.4 add the following:
>
>   "Prepare and submit all Shop Drawings, Samples, and other data under provisions of Section 01340 - Submittals."

Section 01300 - Submittals, Part 1 - General

> 1.03   SHOP DRAWINGS
>
> A. Present in a clear and thorough manner. Title each drawing with Project and Contract name and number; identify each element of drawings by reference to sheet number and detail, schedule, or room number of Contract Documents
>
> B. Identify field dimensions; show relation to adjacent or critical features or Work or products.
>
> C. Sheet Size: 22 by 17 inches or multiples of 8-1/2 by 11 inches.

Section 05420 - Cold-Formed Metal Joist System

> 1.05   SUBMITTALS
>
> A. Submit shop drawings and product data under provisions of Section 01340.
>
> B. Indicate flooring layout, interruptions to grid, special sized panels required, panels drilled or cut-out for services, appurtenances or interruptions, edge details, elevation differences, grilles, and registers.

Section 10270 - Access Flooring

> 1.09   SUBMITTALS
>
> A. Submit shop drawings and product data under provisions of Section 01340.
>
> B. Indicate on shop drawings, component details, framed openings, welds, type and location of fasteners, and accessories or items required of other related work.

Figure I-8-2
Levels of Coverage for General Requirements

I-8-4

(courtesy Construction Specifications Institute Manual of Practice)

Figure 9.5

Division 1 sections should be organized and written in the three-part format, like the sections in Divisions 2 through 16. Administrative provisions may not require Part 2 and Part 3 provisions. In any case, the specifier should write the provisions for Division 1 sections in careful coordination with the provisions of the General Conditions of the Contract, the Supplementary General Conditions, and the Part 1 provisions of sections contained in Divisions 2 through 16. Figure 9.5 shows the relationship and coordination required between the various elements in the contract document process.

Divisions 2 through 16

Divisions 2 through 16 of the specifications are often referred to as the "Technical Specifications." Beginning with Division 2—Site Work, and ending with Division 16—Electrical, the technical specifications are broken down into individual sections, describing specific units of work. These descriptions stipulate the work to be done, as well as materials, assemblies, systems or equipment to be used, and incorporate an expected standard of quality in workmanship, installation, and finish. The "Broadscope" categories in each division are further subdivided into "Mediumscope" and "Narrowscope" listings.

Methods of Specifying

It is not unusual for the specifier to incorporate more than one method of specifying when creating the total specification for a single project. There is no clear rule about using one method of specifying over another. It is clear, however, that the specifier should choose one method as the basis of each section and should not attempt to mix methods in specifying basic units of work. The CSI *Manual of Practice* recognizes four basic types of specifications, which are outlined below.

Descriptive Specifications

Descriptive specifications are defined as written descriptions detailing the required properties of a material, manufacturer's product, assembly of materials or products, or a piece of equipment. The subject of the specification is referred to by its generic description. No manufacturer, trade, or proprietary names are used in this type of specification. The materials are named and qualified. If joined into an assembly, the qualities of that assembly are described.

A typical descriptive specification for concrete mixed at the job site is shown in Figure 9.6. The components are described, weights are compared, and the mixture is specified by proportionate weight of each ingredient, including water.

The specifier should always bear in mind that the contractor to whom the specification is addressed is responsible only for compliance with the exact parameters stated in the specification. While a competent general contractor knows by experience that the concrete ought to perform in certain ways, he fulfills his obligations to the contract for construction by following the specifier's directions for proportioning the mix (illustrated in Figure 9.6). Should the concrete have required an ultimate compressive strength of 2500 pounds per square inch (psi), and if the mix was not specified to achieved that end, the design professional could be responsible to the owner for the cost of replacement or repair.

A second example of the descriptive specification is illustrated in Figures 9.7a and 9.7b. A reinforced flexible flashing is to be used in a masonry cavity wall. Because of restrictions placed by the owner, the

PART 2 - PRODUCTS

2.01 MATERIALS - STANDARD STRUCTURAL CONCRETE

A. Portland Cement: Shall be of domestic manufacture, as approved by Architect. Use only one brand of cement unless otherwise authorized by Architect.

B. Fine Aggregate: Natural bank sand or river sand, as apporved by the Architect from samples, washed and screened so as to produce a minimum percentage of voids.

C. Coarse Aggregate: Gravel or crushed lime stone suitably processed, washed and screened, and shall consist of hard, durable particles without adherent coatings of foreign materials. Aggregate shall range from 1/4" to 1-1/4", well graded between the size limits.

D. Water: Clean, potable, free of injurious amounts of minerals.

E. Admixtures: In accordance with design mix prepared by testing laboratory:

2.02 PROPORTIONING CONCRETE MIX BY VOLUME

A. Cement: 1/2 part

B. Fine Aggregate: 1 part

C. Coarse Aggregate: 2 parts

D. Water: As required to produce minimum slump of 4 inches.

(courtesy American Institute of Architects)

Figure 9.6

specifications must not rely upon proprietary name brand products, but describe the product in such manner as to allow any and all manufacturers who produce such a product to bid competitively. The descriptive specification describes in detail the assembly, its basic materials, and the means of bonding the materials. It also specifies the expected weight of the membrane after assembly. The specification also lists certain expected performance characteristics as to the material's strength and other properties under adverse temperature exposure.

It is not likely that a modern day specifier, familiar with the many proven manufactured products available for the purpose of concealed flexible flashing would wish to research the fine details of each and every ingredient of a proposed product (such as the description of the woven twill and required weight of the cotton fabric written in the descriptive specification in Figure 9.7a). A more satisfactory way of naming the product's performance under stress and weather conditions might be to add certain criteria to the specification as illustrated in Figure 9.7b.

Industry Standard Specifications allow the specifier to reference the requirements for such materials and applications as concrete and flexible flashing. Industry Standard Specifications have relieved the need to rely on such detailed descriptive specifications. There are a number of advantages in the use of the descriptive specification. Some are listed below:

- The contractor has wide discretion in the selection and purchase of materials and individual components.
- Competition among bidders is maximized.
- Approval of material submittals by the design professional offers a substantial basis for judgments to be rendered.

There also are certain disadvantages in descriptive specifying that should be considered:

- Quality and ultimate performance are difficult to predict and control.
- Unskillful specifying can lead to disputes.
- The time required of the specifier to research and write detailed descriptions of components, applications and necessary restrictions of use and performance requirements may be prohibitive.

Proprietary Specifications

The descriptive specification was widely used and greatly preferred in the days when there were few proven published industry standards. Over the years, however, the need for consistent quality and predictable performance has made the proprietary specification more attractive. It is also much easier to write proprietary specifications. Modern manufacturing continues to produce competitive products for building construction, each designed to satisfy a demand for less labor intensive application and greater performance reliability. As these new products have come into the marketplace, the specifier has tended, more and more, to rely upon the use of named brands in specifying the application and quality he seeks. Figure 9.8 illustrates a proprietary specification for flexible membrane flashing in a masonry cavity wall as produced by a well known manufacturer. This product specification accomplishes a similar result as the descriptive specification illustrated in Figure 9.7a with more assurance of quality and performance and less reliance on the technical and communicative skill of the specifier.

PART 2 - PRODUCTS

2.01   MATERIALS - FLEXIBLE FABRIC FLASHING

A. 3 oz. copper base sheet.

B. Sisal fibers: .006 inch diameter, measuring 160 to the inch weighing 5.59 oz. per sq. yd.

C. Cotton Fabric: Closely woven twill having combined thread count in warp and filling of at least 130, weighing at least 6.66 oz. per yd. before saturation.

D. Woven wire mesh: Composed of 21 gauge, plain steel wire fabricated with 2 1/2 meshes per inch in each direction.

D. Asphalt: ASTM 312.

E. Kraft Paper: Weighing no less than 45 lbs per 100 sq. ft., creped, impregnated thoroughly with bitumen conforming to ASTM 450.

2.02   FABRICATION

A. Bond sisal fiber to both sides of copper base with two coats asphalt.

B. Thoroughly embed wire fabric into asphalt on one side of base sheet, cover with one layer kraft paper.

C. Thoroughly embed cotton fabric into asphalt on opposite side of base sheet. Coat fabric with one coat asphalt, apply and embed one layer of kraft paper.

Figure 9.7a

PART 2 - PRODUCTS

2.01 MATERIALS - FLEXIBLE FABRIC FLASHING

    A. 3 oz. copper base sheet.

    B. Sisal fibers: .006 inch diameter, measuring 160 to the inch weighing 5.59 oz. per sq. yd.

    C. Cotton Fabric: Closely woven twill having combined thread count in warp and filling of at least 130, weighing at least 6.66 oz. per yd. before saturation.

    D. Woven wire mesh: Composed of 21 gauge, plain steel wire fabricated with 2 1/2 meshes per inch in each direction.

    D. Asphalt: ASTM 312.

    E. Kraft Paper: Weighing no less than 45 lbs per 100 sq. ft., creped, impregnated thoroughly with bitumen conforming to ASTM 450.

2.02 FABRICATION

    A. Bond sisal fiber to both sides of copper base with two coats asphalt.

    B. Thoroughly embed wire fabric into asphalt on one side of base sheet, cover with one layer kraft paper.

    C. Thoroughly embed cotton fabric into asphalt on opposite side of base sheet. Coat fabric with one coat asphalt, apply and embed one layer of kraft paper.

2.02 PERFORMANCE

    A. Fabricated flexible flashing shall weigh no less than 17 oz. per square yard.

    B. Fabricated membrane shall have bursting strength of no less than 190 lbs. per square inch.

    C. Membrane shall not crack when bent over a 1/2 inch mandrel at 0 degrees F.

Figure 9.7b

Proprietary Specifications identify the desired products by brand name, model number, or trade name and name the manufacturers who produce similar and acceptable products. Sometimes referred to as "single source specifying", this method is considered proprietary, even without mention of the name of the manufacturer, provided the product is only available from one, or a limited number of sources. The proprietary specification provides certain distinct advantages as follows:

- Allows control of product selection.
- Provides technical and performance assurance through manufacturer's data based on product research, testing and performance.
- Provides simplification of the bidding process.
- Allows simplification of technical communication in the OPC relationship.
- Reduces the design professional's exposure to contingent liability for product failure.

The proprietary specification is generally applied in one of two distinct ways. The Closed Proprietary Specification names a single product and manufacturer and offers the contractor little flexibility in the use or proposal to use a product of equal or similar attribute, quality or performance. In some cases, the specified product is the only available product that satisfies the designer's intention and application. In order to assure a reasonable degree of competition among manufacturers of similar products, the specifier will often pre-qualify two or more available products from competing manufacturers and list those products as acceptable for use in the subject project. This approach is known as the Open Proprietary Specification, and to some degree overcomes the disadvantage of reduced or non-existent competition characteristic of the Closed Proprietary Specification.

Performance Specifications

A third type of specification does not require lengthy descriptions of materials, assemblies, applications or fabrication or mix. It is non-proprietary, yet establishes parameters whereby the contractor can understand the function and required results intended for the specified item as well as the criteria by which compliance can be verified. This type of specification is known as the Performance Specification. Figure 9.9 is a performance specification for concrete. Figure 9.6 shows a comparison of descriptive specification methods for the same basic material. The performance specification does not provide the proportions of the materials to be used in the mix, but specifies that the concrete shall, after 28 days attain a minimum compressive strength of 2500 psi.

The Performance Specification makes a statement about the results expected from a material, assembly, or piece of equipment. It also provides criteria whereby compliance with those results can be verified. Figure 9.10 illustrates a performance specification for flexible membrane flashing intended for use in a masonry cavity wall. Figures 9.7a, 9.8, and 9.10 offer a comparison of descriptive, proprietary, and performance specifying for similar application of flexible flashing material.

PART 2 - PRODUCTS

2.01   MATERIALS - FLEXIBLE FABRIC FLASHING

A.   Acceptable Products:

  1. Cop-R-Guard as manufactured by ABC Products, Amherst MA.

  2. Flex-Flash as manufactured by Flexible lashings Co., Dimebox TX.

  3. Copper-Fab as manufactured by Flashing Specialties, Reagan, CA.

  4. Substitutions: In accordance with Section 01600.

B.   Material shall weigh no less than 17 oz. per square yard.

C.   Fabricated flashing shall have bursting strength of no less than 190 lbs. per square inch.

D.   Fabricated flashing shall not crack when bent over a 1/2 inch mandrel at 0 degrees F.

Figure 9.8

2.06   CONCRETE STRENGTH

A. Standard Structural Concrete: Compressive strengths of standard structural concrete shall be capable of minimum allowable compressive strength developed at 28 days as follows:

1. Class AA Concrete: 3750 psi.

2. Class A Concrete: 3000 psi.

3. Class C Concrete: 2500 psi.

4. Class D Concrete: 2000 psi.

B. Non-Structural Concrete: all non-structural concrete used for drives, approaches, walks, curbs, drains, etc. shall have a strength of at least 3000 p.s.i. after 28 days, unless otherwise required by the drawings.

2.07   CONCRETE PROPORTIONING

A. Standard and Lightweight Structural Concrete:

1. The testing laboratory shall establish exact quantities of ingredients required to produce specified concrete.

2. In addition to the above requirements the concrete shall:

a. Have a slump of 4 inches unless otherwise called for on drawings.

b. Work readily into corners and angles of forms and reinforcements without excessive vibration and without permitting materials to segregate or free water to collect on surface.

c. In general, improve workability by adjusting grading rather than by adding water.

Figure 9.9

PART 2 - PRODUCTS

2.01 MATERIALS - FLEXIBLE FABRIC FLASHING

A. Fabricate from 3 oz. copper reinforced with sisal fibers; cotton fabric, composed of closely woven twill having combined thread count in warp and filling of at least 130, weighing at least 6.66 oz. per yd. before saturation; woven wire mesh, composed of 21 gauge, plain steel wire fabricated with 2 1/2 meshes per inch in each direction; asphaltic binder conforming to ASTM 312; covered both sides with kraft paper, weighing no less than 45 lbs per 100 sq. ft., creped, impregnated thoroughly with bitumen conforming to ASTM 450.

B. Fabricated flexible flashing shall weigh no less than 17 oz. per square yard.

C. Fabricated membrane shall have bursting strength of no less than 190 lbs. per square inch.

D. Membrane shall not crack when bent over a 1/2 inch mandrel at 0 degrees F.

Figure 9.10

The advantages of performance specifying are listed below: .

- Improved products and applications are often elicited from innovative industrial producers.
- Constructors competing for the contract have greater flexibility in eliciting competitive bids.
- The specifier has more latitude in combining descriptive specifying techniques with performance criteria (as illustrated in Figure 9.7b).
- This method generally satisfies government and public project non-proprietary requirements.

Although the advantages of performance specifying seem to represent an "ideal" approach, there are also certain disadvantages, the most prominent of which are listed below:

- The specifier must be sure that current technology and manufacturers are capable and willing to meet the criteria of the performance specification. Confirmation may be necessary.
- An incomplete performance specification can result in loss of quality control for the materials, assemblies, equipment, and workmanship that go into a project.
- If performance criteria are the primary means of specifying, many or most of the related contract documents must also be specially written and designed in order not to create ambiguities and conflicts.
- The seeming advantage of encouraging "creative innovation" from manufacturers and competing constructors may be more than can be realistically expected within the time limits set for availability of contract documents and the bidding process.

Reference Standards Specifications

Industry standards have been frequently mentioned as references throughout the contract documents. Industry standards are documented criteria, often produced by industry associations, professional societies, and private research organizations. By general usage throughout the construction industry, these standards have become accepted and applied to describe and further specify the attributes, performance, and accepted usage of a particular material, assembly, or piece of equipment required for the project. Such industry standards, also called Reference Standards, can be included as shown in Figures 9.11a through 9.11b—a typical specification for cast-in-place concrete. Note that reference standards of the American Society of Testing Materials (ASTM) and the American Concrete Institute (ACI) are used most extensively in Part 2— Products.

As can be seen from these illustrations, the frequent use of these and other referenced industry standards from a variety of sources has become an integral part of the common language of the modern day technical construction specification.

As with the other three major methods of specifying recognized by this text, reference standard specifying has certain distinct advantages, some of which are similar to the benefits of other methods, and some of which are unique to reference standard specifying. The more unique advantages can be summed up as follows:

- By skillfully incorporating well-known standards into the specification, the writer can often avoid tedious and lengthy descriptions of materials and applications.

SECTION 03300
CAST-IN-PLACE CONCRETE

PART 1 - GENERAL

1.01   REQUIREMENTS INCLUDED

Poured-in place concrete, foundations and other concrete items specified in other Sections.

1.02   RELATED REQUIREMENTS

A.   Section 02800 - Site Improvements.

B.   Section 03100 - Concrete Formwork.

C.   Section 03200 - Concrete Reinforcement.

D.   Section 03320 - Concrete Topping: Concrete topping and curbs over existing construction.

E.   Section 03346 - Finishing Concrete Surfaces.

1.03   QUALITY ASSURANCE

A.   Reference Standards: Comply with all applicable Federal, State and local codes, safety regulations, Portland Cement Assoc. Standards, Ready Mixed Concrete Assoc. Standards, Texas Aggregates Assoc. Standards and others referred to herein.

B.   Tests and Submittals in accordance with Section 01410.

1.   Mix Design and Tests: The mix design for all concrete be established by a testing laboratory under provisions of Section 01410. All tests shall be performed in accordance with standard procedures as follows:

a.   ASTM C 172 Standard Method of Sampling fresh concrete

b.   ASTM C 31 Standard Method of Making and Curing Concrete compressive and Flexural Strength. Test Specimens in the field.

c.   ASTM C 143 Standard Method of test for Slump of Portland Cement Concrete.

d.   ASTM C 39 Standard Method of test for Compressive Strength of Molded Concrete Cylinders.

2.   Access: The Architect shall have access to all places where materials are stored, proportioned or mixed.

3.   Proportions: The testing laboratory shall submit, prior to the start of concrete work, contemplated proportions and the results of preliminary 7 day compression test. Submit a separate set of proportions and test results for pumpcrete if used.

4.   Slump test shall be made by the testing laboratory of concrete delivered to the site for each set of test cylinders.

5.   Standard test cylinders of all concrete placed in the work shall be made by the testing laboratory. One (1) set of four (4) cylinders shall be taken for each 100 cubic yards or fraction there of poured on each day.

6.   Two (2) cylinders of each set shall be tested at 7 days and two (2) cylinders to be tested at 28 days

7.   Reports of above tests and field quality control tests: Provide copies of test reports:

1 copy to Engineer

2 copies to Architect

2 copies to Contractor

8.   Mill reports: The Contractor shall furnish mill reports of test of cement showing compliance with specifications.

9.   All expenses for concrete design and testing shall be paid by the General Contractor

Section 03300 Page 1

Figure 9.11a

C. Inspection: Inspection of Reinforcing Steel and Concrete Placement: Before any concrete is poured on any particular portion of project, reinforcing steel will be checked and approved by Architect or Engineer. Correct any errors or discrepancies before concrete is placed. Such checking and approval shall not relieve Contractor from his responsibility to comply with the Contract requirements.

1.04 REFERENCE STANDARDS

A. ASTM C33 - Concrete Aggregates.

B. ASTM C150 - Portland Cement

C. ACI 318 - Building Code Requirements for Reinforced Concrete

D. ASTM C494 - Chemical Admixtures for Concrete.

E. ASTM C94 - Ready-Mixed Concrete.

F. ACI 304 - Recommended Practice for Measuring, Mixing, Transporting and Placing Concrete.

G. ACI 305 - Recommended Practice for Hot Weather Concreting.

H. ACI 306 - Recommended Practice for Cold Weather Concreting

I. ACI 301 - Specifications for Structural Concrete for Buildings

J. ACI 311 - Recommended Practice for Concrete Inspection.

1.05 SUBMITTALS

A. Submit product data in accordance with Section 01300.

B. Provide product data for specified products.

C. Submit manufactures' instructions in accordance with Section 01400.

D. Provide shop Drawings showing construction joints.

E. Provide schedule of pouring operations for approval before concreting operations begin.

F. Conform to Mix Design in accordance with 1.03-B.

1.06 PRODUCT DELIVERY, STORAGE AND HANDLING

Store materials delivered to the job and protect from foreign matter and exposure to any element which would reduce the properties of the material.

1.07 COORDINATION

A. Obtain information and instructions from other trades and suppliers in ample time to schedule and coordinate the installation of items furnished by them to be embedded in concrete so provisions for their work can be made without delaying the project.

B. Do any cutting and patching made necessary by failure or delay in complying with these requirements at no cost to Owner.

PART 2 - PRODUCTS

2.01 MATERIALS - STANDARD STRUCTURAL CONCRETE

A. Portland Cement: Type I and III shall conform to "Standard Specifications for Portland Cement" (ASTM C - 150) and shall be of domestic manufacture. Use only one brand of cement unless otherwise authorized by Architect.

B. Fine Aggregate: ASTM C33, natural bank sand or river sand, washed and screened so as to produce a minimum percentage of voids.

C. Normal Weight Coarse Aggregate: ASTM C33, gravel or crushed stone suitably processed, washed and screened, and shall consist of hard, durable particles without adherent coatings. Aggregate shall range from 1/4" to 1-1/4", well graded between the size limits.

Section 03300   Page 2

Figure 9.11b

- This technique allows for the blending of descriptive specifying with performance specifying. In this way, the information included can be used by the contractor in a most economical and efficient manner.
- By incorporating related industry standards, the design professional calls upon the most advanced technology available from recognized specialists in the specified field.
- Properly applied, the referenced standard serves as an additional resource to the design professional's judgment and choice of materials and application.

Unfortunately, not all industry standards are adequate for every purpose. It is vitally important that the specifier study and be intimately acquainted with all of the information contained in the standard to which he refers. He should also be able to produce a copy of that standard if challenged. Even among the most commonly referenced standards there may be certain information that is not in keeping with the design professional's intentions for the subject at hand. For example, although certain provisions within the referenced standard ASTM C 150 may be adequate for the specifier's intention, other provisions published in the same standard may confuse or even conflict with the specifier's intent. Close inspection of ASTM C 150 reveals the fact that the standard for Portland Cement covers not one but five types of Portland Cement. Several of the types have further subcategories, so that there are actually eight distinct types of Portland Cement covered by the document. All are arranged and described in the context of the different applications that may be employed for their use. Clearly, the specifier must be careful to state the type of Portland Cement he intends (see Figure 9.11), rather than to simply specify Portland Cement. As often happens with the "unspecific" use of the reference standard, the contractor may base his contract price on the least expensive of the eight types of material covered by the standard. This least expensive type may not be satisfactory for the designer's intent or the structural adequacy of the building. ASTM C 150 also specifies some 18 other ASTM standards that may be applied to the subject at hand. These other incorporated standards do have a direct bearing on the specification. The specifier must be certain that he is familiar with the provisions of the reference standards because he may otherwise be including specifications contrary to his intent, the owner's budget, and the safety and welfare of those who shall ultimately occupy that building.

Specifying Techniques

Figure 9.12a through 9.12c illustrate Section 01020—Cash Allowances. The Cash Allowance is a commonly used specification technique. A cash allowance provides for certain materials, assemblies or applications to be included in the contract sum provided by the bidder or contractor. It does not restrict or require an exact specification concurrent with the execution of the contract for construction. Cash allowances can be specified to provide certain amounts to be included in the contract sum for the purchase of the subject material, assembly, or piece of equipment. In this case, the amount provided for is usually restricted to the purchase, packaging, pick-up, transportation, delivery, protection, storage, and payment of any required sales or use taxes connected with the identified subject. The contractor may be responsible (by requirements included in the specification) for calculating the entire quantity needed and providing in the contract sum an adequate

SECTION 01020
CASH ALLOWANCES

PART 1 - GENERAL

1.01   REQUIREMENTS INCLUDED

A. Schedule of monetary amounts of allowances in Contract Sum for purchase and delivery of designated products.

B. Costs in Contract Sum other than in Allowance.

C. Procedures for administration of Allowances.

D. The allowances stated herein shall be included in the Base Bid.

1.02   RELATED REQUIREMENTS

Article 4.8 - General Conditions

1.03   UNIT MATERIAL ALLOWANCES

A. For Brick Masonry (Section 04300)

1. For brick masonry type "A" provide a unit price allowance of $ 2000.00_ per one thousand (1000) units as required to complete the installation of masonry according to the drawings.

2. For brick masonry type "B" provide a unit price allowance of $ 1,500.00_ per one thousand (1000) units as required to complete the installation of masonry according to the drawings.

3. For brick masonry type "C" provide a unit price allowance of $ 1,500.00 per one thousand (1000) units as required to complete the installation of masonry according to the drawings.

4. For brick masonry type "D" provide a unit price allowance of $ 2,000.00 per one thousand (1000) units as required to complete the installation of masonry according to the drawings.

5. Contractor (Bidder) is responsible for determining total quantity of brick of each type required including overage for selection, cutting and wastage.

B. Carpet - Glue Down Type (Section 09697)

1. For Carpet (CPT) scheduled type "A", provide a unit price allowance of $ 14.00 per yard for the total volume of type "A" carpet required.

2. For Carpet Tile (CPT) scheduled type "B", provide a unit price allowance of $ 17.00 per yard for the total volume of type "B" carpet required.

3. Contractor (Bidder) is responsible for determining total quantity of carpet of each type required including overage for cutting and wastage.

C. Wall Coverings   (Section 09952)

1. For Vinyl Wall Covering (VWC) scheduled on the drawings, provide a unit price allowance of $ 25.00 per roll to the extent of material required.

2. Contractor (Bidder) is responsible for determining the total quantity of VWC required for the project, including overage required for cutting and wastage.

D. Ceramic Tile

1. For Ceramic Mosaic tile as scheduled for the floors (Section 09311) provide a unit price allowance of $ 2.50 per square foot of tile required.

2. For Ceramic Tile as scheduled for walls (Section 09312) provide a unit price allowance of $ 2.50 per square foot of tile required.

3. Contractor (Bidder) is responsible for determining the total quantity of Ceramic Tile required for the project, including overage required for selection, cutting and wastage.

Section 01020 Page 1

Figure 9.12a

E. Paving Tile

    1. For paving tile as scheduled for certain floors (Section 09314), provide a unit price allowance of $ 7.00 per square foot of tile required.

    2. Contractor (Bidder) is responsible for determining toe total quantity of Paving Tile required for the project, including overage required for selection, cutting and wastage.

1.04   LUMP SUM ALLOWANCES

A. Interior Sinage   (Section 10440): Provide an allowance of $ 500.00 for the purchase of interior signage as required by the Contract Documents.

B. Exterior Signage   (Section 10430): Provide an allowance of $ 2,000.00 for the purchase of exterior signage including building letters as required by the Contract Documents.

C. Landscaping - Section 02900: Provide and allowance of $ 10,000.00 for landscaping plants, materials, accessories, labor, transportation costs, and all other costs incidental thereto.

D. Building Plaque: Provide an allowance of $ 1,000.00 for building plaque including accessories and labor to install.

E. Note: The inclusion of labor and other expenses related to installation is contrary to the General Provisions of Paragraph 1.05.

1.05   COSTS INCLUDED IN ALLOWANCES

A. Unless otherwise specified in the Allowance description in Paragraph 1.03, costs included in allowances shall include cost of product to Contractor or subcontractor, less applicable trade discounts.

B. Delivery to site.

1.06   CONTRACTOR COSTS INCLUDED IN CONTRACT SUM (Not in Allowances)

A. Products handling at site, including unloading, uncrating and storage.

B. Protection of products from elements and from damage.

C. Unless otherwise specified in Paragraph 1.03, Contract Sum shall include labor for installation and finishing.

D. Unless otherwise specified in Paragraph 1.03, Contract Sum shall include other expenses required to complete installation.

E. Contractor overhead and profit.

1.07   ARCHITECT RESPONSIBILITIES

A. Consult with Contractor in consideration of products, suppliers and installers.

B. Select products, obtain Owner's written decision and transmit full information to Contractor:

    1. Manufacturer, product, catalog number and finishes.

    2. Supplier and installer as applicable.

    3. Cost to Contractor, delivered to the site and installed.

C. Prepare Change Order in accordance with Section 01028.

1.08   CONTRACTOR RESPONSIBILITIES

A. Assist Architect in determining suppliers and installers; obtain proposals when requested.

B. Make recommendations for Architect consideration.

C. Promptly notify Architect of any reasonable objections against supplier or installer.

D. On notification of selection execute purchase agreement with designated supplier and installer.

Section 01020 Page 2

Figure 9.12b

E. Arrange for and process shop drawings, product data, and samples.

F. Arrange for delivery. Promptly inspect products upon delivery for completeness, damage, and defects. Submit claims for transportation damage.

G. Install, adjust, and finish products.

PART 2 - PRODUCTS

Not Used

PART 3 - EXECUTION

Not Used

END OF SECTION

Figure 9.12c

provision for the tools, labor, and accessories necessary to incorporate the subject into the work. On the other hand, the cash allowance may be related to the entire cost of a particular unit of work, in which case the intention must be clearly specified (as illustrated by the example in Figure 9.12).

Another similar specifying technique is the use of the Contingency Allowance which provides a specific amount of money to be included in the contract sum to be used or not at the complete discretion of the owner. The very nature of competitive bidding precludes an exact or finite completed cost that can be estimated with 100% accuracy prior to bidding or negotiating procedures or the agreement on a final contract sum. Because of this common uncertainty, a *contingency* is often used to add a percentage of the total estimate—or a certain sum is intended to apply in case the estimate of cost proves to be low when a final determination is made. In many cases, corporate boards and groups of public officials must establish budgets to fund construction projects. Any appropriations from this budget are determined before contracts for construction can be awarded with the full authority of the owner (who may be not a single individual, but many stockholders or the public at large). The contingency allowance provides a ''cushion'' that can be applied to improve, correct, or add to the work without the need to go through a tedious, often futile process of gaining additional appropriations for such expenditures.

The term Nonrestrictive Specification refers to a *technique* of specifying rather than a *method* of specifying. It can be seen that descriptive, performance, and reference standard specifying all can be referred to as nonrestrictive specifications in that no clear restriction to a single proprietary or exclusionary product is stated or implied. Provided a number of alternate but acceptable products are listed, the open proprietary specification could be classified as nonrestrictive. There has been a concerted effort by public sector officials and legislators to enforce standards of specifying so that they do not restrict the acquisition and use of materials and products to certain producers to the unfair and discriminatory exclusion of others. At the same time, this type of specifying also allows for the greatest possible latitude of competition. A typical statute from the volumes of public law is shown in the excerpt from Public Law 92-500, Federal Water Pollution Control Act, Section 204(a)(6) which states:

''. . . no specification for bids in connection with such works shall be written in such a manner as to contain proprietary, exclusionary or discriminatory requirements, other than those based on performance, unless such requirements are necessary to test or demonstrate a specific thing or to provide for necessary interchangeability of parts and equipment, or at least followed by the words 'or equal'. . .''.

The ''Or Equal'' Statement

The statement in the previous example is typical of a sometimes misunderstood and often mis-applied principle that two materials or items of equipment may be exact duplicates of each other and are therefore somehow ''equal'' in application, performance and intended use in the project. Traditionally, the term ''or equal'' has been commonly applied to the closed proprietary specification which names a specific product or products, while loosening the restriction by implying that if the bidder or contractor can provide a product of equal performance, application, use, and quality, the substitute product shall probably be approved. There are many examples of the fallacy in this device of specifying. For instance, consider three manufacturers of aluminum windows. Manufacturer A has been in business for 50 years, is financially secure, well advertised, and continually makes improvements to his window in keeping with the "state of the art". The unique weatherstripping system is patented and the manufacturer's literature indicates that air infiltration measured by ASTM E 283 is less than one tenth of one cubic foot for each square foot of surface area. Product A costs $50. His product is specified with the "or equal" statement following. During the bidding process, one of the bidders requests to substitute the product of Manufacturer B which is "equal" to product A. Manufacturer B sells his window for $30. Upon review of Product B, all features seem to be of similar quality. Weatherstripping seems supple and tight, the five year warranty is similar to that of product A and the literature suggests that the product meets or exceeds the minimum air infiltration requirements of the U.S. Department of Commerce. The product is approved. After some 14 months of occupancy, the owner complains that his windows leak in a blowing rain and seem to exhibit a high degree of air infiltration which is causing unusual consumption of energy. Upon investigating the problem, the design professional discovers that the weatherstripping has failed. He attempts to enforce the warranty and discovers that manufacturer B has gone out of business and the warranty is useless. The contractor's one year warranty has also expired. Obviously the products were not "equal" and the owner either suffers with the failed product or spends many times the "savings" to replace it.

A more satisfactory approach to the specification technique does not rely upon the "or equal" statement, and involves taking the following steps:

- Provide a Division 1 statement in Section 01600—Materials and Equipment, as illustrated in Figures 9.13a and 9.13b.
- Thoroughly investigate no less than three products of manufacturers of substantial means and ability. Determine the reliability of each product by requiring and reviewing qualified testing laboratory data as to attributes that would not be obvious to the casual inspector. List no less than three of those products (if possible) that prove to be "reasonably" equivalent to the needs of the project as being acceptable for the intended use as illustrated in Figure 9.8.
- Write performance criteria in Part 1 of the specification that can be measured by the testing laboratory.

Section 01600—Material and Equipment, is the Division 1 section of the specifications that provides the general parameters for controlling the quality of materials and equipment in the project. Figure 9.13b (paragraph 1.07 from that section) provides a procedure for substitutions to be considered and approved by the design professional. Subparagraph H makes the contractor responsible if the substitute product fails.

SECTION 01600
MATERIAL AND EQUIPMENT

PART 1 - GENERAL

1.01 REQUIREMENTS INCLUDED

 A. Products.

 B. Workmanship.

 C. Manufacturers' Instructions.

 D. Transportation and Handling.

 E. Storage and Protection.

 F. Substitutions and Product Options.

1.02 RELATED REQUIREMENTS

 A. Section 01010 - Summary of Work: Owner-furnished Products. Reference Standards.

 B. Section 01300 - Submittals: Submittal of manufacturers' certificates.

 C. Section 01700 - Contract Closeout: Operation and maintenance data. Warranties and Bonds.

1.03 PRODUCTS

 A. Products include material, equipment and systems.

 B. Comply with Specifications and referenced standards as minimum requirements.

 C. Components required to be supplied in quantity within a Specification section shall be the same, and shall be interchangeable.

1.04 TRANSPORTATION AND HANDLING

 A. Transport products by methods to avoid product damage; deliver in undamaged condition in manufacturer's unopened containers or packaging, dry.

 B. Provide equipment and personnel to handle products by methods to prevent soiling or damage.

 C. Promptly inspect shipments to assure that products comply with requirements, quantities are correct, and products are undamaged.

1.05 STORAGE AND PROTECTION

 A. Store products in accordance with manufacturer's instructions, with seals and labels intact and legible. Store sensitive products in weather-tight enclosures; maintain within temperature and humidity ranges required by manufacturer's instructions.

 B. For exterior storage of fabricated products, place on sloped supports above ground. Cover products subject to deterioration with impervious sheet covering; provide ventilation to avoid condensation.

 C. Store loose granular materials on solid surfaces in a well-drained area; prevent mixing with foreign matter.

 D. Arrange storage to provide access for inspection. Periodically inspect to assure products are undamaged, and are maintained under required conditions.

 E. After installation, provide coverings to protect products from damage from traffic and construction operations, remove when no longer needed.

Figure 9.13a

1.06 PRODUCT OPTIONS

A. Within 10 days after date of Contract, submit complete list of major products proposed, with name of manufacturer, trade name, and model.

B. Options:

1. Products Specified by Reference Standards or by Description Only: Any Product meeting those standards.

2. Products Specified by Naming One or More Manufacturers within a Substitute Paragraph: Submit a request for substitution for any manufacturer not specifically named.

3. Products Specified by Naming Several Manufacturers: Products of named manufacturers meeting specifications; no options, no substitutions allowed.

4. Products specified by naming only one manufacturer: substitutions shall be considered in accordance with Paragraph 1.08..

1.07 SUBSTITUTIONS

A. The listing of product manufacturers in the various sections of the Specifications, or on the drawings, is intended to establish a standard of quality only and is not intended to preclude open, competitive bidding. See Instructions to Bidders for instructions as to proposing substitutions prior to receipt of bids.

B. Equal products of other manufacturers will be acceptable provided the applicable provisions of the GENERAL CONDITIONS and SUPPLEMENTARY GENERAL CONDITIONS are complied with.

C. Substitution requests made by the Contractor after the execution of the Agreement Between Owner and Contractor must be received by the Architect within 10 days of the Order to Proceed with the work.

1. Document each request with complete data substantiating compliance of proposed substitution with Contract Documents. Substitution requests shall include the name of the material or equipment for which it is to be substituted and a complete description of the proposed substitute including drawings, details, samples, performance and test data and any other information necessary for an evaluation, including modifications required for other parts of the Work.

2. Substantiate the motivation of the requested substitution and include any proposed savings in cost that would accrue to the Owner if the substitution were approved.

3. Request constitutes a representation that Contractor:

a. Has investigated proposed product and determined that it meets or exceeds, in all respects, specified product.

b. Will provide the same warranty for substitution as for specified product.

c. Will coordinate installation and make other changes which may be required for Work to be complete in all respects.

d. Waives claims for additional costs or time which may subsequently become apparent.

D. After execution of the Contract Agreement, proposed substitutions will be considered only if there is no increase in cost to the Owner, no decrease in quality, and only when submitted by or through and bearing the approval of the General Contractor.

E. Substitutions will not be considered when they are indicated or implied on shop drawing or product data submittals without separate written request, or when acceptance will require substantial revision of Contract Documents.

F. The burden of proof of the merit of the proposed substitute is upon the Contractor. The Architect's decision of approval or disapproval of a proposed substitution shall be final.

G. Requests for time extensions will NOT be approved for delays due to rejected substitutions. NO substitution will be allowed without the Architect's approval in writing.

H. Should a substitution be approved under the foregoing provisions, and subsequently prove to be defective or otherwise unsatisfactory for the service for which it was intended, the Contractor shall, without cost to Owner, and without obligation on the part of the Architects, replace the same with the material originally specified.

Section 01600   Page 2

Figure 9.13b

Testing of Materials and Systems

To protect the owner's interest and investment, and the reputations of the design and the construction professional, there is no substitute for the safeguard provided in the required testing of various key materials, manufacturer's products, assemblies and equipment that go into the construction of modern buildings. With the major emphasis on economy, the testing of materials to ensure adequacy is one of the few "checks and balances" that are afforded the OPC equation. Testing has come to be more and more of a necessity as construction in the United States has entered the "high tech" age and as the documented evidence of building failures has affected the lives and fortunes of more and more owners, building professionals, contractors and building occupants. Section 01400— Quality Control is the Division 1 section which establishes the criteria for testing of materials.

The National Bureau of Standards

The National Bureau of Standards (NBS), an agency of the United States government, Department of Commerce, Environmental Sciences Administration was officially established on March 3, 1903. From its inception, NBS has been responsible for the custody, preparation, and testing of standards, as well as solving standard problems and determining the physical constants and critical properties of materials. NBS is empowered to render services to scientific societies, colleges and universities, and business firms. NBS has, from the beginning, been instrumental in establishing the basis for most of the industry standards previously discussed. NBS is the creator and custodian of the nation's system of measurement in all things physical and scientific. For a fee, NBS is equipped and qualified to set testing standards, calibrate testing equipment, and certify private testing laboratories as being properly equipped to conduct a variety of tests for building materials, systems, and related areas.

The American Society for Testing Materials

The American Society for Testing Materials, organized in the early 1900's, is a non-profit, educational organization dedicated to the publication of voluntary consensus standards to benefit more than 30,000 members worldwide. ASTM's membership includes engineers, designers, business persons, industrialists, researchers, administrators and consumers from both the private and public sector. The 66 volume *Annual Book of ASTM Standards* contains over 7,000 separate documents dedicated to technical information, specifications and standards dealing with a wide variety of scientific subjects. Originally focused only on materials such as steel and cement, ASTM now develops standards for such diverse subjects as robotics, security systems, textiles, resource recovery, sports equipment, and medical devices. ASTM is organized into 140 technical committees which accomplish the actual writing of standards. ASTM committee members contribute their time and talent to create standards that affect their own work and the work of others.

Cost of Testing

There appear to be at least two distinct "schools of thought" as to how the cost of testing should be administered and financed. Article 7 of AIA Document A201—*General Conditions of the Contract for Construction* is reproduced in Figure 9.14. (For more information on the General Conditions, see Chapter 7). Paragraph 7.7.1 requires that the contractor pay for any testing required by ". . . laws, ordinances, rules, regulations or orders of any public authority having jurisdiction. . .".

7.7 TESTS

7.7.1 If the Contract Documents, laws, ordinances, rules, regulations or orders of any public authority having jurisdiction require any portion of the Work to be inspected, tested or approved, the Contractor shall give the Architect timely notice of its readiness so the Architect may observe such inspection, testing or approval. The Contractor shall bear all costs of such inspections, tests or approvals conducted by public authorities. Unless otherwise provided, the Owner shall bear all costs of other inspections, tests or approvals.

7.7.2 If the Architect determines that any Work requires special inspection, testing, or approval which Subparagraph 7.7.1 does not include, he will, upon written authorization from the Owner, instruct the Contractor to order such special inspection, testing or approval, and the Contractor shall give notice as provided in Subparagraph 7.7.1. If such special inspection or testing reveals a failure of the Work to comply with the requirements of the Contract Documents, the Contractor shall bear all costs thereof, including compensation for the Architect's additional services made necessary by such failure; otherwise the Owner shall bear such costs, and an appropriate Change Order shall be issued.

7.7.3 Required certificates of inspection, testing or approval shall be secured by the Contractor and promptly delivered by him to the Architect.

7.7.4 If the Architect is to observe the inspections, tests or approvals required by the Contract Documents, he will do so promptly and, where practicable, at the source of supply.

7.8 INTEREST

7.8.1 Payments due and unpaid under the Co____ Documents shall bear interest from the da__ ___ due at such rate as the parties may ____ __ or, in the absence thereof, a__ ___ the place of the Project.

7.9 ARBITRATION

7.9.1 All claims, disputes and ___ between the Contractor and the ___ relating to, the Contract Docume__ of, except as provided in Subpa__ spect to the Architect's decisions artistic effect, and except for clai__ waived by the making or acceptanc_ provided by Subparagraphs 9.9.4 an_ cided by arbitration in accordance wi__ Industry Arbitration Rules of the An__ Association then obtaining unless the ____ ___ally agree otherwise. No arbitration arising ___, or relating to the Contract Documents shall include, by consolidation, joinder or in any other manner, the Architect, his employees or consultants except by written consent containing a specific reference to the Owner-Contractor Agreement and signed by the Architect, the Owner, the Contractor and any other person sought to be joined. No arbitration shall include by consolidation, joinder or in any other manner, parties other than the Owner, the Contractor and any other persons substantially involved in a common question of fact or law, whose presence is

required if complete relief is to be accorded in the arbitration. No person other than the Owner or Contractor shall be included as an original third party or additional third party to an arbitration whose interest or responsibility is insubstantial. Any consent to arbitration involving an additional person or persons shall not constitute consent to arbitration of any dispute not described therein or with any person not named or described therein. The foregoing agreement to arbitrate and any other agreement to arbitrate with an additional person or persons duly consented to by the parties to the Owner-Contractor Agreement shall be specifically enforceable under the prevailing arbitration law. The award rendered by the arbitrators shall be final, and judgment may be entered upon it in accordance with applicable law in any court having jurisdiction thereof.

7.9.2 Notice of the demand for arbitration shall be filed in writing with the other party to the Owner-Contractor Agreement and with the American Arbitration Association, and a copy shall be filed with the Architect. The demand for arbitration shall be made within the time limits specified in Subparagraph 2.2.12 where applicable, and in all other cases within a reasonable time after the claim, dispute or other matter in question has arisen, and in no event shall it be made after the date when institution of legal or equitable proceedings based on such claim, dispute or other matter in question would be barred by the applicable statute of limitations.

7.9.3 Unless otherwise agreed i_ ___ the Contractor shall carry on the Work ___ ___rogress during any arbitration _____ ___er shall continue to ___ ___ __ accordance wi__ __

_____ __e is the ____nts for ___ Sub___reto. ___ _he date ___e is no notice to ___ _he Owner-Contractor ____r date as may be established

___ The Date of Substantial Completion of the Work or designated portion thereof is the Date certified by the Architect when construction is sufficiently complete, in accordance with the Contract Documents, so the Owner can occupy or utilize the Work or designated portion thereof for the use for which it is intended.

8.1.4 The term day as used in the Contract Documents shall mean calendar day unless otherwise specifically designated.

8.2 PROGRESS AND COMPLETION

8.2.1 All time limits stated in the Contract Documents are of the essence of the Contract.

AIA DOCUMENT A201 • GENERAL CONDITIONS OF THE CONTRACT FOR CONSTRUCTION • THIRTEENTH EDITION • AUGUST 1976
12   A201-1976   AIA® • © 1976 • THE AMERICAN INSTITUTE OF ARCHITECTS, 1735 NEW YORK AVENUE, N.W., WASHINGTON, D.C. 20006

(courtesy American Institute of Architects)

Figure 9.14

Paragraph 7.7.2 provides that the design professional shall give notice of any required testing not included in the previous paragraph, but it does not clearly state who pays for that testing. This matter must be determined by the design professional and stipulated in appropriate Division 1 sections.

Many owners and design professionals prefer to require that the contractor cover the costs of all testing, and stipulate that the testing laboratory be approved by the design professional. Section 01400—Quality Control is illustrated in Figures 9.15a and 9.15b. This section of Division 1 normally contains the general provisions for testing. When the contractor is required to pay for testing, related procedures are generally included in Section 01400 as illustrated in Figure 9.15c. On the other hand, many owners and design professionals prefer that testing be controlled by the owner, in which case the owner selects the laboratory and pays for the testing. When this approach is used, the provisions stated in Section 01400 should appear as shown in Figure 9.15d. In addition, the design professional may wish to add a Section 01410—Testing Laboratory Services to Division 1 to establish criteria for the testing laboratory.

Once the responsibility for testing materials has been resolved and established by the appropriate Division 1 sections, more detailed testing information should be stated in Part 1 of the individual specification sections.

Disputes

The matter of resolving disputes in the construction process has been discussed in previous chapters. There is growing interest and concern among the many participants in the construction industry on the subject of Risk Management. Risk management implies that disputes can and will be avoided if the principals in the OPC relationship establish sound, well documented, contractual relationships toward the joint goal of producing sound, well-constructed building projects to the profit and credit of all concerned. To successfully avoid risk, the design professional begins with the creation of well thought out, well coordinated, thorough contract documents. Unless the full intention of the contract document requirements is clearly "spelled out" and placed into the Project Manual in a uniform and consistent manner, disputes and misunderstandings are almost inevitable.

The General Conditions of the Contract may name the design professional and establish him as the interpreter of the intent of the contract documents. Figure 7.7 shows a portion of Article 2 of AIA Document A201—*General Conditions of the Contract for Construction*. This article defines the responsibility of the design professional. Good, sound, responsible specifications insure the design professional's ability to fulfill this responsibility to the mutual benefit of all parties to the OPC relationship.

The "Master" Specification

Creating a "master file" of specification sections (generally applicable to the types of projects encountered in professional practice) may be the design professional's best support for producing sound, meaningful specifications. Most design firms, government agencies, and large corporations use master specifications on a mandatory basis. A properly maintained, continually updated master specification file will return dividends more than worth the investment in its creation and maintenance.

SECTION 01400
QUALITY CONTROL

PART 1 - GENERAL

1.01   REQUIREMENTS INCLUDED

A.   General Quality Control.

B.   Workmanship.

C.   Manufacturer's Instructions.

D.   Manufacturer's Certificates.

E.   Manufacturers' Field Services.

F.   Testing of Materials, assemblies to ascertain quality of work.

1.02   RELATED REQUIREMENTS

A.   Section 01010 - Summary of the Work

B.   Section 01020 - Allowances

C.   Section 01300 - Submittals

1.03   QUALITY CONTROL, GENERAL

Maintain quality control over suppliers, manufacturers, products, services, site conditions, and workmanship, to produce work of specified quality and in any event, work conforming to the best standards of the industry or trade.

1.04   WORKMANSHIP

A.   Comply with industry standards except when more restrictive tolerances or specified requirements indicate more rigid standards or more precise workmanship. Conform to Reference Standards specified in individual Sections of the Specifications.

B.   Perform work by persons experienced in the particular unit of Work and who are otherwise qualified to produce workmanship of specified quality. Submit evidence of qualification if required to do so by the individual Section of the Specifications.

C.   Secure products in place in accordance with manufacturer's instructions and recommendations, with positive anchorage devices designed and sized to withstand stresses, vibration, and racking, using such accessories, devices or compounds that are compatible with the material or as recommended by the manufacturer.

1.05   MANUFACTURERS' INSTRUCTIONS

Comply with instructions in full detail, including each step in sequence. Should instructions conflict with Contract Documents, request clarification from Architect before proceeding.

1.06   MANUFACTURERS' CERTIFICATES

When required by individual Specifications Sections, submit manufacturer's certificate, in triplicate, that products meet or exceed specified requirements.

1.07   TESTING OF MATERIALS, SYSTEMS, ASSEMBLIES

A.   Owner will employ, under the provisions of Section 01410 the services of an Independent Testing Laboratory approved by the Architect to perform inspections, tests, and other services required by individual Specification Sections. Employment of Testing Laboratory by Owner, in no way relieves the Contractor of the obligation to perform the Work in strict accordance with the Contract Documents.

B.   Retesting: When the results of the Testing Laboratory's work show that any portion of the Work does not meet the requirements of the Contract Documents or other authority, the Contractor shall pay for retesting of corrected Work until satisfactory results to approval of Architect have been achieved.

Section 01400 Page 1

Figure 9.15a

216

C. Contractor shall cooperate with Testing Laboratory personnel, furnish tools, samples of materials, equipment, storage and assistance as requested.

D. The Contractor shall notify the Architect and the Testing Laboratory 24 hours prior to expected time for operations requiring testing services.

1.08 MINIMUM TESTING REQUIREMENTS

A. Soils Testing: In accordance with requirements of Section 02220 - Structure Base, Fill and Backfill, and Section 02265 - Landscape Grading.

B. Soil Compaction Tests: In accordance with Section 02220 - Structural Base, Fill and Backfilling.

C. Pavement Material and Base: In accordance with requirements of Section 02513 - Asphaltic Concrete Paving, and Section 02514 - Portland Cement Concrete Paving.

D. Concrete Tests: In accordance with Section 03300 - Cast-In-Place Concrete.

E. Other Specified Tests: In accordance with individual Sections of the Specifications.

F. Additional Tests not specified: In such instances where, in the opinion of the Architect, items may not meet the standards specified, additional tests may be required and so ordered by the Architect. If such tests reveal that specified standards have been met, the Contractor shall pay for the tests under the provisions of the Allowance for Testing specified in Section 01020. In the event that such tests reveal that specified standards have not been met, the Contractor shall pay for the tests from his own funds, at no cost to the Owner plus any retesting of corrected material that may be required additionally by the Architect.

PART 2 - PRODUCTS

Not Used

PART 3 - EXECUTION

Not Used

END OF SECTION

Figure 9.15b

1.07 TESTING OF MATERIALS, SYSTEMS, ASSEMBLIES

A. Contractor will employ the services of an Independent Testing Laboratory approved by the Architect to perform inspections, tests, and other services required by individual Specification Sections.

B. Retesting: When the results of the Testing Laboratory's work show that any portion of the Work does not meet the requirements of the Contract Documents or other authority, the Contractor shall pay for retesting of corrected Work until satisfactory results to approval of Architect have been achieved.

C. Contractor shall cooperate with Testing Laboratory personnel, furnish tools, samples of materials, equipment, storage and assistance as requested.

D. The Contractor shall notify the Architect and the Testing Laboratory 24 hours prior to expected time for operations requiring testing services.

E. Provide copies of Testing Laboratory reports as follows:

1. One copy to Owner

2. Two copies to Architect.

3. Retain 3 copies, 1 at jobsite.

1.08 MINIMUM TESTING REQUIREMENTS

A. Soils Testing: In accordance with requirements of Section 02220 - Structure Base, Fill and Backfill, and Section 02265 - Landscape Grading.

B. Soil Compaction Tests: In accordance with Section 02220 - Structural Base, Fill and Backfilling.

C. Pavement Material and Base: In accordance with requirements of Section 02513 - Asphaltic Concrete Paving, and Section 02514 - Portland Cement Concrete Paving.

D. Concrete Tests: In accordance with Section 03300 - Cast-In-Place Concrete.

E. Other Specified Tests: In accordance with individual Sections of the Specifications.

F. Additional Tests not specified: In such instances where, in the opinion of the Architect, items may not meet the standards specified, additional tests may be required and so ordered by the Architect. If such tests reveal that specified standards have been met, the Contractor shall pay for the tests under the provisions of the Allowance for Testing specified in Section 01020. In the event that such tests reveal that specified standards have not been met, the Contractor shall pay for the tests from his own funds, at no cost to the Owner plus any retesting of corrected material that may be required additionally by the Architect.

Figure 9.15c

1.07   TESTING OF MATERIALS, SYSTEMS, ASSEMBLIES

A. Owner will employ, under the provisions of Section 01410 the services of an Independent Testing Laboratory approved by the Architect to perform inspections, tests, and other services required by individual Specification Sections. Employment of Testing Laboratory by Owner, in no way relieves the Contractor of the obligation to perform the Work in strict accordance with the Contract Documents.

B. Retesting: When the results of the Testing Laboratory's work show that any portion of the Work does not meet the requirements of the Contract Documents or other authority, the Contractor shall pay for retesting of corrected Work until satisfactory results to approval of Architect have been achieved.

C. Contractor shall cooperate with Testing Laboratory personnel, furnish tools, samples of materials, equipment, storage and assistance as requested.

D. The Contractor shall notify the Architect and the Testing Laboratory 24 hours prior to expected time for operations requiring testing services.

1.08   MINIMUM TESTING REQUIREMENTS

A. Soils Testing: In accordance with requirements of Section 02220 - Structure Base, Fill and Backfill, and Section 02265 - Landscape Grading.

B. Soil Compaction Tests: In accordance with Section 02220 - Structural Base, Fill and Backfilling.

C. Pavement Material and Base: In accordance with requirements of Section 02513 - Asphaltic Concrete Paving, and Section 02514 - Portland Cement Concrete Paving.

D. Concrete Tests: In accordance with Section 03300 - Cast-In-Place Concrete.

E. Other Specified Tests: In accordance with individual Sections of the Specifications.

F. Additional Tests not specified: In such instances where, in the opinion of the Architect, items may not meet the standards specified, additional tests may be required and so ordered by the Architect. If such tests reveal that specified standards have been met, the Contractor shall pay for the tests under the provisions of the Allowance for Testing specified in Section 01020. In the event that such tests reveal that specified standards have not been met, the Contractor shall pay for the tests from his own funds, at no cost to the Owner plus any retesting of corrected material that may be required additionally by the Architect.

Figure 9.15d

A reasonably complete master specifications system will include the following:

- Pre-written master specification sections filed in "hard" copy and, if available, on electronic media.
- An office manual consisting of notes, bulletins, industry publications and other data. This information should be organized and responsive to the drawings and information contained in the Project Manual.
- A series of checklists for the contents of the individual specification section and the Project Manual.
- A list or file of frequently specified products, design standards and details, and industry reference standards frequently used for associated projects.
- A digest and listing of information about products, materials, systems, codes and standards, research reports, and other information that has a bearing upon the specifications and their content.
- References on costs and the availability of materials and methods.

The primary advantages of a master specification file are summarized below:

- Studies conducted by knowledgeable institutions indicate that savings in technical labor can be cut 50-70% by the use of such a system. The use of electronic media devices makes this system even more efficient.
- A master specification system documenting a wide range of standards and choices expands the decision-making process considerably. A professional design firm is able to save and document the results of research and decisions involving past work.
- Project development in the office can be made more efficient and timely. Use of the master system allows for development of the specifications parallel to the development of drawings and other contract documents.
- Repetitive work can be greatly minimized.
- Errors and omissions can be minimized, thereby reducing the risk of liability.

The "Outline" Specification

Early in the step-by-step development of the modern construction project, an abbreviated specification known as the Outline Specification is often used. Outline specifications cover the essential descriptive provisions of the final specification and serve the purpose of "outlining" or basically describing the information contained in the final document to be produced as part of the contract documents. The outline specification may be thought of as relating to the final specification much as "design development" drawings and sketches relate to final construction drawings. Figures 9.16a and 9.16b show an outline specification for steel windows. This outline specification is prepared by the design professional as he seeks the owner's final approval for the design and budget requirements for a particular project. Figures 9.17a through 9.17c illustrate the final open proprietary specification for steel windows.

SECTION 08510
STEEL WINDOWS

PART 1 GENERAL

A. OUTLINE OF REQUIREMENTS

1. Fixed sash steel windows.

2. Factory applied enamel finish.

B. SYSTEMS DESCRIPTION

Windows, prefinished baked on color, with fixed glazing in steel frames.

C. PERFORMANCE

1. Window components to provide for expansion and contraction caused by a cycling temperature range of 170F degrees without causing detrimental effects to components.

2. Design and size members to withstand dead loads and live loads caused by pressure and suction of wind to a design pressure based on 95 mph, exposure C, category 3, importance factor 1.11. Maximum deformation of frame or sash member: 1/360 of span length.

3. Limit mullion deflection to 1/200 of flexure limit of glass with full recovery of glazing materials, whichever is less.

4. Drain water entering joints, condensation occurring in glazing channels, of migrating moisture occurring within system, to exterior.

5. Limit air infiltration through assembly to 0.10 cu.ft. per sq ft. of assembly surface area, measured at a reference differential pressure across assembly of 0.3 inches water gauge as measured in accordance with ANSI/ASTM E283.

PART 2 PRODUCTS

A. MANUFACTURE

Acceptable Product: 1000 Series Fixed Heavy Intermediate Steel Windows as manufactured by XYZ Architectural Products.

B. MATERIALS

1. Heavy fixed intermediate steel windows shall be manufactured from solid hot rolled steel shapes.

    a. Sections: New billet steel with integral flanges rolled at the mill.

    b. Perimeter frames shall have unobstructed glazing surface of at least 3/4 inch.

    c. Glazing rebate surfaces shall be perpendicular to the web or stem of the section. Tapered rebate surfaces are not acceptable.

    d. Provide 3 anchors per jamb.

2. Combined weight of frame shall be no less than 3.5 pounds per lineal foot.

3. Muntins: Steel Tees:

    a. Hot rolled from new billet steel with integral flanges rolled at the mill.

    b. Glazing rebate surfaces shall be as specified in A above.

    c. 1 3/8 inch tee shall weigh no less than 1.55 pounds per lineal foot.

Section 08510 Page 1

Figure 9.16a

C. FACTORY FINISHING

1. Hot dip galvanize components after fabrication.

2. Steel window frames and muntins shall be zinc-phosphate treated in a continuous five stage process as a preparation for painting.

   a. Following pre-treatment, one coat of primer is applied and oven cured.

   b. Following prime coat and baking, all exposed surfaces shall be given two coats of acrylic enamel.

3. Finish color as selected by Architect.

4. Apply one coat of bituminous paint or zinc-chromate paint to concealed steel surfaces in contract with cementitous or dissimilar materials.

5. Apply strippable protective coating to finished surfaces prior to shipping from factory.

END OF OUTLINE SECTION

Section 08510 Page 2

Figure 9.16b

```
                          SECTION 08510
                          STEEL WINDOWS

PART 1  GENERAL

1.01  REQUIREMENTS INCLUDED

    A.  Fixed sash steel windows.

    B.  Factory applied enamel finish.

1.02  REQUIREMENTS INSTALLED BUT SPECIFIED IN OTHER SECTIONS

    A.  Section 07900 - Joint Sealants: Sealants for use surrounding window frames.

    B.  Section 08800 - Glass and Glazing: Glazing of steel windows.

1.03  RELATED REQUIREMENTS

    A.  Section 04300 - Masonry: Masonry openings at windows.

    B.  Section 06100 - Rough Carpentry:  Wood perimeter shims.

    C.  Section 07900 - Sealants:  Perimeter sealant and back-up materials.

    D.  Section 08800 - Glass and Glazing.

    E.  Section 09260 - Gypsum Wallboard Systems: Adjacent finishes.

1.04  SYSTEMS DESCRIPTION

    Windows, prefinished baked on color, with fixed glazing in steel frames.

1.05  PERFORMANCE

    A.  Window components to provide for expansion and contraction caused by a cycling temperature range of 170F
        degrees without causing detrimental effects to components.

    B.  Design and size members to withstand dead loads and live loads caused by pressure and suction of wind to a
        design pressure based on 95 mph, exposure C, category 3, importance factor 1.11.  Maximum deformation of
        frame or sash member: 1/360 of span length.

    C.  Limit mullion deflection to 1/200 of flexure limit of glass with full recovery of glazing materials,
        whichever is less.

    D.  Drain water entering joints, condensation occurring in glazing channels, of migrating moisture occurring
        within system, to exterior.

    E.  Limit air infiltration through assembly to 0.10 cu.ft. per sq ft. of assembly surface area, measured at a
        reference differential pressure across assembly of 0.3 inches water gauge as measured in accordance with
        ANSI/ASTM E283.

1.04  REFERENCES

    A.  ASTM A36 - Structural Steel.

    B.  ANSI/ASTM E283 - Rate of Air Leakage through Exterior Windows, Curtain Walls and Doors.

    C.  ANSI/ASTM E330 - Structural Performance of Exterior Windows, Curtain Walls, and Doors by Uniform Static Air
        Pressure Difference.

    D.  FS TT-P-645 - Primer, Paint, Zinc Chromate, Alkyd Type.

1.05  SUBMITTALS

    A.  Submit shop drawings and product data in accordance with Section 01300.

    B.  Include materials, sections, finish, wall opening and component dimensions; wall opening tolerances required;
        anchorage and fasteners; affected related work and installation requirements.

    C.  Submit manufacturer's installation instruction in accordance with Section 01600.
```

Figure 9.17a

1.06 SAMPLES

A. Submit samples in accordance with Section 01300.

B. Submit one sample assembly, 18 inches high x 24 inches wide illustrating window frame sections, corner section, mullion section, of fixed glass assembly.

1.07 DELIVERY, STORAGE AND HANDLING

A. Deliver, handle, store and protect window units in accordance with Section 01600.

B. Provide wrapping or protective coating to protect prefinished aluminum surfaces.

1.08 WARRANTY

A. Provide one year manufacturer's warranty in accordance with Section 01700.

B. Warranty: Cover complete window system for failure to meet specified requirements.

PART 2 PRODUCTS

2.01 MANUFACTURE

A. Acceptable Product: 1000 Series Fixed Heavy Intermediate Steel Windows as manufactured by XYZ Architectural Products.

B. Substitutions: In accordance with Section 01600.

2.02 MATERIALS

A. Heavy fixed intermediate steel windows shall be manufactured from solid hot rolled steel shapes.

   1. Sections: New billet steel with integral flanges rolled at the mill.

   2. Perimeter frames shall have unobstructed glazing surface of at least 3/4 inch.

   3. Glazing rebat surfaces shall be perpendicular to the web or stem of the section. Tapered rebate surfaces are not acceptable.

   4. Provide 3 anchors per jamb.

   5. Combined weight of frame shall be no less than 3.5 pounds per lineal foot.

B. Muntins: Steel Tees

   1. Hot rolled from new billet steel with integral flanges rolled at the mill.

   2. Glazing rebate surfaces shall be as specified in A above.

   3. 1 3/8 inch tee shall weigh no less than 1.55 pounds per lineal foot.

2.03 FABRICATION

A. Fabricate steel windows in accordance with approved shop drawings.

B. Prior to fabrication, all hot rolled steel sections shall be cleaned by shot blasting.

C. Corners of frames shall be mitered or coped then solidly welded in accordance with AWI standards. Exposed and contact surfaces shall be finished smooth flush with adjacent surfaces.

D. Steel tee muntins shall be tenioned and welded to the perimeter frame. Muntin intersections shall be slotted and cross notched.

E. Fabricate windows allowing for minimum clearances and shim spacing around perimeter of assembly, yet enabling installation.

F. Develop drainage holes with moisture pattern to exterior.

G. Prepare components to receive anchor devices. Fabricate anchorage items as required by drawings.

Figure 9.17b

2.04 FACTORY FINISHING

   A. Hot dip galvanize components after fabrication.

   B. Steel window frames and muntins shall be zinc-phosphate treated in a continuous five stage
       process as a preparation for painting.

       1. Following pre-treatment, one coat of primer is applied and oven cured.

       2. Following prime coat and baking, all exposed surfaces shall be given two coats of acrylic enamel.

   C. Finish color as selected by Architect.

   D. Apply one coat of bituminous paint or zinc-chromate paint to concealed steel surfaces in contract with
       cementitous or dissimilar materials.

   E. Apply strippable protective coating to finished surfaces prior to shipping from factory.

2.05 GLASS AND GLAZING MATERIALS

   A. Glass and Glazing Materials: Specified in Section 08800.

PART 3 EXECUTION

3.01 INSPECTION

   A. Verify wall openings and adjoining air seal materials are ready to receive work of this Section.

   B. Field verify openings prior to fabrication.

   C. Beginning of installation means acceptance of existing conditions.

3.02 INSTALLATION

   A. Install window frames, in accordance with manufacturer's instructions.

   B. Use anchorage devices to securely attach frame to structure.

   C. Align window frame plumb and level, free of warp of twist. Maintain dimensional tolerances, aligning with
       adjacent work.

   D. Pack fibrous insulation in shim spaces at perimeter to maintain continuity of thermal barrier in accordance
       with Section 07115.

   E. Install perimeter sealant and backing materials in accordance with Section 07900.

3.03 PROTECTION

   A. Protect against damage by other Trades. Replace any defaced, defective steel work or broken glass caused by
       improper installation at no cost to Owner.

   B. After setting sills, immediately protect with board or other approved non-staining covering. Maintain
       protection in place until completion of masonry and plastering.

3.04 CLEANING

   A. Remove protective material from prefinished steel surfaces.

   B. Wash down exposed surfaces using a solution of mild detergent in warm water, applied with soft, clean wiping
       cloths. Take care to remove dirt from corners. Wipe surfaces clean.

                                        END OF SECTION

                                     Section 08510 Page 3

Figure 9.17c

Chapter 10
DRAWINGS

While there is no record of the first architectural or engineering drawing, it is clear that some form of graphic illustration must have been used to guide some of man's earliest construction projects. The term "drawing" implies much more than just the process of placing lines on a writing surface. In many languages (e.g., Latin, French, and Italian), the word for drawing also means designing. The Greeks and the Chinese use the same word to mean drawing, painting and writing. Samuel Johnson's *Dictionary of the English Language*, printed in 1755, describes a drawing as a "delineation, representation, sketch or outline". Architects' or engineers' drawings have long been the basic means by which the ideas and instructions of the design professional are communicated to those who accomplish the work of construction.

Engineering and Architectural Graphics

With the dawn of the Machine Age came what we know today as Engineering Drawing. By this time, building construction was a well developed industry involving the coordination of many trades under the architect's supervision. The architect used simple geometric drawings and details to establish the basic principles of the architectural design and personally coordinated and supervised the construction work. The mass production of industrial machines, on the other hand, required highly detailed and measured drawings to communicate the exact shape, size, material, and assembly of the machine's components. In response to this need, the art of "mechanical" drawing was developed by engineers who gave meaning to such terms as "scale" and "descriptive geometry". Soon such graphic techniques as orthographic, axonometric, oblique, and perspective projection were developed. Using these principles, the object to be constructed could be "built" on paper, and the drawing used as an exact pattern to guide the technician who would make the machine. Architects soon adopted many of these engineering techniques to produce drawings that would faithfully depict the building and its component parts. These improved drawings significantly reduced the time required of the architect to actually direct the detailing at the job site during construction.

Reproduction of Drawings

Modern building construction and modern manufacturing require that the drawings of the design professional be reproduced in quantity for distribution among the many related trades and crafts required for the project. The simple ability to economically reproduce quantities of architectural drawings has had a significant impact on building construction and manufacturing in the modern age.

Graphic Media

The design professional's drawings once created on linen, are today drawn—either by hand or by computer—on vellum, or more frequently on thin but sturdy, dimensionally stable mylar (plastic) sheets. Mylar is translucent which allows for reproduction, and has a surface that is particularly adapted to ink lines produced by modern drafting pens. Plastic pencil "lead" has been developed specifically for the mylar surface which allows for hand work that is relatively free of graphite dust and smearing that sometimes occurs with conventional graphite leads. The tough plastic surface allows for machine erasures with a minimum of the kind of damage that may occur on the surface of paper or linen.

Blue Prints

Blue Print is a familiar term commonly used to describe reproductions of the design professional's drawings. True blue prints are seldom used in construction today. The blue printing process owes its discovery to the development of photography. It requires an original drawing on transparent media, called the "tracing". The tracing is placed directly over a second sheet, called the "print", which has been sensitized with a mixture of ferric ammonium citrate and potassium ferricynide. The "sandwiched" combination is then exposed to a strong light source which, by the sensitivity of the chemical emulsion, creates a reverse or negative image of the tracing on the print. The lines of the drawing, being opaque, are not exposed, and thus appear as white (or the color of the print paper) on a background of blue.

In the early days of blue printing, the prints were produced in flat frames and exposed to sunlight. The chemical emulsion was applied by hand to the print media and after exposure washing in water was all that was necessary to produce the print. Later it was found that a bath of potassium dichromate would darken the exposed emulsion and greatly improve the contrast between the light and dark areas of the print. Once developed and dried, the blue print exhibits a remarkable "life", seldom fading, thus providing use for many years. As the demand for blue prints increased, a machine was developed to reproduce them.

The process of blue printing was discovered by Sir John Herschel, an Englishman, in 1842. His discovery was a means of reproducing drawings which was not substantially improved until the middle of the twentieth century when the White Print came into general use.

White Prints

The white print, unlike the blue print, is a positive image—dark lines on a light background. The white print process was first developed by Gustav Kogel in 1917. Like blue printing, white printing is also a photoreactive process. Because white printing involves a chemical process that produces a dye in the image, it is possible to create a number of different line colors and use a number of different textures, colors and weights of paper as the base of the print. Common, commercially available colors include black, blue, brown (sepia), green, and red. The flexibility and color range in the use of white printing expands the creativity of the design professional's presentation.

"Working" Drawings

The term *Working Drawings* is often used to refer to the construction drawings which are part of the contract documents. Working drawings serve to illustrate portions of the work that are difficult to describe in any other way. Drawings show the relationship of the materials, including sizes, shapes, locations, and connections. The drawings may include schematic diagrams showing such elements as mechanical and electrical systems. They may also include schedules of structural elements, equipment, finishes, and other similar items.

The design professional normally approaches the project by accomplishing an ordered series of activities. The end result is the final design of the building and the documentation of the project by means of contract documents. Likewise, the construction drawings are developed in a systematic way during that process of project development. In order to understand how the construction drawings are developed, it is helpful to review the design professional's responsibilities.

Figure 10.1 illustrates a professional service/phase matrix involving as many as nine phases of service. The basic five phases of service, considered by most to be the minimum requirement of any project, are generally characterized as shown in Figure 10.1.

- Phase 3—The Schematic Phase.
- Phase 4—The Design Development Phase.
- Phase 5—The Contract Documents Phase.
- Phase 6—The Bidding or Negotiating Phase.
- Phase 7—The Construction Administration Phase.

The Construction Drawings are the product of other drawings prepared in Phases 3 and 4 as listed above. Phase 3, the schematic phase of the design professional's service is sometimes referred to as the Preliminary Design phase. It is at this level that the general design and budget parameters of the project are determined. The program of design stipulating the space and functional requirements is also confirmed and evaluated at this stage, and budget requirements and other limiting factors are addressed. The design professional may determine several design alternatives, each of which requires drawings in the form of sketches. Once the owner and design professional have agreed on a design approach, preliminary sketches are prepared, and generally consist of the following:

- Site plan(s).
- Diagrammatic floor plans of building(s).
- Diagrammatic cross section(s) through buildings.
- Building Elevations.
- Notes and explanations.
- Perspective sketches (Optional, usually provided as an extra service).
- Architectural Model (Optional, usually provided as an extra service).

A preliminary cost estimate may be prepared based on available current square foot and systems costs. An appropriate contingency may be included to allow for variations and unanticipated costs, fees, and expenses. Owner's approval and acceptance of the schematic phase is desirable before the next phase of the work begins.

The next phase, called the Design Development Phase, may be thought of as the study phase of the work. At this point, the design professional studies and refines all aspects of the project design by establishing the

PHASE/SERVICE MATRIX

	PHASE 1: PREDESIGN SERVICES (1)	PHASE 2: SITE ANALYSIS SERVICES (2)	PHASE 3: SCHEMATIC DESIGN SERVICES (3)	PHASE 4: DESIGN DEVELOPMENT SERVICES (4)	PHASE 5: CONSTRUCTION DOCUMENTS SERVICES (5)	PHASE 6: BIDDING OR NEGOTIATIONS SERVICES (6)	PHASE 7: CONSTRUCTION CONTRACT ADMINISTRATION SERVICES (7)	PHASE 8: POST-CONSTRUCTION SERVICES (8)	PHASE 9: SUPPLEMENTAL SERVICES (9a)	PHASE 9 (CONT'D): SUPPLEMENTAL SERVICES (9b)
A	01 Project Administration	01 Project Administration	01 Project Administration	01 Project Administration	01 Project Administration	01 Project Administration	01 Project Administration	01 Project Administration	61 Special Studies	79 Materials and Systems Testing
B	02 Disciplines Coordination/Document Checking	02 Disciplines Coordination/Document Checking	02 Disciplines Coordination/Document Checking	02 Disciplines Coordination/Document Checking	02 Disciplines Coordination/Document Checking	02 Disciplines Coordination/Document Checking	02 Disciplines Coordination/Document Checking	02 Disciplines Coordination/Document Checking	62 Renderings	80 Demolition Services
C	03 Agency Consulting/Review/Approval	03 Agency Consulting/Review/Approval	03 Agency Consulting/Review/Approval	03 Agency Consulting/Review/Approval	03 Agency Consulting/Review/Approval	03 Agency Consulting/Review/Approval	03 Agency Consulting/Review/Approval	03 Agency Consulting/Review/Approval	63 Model Construction	81 Mock-up Services
D	04 Owner-supplied Data Coordination	04 Owner-supplied Data Coordination	04 Owner-supplied Data Coordination	04 Owner-supplied Data Coordination	04 Owner-supplied Data Coordination	04 Owner-supplied Data Coordination	04 Owner-supplied Data Coordination	04 Owner-supplied Data Coordination	64 Life Cycle Cost Analysis	82 Still Photographs
E	05 Programming	13 Site Analysis and Selection	21 Architectural Design/Documentation	21 Architectural Design/Documentation	21 Architectural Design/Documentation	34 Bidding Materials	41 Office Construction Administration	50 Maintenance and Operational Programming	65 Value Analysis	83 Motion Pictures and Videotape
F	06 Space Schematics/Flow Diagrams	14 Site Development Planning	22 Structural Design/Documentation	22 Structural Design/Documentation	22 Structural Design/Documentation	35 Addenda	42 Construction Field Observation	51 Start-up Assistance	66 Quantity Surveys	84 Coordination with Non-Design Professionals
G	07 Existing Facilities Surveys	15 Detailed Site Utilization Studies	23 Mechanical Design/Documentation	23 Mechanical Design/Documentation	23 Mechanical Design/Documentation	36 Bidding/Negotiations	43 Project Representation	52 Record Drawings	67 Detailed Construction Cost Estimates	85 Special Disciplines Consultation
H	08 Marketing Studies	16 On-site Utility Studies	24 Electrical Design/Documentation	24 Electrical Design/Documentation	24 Electrical Design/Documentation	37 Analysis of Alternates/Substitutions	44 Inspection Coordination	53 Warranty Review	68 Energy Studies	86 Special Building Type Consultation
I	09 Economic Feasibility Studies	17 Off-site Utility Studies	25 Civil Design/Documentation	25 Civil Design/Documentation	25 Civil Design/Documentation	38 Special Bidding Services	45 Supplemental Documents	54 Postconstruction Evaluation	69 Environmental Monitoring	
J	10 Project Financing	18 Environmental Studies and Reports	26 Landscape Design/Documentation	26 Landscape Design/Documentation	26 Landscape Design/Documentation	39 Bid Evaluation	46 Quotation Requests/Change Orders		70 Tenant-related Services	
K		19 Zoning Processing Assistance	27 Interior Design/Documentation	27 Interior Design/Documentation	27 Interior Design/Documentation	40 Construction Contract Agreements	47 Project Schedule Monitoring		71 Graphics Design	
L			28 Materials Research/Specifications	28 Materials Research/Specifications	28 Materials Research/Specifications		48 Construction Cost Accounting		72 Fine Arts and Crafts Services	
M	29 Project Development Scheduling	29 Project Development Scheduling	29 Project Development Scheduling	29 Project Development Scheduling	30 Special Bidding Documents/Scheduling		49 Project Closeout		73 Special Furnishings Design	
N	31 Project Budgeting	31 Project Budgeting	32 Statement of Probable Construction Cost	32 Statement of Probable Construction Cost	32 Statement of Probable Construction Cost				74 Non-Building Equipment Selection	
O	33 Presentations	33 Presentations	33 Presentations	33 Presentations	33 Presentations				75 Project Promotion/Public Relations	
P									76 Leasing Brochures	
Q									77 Expert Witness	
R									78 Computer Applications	

NOTE: Services marked with ● are similarly found under the description of "Basic Services" in AIA Document B141. All services in this chart are contained in AIA Document B162.

Figure 10.1

materials and methods of construction and the environmental and other systems to be employed. He also identifies regulatory conditions and similar requirements. It is during this phase that most of the critical decisions regarding size, shape, and function are finalized, as well the selection of materials, systems, applications, and modifications. The drawings produced at this phase consist of the following:

- Site plan(s) showing the following:
  - —Final grading and extent of site improvements.
  - —Paving and drainage structures.
  - —Schematic utility locations and connection to building.
- Diagrammatic floor plans of building(s).
  - —Major dimensions.
  - —Structural features and requirements.
  - —Schedules of finishes, windows, and doors.
  - —Finished carpentry, millwork, and similar features.
  - —Equipment.
  - —Furnishings (if applicable).

- Major wall sections with dimensions and material indications.
- Exterior elevations with finish and material indications.
- Notes and explanations.
- Material samples as applicable.
- Interior perspective sketches (optional and extra service).

Figures 10.2a through 10.2e are a partial set of preliminary drawings of a small office building. These drawings are typical of those that might be produced at the Design Development Phase of the design professional's service. These figures are for illustrative purposes only. An actual project might require more drawings and much more detail.

At this stage, a second, more detailed cost estimate may be prepared based on current unit and systems costs, with ample contingency for current construction costs, fees and other anticipated expenses. The owner's approval and acceptance of the design development phase is desirable before the next phase of the work is begun.

The Construction Documents Phase of the service involves just what the title implies. It is during this phase that the design professional and his consultants (if any) prepare the final version of the contract documents which include the final construction ("working") drawings.

Organizing the "Set" of Construction Drawings

The number of drawings and kind of information required in the final set of drawings vary with the type, character, size and complexity of the project type. The organization of the "set" may also vary depending on the size and composition of the prime design professional's staff. Many major design firms employ staff professionals representing most of the major design disciplines that are required to produce the final work. Medium-sized firms tend to maintain one or more of the required disciplines on staff and hire others as outside consultants according to the needs of the individual project. Regardless of how the prime design professional maintains or assembles the various disciplines required to finally design the project, the organization of the construction drawings should follow a logical, organized, interdisciplinary format. In this way, it is relatively easy and convenient for the constructor(s) to find information and determine the scope, sequence, and full extent of the work. Certain "rules of thumb" and guidelines apply to the basic

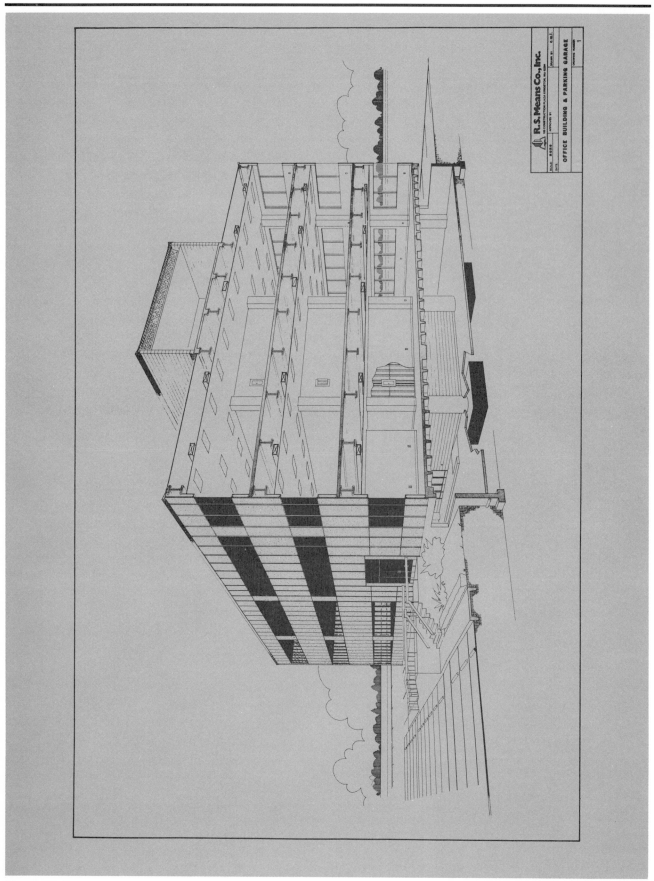

Figure 10.2*a*

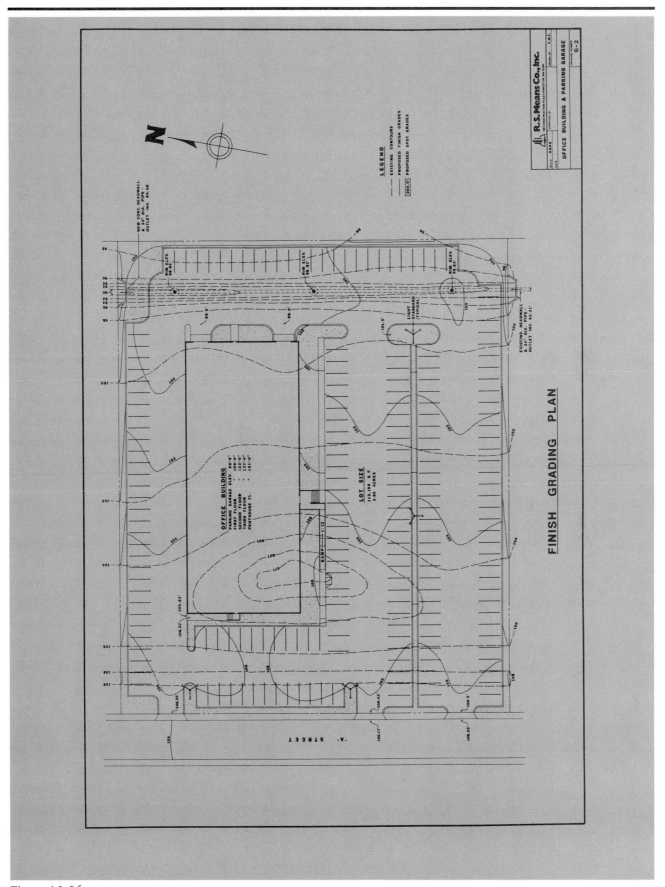

Figure 10.2b

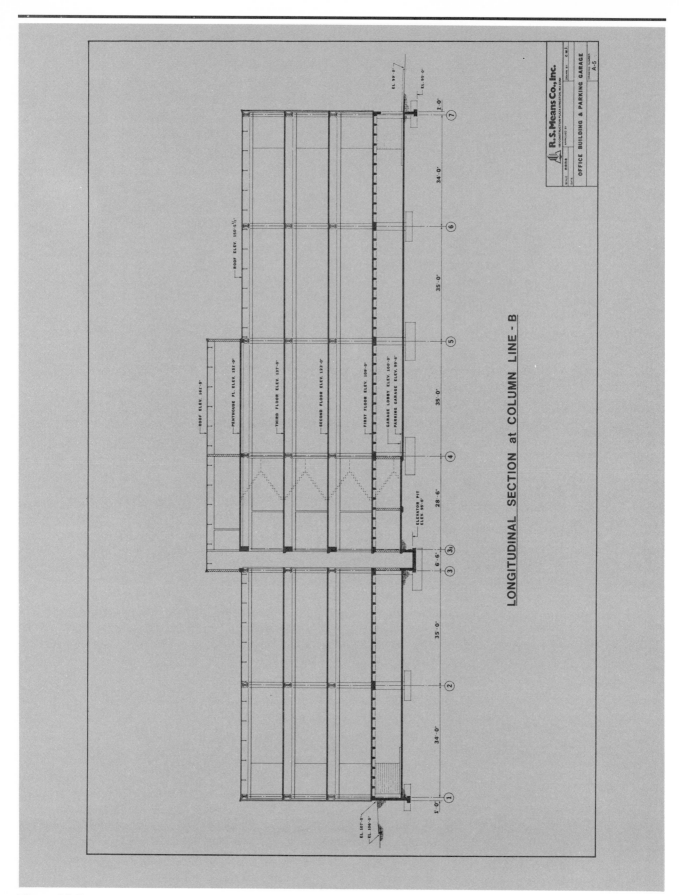

LONGITUDINAL SECTION at COLUMN LINE - B

Figure 10.2c

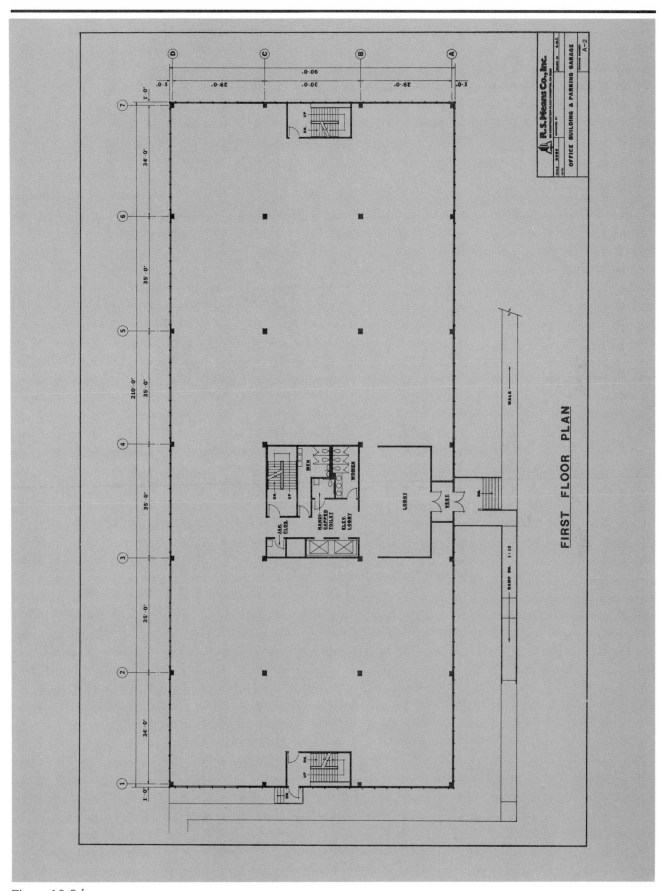

Figure 10.2d

235

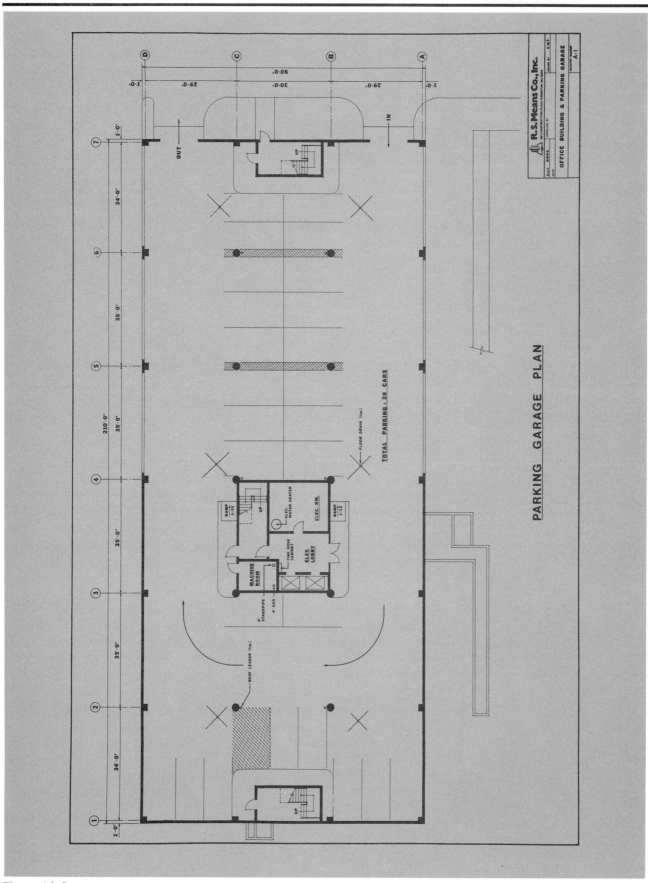

Figure 10.2e

organization of the set as follows:

- Determine the various design disciplines that will be employed to complete the Contract Documents. The disciplines may include, without being limited to the following:
  - —Architecture (A)
  - —Civil Engineering (C)
  - —Structural Engineering (S)
  - —Mechanical Engineering (M&P)
  - —Electrical Engineering (E)
  - —Acoustical Engineering (Ae)
  - —Environmental Engineering. (Ee)
  - —Landscape Architecture. (L)
  - —Interior Design. (I)
  - —Other Specialties. (X)

- Observe the probable sequence of the work and generally organize sub-sets of drawings along the lines of the various disciplines and the sequence of the work:
  - —Site Preparation
  - —(C) Civil Engineering
    - (aa) Landscape
    - (ab) Special Site Features

  - —Foundation & Superstructure
  - —(S) Structural Engineering

  - —Architectural Features
  - —(A) Architecture

  - —Plumbing
  - —(M) Mechanical Engineering

  - —Heating, Ventilating and Air Conditioning

  - —Equipment (X)

- Create two distinct page numbering systems.
  The primary system should number drawings as they occur sequentially within the primary set, each recognizing the placement within the primary set. (i.e., Drawing No. 10 of 50) Note: This system requires that the primary numbering system not be applied until the entire set of drawings is complete. The secondary system should use a prefix letter denoting the sub-category or sub-set and the drawing number within the sub-set (i.e., S4 of 10S).

The procedures outlined above have certain distinct advantages in organizing and preparing the drawings to be included in the primary set. Among these benefits are the following:

- Sub-sets can be prepared independently of other sub-sets involving other disciplines.
- Drawings within the sub-set can be assigned a sub-set number at an early date for purposes of cross-referencing as the drawings are completed.
- Drawings are organized in a consistent and uniform way into sub-sets with clear divisions based on design discipline. This approach tends to reduce the time required for bidders, estimators, subcontractors, material suppliers, and other users who must search for and use pertinent information.

- Being able to determine the position of the individual drawing within the primary set and sub-set allows the user to re-assemble drawings that may be disassembled during the bidding or negotiation processes. It is easy to discover if a drawing is missing.
- Cross-referencing within the sub-set tends to reduce the potential for error, omission and confusion when unforeseen changes are made or additional sheets added to the sub-set.

Figure 10.3 is a typical drawing sheet that may be used by the design professional. The design of title blocks may vary considerably from office to office. Many design professionals consider the graphic design of such sheets as part of the "logo" expressing the identity or personality of the design professional.

Systems Production of Drawings

The preparation of drawings required for a modern building complex is the single most costly requirement that the design professional must consider when negotiating his compensation with the owner. Advancements in the technology of reproduction (including printing, lithography and photography) have all contributed to reduce the time and expense required to produce professional drawings.

Printing
The plastics and plastic adhesives that are available today have had a major impact on the production of professional drawings. Among these innovations is the thin mylar transparent sheet backed with a transparent film of adhesive. This process enables the design professional to create and stockpile a library of construction details, title blocks, general notes, schedule forms, symbol and material legends and other graphics that are repeatedly used in the drawings he creates. These items can be placed on the drawing, by use of the adhesive backing. Since they no longer need to be individually re-drawn, significant manhours are saved. Modern lithography also allows for the pre-printing of drawing sheets with borders, title blocks, design professional identification, and other common but repetitive features.

Diazo Reproducibles
The diazo reproduction on transparent media, commonly called a "sepia" because of its familiar brown color, has expanded the design professional's ability to save manhours. This process can be used to "model" drawings that serve as a base for other drawings. For instance, the floor plan of the building is common to much of the diagrammatic work and layout of the mechanical and electrical disciplines. The diazo reproducible on a stable mylar base provides a handy "footprint" of the basic building floor plan, site plan, or building section. Other disciplines can use this basic plan to complete their work.

Process Camera Work
The modern process camera was developed as a natural adjunct to the photo based lithographic printing process. This process has made an "antique" of the direct application printing press used since the 16th century. The photographic preparation necessary for the lithographic process requires little if any sensitivity to intermediate tone. When shades and shadows need to be printed, the effect is accomplished by the use of "half-tone" screens mounted at the image area of the camera. The camera with greatly enhanced lighting, optics, and exposure control allows the design professional to create drawings photographically in a number of ways. Details can be rapidly drawn at

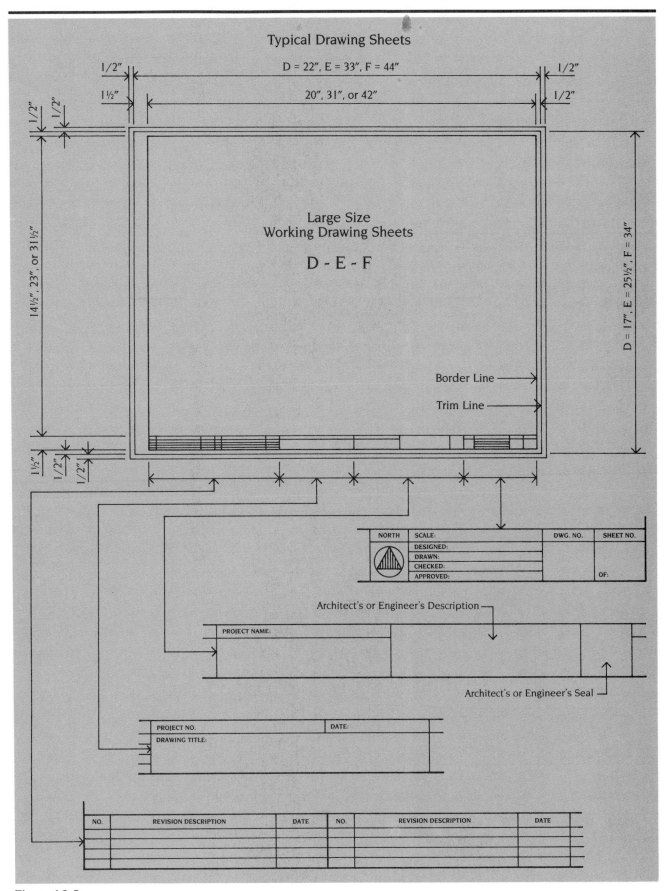

Typical Drawing Sheets

D = 22", E = 33", F = 44"

20", 31", or 42"

1/2"   1/2"

1 1/2"   1/2"

1/2"   1/2"

14 1/2", 23", or 31 1/2"

D = 17", E = 25 1/2", F = 34"

Large Size
Working Drawing Sheets

D - E - F

Border Line

Trim Line

1 1/2"   1/2"   1/2"

NORTH	SCALE:		DWG. NO.	SHEET NO.
	DESIGNED:			
	DRAWN:			
	CHECKED:			
	APPROVED:			OF:

Architect's or Engineer's Description

PROJECT NAME:		

Architect's or Engineer's Seal

PROJECT NO.	DATE:
DRAWING TITLE:	

NO.	REVISION DESCRIPTION	DATE	NO.	REVISION DESCRIPTION	DATE

Figure 10.3

large scale and reduced for final reproduction. Appropriate supporting graphics such as maps, tables, drawings, and photographs can be incorporated into the professional drawing photographically. Double and triple exposures allow composite graphics to be combined into one drawing.

Overlay Drafting

The overlay system of drawing production first became popular in the late 1960's and continues to be of significant value to the design professional. The basic concept is to separate the various types of information and graphics normally placed on a single drawing onto different layers which when overlaid and printed together in register, makes a reproduction of all of the information contained on each layer. The floor plan of a building is either drawn or reproduced many different times within a set of drawings. By using the overlay system, the floor plan, drawn but one time, becomes the "footprint" or background for other drawings. The "footprint" becomes the base layer for a number of other drawings. A second layer may contain all dimension lines and nomenclature. Many of the other drawings using the base "footprint" do not require that the dimensions be reproduced. A third layer may contain symbols that are unique to only one of the disciplines; another layer may incorporate the room titles, door and window symbols, and other nomenclature. By printing the different layers in various combinations and utilizing either the camera or the diazo reproducible or both, much of the basic information common to a number of different drawings can be drawn once, and used again and again for parallel purposes.

Assuring exact register (one layer aligned with the other) is essential. There are two basic methods by which register can be accomplished, one of which is more practical than the other. In the first more "primitive" method, register marks are strategically placed in identical locations on each sheet so that the draftsperson can register the layers visually by imposing one directly over the other. The second method, commonly called the "pen-graphics" method requires that a series of uniform sized holes, uniformly spaced, be punched into the top of each drawing sheet. Pins, or short posts of similar diameter and spacing are firmly and securely placed at the top of the drawing board, and as each drawing is uniformly placed over the posts, exact register is achieved. By using clear plastic posts in the diazo reproduction machine, reproductions can be made of combined layers, assuring complete register in the printing process as well.

Computer Aided Drafting

The computer as a production tool for creating contract documents is a relatively new, but promising innovation. Computer capabilities promise to "revolutionize" the art of drawing as well as the production of written documents. The primary advantage of the computer is its ability to accomplish a great number of operations with tremendous speed and accuracy. The second major advantage is the computer's ability to "remember" and reproduce a series of commands.

Computer aided drafting (CAD) has been developed and available to the design community since the early 1960's. Originally developed as a tool for industry in the design and manufacture of automobiles and aircraft, CAD has only recently started to become "affordable" to the average design professional. CAD utilizes the computer's ability to remember the coordinates of points, each with a specific location on a geometric grid.

A line can be described between any two points and then drawn by a computer driven plotter or similar device. In the earliest application of the technique, the programs required to produce even simple drawings on the computer required large amounts of electronic "storage". Thus, only large, "mainframe" computers could be used. The technological advancements of the past two decades have allowed CAD programs to be run on both "micro" and "mini" computers. Recent research reveals that by the year 1995, 85 percent of all of the drawings produced by design professionals will be produced by computer.

Graphic Standards

It is not the purpose of this volume to attempt to teach the art of preparing professional drawings, for that subject is best learned in the workplace. However, this text does endeavor to list and discuss the many attributes of drawings, and the most valuable techniques and resources. Certain standards have been developed so that the "language" of drawings can be understood by all. These standards help to establish consistency and uniformity in the industry. For drawings, graphic symbols provide a method for such understanding by representing what otherwise would require a great deal of text. Graphic symbols are a common resource or tool, used to represent, illustrate, direct, emphasize, and abbreviate information conveyed throughout the drawings. Figures 10.4a and 10.4b illustrate many of the typical symbols commonly used among today's practitioners.

Schedules

The use of schedules on the drawings and in the specifications is an excellent device for placing a volume of information in a limited space with a minimum of words. The primary schedules used with the architectural drawings are the Finish Schedule as illustrated in Figure 10.5 and the Door Schedule, as illustrated in Figure 10.6.

Relating Drawings and Specifications

The coordination of information in the drawings and the specifications is a critical legal responsibility of the design professional. The object of the contract documents is to describe, as completely as time and economics will permit, the requirements of the work needed to complete the building or project. By definition, drawings are graphic illustrations of the work to be accomplished. Drawings should illustrate the relationships between materials and indicate the following:

- Location of each material, assembly, component and accessory.
- Identification of all components and pieces of equipment.
- Dimensions of the construction and sizes of field assembled components.
- Details and diagrams of connections.

Specifications, on the other hand, describe requirements for the physical qualities, (composition—both physical and chemical), of materials, assemblies, equipment and other components. Specifications also establish a minimum standard for workmanship in both the manufacture and installation of these items.

The question is constantly raised in the field as to which takes precedence—the drawings or the specs? The answer is that drawings and specifications are complementary and neither implies information that is more important nor with precedence over the other. The General Conditions of the Contract implies that all contract documents are complementary and establishes the design professional as the

Architectural Symbols in Section

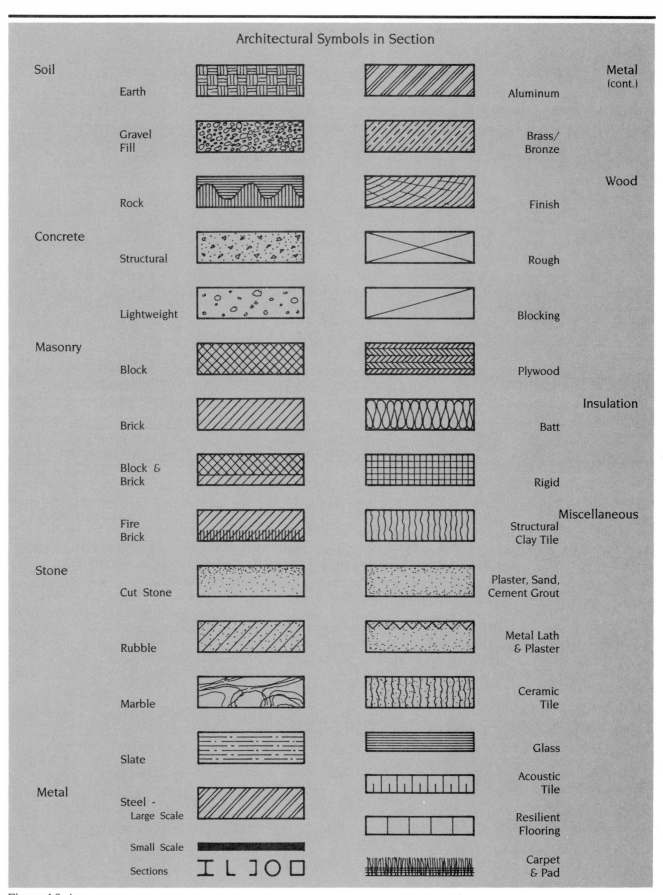

Soil
- Earth
- Gravel Fill
- Rock

Concrete
- Structural
- Lightweight

Masonry
- Block
- Brick
- Block & Brick
- Fire Brick

Stone
- Cut Stone
- Rubble
- Marble
- Slate

Metal
- Steel - Large Scale
- Small Scale
- Sections

Metal (cont.)
- Aluminum
- Brass/ Bronze

Wood
- Finish
- Rough
- Blocking
- Plywood

Insulation
- Batt
- Rigid

Miscellaneous
- Structural Clay Tile
- Plaster, Sand, Cement Grout
- Metal Lath & Plaster
- Ceramic Tile
- Glass
- Acoustic Tile
- Resilient Flooring
- Carpet & Pad

Figure 10.4a

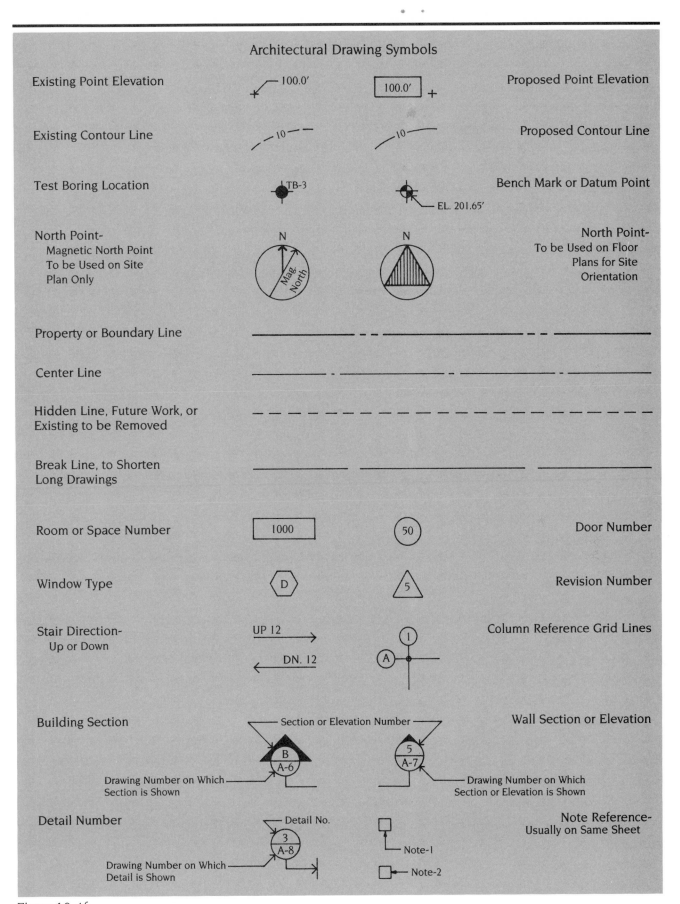

Architectural Drawing Symbols

Existing Point Elevation — 100.0'

100.0' — Proposed Point Elevation

Existing Contour Line — 10

10 — Proposed Contour Line

Test Boring Location — TB-3

EL. 201.65' — Bench Mark or Datum Point

North Point-
Magnetic North Point
To be Used on Site
Plan Only — N Mag. North

N — North Point-
To be Used on Floor
Plans for Site
Orientation

Property or Boundary Line

Center Line

Hidden Line, Future Work, or
Existing to be Removed

Break Line, to Shorten
Long Drawings

Room or Space Number — 1000

50 — Door Number

Window Type — D

5 — Revision Number

Stair Direction-
Up or Down — UP 12, DN. 12

1 A — Column Reference Grid Lines

Building Section — Section or Elevation Number — B A-6
Drawing Number on Which Section is Shown

5 A-7 — Wall Section or Elevation
Drawing Number on Which Section or Elevation is Shown

Detail Number — Detail No. 3 A-8
Drawing Number on Which Detail is Shown

Note-1, Note-2 — Note Reference-
Usually on Same Sheet

Figure 10.4b

PROJECT

PAGE ____ OF ____

DATE

BY

ARCHITECT

ROOMS		FLOORS							BASES						WAINSCOTS					WALLS						CEILING							REMARKS
ROOM NAME		MATERIALS							MATERIALS						MATERIALS				HT.	MATERIALS						MATERIALS					MTG	
		1	2	3	4	5	6	P	1	2	3	4	5	P	1	2	3	4	P		1	2	3	4	5	W P	1	2	3	4	5	P F S	

Figure 10.5

244

Means Forms
DOOR AND FRAME SCHEDULE

PROJECT		ARCHITECT			PAGE	OF
LOCATION		OWNER			DATE	
					BY	

DOOR NO	DOOR								FRAME						FIRE RATING		HARDWARE		REMARKS
	SIZE			MAT.	TYPE	GLASS	LOUVER	MAT.	TYPE	DETAILS			LAB	CON	SET NO.	KEYSIDE ROOM NO.	
	W	H	T							JAMB	HEAD	SILL					

Figure 10.6

interpreter of the intentions of the documents. The Supplemental General Conditions usually require the contractor to report to the design professional any inconsistency, conflict, omission or error in the documents.

There are several "rules of thumb" for coordinating the information (primarily the drawings and specifications) contained in the contract documents. Some guidelines are listed below:

- Drawings illustrate; specifications describe. Avoid placing information on the drawings that could contradict the specifications. Example: A note on a wall section should say simply "Metal Flashing". The corresponding specification found in Section 07600—Flashing and Sheet Metal, should state "32 oz. copper flashing with seams locked and soldered". At the same time, avoid statements in the specifications that may contradict the drawings. Example: In Section 05500—Metal Fabrications, there might be the following statement: "Anchor bolts, ASTM A 36 steel". A note on the drawings should state "1/2 inch diameter anchor bolts, placed on 36 inch centers".

- Avoid statements such as "see specifications" on the drawings, or "as shown on the drawings" in the specifications. Imagine the confusion if Section 05500 of the specifications stated, "Anchor bolts, size as shown on the drawings" and the corresponding note on the drawings stated, "Anchor bolts, see specifications".

- Provide the primary information *once* in the most appropriate and conspicuous location. Secondary or repetitive information should be provided by reference to the primary note or location of the note. Repeating information again and again is not only redundant, but may lead to confusion, and errors when changes made in one location are not made in all the others.

- Be consistent with the use of terminology in both drawings and specifications. A "service sink" shown on the drawings should not be referred to as a "janitor's sink" in the specifications. A "bituminous surface course" in one location should not be an "asphalt topping" in another.

- Establish office standards, preferably in a printed manual distributed to each member of the professional team. Such a manual should contain standards for terminology, symbols, abbreviations, graphic representations of textures and materials, style of hand lettering, uniformity of line weight, and other attributes clearly established and enforced as to general use.

In summarizing the discussion on drawings, it is important to emphasize the need for care and coordination in the planning and preparation of all of the contract documents. Each document has a special purpose, content and intended use. The complete and properly prepared package is required to serve as a proper basis for bidding and construction.

Chapter 11

ADMINISTRATION OF THE CONTRACT FOR CONSTRUCTION

Few undertakings exceed the requirements for skill, judgment and expertise in organizing, scheduling, supervising, coordinating, administering and record keeping that are involved in the construction of a modern building. The sensitive interrelationships of the owner, the design professional, the contractor, and the subcontractor produce tremendous exposure to liability and financial risk because of the potential for errors and omissions in design and construction, injury on the job, and possible failure of materials and assemblies (and workers) to perform as expected.

Building construction has become an extremely complex endeavor involving the careful orchestration of large capital expenditures, the employment of specialized design and engineering resources as well as construction management expertise. In addition, a variety of crafts, trades and labor must be coordinated. All of these elements must come together in the assembly of a variety of materials and systems. The finished product must be delivered within a specified period of time for a pre-arranged cost if a project is to be "successful". At no time in history has the building process been more complicated by a combination of government regulation and economic factors. In its zeal to protect, government has created law that regulates location, size, shape, structure, envelope, ingress and egress, and even the ultimate use of the modern building. At the same time, government has come to regulate the wages, work, and safety conditions, record keeping, and accountability of those who employ and manage. Because of its size and influence on the general economy, building construction is extremely sensitive to changes in the general "health" of business and commerce.

Figure 11.1 illustrates the interrelationships of function and the flow of money, effort, resource, and records that must occur between owner, design professional, constructor, and community (government) during the construction of a modern building. These relationships, although they may vary greatly from project to project, may be thought of as a wheel kept constantly turning by the transfer of energy from one spoke to another in a single coordinated direction. The failure of any sector to transfer "energy" to the next sector, or any reversal of the flow will slow or perhaps even stop the progress of construction. Much like any machine, a major expenditure of collective energy is required to "start" the construction "wheel" in rotation, and a continuous transfer of energy is needed to maintain the rotation. Any "breakdown" of the component parts will cause the process to slow, or even stop. In order to start up again, considerable extra energy and cost must be expended to overcome the inertia, reach its former momentum, and then continue that motion through the process of completion.

The Community

The community in which the project is constructed, acting through the authority of its elected officials, is an outside, but interested third party to the contract for construction. Figures 11.2 and 11.3 illustrate two types of local municipal government prevalent in the United States. Municipal government has the primary responsibility for establishing zoning regulations and building codes. It is their purpose to regulate building design and construction for the physical and economic well being of the community at large. Figure 11.4 illustrates the process of municipal control of the building process. It begins (after zoning and planning requirements are met) with the application for and issuance of a building permit, and subsequently a final certificate of occupancy.

The Function of Government

The fundamental purpose of government in the United States is to represent and safeguard the public interest, health and economy, to provide basic services, and to establish and maintain order. The function of local government in building construction is established by legislation which gives cities the ability to:

- Adopt zoning regulations, which are usually administered by an appointed commission of knowledgeable and responsible citizens. The primary responsibility of such commissions is to control land use in terms of function and potential nuisance, e.g., limiting the height of buildings and building density. Secondary objectives of a zoning commission may be to preserve a percentage and quality of free or open space for the enjoyment and benefit of the community and to establish guidelines for community planning for future growth, communication, transportation and basic utility and sanitary services.
- Establish ordinances, building codes, and other authority under the administration of an appointed building official, as well as regulations regarding the type, occupancy, and appropriate construction of buildings in accordance with zoning requirements and safe practice concerning the safety and welfare of building occupants and the public at large.

Taxation and Fees

The functions of government are funded by various taxes collected in a variety of ways and by fees collected for the services it renders. In regard to building construction, most municipalities require the issuance of a Building Permit prior to commencement of construction. This process involves collection of a fee based on the size and value of the construction. The fee covers the cost of review and approval of the construction documents as well as periodic inspection of the work by the Building Official. Certain portions of the building such as plumbing, mechanical, and electrical work may require issuance of additional permits and licensing of certain associated subcontractors based on requirements for knowledge of the trade and workmanship, amount of experience, and understanding of the building and life safety codes that are associated with that work. In some jurisdictions, licensing of the

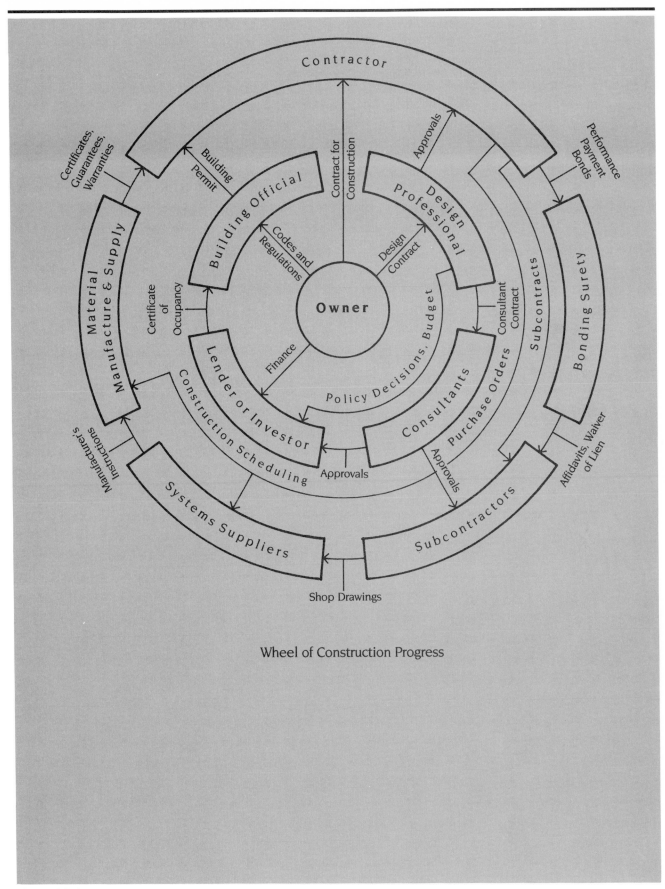

Wheel of Construction Progress

Figure 11.1

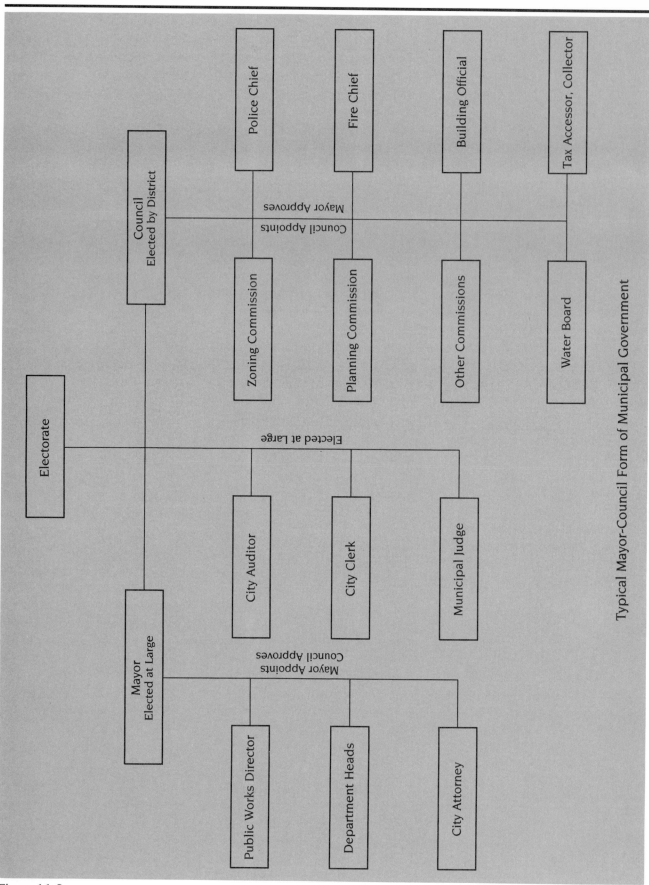

Typical Mayor-Council Form of Municipal Government

Figure 11.2

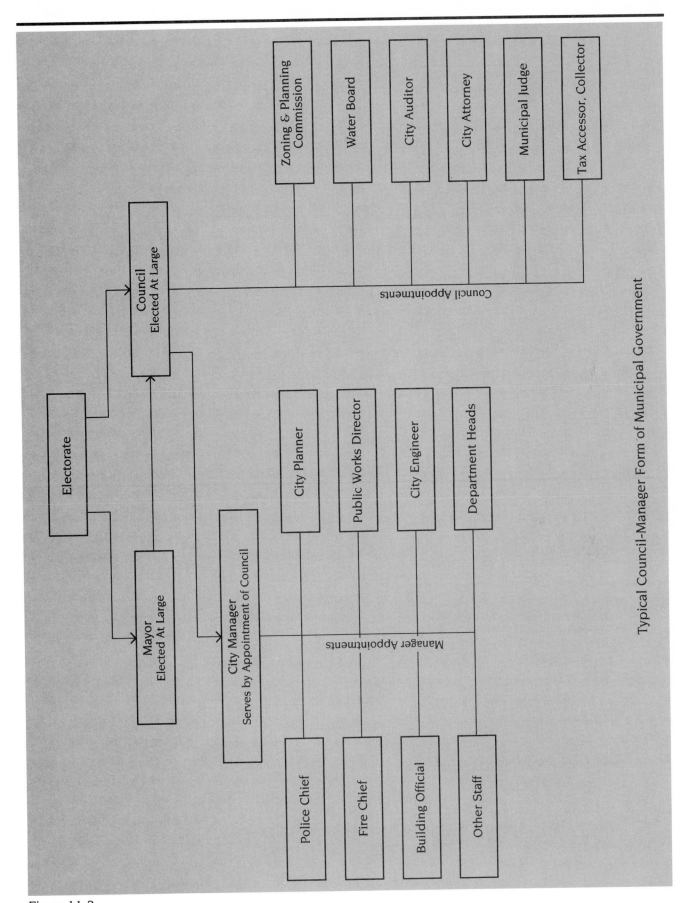

Typical Council-Manager Form of Municipal Government

Figure 11.3

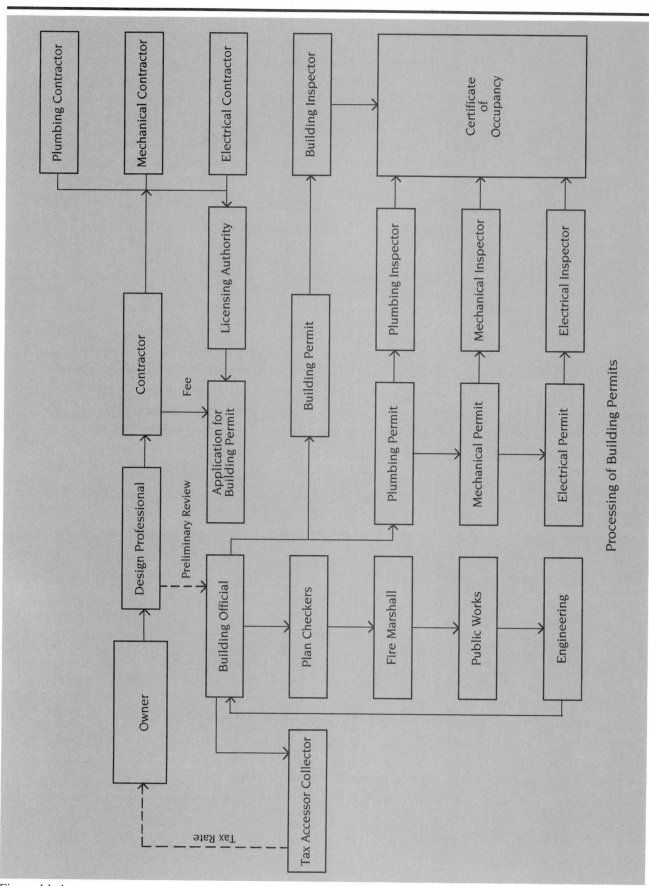

Processing of Building Permits

Figure 11.4

252

general contractor and other major subcontractors may be required. The building permit establishes the relative value of the improved property which is entered upon the tax record for the purpose of collecting property taxes. Meters are installed to collect fees for utilities such as water, gas, and electricity. Other forms of taxation may include sales tax on certain materials, as well as tax on income. It is generally the private owner who generates the majority of tax revenues to the community. Publicly owned buildings are usually exempt from payment of property, sales and other taxes.

Approval of the proposed building (by the municipal building department) subsequent to the issuance of a building permit may require reviews by the departments which administer public utility services, engineering, traffic and transportation, zoning, and or city planning, fire protection, police, and health and sanitation. These reviews confirm compliance with building codes and other applicable ordinances. Once the appropriate permits are issued, various members of the building inspection department may make required periodic visits and inspections of the work. These officials may have the authority to issue citations for the violation of codes and ordinances as well as to refuse to issue the Certificate of Occupancy which is usually required before permanent utilities can be turned on and occupancy of the building can take place. The building official has the power to demand testing of materials and assemblies to confirm compliance with codes and other regulations. The cost of such tests must therefore be included as part of the project cost. Contract documents usually provide contractor responsibility for the cost of building permits and testing required by government authorities (Refer to Paragraph 7.7.1, Article 7 of AIA Document A201—*General Conditions of the Contract for Construction* for details relative to the Contractor's responsibility for testing. The Supplemental General Conditions may expand upon these responsibilities for the individual project.) See Chapter 9 for a discussion of testing requirements that are included in a technical specification.

Financing the Construction Process

Today's building owner, unless he is able to pay cash for the cost of land and improvements, must borrow to finance such a project. Borrowing to partially finance the cost of construction involves a business device called *leveraging* to achieve the liquid funding necessary to pay for the cost of the land and improvements.

Leveraging (in the case of the private owner) is borrowing, where the accepted value of the land and proposed improvements, plus other items of value (if necessary) are used as *collateral*. Based on that collateral, an investor loans an agreed amount of money which is used to finance, in part or whole, the cost of the improvements. The lender is usually a bank, a savings and loan or other similar institution with the financial resources to make long term loans for construction purposes. As a matter of sound business policy, loans for real estate and construction purposes are usually made on the basis of a *margin*. A margin is the maximum amount of funds loaned, and represents a percentage, usually no less than 50 percent or more than 90 percent, of the total value of the land and improvements. The owner must, therefore, invest funds of his own, called *equity*, to make up the difference between the amount borrowed and the total cost of land and improvements. The legal instruments normally used for such construction leveraging (depending upon the laws and procedures of the individual state) are the *Promissory Note* and the *Deed of Trust*. The promissory note sets forth the amount and conditions of the obligation, and the deed of trust collateralizes the property and allows the lender to foreclose or seize title to the property in the case of default on payment or other conditions set forth in the note.

Leveraging new construction involving publicly owned property by a municipality, county, or other form of taxation district, is accomplished by selling *General Obligation Bonds*. These are interest-bearing instruments of investment, sold by the public entity, purchased by investors, on which the public entity, from tax or other revenues, promises to repay principal and interest under fixed terms over a specific period of time. General Obligation Bonds cannot normally be sold unless public approval is granted through a special election, called a *Referendum*. Once approved, the obligation created becomes a matter of law, placing the repayment of bonds ahead of any other expenditure of public funds. In the case of General Obligation Bonds, the investor does not have the protection of the property as collateral. Nevertheless, he is protected as a matter of general public obligation, or public trust.

The banker, lender, or investor from whom the leverage funds are derived becomes indirectly interested in the project's development. During construction, for instance, the lender (on private projects) may wish to control the disbursement of funds to the construction process, and may require an accounting of the progress of the work to be made on a monthly basis. The public investor who purchases bonds, as a matter of courtesy, may be issued a progress report by the owner or the agency who acts as the bond broker.

The OPC Relationship—Duties and Objectives

The OPC (Owner-Professional-Contractor—see Chapter 1 for a complete discussion) relationship, and the duties of each party have been discussed at length in earlier chapters of this book. It is appropriate at this point to recognize and profile the various representatives of each of these parties—who may be employed to carry out the duties and responsibilities of their respective employers on the job site, either by continuous or part-time on-site representation. Following is a review of the overall roles and responsibilities of each of the major participants, along with the members of their support staff.

The Owner's Duties and Objectives

The owner is the source of the project's capital and direction. He initiates the project by identifying a need, and then arranging the financial resources to accomplish that need. The owner retains the design professional who confirms the owner's need and draws up a program of design and improvement within the scope of the owner's financial capacity. Contract documents are drawn up by the design professional, competitive bids or negotiations for construction are arranged, the contract for construction is agreed upon, and construction begins.

Most owners in building construction today are corporate entities. The owners who make, by far, the largest contribution to total building construction, consist of boards of directors of major corporations, municipal councils, county commissions, school boards, boards of governors, state legislatures, and the government of the United States. This is not to ignore the individual owner who is, for the most part, the homeowner, small businessman and, in many instances, the individual private investor.

The owner, whether corporation or individual, has at least three primary, and three secondary goals in commissioning the design and construction of a modern building. The primary goals of an owner may be:

- Construction of a building that will house some function vital to certain needs and objectives.
- Creation of maximum space and utility for minimum expenditure of capital.
- A resulting building of beauty and functional efficiency, which reflects the owner's objectives, character and personality.

The secondary objectives of the owner may be:

- A cost savings over the existing operation or facility, or an alternative suitable to his needs and objectives.
- Structured shelter from taxation.
- Recognition in the community.

Figure 11.5 shows the typical organization and immediate resources needed by the Owner. It includes employment of the design professional and selection of the constructor.

Among the owner's duties and responsibilities are:

- Provision of adequate funds, a site, and information necessary to define his need.
- Employment of competent professionals to design and engineer the project.
- Selection and employment of construction professionals to build the project.
- Administration of the budget and payment of monies earned and due.
- Rendering of approvals and instructions when appropriate.
- Coordination of separate items of work.
- Inspection and acceptance of the completed project.

The Design Professional's Duties and Objectives

The design professional, like the owner, is seldom a single individual, but a carefully coordinated team of professionals, each a specialist in certain disciplines. Together this group establishes the building's design under the direction, responsibility, and coordination of the architect or engineer identified as the prime design professional. Figure 11.6 is a diagram of the design professional's organization, resources, and disciplines.

The primary objectives of the design professional are as follows:

- To serve the owner's needs and objectives competently and completely at an adequate profit to himself and his associates.
- To create a design that can be delivered within the owner's budget requirements, that will serve adequately for many years, and that will satisfy the concerns and regulations of the community in which it is constructed.
- To be recognized as a participant in a successful project that will bring credit to himself and all who participated in the endeavor.

The design professional, by training and experience, is the appropriate administrator of decisions and the author of documentation that delineates the final design of the project. As such, he is the logical party to make judgments and recommendations to the owner regarding

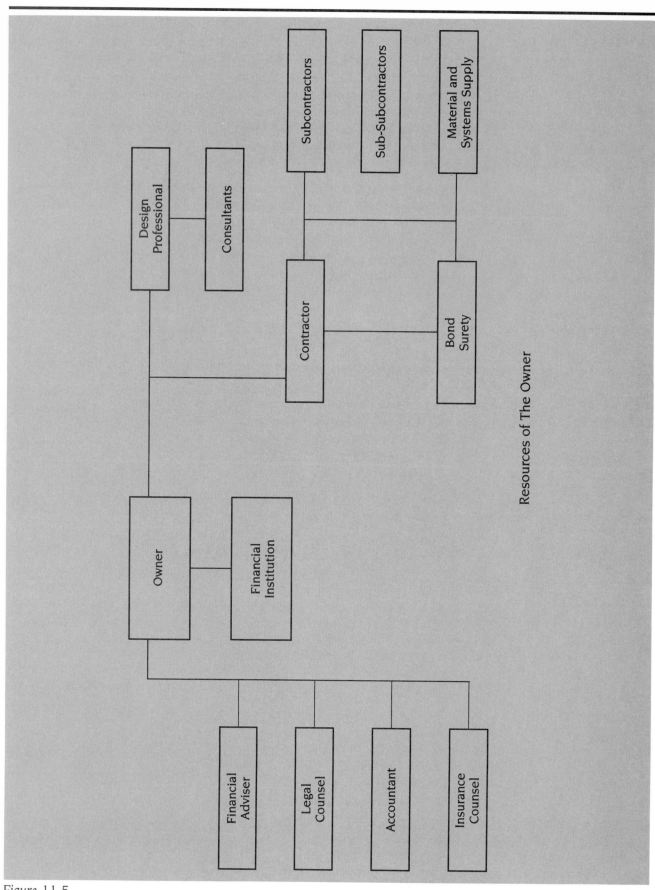

Resources of The Owner

Figure 11.5

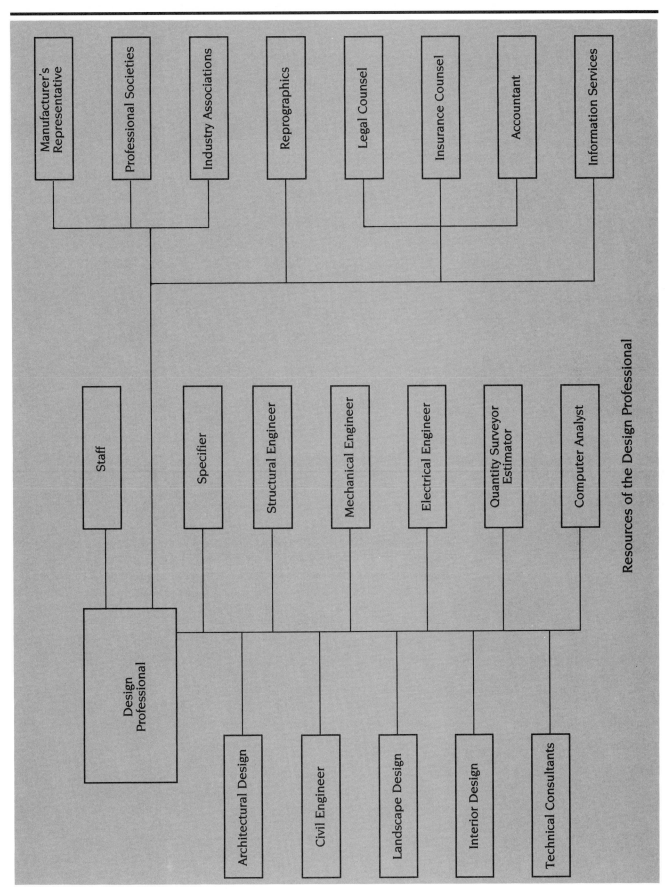

Resources of the Design Professional

Figure 11.6

257

appropriate materials, size, shape, function, arrangement of the envelope, and the immediate environment of the building and site. In principle, he is an extension of the owner, implementing the owner's resources to accomplish the owner's objectives. Once the design is complete and documented, and the constructor has been chosen and the construction begun, the design professional is the owner's representative, participating in the process by observing and administrating the contract for construction.

The Constructor's Duties and Objectives

The building's constructor, identified by the contract for construction as the (general) contractor, is the implementer of the construction process. Figure 11.7 shows the resources and organization of the typical general contractor—including personnel, subcontract resources, and source of supply. Such organizations vary greatly depending upon the size of the company and its capacity to accomplish work with "in-house" employees and equipment. The illustration is based on the typical medium-sized contractor and assumes that the contractor is capable of performing approximately 20% of the work with his own forces, with 80% accomplished by subcontractors.

It is the contractor's duty to organize and provide the labor, skills, supervision, materials, systems, equipment, tools and other resources necessary for the proper construction and completion of the project. The contractor's primary responsibilities may be:

- To adequately estimate the cost and time required to construct the proposed building, keeping in mind that the final result must be acceptable to both the owner and the design professional. To be selected over the competition, while at the same time maintaining an adequate margin and profit potential.
- To administrate the construction process, management and procurement of the material, systems, means, resources and personnel required to construct the building while maintaining or exceeding the profit objectives established when the contract sum was offered.
- To complete the work in a competent, efficient and timely manner that will bring credit to himself and his organization.

In the typical contract for construction, the contractor, and the contractor alone, is responsible for the means and methods of construction. He is responsible for observing and adhering to the full intent and content of the contract documents, authored by the design professional. The contract documents establish the duties and responsibilities of the owner, design professional, contractor, subcontractor, and sub-subcontractor. They also illustrate the building and its components and establish the quality of materials, components, assemblies, equipment, workmanship and delivery requirements of the project. The contractor has full discretion (with certain controls for the owner's approval and protection) to pursue and execute the work in the most appropriate and expeditious manner available under the guidance of the contract documents.

The Construction Manager

Because of the complexity of modern building construction, some owners—both private and public—may wish to hire an independent *Construction Manager* to represent their interests during the critical construction phase of the project. In this role, the construction manager serves as liaison between owner, design professional, contractor and

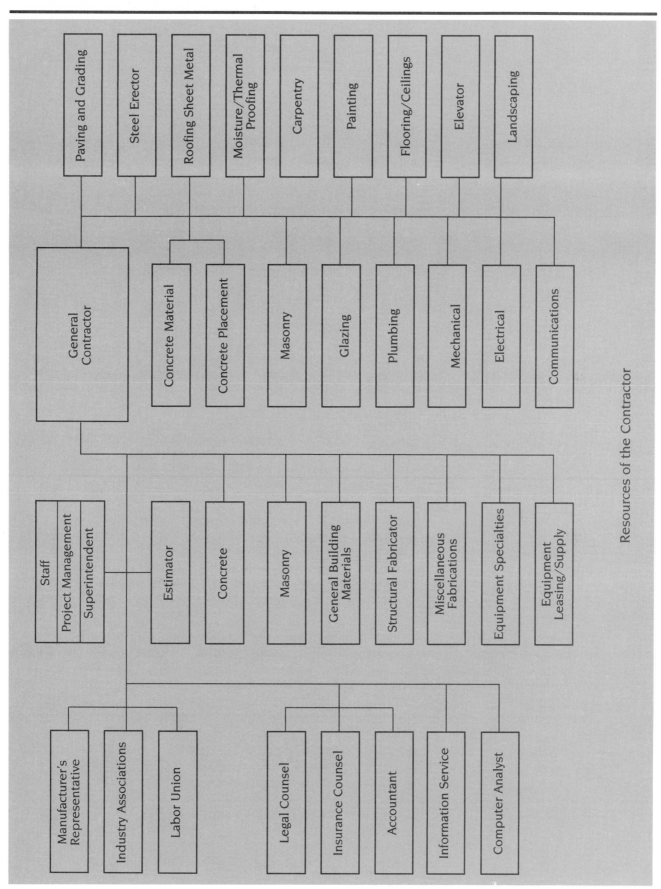

Figure 11.7

Resources of the Contractor

building official. In some respects, the construction manager's duties may overlap, and even conflict with the responsibility of the design professional. Appropriate measures must be taken in modifying the contract documents to avoid any conflict or confusion. Paragraph 1.5.4 of AIA document B 141—*Standard Form of Agreement Between Owner and Architect* makes clear the fact that unless otherwise provided, the design professional . . ."shall not be required to make exhaustive or continuous on site-inspections to check the quality or quantity of the Work. . .". The duties of the construction manager, employed by the owner, include "exhaustive and continuous on site inspections to check the quality and quantity of the Work", and reporting of these inspections. Depending on the type of contract, the construction manager may be an independent construction professional, with the design professional acting under an extension to the basic services agreement, or in certain contracting methods, may be employed instead of a general contractor. In this latter case, the construction manager is responsible for coordinating the work under a series of subcontracts (or multiple prime contracts) and purchase orders for materials and manufactured items.

The Owner's Representative

The owner, particularly the corporate owner, may wish to employ, if not a construction manager, an *Owner's Representative*. The role of an owner's representative is to be available on a full-time basis to represent the owner's interests in the work. In addition, this representative would see that the owner's duties and responsibilities, special work and separate contracts, and other related duties and privileges are carried out, properly coordinated and completed according to the provisions of the various contracts and agreements. A typical profile of an owner's representative may be as follows:

- An Architect or Engineer.
- If not a licensed professional, someone with training and experience in building construction and administration.
- An individual with an eye for detail and keen powers of observation.
- Someone with a distinct and proven ability to draw up and maintain records, conduct and chair meetings, and capable of understanding the content, meaning and application of the various contract documents.

Representatives of the Design Professional

A design professional's representative, or Construction Administrator, may be employed to assist in the many responsibilities of the design professional during the construction process. Such an individual, sufficiently experienced and qualified, can be a valuable source of information and criticism regarding the continuing quality standards of the design professional's practice. This representative can also act as an observer and reporter on the construction process of particular projects. Figure 11.8 illustrates AIA Document B352—*Duties, Responsibilities and Limitations of Authority of the Architect's Project Representative.* A qualified project representative should:

- Have experience in building construction as contractor or contractor's superintendent.
- Be familiar with all aspects, materials and methods, of the particular types of construction he is asked to observe.

- Be intimately familiar with the contract documents of the project, particularly the drawings and specifications.
- Have a keen eye for detail and know the proper sequence of construction, as well as the provisions of and schedule for inspections of various portions of the work before they are covered.
- Finally, his integrity, background and general character should be above reproach.

The Construction Superintendent

The Construction Superintendent plays a key role in the ultimate success and quality of the construction project. This is true regardless of the capability, integrity and experience of other representatives of the owner and design professional. The construction superintendent is the coordinator of the contractor's responsibilities. He implements the construction schedule, marshals the manpower and effort of workers on the job, receives materials, and arranges for the storage, inventory and protection of the construction materials. He coordinates the work of subcontractors and sub-subcontractors and communicates with the design professional and his staff, as well as the construction manager and owner's representatives. A construction superintendent should:

- Be thoroughly experienced in building construction and possess strong leadership ability in the field.
- Have a good rapport with the various elements of the construction industry.
- Be able to direct, communicate effectively with worker and professional alike, and display a strong sense of responsibility and trust.
- Be able to maintain positive control during times of crisis, criticism, dispute and emergency.
- Be familiar with all aspects of applicable building codes, government regulations, industry standards, safety requirements and procedures.
- Be thoroughly knowledgeable of required and applicable labor rates and requirements, equal opportunity requirements and procedures, rules and regulations concerning hiring practices, and other labor-related legislation and procedures.
- Have a thorough understanding of the requirements and intent of the contract documents.
- Be able to plan ahead and anticipate the needs of the project several weeks or months beyond the work in progress. Planning ahead is necessary to coordinate the activities of many different workers, tradesmen, subcontractors, suppliers and others involved in executing the work.

Contractor's Project Manager

Many contractors responsible for a number of concurrent projects may employ executive assistants with title of *Project Manager*. The project manager performs a variety of middle management functions in the construction process, serving as a liaison between field and office. The project manager may supervise the ordering of material and equipment as well as the subcontracting record keeping, correspondence, and handling of submittals and other communications.

DUTIES, RESPONSIBILITIES AND LIMITATIONS OF AUTHORITY OF THE ARCHITECT'S PROJECT REPRESENTATIVE

AIA DOCUMENT B352

Recommended as an Exhibit When an Architect's Project Representative is Employed

1. GENERAL

1.1 The Architect and the Architect's Project Representative have authority to act on behalf of the Owner only to the extent provided in contractual agreements to which the Architect is a party. The Project Representative shall confer with the Architect at intervals and on occasions appropriate to the stage of construction. The Project Representative shall communicate with the Owner through, or as directed by, the Architect; and shall not communicate with Subcontractors unless authorized by the Contractor and the Architect.

2. DUTIES AND RESPONSIBILITIES

2.1 Observe the progress and quality of the Work as is reasonably necessary at that stage of construction to determine in general that it is proceeding in accordance with the Contract Documents. Notify the Architect immediately if, in the Project Representative's opinion, Work does not conform to the Contract Documents or requires special inspection or testing.

2.2 Monitor the construction schedule and report to the Architect conditions which may cause delay in completion.

2.3 Review Contract Documents with the Contractor's superintendent. Obtain necessary interpretations from the Architect and transmit them to the Contractor.

2.4 Consider the Contractor's suggestions and [recom]mendations, evaluate them and submit the[m with recom]mendations, to the Architect for a f[inal decision.]

2.5 Attend meetings as d[irected and] report to the Architect on th[e . . .]

2.6 Observe tests required [. . .] Record and report to the Ar[chitect . . .] and, where applicable, the res[ults . . .] to be paid by the Owner.

2.7 Maintain records at the co[nstruction site in an or]derly manner. Include correspo[ndence, agree]ments, Change Orders, Construct[ion Change Direc]tions, Architect's Supplemental I[nstructions, field] site conferences, Shop Drawings, P[roduct Data and] supplementary drawings, color sch[edules, Applications for] payment, and names and addresses [of Sub]contractors and principal material sup[pliers.]

2.8 Keep a diary or log book recordin[g the] Project Representative's time and activities related to the Project, weather conditions, nature and location of Work being performed, verbal instructions and interpretations given to the Contractor, and specific observations. Record any occurrence or Work that might result in a claim for a change in Contract Sum or Contract Time. Maintain a list of visitors, their titles, and time and purpose of their visit.

2.9 Assist the Architect in reviewing Shop Drawings, Product Data and Samples. Notify the Architect if any portion of the Work requiring Shop Drawings, Product Data or Samples is commenced before such submittals have been approved by the Architect. Receive and log Samples which are required to be furnished at the site, notify the Architect when they are ready for examination, and record the Architect's approval or other action. Maintain custody of approved Samples.

2.10 Observe the Contractor's Record Drawings at intervals appropriate to the stage of construction and notify the Architect of any apparent failure by the Contractor to maintain up-to-date records.

2.11 Review Applications for Payment submitted by the Contractor and forward them to the Architect with recommendations for disposition.

2.12 Review the list of items to be completed or corrected which is submitted by the Contractor with a request for issuance of a Certificate of Substantial Completion. Inspect the Work and if the list is accurate, forward it to the Architect for final disposition; if not, so advise the Architect, and return the list to the Contractor for correction.

2.13 Review and report to the Archite[c]t on conditions of the portions of the Project bein[g . . . complet]ed or utilized by the Owner or separate [. . . to m]inimize the possibility of claims f[. . .]

2.14 A[ssist . . . completio]n of the Work. [. . . f]or transmittal [. . . Con]tractor is re[. . . W]ork.

[. . .]cuments. [. . . e]xcept as [. . .]r third [. . . b]y the [. . . du]ties of the Contractor's [. . . sub]contractors.

[. . . advi]se on, or issue directions concerning, aspects of construction means, methods, techniques, sequences or procedures, or safety precautions and programs in connection with the Work.

3.7 Authorize or suggest that the Owner occupy the Project in whole or part.

3.8 Issue a Certificate for Payment or Certificate of Substantial Completion.

3.9 Prepare or certify to the preparation of Record Drawings.

3.10 Reject Work or require special inspection or testing except as authorized in writing by the Architect.

3.11 Order the Contractor to stop the Work or any portion thereof.

AIA DOCUMENT B352 • ARCHITECT'S PROJECT REPRESENTATIVE • MAY 1979 EDITION • AIA® • © 1979
THE AMERICAN INSTITUTE OF ARCHITECTS, 1735 NEW YORK AVE., N.W., WASHINGTON, D.C. 20006

B352 — 1979

(courtesy American Institute of Architects)

Figure 11.8

262

Subcontractors

In today's highly specialized world, a great percentage of buildings may be constructed by subcontractors selected, contracted, and supervised by the contractor. Although this practice is convenient for the contractor, reducing his continuing overhead cost of personnel and inventory, subcontracting can also pose some difficulties. Among the challenges are: getting some subcontractors to return to the job site for completion of minor items or repair of damage, and the problems of coordinating many trade activities in a complicated sequence of work.

The general contractor is responsible for the entire project. Portions of the contract sum may be retained by the owner until the project is completed, including "punch list" items discovered by the owner's representative and/or the design professional. For example, a building project is valued at $1,000,000. A retainage of 5% would amount to $50,000. In a project of this size, the painting subcontract could amount to $50,000. If the contractor followed suit with his subcontractors and retained 5% of the contract sum against final completion, the amount retained from the painting subcontract would be only $2,500.00. A busy painter, working in an active job market may find it costly to return to a project for touch-up work at the contractor's convenience when such a small sum is outstanding. He may instead choose to return at his own convenience making it difficult for the contractor to finish the building on time. If substantial portions (approaching 100%) of the work are accomplished by subcontractors, and the retainage is 5% or less, it may be difficult, if not impossible to complete the work on a timely basis. For this reason, many owners and design professionals choose to qualify bidders on the basis that 20% or more of the work be accomplished using the contractors' own forces.

It is difficult for the contractor, subject to the competitive bidding process, to readily identify the subcontractors he intends to employ at the time the bids are due. Competition is keen for subcontractor awards, and confidentiality is not always strictly observed among competing subcontractors. A practice known as "shopping" often takes place. In this practice, a contractor may reveal the sub-bid proposal of one subcontractor to another in an effort to force the price of that work down, and thus increasing his own potential profit. This practice has become so widespread that many astute subcontractors will wait until the last minutes before the candidate contractor seals the bid to the owner to reveal his price for the subcontract work. Most general requirements (Division 1 of the specifications) require the contractor to provide a list of proposed subcontractors within 10 days or so of the bid opening for the owner's and/or design professional's approval before executing the contract for construction. This practice is in the owner's best interest and tends to help prevent subcontractors with a questionable reputation or inferior credit rating from becoming involved in the project.

Manufacturers and Materials

The specifications are frequently written in such a way as to give the contractor the widest possible latitude in achieving competition in the price of materials, assemblies, equipment, and other components of the building. In the case of public contracts, non-proprietary specifying is often a requirement. It is common practice to require the apparent low-bidder, prior to award of contract, to draw up a listing by CSI number of the materials and manufacturers he intends to use for the building construction. This listing is submitted to the design professional for approval.

Project Meetings

Project meetings can be time consuming, expensive, and inconvenient, but they are also necessary to the enormous task of coordinating the project. Such meetings are essential to the collective interests of the OPC relationship, and are to be preserved and enforced. Properly prepared Division 1 sections will require certain meetings to be attended by all concerned parties from time to time during the project development.

Pre-Bid Conference: The pre-bid conference allows questions, bidding instructions, and other pertinent information to be discussed among the competitors, their major subcontractors, the owner's representative, and the design professional who has prepared the contract and bidding documents. Much time can be saved if all attend, as confusion and potential misunderstandings can be cleared up at such meetings.

Pre-Construction Conference: A pre-construction conference may be held prior to the order to proceed with construction. Such a meeting is often helpful in clearing up any unfulfilled submittal or qualification items as well as to establish construction scheduling, coordination of the work, and any remaining uncertainty as to the role to be played by the various members of the construction "team".

Coordination Meetings: The general contractor should call frequent meetings between his superintendent, project manager, and major subcontractors in order to better schedule start dates and coordination between the work of different trades, much of which will take place at the same time in the same space.

Progress Meetings: The owner and the design professional may find it useful to hold monthly, or even weekly progress meetings with the contractor and his superintendent. Such a meeting provides an opportunity to discuss monthly pay requests, the current percentage of completion, concerns of the owner and the design professional's representatives, and the overall progress of the work. This practice can do much to prevent future disputes and legal problems, with corresponding negotiation and compromise.

Transmittals

The need to transmit information, instructions, drawings, samples, and correspondence between the various elements in the construction process is both significant and frequent. Time is the essence of the contract and documentation must be kept of the transactions. Figure 11.9 illustrates a Means Letter of Transmittal. This (or a similar) form allows the sender to communicate considerable information about the particular transmittal including: the date, name of the individual and company to whom it is addressed, the nature and purpose of the transmittal, and the action that is required as a result. Also included are a description of what is being transmitted and a provision for any remarks or explanations.

▲ Means Forms

**LETTER
OF TRANSMITTAL**

FROM:

_____

_____

_____

_____

TO: _____

_____

_____

_____

DATE _____

PROJECT _____

LOCATION _____

ATTENTION _____

RE: _____

_____

_____

_____

_____

Gentlemen:

　　　　WE ARE SENDING YOU　　☐ HEREWITH　　　☐ DELIVERED BY HAND　　　☐ UNDER SEPARATE COVER

VIA _____ THE FOLLOWING ITEMS:

☐ PLANS　　　☐ PRINTS　　　☐ SHOP DRAWINGS　　　☐ SAMPLES　　　☐ SPECIFICATIONS

☐ ESTIMATES　☐ COPY OF LETTER　　☐ _____

COPIES	DATE OR NO.	DESCRIPTION

　　　THESE ARE TRANSMITTED AS INDICATED BELOW

☐ FOR YOUR USE　　　　　　　☐ APPROVED AS NOTED　　　　　☐ RETURN _____ CORRECTED PRINTS

☐ FOR APPROVAL　　　　　　　☐ APPROVED FOR CONSTRUCTION　☐ SUBMIT _____ COPIES FOR_____

☐ AS REQUESTED　　　　　　　☐ RETURNED FOR CORRECTIONS　　☐ RESUBMIT_____ COPIES FOR_____

☐ FOR REVIEW AND COMMENT　☐ RETURNED AFTER LOAN TO US　　☐ FOR BIDS DUE_____

☐ _____

REMARKS: _____

_____

_____

_____

_____

_____

IF ENCLOSURES ARE NOT AS INDICATED,
PLEASE NOTIFY US AT ONCE.

SIGNED: _____

Figure 11.9

The transmittal form or letter serves several functions explained as follows:

- It establishes what, when, why, and how a significant piece of information is transmitted.
- It establishes the date and fact of transmittal. Such a record is useful should data be lost, misplaced, or misdirected.
- It provides a permanent record of the sender's compliance with his responsibilities under the contract for construction.

Submittals

Other chapters have addressed the subject of submittals in various contexts. The following is a review of some of the submittals that may be required of the contractor during the construction process:

- Samples of materials and finishes.
- Samples of manufactured assemblies.
- Manufacturer's literature, installation or application instructions, maintenance data and similar information.
- Certification that a material, assembly, or piece of equipment is in compliance with the requirements of the contract documents.
- Test results that may be required by the building inspector or by a specification provision.
- Shop drawings indicating the fabrication, assembly, installation, and other physical aspects of a construction component.
- Progress schedules, construction sequence, compliance with time requirements, and other data concerning the completion of the work.
- Requests for clarification, information, action, approval or any other interaction between the participants in the construction process.

The process of requesting, receiving, and processing submittals during construction serves a number of major purposes. In general, submittals document compliance with the intent and requirements of the contract documents. When submittals are required, the contractor must prevail upon his subcontractors, vendors, selected manufacturers, and others to document the materials, assemblies, equipment, and/or systems as needed. The design professional generally writes specifications and creates drawings that are generic in order to allow a wide margin for competition in price and labor. The various submittals, when transmitted according to the requirements of the contract documents, allow the design professional the opportunity to either confirm or reject the proposed product. If the proposal is rejected, the design professional can communicate his objection, and indicate why and on what basis the submittal is unsatisfactory. Figure 11.10 shows the form and content of a stamp typically used by design professionals to indicate their actions regarding a particular submittal. The statement made by the approval stamp is, in effect, a disclaimer. The design professional's approval acknowledges general compliance with the intent of the contract documents. The design professional does not assume any responsibility for the correctness of dimension, correlation of job site conditions, or construction means and methods. This statement is generally in accord with Article 2.2 of the General Conditions which sets forth the design professional's responsibilities regarding administration of the contract for construction.

Samples

Submittals of materials and product samples illustrating color, texture, composition, and other attributes allows the design professional to approve and confirm the actual material that will be used in the construction. If the approved samples are kept at the job site, they can also provide a basis of comparison to confirm that the requirements and intent of the contract documents have been met. Many products made by different manufacturers are similar in nature, but competitive in price and availability. The contractor will choose the product he intends to use, but if required, must seek the design professional's approval before the material is ordered or otherwise committed to the project. In most instances the design professional specifies the material or product in such a way that any one of several products may satisfy the design requirement. Approved samples confirm agreement between design professional and contractor on a particular product.

Manufacturers' Literature

Many products used in building construction have been carefully formulated, designed, and manufactured for specific applications and uses. In many instances, the design professional will require that manufacturer's literature regarding specific products be submitted prior to approval. In this way, the manufacturer's responsibility for the use and reliability of the product is reasonably assured. The huge commitment of capital expended by a manufacturer to develop and produce the product, and make it available to the market, means that he has, in all likelihood, tested and explored the limits and capabilities of the product. Chances are, the product has been classified among

☐ NO EXCEPTION TAKEN   ☐ EXCEPTIONS NOTED

☐ SUBMIT SPECIFIED ITEM   ☐ REVISE & RESUBMIT

Checking is only for general conformance with design concept of project and general compliance with Contract Documents. Contractor is responsible for confirming and correlating dimensions at job site: for information which pertains to fabrication processes of construction techniques and for coordination of work of all trades. Checking of shop drawings shall not relieve Contractor of responsibility for deviation from requirements of Contract Documents nor for errors or omissions in shop drawings.

BY: _____   DATE: _____

WALLER S. POAGE, ARCHITECT

Figure 11.10

commonly accepted industry standards and comes with general warranties and limited guarantees as to its performance and use when installed, assembled, or applied in accordance with the manufacturer's instructions and recommendations. The manufacturer is generally the best source of information as to the methods, advantages, disadvantages and limitations of the product's use and what accessory items, tools, fasteners, adhesives and other processes should be employed in its application or installation. By requiring the contractor to use, apply, or install the product in strict accordance with the manufacturer's instructions and recommendations, the design professional provides himself and the owner with an additional layer of protection against the failure of building components. This is accomplished by adding the manufacturer to those responsible for the performance and compatibility of a specified product used in the building's construction. The implications of manufacturer's guarantees and warranties are discussed in some detail in subsequent paragraphs.

Certifications

A *Certificate* is a document which serves as evidence or testimony as to the status, qualification, privilege, or truth of a matter that must be substantiated. Certificates play an important role in establishing solid evidence that a certain requirement of the contract is, has, or can be met in a particular way. It is often necessary to require a manufacturer to certify in writing that his material has been used in a project in accordance with his best intent for that product and that the installation or application has been accomplished in accordance with the proper methods and intent of that product. In many instances, certification by a contractor, subcontractor, manufacturer, or vendor is the most mutually satisfactory method whereby the owner can be assured that certain building components meet or exceed his performance expectations.

Test Results

Testing is the most satisfactory method of assuring the adequacy and performance capability of a preparation, a material, a mixture of materials, an assembly, or fabrication of components. It is also a way to judge the operation of a system or piece of equipment, or the stability of a structural component used in building construction. The types and capabilities of testing and the responsibility for this aspect of the project are discussed in Chapters 7 and 9 of this book.

In the absence of certification, testing is often required by the building official to prove that a certain component meets or exceeds the requirements of the building code. In other cases, the design professional requires testing of certain items to confirm compliance with the contract documents as construction proceeds. Such tests, common to most building projects may include the following:

- Testing of the quality, bearing capacity, nature and composition of soils and subsoils.
- Testing of mixtures such as asphalt, concrete, and mortar for structural and other performance properties once they are mixed, placed, and cured.
- Testing of structural and other components for performance under conditions of stress, strain, compression and tension.
- Testing of joining methods such as welding, gluing, fastening, and other means of connecting materials and components.

- Testing of various materials for thermal expansion and contraction, hardness, flame spread and support, smoke contribution when subjected to fire, and similar properties.
- Testing of various materials and assemblies for thermal and acoustical properties.
- Testing of various materials, assemblies and enclosures for resistance to fire and smoke.
- Testing of various materials for compatibility when used in conjunction with other materials.
- Testing of piping assemblies for resistance to pressure and leaks.
- Testing of mechanical and electrical systems.

Shop Drawings

Shop drawings prepared under the direction of the contractor confirm the design and detailing of fabricated components, equipment, assemblies, and systems by illustrating the exact properties, dimensions, materials, finishes, installation methods, and/or other attributes of construction elements that are to be provided. As with other types of submittals, shop drawings give the design professional and the contractor the opportunity to communicate and agree upon construction details. The design professional's approval of shop drawings indicates agreement, but (as the design professional's approval stamp in Figure 11.10 indicates) does not waive the contractor's responsibility to meet the requirements of the contract documents.

Schedules

The art and technique of scheduling the modern construction project is a science worthy of a separate volume unto itself. For the purposes of this discussion, it is sufficient to touch briefly upon the requirements for construction schedule preparation and submittal in terms of the contract documents.

As discussed in the General Conditions of the Contract, time is the "essence" of the contract. When the contract for construction is executed, the contractor has usually agreed to complete the work in a specific number of calendar days. The construction schedule required by the design professional serves a number of purposes as follows:
- It confirms the contractor's commitment as to when construction shall be complete.
- It provides a "road map" of how and in what sequence the work will be achieved.
- It provides a ready reference as to the timeliness of the construction progress at the time of each monthly pay request.
- It shows the impact of changes to the contract on the time of completion.
- It serves as a planning guide to all participants in the construction process.

Figure 11.11 is a simple bar-graph type construction schedule that plots various kinds of work on a straight line basis over time plotted in terms of months. Figure 11.12 is an example of a more sophisticated construction schedule prepared by use of network scheduling which identifies the "critical path" of the construction process. This critical path method (CPM) considers the earliest and latest starting dates that various sequences of the work can be accomplished while keeping in proper sequence with other trades.

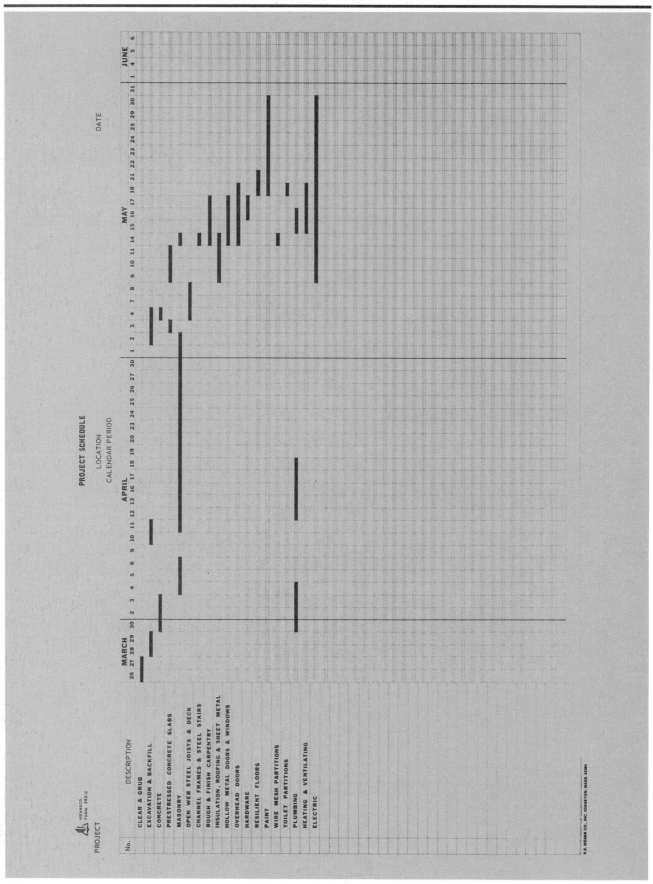

Figure 11.11

270

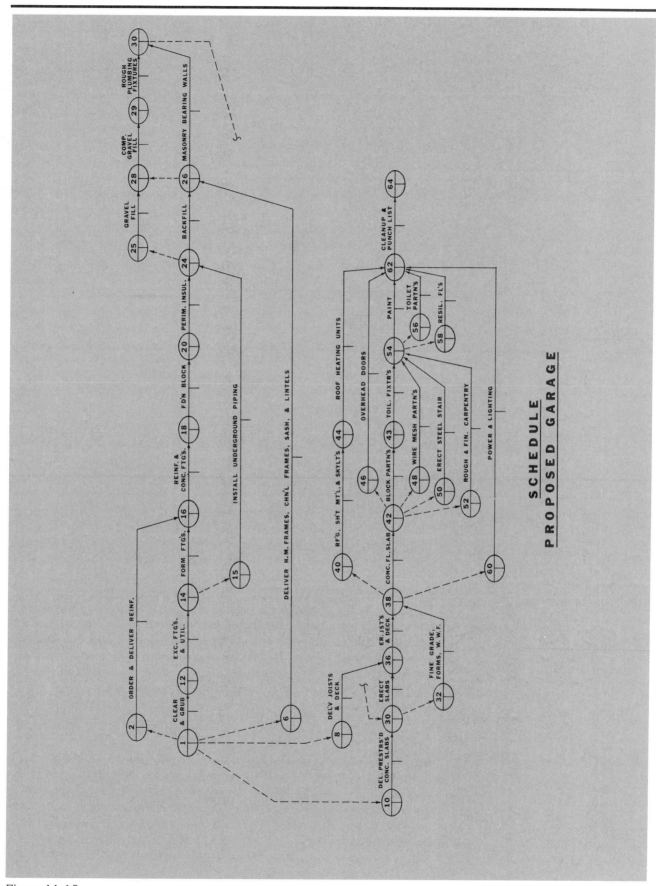

Figure 11.12

In the early 1900's the growth of industry led to the creation of organizations like the National Bureau of Standards and American Society for Testing Materials. At this time, Henry L. Gantt and Fredrick W. Taylor began to work with graphic representations of work versus time. Their technique soon became known as Gantt Charts and are the forerunners of today's bar charts of activity vs. time (as illustrated in Figure 11.11).

The basic problem with construction scheduling by the bar chart method is that the simple bar graph is limited in terms of the information it can present. A major drawback is its inability to present opportunities for saving time and money. Preparation of a bar chart is often influenced by an assumed completion date rather than a predicted and more realistic date based on a network of events. The network, or CPM method (illustrated in Figure 11.12) considers each event from the standpoint of earliest start and completion date. It then relates subsequent events that can take place concurrently, along with the earliest and the latest dates that they can begin. By placing all of the events in a graphic network the best possible completion date for the entire project can be predicted.

The Critical Path Method (CPM) of planning and scheduling apparently began in the mid 1950's when the E.I. Du Pont Company first used a computer to schedule and correlate management of the company's engineering functions for an expanded building program. The resulting computerized scheduling technique became known as the *Kelley-Walker Method*. This procedure was the forerunner of what we know today as CPM. In the late 1950's, the Special Projects Office of the U. S. Navy Bureau of Ordinance developed a similar program called *Program Evaluation Research Task* (PERT) to assist with the development of the Polaris missile program. Today variations and combinations of CPM and PERT are used to generate very sophisticated construction schedules. Compared to traditional methods, such schedules can help to reduce construction time by as much as 40%.

Mock-Ups

Often, the design of a particular building requires the assembly of certain materials and systems whose workmanship, detailing, finish or other physical characteristics are critical to the quality and objectives of the designer's art and intention. This critical attention to detail usually applies to systems and components that require either a mix of basic ingredients, such as concrete or precast concrete, or the assembly of many pieces such as occurs with various kinds of masonry. A "mock-up", or sample panel or section of certain critical design components, can be helpful to both designer and contractor and may be constructed for approval by the design professional. This sample may serve as a standard of quality and consistency for the actual work. Sometimes the "mock-up" is constructed in such a way that it can later be incorporated into the work. In other cases, the mock-up is placed at some conspicuous location on the site where it remains for study and comparison until it no longer serves a useful purpose. It is then discarded. Mock-ups may be required of any number of different

systems including those listed below:
- Architectural Precast Concrete Panels
- Masonry
- Window Wall
- Plaster Work
- Ornamental Metal
- Special Architectural Features
- Special Finishes
- Millwork
- Woodwork
- Windows
- Doors

Requests and Certificates for Payment

The Contract Documents normally make provision for the contractor to be paid on a specific periodic basis. Most contracts provide the owner the right to retain a certain percentage of the amount due. This withheld amount, or "retainage", gives the owner a slight leverage toward the matter of final completion and closeout of the contract. Depending upon the nature of the project, whether it is public or private work, and any local law regulating the owner's rights to retain such a percentage, most contracts recognize an adequate retainage to be between 5% and 10%. The contract language concerning retainage may appear as follows:

"On or about the tenth day of each month, the contractor shall be paid an amount equal to 90 percent of the value, based on the Contract prices of labor and materials incorporated in the work and 50 percent of materials suitably stored at the site up to the first day of that month, as estimated by the Architect, less the aggregate of previous payments; and upon substantial completion of the entire work, a sum sufficient to increase the total payments to 95 percent of the Contract price."

Article 9 of AIA Document A201—*General Conditions of the Contract for Construction* relates to payments made to the contractor and conditions of completion. It is common practice for the contractor to be paid 90% to 95% of all amounts due, and for the owner to withhold the difference as "retainage", an amount which is not paid until Substantial Completion.

Payment for materials delivered and suitably stored at the site (prior to installation) varies depending upon the locality and other factors. In 1980, the high losses from theft prompted many insurance carriers to exclude any material from theft coverage if it has not been incorporated into the work. For this reason, many owners will not pay the contractor for material not yet "in-place". The design professional should determine the owner's policy on this matter and specify (or exclude) provisions for such payments in the contract documents. In this way, bidders know what to expect when submitting proposals.

Figure 11.13 illustrates AIA Document G702—*Application and Certificate for Payment*. As this form is designed, each application builds upon the information provided in the previous application. The application form is initiated by the contractor, who first prepares a form similar to the *Continuation Sheet* (AIA Document G703 shown in Figure 11.14). The continuation sheet lists each item established in the *Schedule of Values*. Column D provides space for the total value of work completed as of the previous application. Column E lists the value of work completed for each item since the last application. Column F provides space to add the value of materials that are stored on the site, but not yet installed in the job. By dividing the amount for each item under Column C by the value of the same item under Column G, a percentage of completion can be derived for each item recorded in the % (G-C) column. By subtracting the value of each item listed under the first G column from the corresponding column of C, a value is obtained that represents the balance to be completed. This figure can be recorded in Column H. By applying the retainage factor (to calculate the amount held by the owner until substantial completion), the retainage value for each item on the schedule of values can be obtained and then recorded in Column I. Each column is added and crosschecked, and the total of each column is recorded at the bottom of the sheet. Larger projects may require several sheets.

The "Application for Payment" portion of AIA Document G702 is completed by the contractor, and the "Certificate For Payment" portion is completed by the design professional. In the "Application" portion of the form, space is provided to record the total impact of change orders made prior to the current application period. Separate columns are provided to separate additions and deductions to the contract during previous application periods. Another space allows for a record of any current and total change orders.

The current status of the contract sum and the amount due the contractor can be determined next. The Original Contract Sum is the amount recorded in the Contract for Construction. Next, costs are entered from the adjacent Change Order Summary that appears on the same sheet. The "Total Completed and Stored to Date" is taken from the total of Column G on the continuation sheet (AIA Document G703). Total retainage through the current application is calculated. "Total Earned Less Retainage" is determined and recorded as instructed. The total of payments made to date is recorded and the amount of the current payment due is then calculated. The balance to finish is also calculated as instructed, and recorded. The contractor signs the application in the presence of a Notary Public. The application is then transmitted to the design professional, who verifies the contractor's numbers based on his own records and observations. The amount verified and approved by the design professional as due and payable to the contractor is recorded in the space provided. The application is then transmitted to the owner and payment is made to the contractor.

The design professional has the responsibility of certifying the contractor's applications for payment. The design professional should be aware that in the event that the contractor is certified for amounts that in effect overpay him for the value of the work, the DP could be liable for losses sustained by surety in the event that the contractor should default and surety be called upon to complete the work.

Substantial Completion

Substantial Completion is defined in paragraph 9.8 of AIA Document A201—*General Conditions of the Contract for Construction* (see Chapter 7). When this stage of the construction is reached, all work should be finished with only minor items, if any, left to be completed.

APPLICATION AND CERTIFICATE FOR PAYMENT   AIA DOCUMENT G702   (Instructions on reverse side)

PAGE ONE OF   PAGES

Distribution to:
☐ OWNER
☐ ARCHITECT
☐ CONTRACTOR
☐ ☐

TO (OWNER):

PROJECT:

APPLICATION NO:

PERIOD TO:

FROM (CONTRACTOR):

VIA (ARCHITECT):

ARCHITECT'S
PROJECT NO:

CONTRACT FOR:

CONTRACT DATE:

Application is made for Payment, as shown below, in connection with the Contract.
Continuation Sheet, AIA Document G703, is attached.

1. ORIGINAL CONTRACT SUM .... $
2. Net change by Change Orders .... $
3. CONTRACT SUM TO DATE (Line 1 ± 2) .... $
4. TOTAL COMPLETED & STORED TO DATE .... $
   (Column G on G703)
5. RETAINAGE:
   a. ____ % of Completed Work $ _____
      (Column D + E on G703)
   b. ____ % of Stored Material $ _____
      (Column F on G703)
   Total Retainage (Line 5a + 5b or
   Total in Column 1 of G703) .... $
6. TOTAL EARNED LESS RETAINAGE .... $
   (Line 4 less Line 5 Total)
7. LESS PREVIOUS CERTIFICATES FOR
   PAYMENT (Line 6 from prior Certificate) .... $
8. CURRENT PAYMENT DUE .... $
9. BALANCE TO FINISH, PLUS RETAINAGE .... $
   (Line 3 less Line 6)

CONTRACTOR'S APPLICATION FOR PAYMENT

CHANGE ORDER SUMMARY

Change Orders approved in
previous months by Owner

TOT...

Approved this Month

Number	Date Approved

TOTALS

Net change by Change Orders

The undersigned Contractor certifies th... information and belief the Work covere... completed in accordance with the Contr... paid by the Contractor for Work for whi... issued and payments received from the ... herein is now due.

CONTRACTOR:

By:

State of: County of:
...bscribed and sworn to before me this   day of   ,19
...tary Public:
Commission expires:

...UNT CERTIFIED .... $
...h explanation if amount certified differs from the amount applied for.)
...TECT:

By: Date:
This Certificate is not negotiable. The AMOUNT CERTIFIED is payable only to the Contractor named herein. Issuance, payment and acceptance of payment are without prejudice to any rights of the Owner or Contractor under this Contract.

ARCHITECT'S CERTIFICATE

In accordance with the Contract Documents, based... data comprising the above application, the Architect... best of the Architect's knowledge, information and be... indicated, the quality of the Work is in accordance wit... the Contractor is entitled to payment of the AMOUN...

AIA DOCUMENT G702 • APPLICATION AND CERTIFICATE FOR PAYMENT • MAY 1983 EDITION • AIA® • © 1983
THE AMERICAN INSTITUTE OF ARCHITECTS, 1735 NEW YORK AVENUE, N.W., WASHINGTON, D.C. 20006

G702-1983

(courtesy American Institute of Architects)

Figure 11.13

CONTINUATION SHEET

AIA DOCUMENT G703   (Instructions on reverse side)   PAGE   OF   PAGES

AIA Document G702, APPLICATION AND CERTIFICATE FOR PAYMENT, containing
Contractor's signed Certification is attached.
In tabulations below, amounts are stated to the nearest dollar.
Use Column I on Contracts where variable retainage for line items may apply.

APPLICATION NUMBER:
APPLICATION DATE:
PERIOD TO:
ARCHITECT'S PROJECT NO:

A	B	C	D	E	F	G		H	I
			WORK COMPLETED						
ITEM NO.	DESCRIPTION OF WORK	SCHEDULED VALUE	FROM PREVIOUS APPLICATION (D + E)	THIS PERIOD	MATERIALS PRESENTLY STORED (NOT IN D OR E)	TOTAL COMPLETED AND STORED TO DATE (D+E+F)	% (G ÷ C)	BALANCE TO FINISH (C – G)	RETAINAGE

SAMPLE

AIA DOCUMENT G703 • APPLICATION AND CERTIFICATE FOR PAYMENT • MAY 1983 EDITION • AIA® • © 1983
THE AMERICAN INSTITUTE OF ARCHITECTS, 1735 NEW YORK AVENUE, N.W., WASHINGTON, D.C. 20006

G703-1983

(courtesy American Institute of Architects)

Figure 11.14

The "Punch List"

At the point of presumed substantial completion, notice is given by the contractor, together with a list of items that remain to be completed. The design professional will then inspect the work, make notes of his observations, and prepare an independent list of items to be completed, repaired, or replaced. This list of items is often called the "punch list". The contractor must then correct these deficiencies before receiving final payment. The term "punch list" comes from a nineteenth century custom whereby the superintendent used a special paper punch as his "seal", and punched a hole beside each item as it was completed, repaired, or replaced.

Certificate of Substantial Completion

Once the contractor and the design professional agree that Substantial Completion has been reached, AIA Document G704—*Certificate of Substantial Completion* is signed by the design professional, the contractor, and the owner. Provisions are made for the owner and contractor to agree on the disposition of security, maintenance, heat, utilities, any damage to the work that may occur after the date of Substantial Completion, and insurance coverage required beyond that date. Normally, the owner takes possession of the property and makes arrangement for the items named above. However, depending upon the nature and extent of the work that remains to be completed, alternate arrangements may need to be made through the time of final completion. A number of functions must take place at the time of Substantial Completion.

One of these functions is the notification of the Surety who has provided the Performance Bond and the Payment Bond for materials and labor. Arrangements must be made that are in keeping with the surety's responsibility to the owner.

Completion of AIA Document G706A—*Contractor's Affidavit of Release of Liens* and AIA Document G706—*Contractor's Affidavit of Payment of Debts and Claims* is the other function that must be performed at this time. An affidavit is, in the legal sense, an oath sworn before a public official. Using an affidavit such as AIA Document G706, the contractor testifies that he has paid in full all obligations for materials, equipment, labor, and services performed. The affidavit also includes statements that the contractor has resolved all known indebtedness and claims against him (for which the owner or surety may be held responsible) that are in any way connected with the performance of the Contract for Construction. If the contractor cannot so warrant, arrangements may be made to continue to withhold funds from the retainage; or, the contractor may provide additional bonding in an amount sufficient to cover any outstanding obligations, claims, or both. Supporting documents should include the following:

- Consent of surety to a reduction in and partial release of retainage or final payment.
- Separate releases or waivers of liens from subcontractors and material and equipment suppliers to the satisfaction of the owner.

One of the owner's greatest areas of vulnerability during the construction process is a claim from a third party who has not been paid for the work, materials, or equipment that he has provided for the project. The construction contract is an agreement between the owner and the contractor; thus it is the contractor alone who is paid for the work of all those he employs to accomplish the project. While it is the contractor's duty to pay others, there is nothing in the contract to guarantee that such payment will in fact take place. The owner's vulnerability comes from the lien rights provided by law for each mechanic and materialman who does any work on the project. Although the surety has provided a bond as additional protection for the owner, the most satisfactory method of assuring that no liens shall be filed is to require that waivers of such lien rights be obtained from all concerned prior to release of any retainage or final payment.

Project Closeout

There is an expression, "Building construction is much like reading a very dull book; it is easy to start but difficult to finish...". However the process of closing out a project is as critical to the owner's interest as any stage of the project. Procedures that are necessary to assure compliance with the contract documents include the following:

Documentation: As project construction nears completion, the contractor is generally remanded to collect all documentation required by the contract documents. The following items may be included:
- Guarantees
- Warranties
- Affidavits attesting that all payrolls and bills have been paid (waivers of lien).
- Consent of surety to final payment.
- Certificates of inspection.
- Operating manuals for: mechanical equipment and controls; electrical equipment and controls; other service equipment including parts list, operating instructions, maintenance instructions, and equipment warranties.
- Keys and keying schedule.
- Project Record Drawings.
- Miscellaneous items required by the contract documents.

Such documentation should be in accordance with the number of copies specified, and should be delivered to the owner upon completion of the Project.

Certifications: When the contractor considers that the work has reached final completion, he is usually required to submit written certification that the Contract Documents have been reviewed, that the work has been inspected by local authorities, and that the work is complete in accordance with the Contract Documents and ready for the design professional's inspection.

Code Compliance: In addition to the submittals that may be required by the conditions of the contract, the contractor should provide any information and certifications that may be required by governing authorities.

Final Accounting: The contractor should submit a final statement of accounting stating the total adjusted Contract Sum, total amount of previous payments, and a statement of the sum including retainage that may be remaining due.

Final Change Order: Upon receipt of the required data, the design professional should issue a final change order reflecting any approved adjustments to the contract sum not previously made by change order.

Final Cleaning: These operations are generally required prior to Substantial Completion and again prior to Final Inspection. Specifically, final cleaning entails:

- Cleaning of interior and exterior surfaces that are exposed to view. Removal of stains, foreign substances, and temporary labels.
- Polishing of transparent and glossy surfaces, and vacuuming of carpeted and soft surfaces.
- Cleaning of equipment and fixtures.
- Cleaning or replacement of filters on mechanical equipment.
- Cleaning of roofs, and verification that drainage systems are clean and free of all debris.
- Cleaning of site: sweeping of paved areas, raking and cleaning of other surfaces.
- Removal of waste and surplus materials, rubbish, and construction equipment from the buildings and from the site.

Project Record Documents: The contractor is generally required to store and maintain project record documents separately from those used for construction. Such records should be maintained on a daily basis with the caution that no work be permanently concealed until the required information (such as size of components, dimensions as to location and other "as built" information) has been recorded.

Systems Demonstration and Product Certification: Prior to final inspection, the contractor should demonstrate the operation of each system to the design professional and owner and (as required) instruct the owner and his personnel in the adjustment and maintenance of each piece of equipment and other systems. The operation and maintenance data are used as the basis of instruction. The contractor may be required to provide these additional certifications:

- That an authorized representative of each manufacturer of certain materials and/or equipment installed in the work has personally inspected the installation and operation of his material systems, and/or equipment and determined that they are correctly installed and operating properly.
- That inspections and testing have been accomplished for work which is not concealed and for work which is concealed during the course of construction. Inspections should be made both prior to concealment and after completion of the installation.

Warranties and bonds: The contractor is usually required to provide duplicate, notarized copies of all warranties and bonds including those furnished by subcontractors, suppliers, and manufacturers.

Spare parts and maintenance materials: It is not unusual for the contractor to be required to provide spare parts and maintenance materials for specific items which are usually specified in an individual section of the specifications.

Certificate of Occupancy

The Certificate of Occupancy is issued by the building official. It is not only a means of certifying that the finished project meets or exceeds all code requirements, but it is usually a mandatory requirement before the utilities of water, natural gas, and electricity can be delivered on a permanent basis to the owner. The Certificate of Occupancy assures code compliance from the contractor and major subcontractors.

Chapter 12
PROJECT RECORDS

This final chapter is devoted to the importance of record keeping throughout the construction process. It has been shown that there are easily thousands of decisions that must be made and consequently documented in the collective effort that is required to erect a modern building. Without proper methods for recording these developments and transactions, the progress of the project may be jeopardized.

The Record Keeping Process

Timely, informative, communicative, and accurate record keeping is not only desirable but essential to the success of today's construction project. Proper record keeping is also a key ingredient in the fortunes and success of all concerned participants including the owner, the design professional, the contractor, and the many others who become indirectly involved in the construction process. The advantages of record keeping are many. Among the most obvious benefits are the following:

- Each party to the construction process is linked to the combined effort by a contract or similar instrument which stipulates a promise and requires some form of consideration. Thus, there is a legal obligation on the part of both parties. Record keeping is the most convenient method of substantiating the fulfillment of an obligation and proper payment for that item or service, while documenting compliance with the requirements of the contract documents. Precise and complete records made and kept by all parties to the construction effort will, by no means, eliminate the possibility of dispute and litigation. It is, however, safe to say that without such records, frustrating and expensive disputes are far more likely.
- Documenting all modifications, submittals, approvals, agreements and other transactions expedites the collective work and coordination of all parties to the construction process.
- Written communications between parties to the contract for construction are the most effective method of efficiently managing the construction process. Compliance with contract document requirements is recorded in these types of records.
- Recording the exact location of items that are concealed by construction is extremely important. Such records are used by the owner during the life of the project for maintenance and safety purposes. This kind of documentation often proves invaluable should additions and alterations be made to the project in the future.

The American Institute of Architects publishes hundreds of prepared documents which can be used throughout design and construction. These documents can prove valuable as time-saving instruments to all building professionals. Only a portion are described and mentioned in this book. The AIA should be consulted for the latest versions of these and other documents.

Pre-Construction Submittals

The contract documents require the contractor to submit a significant amount of written information prior to the commencement of the construction process. Pre-construction submittals generally consist of documents describing how and by whom the construction process is to be conducted. Also included are certification of owner protection and other controls that should be approved before construction begins.

Bonds

The bonding or surety company (for projects where bonding is required) has a responsibility to the owner that may transcend the period of construction. In most jurisdictions, the contractor's general warranty of the completed work applies to a minimum one year period. Individual warranties for some specific building components may cover longer periods. If a guarantee or warranty needs to be enforced, or if the contractor should be unable or unwilling to fulfill such obligations, the bonding company could be called upon to do so.

Performance Bond

The *Performance Bond* (AIA Document A312) provides a guarantee from a surety that the contract for construction will be fulfilled in the event of failure or default by the contractor. The performance responsibility includes any guarantees and warranties that may be required of the contractor by the contract documents. Should the building or any portion thereof experience a failure resulting from faulty workmanship by the contractor, the bonding company's responsibility may transcend the period of construction and the general warranty period and extend to the limit of any statutes of limitations that may exist in the jurisdiction of the project. For this reason, the bond becomes a valuable permanent record to be retained by the owner, the design professional, and the contractor.

Labor and Material Payment Bond

Previous chapters have noted the importance to the owner of obtaining releases of lien from the contractor, various subcontractors, material suppliers, and others who may have a claim for payment before the project is closed out and the final payment made. Even though a diligent effort may have been made to obtain waivers of lien from all potential claimants, it is always possible that liens may be filed after the contract closeout. Many jurisdictions have established statutes of limitation that allow an alleged creditor to make a claim after total payment has been made and the contract closed out. Some unforeseen claims may come from tax authorities who have not been satisfied by the amounts paid by the contractor or those he employs. For example, under federal law, the Internal Revenue Service requires any employer to be responsible for withholding and paying certain payroll taxes. If the contractor or any subcontractor fails to pay such taxes, a federal tax lien could be filed against the owner's property. As is often the case, unsatisfied tax liability may not appear until some time after the work has been completed. If the responsible party does not satisfy the claim by the taxing authority, the bonding company has an obligation to protect the owner. The *Labor and Material Payment Bond* (AIA Document A311) is used for this purpose.

Certificate of Insurance

Under the insurance requirements stated in most General Conditions of the Contract (and in any supplemental conditions), the contractor's insurance carrier must submit certification that adequate insurance has been provided and is in force at the time construction begins. Some insurance coverage, such as the various bond requirements, may transcend the period of construction for several potential loss categories. For example, if a worker developed an illness or incapacity that could be proven to be related to work on a project, such a claim could be made after completion of the project (within the limits of any jurisdictional statute of limitation that may apply). In other cases, damage to the building proven to result from a failure during construction may be covered by the contractor's liability insurance (in force during the construction process).

List of Subcontractors

An owner or design professional may sometimes require that a contractor provide a list of proposed subcontractors for a project. This approach gives the owner or design professional the chance to make any reasonable objection to any subcontractor named. As a permanent record, the list of subcontractors is a valuable directory for the owner's use in maintaining, repairing, replacing, or altering building components throughout the life of the project.

The owner's concern with approving subcontractors is not without foundation. Major subcontracts for mechanical and electrical work alone may involve as much as 30% to 40% of the total contract sum. Any failure of one of these subcontractors could jeopardize the contractor's ability to complete the project. It is becoming a common practice to stipulate in the contract documents that major subcontractors be bonded. Major subcontractors may also be required to carry specified limits on liability insurance.

Schedule of Values

The schedule of values is a breakdown of the contract sum by category of work. Figure 12.1 illustrates a sample schedule of values with work categories listed according to the CSI format. The Schedule of Values is discussed more thoroughly in Chapter 11, "Administration of the Contract for Construction".

The schedule of values becomes the basis by which periodic payments are made to the contractor. As work in the various categories is completed, the contractor and design professional may certify the percentage of completion and the amount of material received by the contractor. At the time of each periodic payment, an accounting is made of the amount of work accomplished since the last application for payment was made. The current level of completion is computed and an assessment is made of previous payments and retainage, in order to compute the amount that may be due the contractor. AIA Document

CONTRACT BREAKDOWN	CONTRACT AMOUNT	PREVIOUS ESTIMATE	THIS ESTIMATE	%	BALANCE
Insurance					
Move In & Bond					
Contingency Fund					
Site Sub-Grade Work					
Drilled Piers					
Concrete & Finish					
Form Work					
Structural Steel					
ReBars & Mesh					
Waterproof, Dampproof & Caulk					
Masonry					
Finish Carpentry					
Demolition					
Rough Carpentry					
Millwork					
Hardware					
Lath & Plaster					
Metal Doors & Frames					
Aluminum Glass & Glaze					
Acoustical Ceilings					
Resilient Floor & Base					
Painting & Vinyl					
Toilet Stalls					
Drywall Partitions					
Roofing & Sheet Metal					
Plumbing Pipe					
Air Conditioning Pipe					
Plumbing Equipment					
Air Conditioning Equip					
Duct Work					
Controls					
Insulation					
Test & Balance					
Fire Protection					
Fire Alarm					
Electrical Fixtures					
Panels & Switches					
Conduit & Rough-In					
Wire					
Job Clean Up					
Poured Roof Deck					
Cubical Track					
Building Insulation					
Folding Doors					
Carpet					
Seamless Floors					
Supervision					
Temporary Facilities					
Contract Sum					
List Change Orders:					
Change Order No. 1					
Change Order No. 2					
etc.					
TOTALS					

Work completed to date . . . .
Stored Material (See attached) . . . . .
Subtotal . . . .
Less 10% Retainage . . . .
Subtotal . . . .
Less Previous Estimates. . . . .
TOTAL AMOUNT DUE THIS ESTIMATE

Figure 12.1

A702—*Application and Certificate for Payment* and AIA Document G703—*Continuation Sheet* are shown in Figures 11.13 and 11.14. The Continuation Sheet can be used to record the schedule of values and a summary of work completed at the time of each periodic payment. The Application and Certification for Payment is used to compile the data from the schedule of values, and to determine the current payment due which is certified by the design professional or construction manager.

Construction Schedule

The construction schedule sets forth the contractor's estimate of completion for the project. One of the functions of this document should be to indicate the approximate degree of completion that the owner can expect at each period of application and certification of payment. Figures 11.11 and 11.12 are examples of different types of schedules. Figure 11.11 shows a bar graph which breaks down the work in a format similar to that of the schedule of values. Figure 11.12 is a more sophisticated construction schedule based on networking construction events to determine the "critical path" of construction activity. The "critical path" details the optimum sequence and duration of the construction process.

Construction Submittals

Most required submittal documents provide verification or certification of specific construction specifications requirements. Submittals often required of the contractor include material samples, manufacturers' literature and certification, test results, shop drawings, and schedules of progress (see Chapter 11). Such documentation serves a two-fold purpose. First, submittals provide data as a basis for the design professional to approve of materials, payments, and other components of the project. Second, as permanent project records, submittals may provide valuable information for the owner's use during the life of the project for maintenance, replacement, future additions, and alterations.

While project data demands a high priority among project records, the job file is no less important. The job file is the repository of all written communication between the parties to the contract for construction. The job file should organize and make available all correspondence between the parties including transmittal records, legal notices, memos, written instructions, and the minutes of project meetings. While it may not be considered part of the contract documents, the job file, when properly administered and organized, may serve as a "diary" of the construction process. The data in the job file provide a wealth of information, such as recall of agreements, instructions, and transactions that take place during the course of the project.

Correspondence

Correspondence is any form of written communication that occurs between any two or more of the parties to the contract for construction. Correspondence may be in the form of letters, memos, or any other written communication, and should be kept in the job file.

Transmittal Records

Transmittals are used to direct a piece of information to its intended party or parties in the approval or notification process. The job file is the proper repository for transmittal forms once they have served their purpose. The contract documents often specify time requirements for submittals (i.e., shop drawings and manufacturer's literature). The organized handling and filing of transmittals by both the contractor and the design professional can settle arguments and disputes that result from delays that may or may not have been caused by the approval process. A well documented job file containing complete records with dates indicating when information was transmitted, how, or by what means it was transmitted, and the date it was received and processed, can serve as evidence in such disputes.

Notices

The contract documents often require formal written correspondence (in the form of legal notices) from the parties to the Contract for Construction. Legal notices establish evidence of necessary communication related to several critical provisions of the Contract for Construction. For example, the Notice to Proceed, usually issued by the design professional, establishes the official date when construction begins. The Notice to Proceed can therefore be fundamental in establishing the date of Substantial Completion. Other legal notices may be required if either party to the contract needs to inform the other of any requirement not fulfilled according to the agreement. Such notices should become part of the job file and, if necessary, serve as evidence of the procedures necessary to establish compliance with the legal duties of the parties to the contract for construction.

Supplemental Instructions

From time to time, the design professional or the construction manager must issue supplemental instructions to the contractor regarding some aspect of the construction process. These supplemental instructions should become part of the contract documents, and therefore must be carefully handled within the procedures set forth in the agreement for such information. It is not good policy to rely upon verbal agreements in the construction process. All related communication should instead be put in writing. A written record establishes the facts in the case of potentially costly disputes. AIA Document G710—*Architect's Supplemental Instructions* is designed to record and transmit supplemental instructions given during the construction process. AIA Document G711—*Architect's Field Report* is designed to document the design professional's compliance with the duty of periodic job site inspection. AIA Document G713—*Construction Change Authorization* is intended to document any agreement made during the construction process that facilitates a change and causes a change in the contract sum. As a matter of procedure, this document is normally used in order to avoid delay in the project while an official Change Order is being processed. Figure 12.2 illustrates a Means Contract Change Order, a document for creating modifications to the contract for construction.

Minutes of Meetings

Written notes taken during meetings between the parties to the Contract for Construction are important records. Copies of these notes, or "minutes" should be kept in the job files of the owner, design professional and contractor. Like other similar documentation, such records minimize potential misunderstandings, disputes, delays, and litigation that may occur after construction.

Means Forms

**CONTRACT
CHANGE ORDER**

FROM:

_____

_____

_____

TO:

_____

_____

_____

_____

CHANGE ORDER NO.		
DATE		
PROJECT		
LOCATION		
JOB NO.		
ORIGINAL CONTRACT AMOUNT	$	
TOTAL PREVIOUS CONTRACT CHANGES		
TOTAL BEFORE THIS CHANGE ORDER		
AMOUNT OF THIS CHANGE ORDER		
REVISED CONTRACT TO DATE		

Gentlemen:

This CHANGE ORDER includes all Material, Labor and Equipment necessary to complete the following work and to adjust the

total contract as indicated;

☐ the work below to be paid for at actual cost of Labor, Materials and Equipment plus _____ percent (_____%)

☐ the work below to be completed for the sum of _____

_____ dollars ($_____)

_____

_____

_____

_____

_____

_____

_____

_____

_____

_____

_____

_____

_____

_____

_____

_____

_____

_____

CHANGES APPROVED

The work covered by this order shall be performed under the same Terms and
Conditions as that included in the original contract unless stated otherwise above.

By_____

By_____

Signed_____

By_____

Figure 12.2

The Schedule of Values

The *Schedule of Values* (shown in Figure 12.1) is fundamental to the entire construction process. It is the basis for periodic payment to the contractor and has a direct bearing on the construction schedule. The Schedule of Values is the key element in the accounting process for completion of the project.

Accounting Records

The Contract for Construction most often requires that accounting records be maintained and available for review if necessary for legal or tax purposes. In public projects, the law may demand that the contractor (and subcontractors) pay workers according to established minimum wage requirements. Payroll and other accounting records may have to be reviewed by authorities to establish compliance with the law. The contractor's insurance carrier may require an audit of payroll records to establish premiums for worker's compensation insurance. The contractor's financial records of overhead, labor and material costs may also become part of the Contract for Construction where the contractor's compensation is based on cost plus a fee.

Subcontracts

The subcontractor's financial records are as much a part of the project requirement as are those of the contractor. The subcontractor must conform to any minimum wage scale or worker's compensation insurance requirements. Records of payment to subcontractors (by the contractor) become part of the procedure of waiver of lien, compliance with the law, and good business policy.

Construction Records

The contractor, in order to fulfill his contract obligation to the owner, is responsible (either directly or indirectly) for the employment of all labor and the purchase of all materials and products to be incorporated into the project. He has an obligation to see that all participants are paid according to the various contracts and laws regarding the construction process. At the time of periodic payment, and particularly the time of final payment, the contractor may be required to show documented proof of compliance with the compensation requirements regarding labor, purchase of materials, and payment of federal, state, and local taxes. Furthermore, the contractor may be required to prove that he has met all other contract document requirements including building codes, zoning restrictions, and other statutory requirements having jurisdiction over the project. Proper record keeping during the construction process is the key to the contractor's ability to substantiate such compliance.

Time Sheets

Figure 12.3 is a Means Daily Time Sheet form. The contractor and the subcontractor can use this type of form to establish a record of labor performed during construction. The cost of labor in a typical construction project can be 50% or more of the total cost; thus, management of labor on a daily basis is fundamental to preserving the contractor's profit margin. Carefully maintained labor records enter the process of cost accounting and are fundamental to the contractor's ability to manage the project, while complying with the law, union, and insurance requirements.

Means Forms

DAILY TIME SHEET

PROJECT

FOREMAN

WEATHER CONDITIONS

TEMPERATURE

DATE

SHEET NO.

NO.	NAME		DESCRIPTION OF WORK							TOTALS		RATES		OUTPUT	
										REG-ULAR	OVER-TIME	REG-ULAR	OVER-TIME		
		HOURS													
		UNITS													
		HOURS													
		UNITS													
		HOURS													
		UNITS													
		HOURS													
		UNITS													
		HOURS													
		UNITS													
		HOURS													
		UNITS													
		HOURS													
		UNITS													
		HOURS													
		UNITS													
		HOURS													
		UNITS													
		HOURS													
		UNITS													
		HOURS													
		UNITS													
		HOURS													
		UNITS													
		HOURS													
		UNITS													
		HOURS													
		UNITS													
	TOTALS	HOURS													
	EQUIPMENT	UNITS													

Figure 12.3

Material Cost Records

Records of the purchase of materials, assemblies and equipment are also important to cost accounting. Prices of items purchased for construction vary considerably. AIA Document G605—*Purchase Order* can be used by a purchaser (such as the contractor) of project materials. This form, when accepted by both purchaser and vendor (seller), is a type of contract that records who ordered the items and from what source. It also records when the transaction was made, the price that was agreed upon, and the terms by which payment shall be made. Additional information might include any discounts offered for early payment and the anticipated date and method of delivery. Once the transaction is complete, the vendor presents an invoice to the contractor for payment. This invoice can be compared to the purchase order to confirm that the transaction has been completed within the agreed upon terms.

Daily Construction Report

Figures 12.4a and 12.4b are examples of a Means Daily Construction Report form, designed to provide daily records of all activities at the job site. These daily records, when accurate and up to date, can provide a valuable foundation to support the other documents and records that the contractor must keep.

The Daily Construction Report can have an important influence on the contractor's financial records, the construction schedule, and applications for payment. This form is also reviewed during any audit that may be requested to determine compliance with contract obligations and other legal requirements.

Job Progress Report

Figure 12.5 is a Means Job Progress Report form, designed to provide a periodic computation of work completed by certain key dates during the construction process. As a continuing record, developed and updated periodically, the Job Progress Report can be the basis of periodic application for payment (see Figure 11.13), as well as the contractor's accounting system.

Field Inspection Reports

AIA Document G711—*Architect's Field Report* can be used by the design professional to record observations at the job site when periodic inspection of the work is made. This form presents information from the design professional's point of view just as job progress reports record the contractor's observations. Periodic payments to the contractor rely on an agreement by both parties of the percentage of work completed. Often that amount is the result of a compromise between the contractor and the design professional, based on the observations each has recorded.

Progress Photographs

Progress photographs are supplemental to other, written records of the progress of construction. While photographs may not always be required by the construction documents, they perform a valuable function in the documentation of a project. A photograph can rectify a dispute about what may have occurred after the fact. Progress photos taken on a regular basis, may prove to be a minor overhead cost when compared to the major cost of delay or litigation that may result from a dispute that cannot be settled without photographic evidence.

Means Forms

DAILY CONSTRUCTION REPORT

JOB NO.

DATE

PROJECT

SUBMITTED BY

ARCHITECT

WEATHER

TEMPERATURE   AM   PM

CODE NO.	WORK CLASSIFICATION	FOREMEN	MECHANICS	LABORERS	SUBCONTRS	TOTAL HOURS	DESCRIPTION OF WORK
	General Conditions						
	Site Work: Demolition						
	Excavation & Dewatering						
	Caissons & Piling						
	Drainage & Utilities						
	Roads, Walks & Landscaping						
	Concrete: Formwork						
	Reinforcing						
	Placing						
	Precast						
	Masonry: Brickwork & Stonework						
	Block & Tile						
	Metals: Structural						
	Decks						
	Miscellaneous & Ornamental						
	Carpentry: Rough						
	Finish						
	Moisture Protection: Waterproofing						
	Insulation						
	Roofing & Siding						
	Doors & Windows						
	Glass & Glazing						
	Finishes: Lath, Plaster & Stucco						
	Drywall						
	Tile & Terrazzo						
	Acoustical Ceilings						
	Floor Covering						
	Painting & Wallcovering						
	Specialties						
	Equipment						
	Furnishings						
	Special Construction						
	Conveying Systems						
	Mechanical: Plumbing						
	HVAC						
	Electrical						

Page 1 of 2

Figure 12.4a

Means Forms

EQUIPMENT ON PROJECT	NUMBER	DESCRIPTION OF OPERATION	TOTAL HOURS

EQUIPMENT RENTAL - ITEM	TIME IN	TIME OUT	SUPPLIER	REMARKS

MATERIAL RECEIVED	QUANTITY	DELIVERY SLIP NO.	SUPPLIER	USE

CHANGE ORDERS, BACKCHARGES AND/OR EXTRA WORK

VERBAL DISCUSSIONS AND/OR INSTRUCTIONS

VISITORS TO SITE

JOB REQUIREMENTS

Page 2 of 2

Figure 12.4*b*

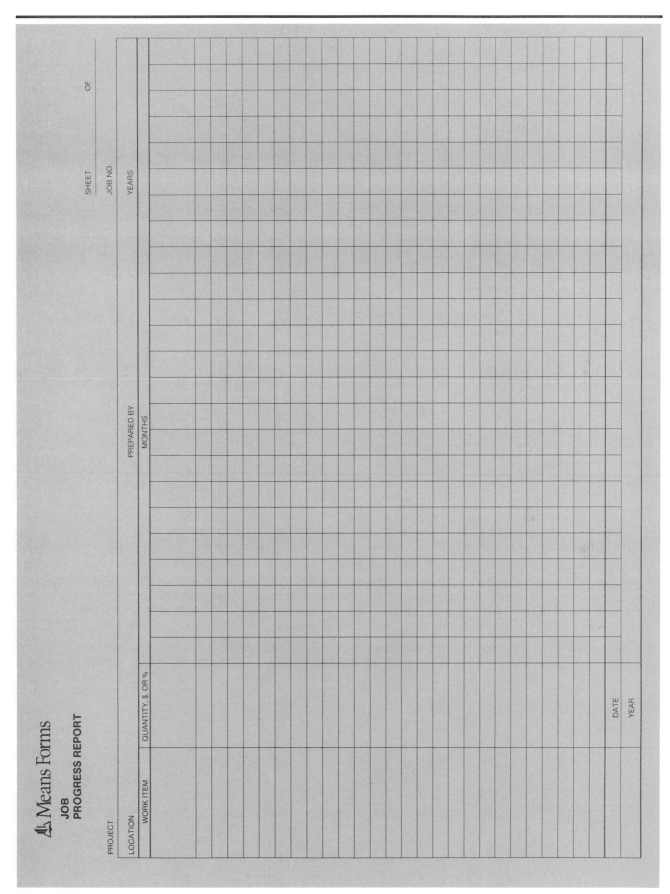

Figure 12.5

293

"As Built" Drawings

A modern building project is a complicated organism composed of many interrelated systems that may be usefully compared to the functions and components of the human body. The supporting structure or "skeleton" may be thought of as the "bones" of the building, the enclosing envelope as the "skin", the plumbing, mechanical and electrical components as the "veins and arteries". The drawings prepared by the design professional illustrate the work to be done. Many of the components are often represented schematically for convenience. As the construction proceeds, the final design and location of many vital building components are decided. "As built" drawings are a product of this process; they record the size, configuration, and location of materials and methods used, and serve as a permanent record for the owner as he maintains, uses, and perhaps alters the building during its useful "life".

Creating and maintaining "as built" data during construction is often a requirement of the contract documents. It need not be a difficult or expensive function, provided the contractor keeps accurate and useful documents and records throughout the building process. Most final design data relating to material, configuration, size and location of various components will be shown on shop drawings or manufacturer's literature. Other information can be recorded with photographs and sketches made during placement, before subsequent operations conceal such items as mechanical and electrical components. The constant influx of data is recorded on special copies of the drawings and specifications that may be provided by the design professional. This process allows for a final compilation and permanent record of "as built" data at the time of completion. The finalized version should be recorded by competent drafters on reproductions of the design professional's documents, and preserved for future reference.

Modifications to the Contract

The contract for construction makes provision for changes or modifications in the work. Such modifications can involve additions to the project, changes in material or equipment, or the deletion of some portion of the work. The design professional may recommend a change that would improve the design or function of the project or correct a condition that becomes apparent once construction has begun. The contractor may also recommend a change to expedite the work, substitute an item for one that becomes unavailable, improve the work, or produce a cost savings. Article 12 of the AIA Document—*General Conditions of the Contract for Construction* states the procedures to be used to make changes. To alter the Contract for Construction, the owner, the design professional, and the contractor must draw up a written agreement.

The Request for Proposal

In most cases, an anticipated modification in the Contract for Construction will require a change in the contract sum, the number of calendar days required for construction, or both. AIA Document G709—*Proposal Request* is prepared by the design professional allows the contractor to respond formally with a disclosure of the information necessary to accomplish a change. Such information is transmitted to the owner via the design professional and the anticipated work is either accepted, modified, or rejected.

Construction Change Authorization

Documenting contract modifications may require considerable time for study, negotiation, agreement, and finally, three-way approval. When delays are inevitable and the owner is willing to accept a change with certain conditions, the design professional may issue a *Construction Change Authorization* (AIA Document G713). This form allows the contractor to proceed with the change on the basis that the finally negotiated cost and time extension shall not exceed certain limits established in the authorization document.

Change Orders

Figure 12.2 illustrates a Means Contract Change Order, which has been previously discussed in this text. The Change Order is used to document the modification to the Contract for Construction. Change orders should be carefully documented, placed in consecutive order, and coordinated with each current application for payment. (See Figure 11.13.)

Close-Out Documents

All documents and procedures described below are included for demonstration purposes. Actual documents and procedures may vary from project to project depending on contractual obligations, municipal, legal, and/or other requirements.

Figures 12.6a through 12.6c illustrate an example of Section 01700— *Project Closeout*, typically included in Division 1—General Requirements of the Specifications. This section specifies the normal procedures for closing out the Contract for Construction for typical projects. Figures 12.7a and 12.7b illustrate Section 01720, *Project Record Documents*. This is a companion section to 01700, also included in Division 1. This section specifies the procedures and data generally required of the contractor.

The General Conditions of the Contract define *Substantial Completion* as that point in the construction when the project is complete enough for the owner to take possession of the building. When the contractor believes that Substantial Completion has been achieved, he notifies the design professional, who then makes an inspection for confirmation. If the design professional agrees, the owner and the surety who has issued the performance and payment bonds may be notified by a *Certificate of Substantial Completion* (AIA Document G704). Subject to any items requiring completion (that may be listed in the design professional's "punch list"), the owner may receive a semi-final *Application and Certification for Payment*. The owner may then pay the contractor an amount including retainage to bring the sum of all payments to 95% or more of the contract sum (or as negotiated and specified in the contract). This payment may be contingent on the contractor's certification that all debts and claims have been paid, together with an affidavit of release or waiver of liens. Under the provisions of the bonds provided by the surety, the owner may be required to withhold the retainage until the surety has issued a consent for its release. Other documents such as AIA Document G706—*Contractor's Affidavit of Payment of Debts and Claims* and AIA Document G706a—*Contractor's Affidavit of Release of Liens*, may provide some legal protection for both owner and surety (as well as for the contractor) when the contractor is paid a substantial amount of the retainage. AIA Document G707A—*Consent of Surety to*

SECTION 01700
CONTRACT CLOSEOUT

PART 1 - GENERAL

1.01   REQUIREMENTS INCLUDED

    A. Closeout Procedures.

    B. Final Cleaning.

    C. Operation and Maintenance Data.

    D. Systems Demonstration.

    E. Guarantees, Warranties and Bonds.

1.03   RELATED REQUIREMENTS

    A. Conditions of the Contract: Fiscal provisions, legal submittals and other administrative requirements.

    B. As the construction of the Project nears completion, collect all guarantees, warranties, affidavits that all payrolls and bills have been paid, Consent of Surety to final payment, certificates of inspection, operating manuals, keys and keying schedule, Project Record Drawings and other items required, in the number of copies specified, to be delivered to the Owner upon completion of the Project.

    C. When Contractor considers Work has reached final completion, submit written certification that Contract Documents have been reviewed, Work has been inspected, and that Work is complete in accordance with Contract Documents and ready for Architect's and Engineer's inspection.

    D. In addition to submittals required by the conditions of the Contract, provide submittals required by governing authorities, and submit a final statement of accounting giving total adjusted Contract Sum, previous payments, and sum remaining due.

    E. Architect will issue a final Change Order reflecting approved adjustments to Contract Sum not previously made by Change Order.

1.04   FINAL CLEANING

    A. Execute prior to Substantial Completion and again prior to Final Inspection.

    B. Clean interior and exterior surfaces exposed to view; remove temporary labels, stains and foreign substances, polish transparent and glossy surfaces, vacuum carpeted and soft surfaces. Clean equipment and fixtures to a sanitary condition, clean or replace filters of mechanical equipment. Clean roofs, and verify that drainage systems are clean and free of all debris of any kind.

    C. Clean site; sweep paved areas, rake clean other surfaces.

    D. Remove waste and surplus materials, rubbish, and construction facilities from the Project and from the site.

1.05   PROJECT RECORD DOCUMENTS

    A. Store Project Record Documents separate from those used for construction and in accordance with Section 01720.

    B. Keep documents current; do not permanently conceal any work until required information has been recorded.

    C. At Contract closeout, submit documents with transmittal letter containing date, Project title, Contractor's name and address, list of documents, and signature of Contractor.

Example Project

Figure 12.6a

1.06   OPERATION AND MAINTENANCE DATA

   A.   General Contractor shall provide data for:

      1.   Specialties - Division 10.

      2.   Equipment - Division 11.

      3.   Furnishings - Division 12.

      4.   Mechanical equipment and controls - Division 15.

      5.   Electrical equipment and controls - Division 16.

   B.   Submit minimum of 3 sets of required information prior to final inspection, bound in 8-1/2 x 11 inch three-ring side binders with durable plastic covers. If a system is accepted prior to final acceptance of Contract, submit 1 set at time of system acceptance and the other 2 sets prior to final acceptance.

   C.   Provide a separate volume for each system, with a table of contents and index tabs for each volume.

   D.   Part 1: Directory, listing names, addresses, and telephone numbers of: Architect, Architect's Consultants, Contractor, Subcontractors, Manufacturers, Material Suppliers and any other entity related to the work.

   F.   Part 2: Operation and maintenance instructions, arranged by system. For each system, list:

      1.   Identify parties listed in Part 1 who are associated with the subject system.

      2.   Appropriate design criteria.

      3.   List of equipment.

      4.   Parts list.

      5.   Operating instructions.

      6.   Maintenance instructions, equipment.

      7.   Maintenance instructions, finishes.

      8.   Shop Drawings and product data.

      9.   Warranties and Guarantees.

.07   SYSTEMS DEMONSTRATION AND PRODUCT CERTIFICATION

   A.   Prior to final inspection, demonstrate operation of each system to Architect and Owner.

   B.   Instruct Owner's personnel in operation, adjustment, and maintenance of equipment and systems, using the operation and maintenance data as the basis of instruction.

   C.   Prior to Final Acceptance of the Work, for items so designated in individual specification Sections, an authorized representative of each manufacturer of materials and/or equipment installed in the Work shall personally inspect the installation and operation of his materials systems, and/or equipment to determine that they are correctly installed and operating properly.

      1.   Inspection and testing shall be accomplished:

         a.   For work which will be concealed: during the course of the Work, after completion of installation and prior to concealment.

         b.   For work which will not be concealed: at completion of the Work.

      2.   Each representative shall submit a signed statement to the Architect, through the General Contractor, certifying to his personal inspection and to the correct installation and proper operation of materials, systems and/or equipment. Their certification shall list the items included.

      3.   The General Contractor shall transmit all such certifications to the Architect at or prior to the Final Acceptance Inspection. The transmittal shall include a list of all certifications included.

Example Project

Figure 12.6b

1.08   WARRANTIES, GUARRANTIES AND BONDS

A. Provide duplicate, notarized copies. Execute Contractor's submittals and assemble documents executed
    by subcontractors, suppliers, and manufacturers. Provide table of contents and assemble in binder
    with durable plastic cover.

B. Submit material prior to final application for payment.   For equipment put into use with Owner's
    permission during construction, submit within 10 days after first operation. For items of Work
    delayed materially beyond Date of Substantial Completion, provide updated submittal within ten days
    after acceptance, listing date of acceptance as start of warranty period.

1.09   SPARE PARTS AND MAINTENANCE MATERIALS

Provide products, spare parts, and maintenance materials in quantities specified in each section, in addition
to that required for completion of Work. Coordinate with Owner, deliver to Project site and obtain receipt
prior to final payment.

1.10   DELIVERY SCHEDULE

A. Keys and Keying Schedule, and one copy of equipment operating manuals shall be delivered at the time
    of the Substantial Completion Inspection for each separately accepted portion of the Work.

    1. Deliver Keys and Keying Schedule to the Owner, with copy of signed receipt to the Architect.

    2. Deliver other items to the Architect for his transmittal to the Owner.

B. Deliver all other items at the Final Inspection.

PART 2 - PRODUCTS

Not required.

PART 3 - EXECUTION

Not Required

END OF SECTION

Example Project

Figure 12.6c

298

SECTION 01720
PROJECT RECORD DOCUMENTS

PART 1 - GENERAL

1.01   REQUIREMENTS INCLUDED

A.   Maintenance of Record Documents and Samples.

B.   Submittal of Record Documents and Samples.

1.02   RELATED REQUIREMENTS

A.   Section 01300 - Submittals: Shop drawings, product data, and samples.

B.   Section 01700 - Contract Closeout: Closeout procedures.

C.   Individual Specifications Sections: Manufacturer's certificates and certificates of inspection.

1.03   MAINTENANCE OF DOCUMENTS AND SAMPLES

A.   Contractor shall maintain at the site for Owner, one record copy of:

1.   Contract Drawings.

2.   Specifications.

3.   Addenda.

4.   Change Orders and other modifications to the Contract.

5.   Reviewed shop drawings, product data, and samples.

6.   Inspection certificates.

7.   Manufacturer's certificates.

B.   Store Record Documents and samples in Field Office apart from documents used for construction. Provide files, racks, and secure storage for Record Documents and samples.

C.   Label and file Record Documents and samples in accordance with Section number listings in Table of Contents of this Project Manual. Label each document "PROJECT RECORD" in neat, large, printed letters.

D.   Maintain Record Documents in a clean, dry and legible condition. Do not use Record Documents for construction purposes.

E.   Keep Record Documents and samples available for inspection by Architect.

1.04   RECORDING

A.   Record information on a set of blue line prints of drawings and bound Project Manual provided by Owner.

B.   Provide felt tip marking pens, maintaining separate colors for each major system, for recording information.

C.   Record information concurrently with construction progress. Do not conceal any work until required information is recorded.

D.   Contract Drawings and Shop Drawings: Legibly mark each item to record actual construction, including:

1.   Measured locations of internal utilities and appurtenances concealed in construction, referenced, by dimension and otherwise, to visible and accessible features of construction.

2.   Field changes of dimension and detail.

3.   Changes made by modifications.

4.   Details not on original Contract Drawings.

5.   References to related shop drawings and Modifications.

Example Project

Figure 12.7a

E. Specifications: Legibly mark each item to record actual construction, including:

   1. Manufacturer, trade name, and catalog number of each product actually installed, particularly optional items and substitute items.

   2. Changes made by Addenda and Modifications.

F. Other Documents: Maintain manufacturer's certifications, inspection certifications, field tests and start up, records, and other information required by individual Specifications sections.

1.05 "AS BUILT" DRAWINGS

A. General Contractor shall have drafted, a set of "as-built" drawings of the project, on reproducible media, for Owner's final record.

B. Using data accumulated on blue line prints as specified in paragraph 1.04, place all information on a set of sepia reproducible drawings furnished by the Owner,

C. Use only experienced draftspersons for this work.

D. Use industry standards for drafting, keep lines and lettering uniform, legible.

1.06 SUBMITTALS

A. At Contract closeout, deliver Record Documents and samples under provisions of Section 01700.

B. Transmit with cover letter in duplicate, listing:

   1. Date.

   2. Project title and number.

   3. Contractor's name, address, and telephone number.

   4. Number and title of each Record Document.

   5. Signature of Contractor or authorized representative.

PART 2 - PRODUCTS

   Not Used.

PART 3 - EXECUTION

   Not Used.

END OF SECTION

Example Project

Figure 12.7b

Reduction in or Partial Release of Retainage may be issued to the owner before any retainage is paid to the contractor.

Once the contractor has complied with all required provisions of the Project Closeout, and all items shown on the semi-final punch list have been completed, the design professional may issue a final Certificate for Payment. This document notifies the owner that he can, subject to the consent of the surety, release an amount to the contractor that will bring the total payments to 100% of the Contract Sum.

Certificate of Occupancy

The General Conditions of the Contract for Construction require the contractor to be responsible for the acquisition of building permit(s), and for compliance with all codes, ordinances and other matters of regulation and authority of the building official. Many jurisdictions require a *Certificate of Occupancy* to be issued by the building official before the owner will be allowed to occupy the completed project. The *Certificate of Occupancy* is the building official's certification that the building meets the requirements of the building code and/or other applicable ordinances and therefore, when required, must be considered as an important and integral part of the finalization of the project. The design professional may wish to issue the final *Certificate for Payment* subject to issuance of such a document by the municipality or other jurisdiction in which the project is located.

Summary

It has been the purpose of this text to review the process of building construction from the standpoint of the interrelated functions of Owner, (Design) Professional and Constructor expressed in terms of what we have called the OPC Relationship. This basic relationship has been seen in terms of the duties of the primary parties to the Contract for Construction (i.e., the owner and constructor). The professional is directly related to the owner by separate agreement, and indirectly to the constructor by virtue of the design professional's responsibility to the owner.

The owner may choose to be represented in the construction process solely by the design professional, or he may choose to employ a construction administrator, or construction manager, to oversee the fulfillment of the contract, in addition to the services provided by the design professional.

The constructor, identified as the contractor by the contract documents, in order to fulfill his obligation under the contract for construction, becomes entirely responsible for the construction process and its completion. The contractor is responsible by separate agreement for subcontractors, material and equipment suppliers and others who supply and process the work of construction.

The design professional acts as the interpreter of the content and intent of the contract documents, and in concert with other professionals, advises the owner. One of the primary duties of the design professional is to periodically observe the construction process and report to the owner on the contractor's apparent conformity with the requirements of the contract documents. The design professional either employs professional specialists or separately contracts with professional consultants to implement specialized technical design.

The instruments by which the building process is organized and implemented, commonly called *Plans, Specs, and Contracts* are usually created by the design professional. These instruments are formally named the *Contract Documents*. Basic to the contract documents are the defined responsibilities of each member of the OPC relationship, a complete description of the work to be done, and provision for such ancillary requirements as bonding, insurance, administrative requirements, evidence of conformity to design and specifications, and instructions for record keeping.

Under the code of common conduct and responsibility is an unwritten element of mutual faith that relies on all of the parties to adhere to the principals of common law, generally accepted "good" practices of the construction industry, and the integrity that is characteristic of that which we call professionalism. The construction industry is far from being a "perfect" science. Far too often, building construction can be compared to a poor novel in that it is easy to start, but difficult to complete.

APPENDIX

Professional Associations

ARI   Air-Conditioning and Refrigeration Institute
1815 North Fort Myer Drive
Arlington, VA 22209

ADC   Air Diffusion Council
230 North Michigan Avenue
Chicago, IL 60601

AMCA   Air Movement and Control Association
30 West University Drive
Arlington Heights, IL 60004

AA   Aluminum Association
818 Connecticut Avenue, N.W.
Washington, DC 20006

ACI   American Concrete Institute
Box 19150
Reford Station
Detroit, MI 48219

ACEC   American Consulting Engineers Council
1015 15th Street, N.W.
Washington, D.C. 20005

AIA   American Institute of Architects
1735 New York Avenue, N.W.
Washington, D.C. 20006

AISC   American Institute of Steel Construction
400 North Michigan Avenue
Eighth Floor
Chicago, IL 60611

AISI   American Iron and Steel Institute
1000 16th Street, N.W.
Washington, DC 20036

ANSI   American National Standards Institute
1430 Broadway
New York, NY 10018

APA   American Plywood Association
Box 11700
Tacoma, WA 98411

ASCE   American Society of Civil Engineers
345 East 47th Street
New York, NY 10017

ASHRAE	American Society of Heating, Refrigerating and Air Conditioning Engineers 1791 Tullie Circle, N.E. Atlanta, GA 30329
ASME	American Society of Mechanical Engineers 345 East 47th Street New York, NY 10017
ASTM	American Society for Testing and Materials 1916 Race Street Philadelphia, PA 19103
ASPA	American Sod Producers Association Association Building Ninth and Minnesota Hastings, NE 68901
AWWA	American Water Works Association 6666 West Quincy Avenue Denver, CO 80235
AWS	American Welding Society 550 LeJeune Road Miami, FL 33135
AWPA	American Wood-Preservers' Association 7735 Old Georgetown Road Bethesda, MD 20014
AWI	Architectural Woodwork Institute 2310 South Walter Reed Drive Arlington, VA 22206
AI	Asphalt Institute Asphalt Institute Building College Park, MD 20740
AGC	Associated General Contractors of America 1957 E Street, N.W. Washington, DC 20006
CLFMI	Chain Link Fence Manufacturers Institute 1101 Connecticut Avenue, N.W. Washington, DC 20036
CSI	Construction Specifications Institute 601 Madison Street Alexandria, VA 22314
CRSI	Concrete Reinforcing Steel Institute 933 Plum Grove Road Schaumburg, IL 60195
CDA	Copper Development Association 57th Floor, Chrysler Building 405 Lexington Avenue New York, NY 10174
EJCDC	Engineers' Joint Contract Documents Committee American Consulting Engineers Council 1050 15th Street, N.W. Washington, DC 20005

EJMA	Expansion Joint Manufacturers Association 707 Westchester Avenue White Plains, NY 10604
FM	Factory Mutual System 1151 Boston-Providence Turnpike Norwood, MA 02062
FS	Federal Specification General Services Administration Specifications and Consumer Information Distribution Section (WFSIS) Washington Navy Yard, Bldg. 197 Washington, DC 20407
FGMA	Flat Glass Marketing Association 3310 Harrison White Lakes Professional Building Topeka, KS 66611
GA	Gypsum Association 1603 Orrington Avenue Evanston, IL 60201
IEEE	Institute of Electrical and Electronics Engineers 345 East 47th Street New York, NY 10017
IMIAC	International Masonry Industry All-Weather Council International Masonry Institute 815 15th Street, N.W. Washington, DC 20005
ML/SFA	Metal Lath/Steel Framing Association 221 North LaSalle Street Chicago, IL 60601
MIL	Military Specification Naval Publications and Forms Center 5801 Tabor Avenue Philadelphia, PA 19120
NAAMM	National Association of Architectural Metal Manufacturers 221 North LaSalle Street Chicago, IL 60601
NEMA	National Electrical Manufacturers' Association 2101 L Street, N.W. Washington, DC 20037
NEBB	National Environmental Balancing Bureau 8224 Old Courthouse Road Vienna, VA 22180
NFPA	National Fire Protection Association Battery March Park Quincy, MA 02269

NFPA	National Forest Products Association 1619 Massachusetts Avenue, N.W. Washington, DC 20036
NSPE	National Society of Professional Engineers 1420 King Street Alexandria, VA 22314
NSWMA	National Solid Wastes Management Association 1120 Connecticut Avenue, N.W. Washington, D.C. 20036
PCA	Portland Cement Association 5420 Old Orchard Road Skokie, IL 60077
PS	Product Standard U. S. Department of Commerce Washington, DC 20203
SIGMA	Sealed Insulating Glass Manufacturers Association 111 East Wacker Drive Chicago, IL 60601
SMACNA	Sheet Metal and Air Conditioning Contractors' National Association 8224 Old Court House Road Vienna, VA 22180
SDI	Steel Deck Institute Box 3812 St. Louis, MO 63122
SDI	Steel Door Institute 712 Lakewood Center North Cleveland, OH 44107
SJI	Steel Joist Institute 1703 Parham Road Suite 204 Richmond, VA 23229
SSPC	Steel Structures Painting Council 4400 Fifth Avenue Pittsburgh, PA 15213
TAS	Technical Aid Series Construction Specifications Institute 601 North Madison Street Alexandria, VA 22314
TCA	Tile Council of America, Inc. Box 326 Princeton, NJ 08540
UL	Underwriters' Laboratories, Inc. 333 Pfingston Road Northbrook, IL 60062
WCLIB	West Coast Lumber Inspection Bureau Box 23145 Portland, OR 97223

Note: AIA documents can be ordered from architectural bookstores or from the address given in the Acknowledgments to this book. EJCDC documents can be obtained from member organizations such as: National Society of Professional Engineers, American Consulting Engineers Council, and the American Society of Civil Engineers. Select EJCDC documents can also be obtained from the Construction Specifications Institute. The addresses of all of these organizations are provided in the above list.

GLOSSARY OF TERMS

Addenda
Plural form of Addendum.

Addendum
Document describing an addition, change, correction or modification to Contract Documents. An addendum is issued by the design professional during the bidding period or prior to the award of contract, and is the primary method of informing bidders of modifications to the work during the bidding process. Addenda become a part of the Contract Documents.

Advertisement for Bids
Published notice of an owner's intention to award a contract for construction to a constructor who submits a proposal according to Instructions to Bidders. In its usual form, the advertisement is published in a convenient form of news media in order to attract constructors who are willing to prepare and submit proposals for the performance of the work.

AFL-CIO
A major union, formed by the merger of AFL (American Federation of Labor) and CIO (Committee for Industrial Organizations) under the leadership of John L. Lewis in 1955. The AFL-CIO represents the interests of various types of member-workers in industry and other endeavors (construction) for the purpose of negotiating with management for wages, benefits and other material interests of worker-employees.

Agreement
A consensus of two or more parties concerning a particular subject. Regarding matters of construction, the term "agreement" is synonymous with contract. An example is the Agreement between Owner and Contractor.

Allowance
A stated requirement of the Contract Documents whereby a specified sum of money is incorporated, or allowed, into the Contract Sum in order to sustain the cost of a stipulated material, assembly, piece of equipment or other part of a construction contract. This device is convenient in cases where the particular item cannot be fully described in the contract documents. The allowance can be stated as a Lump Sum or as a Unit Sum and includes specific instructions as to whether or not the cost of material and required installation is to be included in the amount of the allowance. In the case of the Unit Cost Allowance,

the constructor (bidder) is responsible for determining the quantity to be applied; in this way, a sum can be calculated that will cover the material required by the Contract Documents.

All Risk Insurance

An insurance policy which can be written separately to add coverage against certain specific risks of damage or loss from any number of potential events. These risks represent potential losses in excess of coverage provided by other forms of insurance purchased for the purpose of protecting the owner, design professional and contractor during and after the construction process.

Alternate

A specified item of construction that is set apart by separate sum. An alternate may or may not be incorporated into the Contract Sum at the discretion and approval of the owner at the time of contract award.

American Federation of Labor

A labor organization or union formed in the United States under the leadership of Samuel Gompers in 1886. The American Federation of Labor provided an ''umbrella'' organization the purpose of which was to represent to management the interests of workers in various trades, crafts and other skilled disciplines related to manufacture and construction.

Application for Payment

A statement prepared by the contractor stating the amount of work completed and materials purchased and properly stored to date. This statement includes the sum of previous payments and current payment requested in accordance with payment provisions of the Contract Documents.

Arbitration

A procedure whereby disputes regarding matters of contract responsibility can be mediated without litigation in a court of law. Under arbitration, a panel of knowledgeable arbitrators reviews the evidence and testimony of the parties to the dispute. The parties to the contract would have agreed in advance to accept the decision rendered by the panel of arbitrators.

Architect

A design professional who, by education, experience and examination, is licensed by state government to practice the art of building design and technology. Derived from the root words ''arch'' and ''technology'', this term is roughly translated as ''technician of the arch''.

As Built Drawings

Record drawings made during construction. As built drawings record the locations, sizes and nature of concealed items such as structural elements, accessories, equipment, devices, plumbing lines, valves, mechanical equipment and the like. These records (with dimensions) form a permanent record for future reference.

Bar Graph

Graphical representations of simultaneous events charted with reference to time. A technique developed by Henry Gantt and Frederick W. Taylor around 1900. Early forms were called ''Gantt Charts''. A bar graph is a simplified method of charting events that occur in sequence, such as the processes of building construction. The horizontal axis of the chart is scaled to increments of time; the various events are charted vertically. The duration of the event is charted by a horizontal line or bar beginning at the time the event is scheduled to begin and ending at the time the event is scheduled to be complete. At any point in time, the reader can observe the number of events that are occurring simultaneously.

Bid

A term commonly used for a complete and properly executed proposal to perform work that has been described in the Contract Documents and submitted in accordance with Instructions To Bidders.

Bid Bond

A form of Bid Security purchased by the bidder from a Surety. A bid bond is provided, subject to forfeit, to guarantee that the bidder will enter into a contract for construction within a specified time and furnish any required bonds such as Performance Bond and Payment Bond.

Bidding Documents

Documents usually including Advertisement or Invitation To Bidders, Instructions To Bidders, Bid Form, form of Contract, forms of Bonds, Conditions of Contract, Specifications, Drawings and any other information necessary to completely describe the work by which candidate constructors can adequately prepare proposals or Bids for the owner's consideration.

Bid Opening

A formal meeting held at a specified place, date and hour at which sealed bids are opened, tabulated and read aloud.

Bidding Requirements

Those instructions included in the Bidding Documents which consist of the Invitation or Advertisement for bids, Instructions to Bidders, Bid Form, and Bid Bond.

Bid Security

A Bid Bond or other form of security such as a Cashier's Check that is acceptable to the owner. Bid security is provided as guarantee that bidder will enter into a contract for construction within a specified time and furnish any bonds and other requirements of the Bid Documents.

Blue Print

A paper sensitized with a mixture of ferric amonimum citrate and potassium ferricynide used for preparing reproductions of drawings. When subjected to a strong light source and washed in a solution of potassium dichromate, the exposed portion will turn a dark blue color. By placing the drawing over the sensitized medium, and performing the light exposure, the dark image on the drawing blocks a corresponding area on the print. When developed, the original is reproduced in reverse image.

Bonds

Written documents, given by a surety in the name of a principal to an obligee to guarantee a specific obligation. In construction, the principal types of bonds are the Bid Bond, the Performance Bond and the Payment Bond.

Bonus Provisions

Provisions in the contract for construction by which the owner may offer monetary rewards to the contractor for achieving some savings that benefit the owner. For example, a stipulated bonus may be offered for early completion of the work, or the achievement of some savings in construction cost.

Breach
A term applied to the failure of one or more parties to a contract to perform according to the exact terms of the contract.

Broadscope
A term describing the content of a section of the specifications, as established by the Construction Specifications Institute. A broadscope section covers a wide variety of related materials and workmanship requirements (narrowscope specifications denote a section describing a single material; mediumscope denotes a section dealing with a family of materials).

Building Codes
The minimum legal requirements established or adopted by a government such as a municipality. Building codes are established by ordinance, and govern the design and construction of buildings.

Building Official
An appointed officer of a body of government, responsible for enforcing the Building Code. Sometimes called the Building Inspector, the building official may approve the issuance of a Building Permit, review the Contract Documents, inspect the construction and approve issuance of a Certificate of Occupancy.

Building Permit
A written authorization required by ordinance for a specific project. A building permit allows construction to proceed in accordance with construction documents approved by the building official.

Cash Allowance
A specified sum of money to be included into the Contract Sum for an element, group of elements, assembly, system, piece of equipment or other described item to be included into the work under specified conditions.

Certificate
A written document appropriately signed by responsible parties testifying to a matter of fact in accordance with a requirement of the Contract Documents.

Certificate of Insurance
A written document appropriately signed by a responsible representative of the insurance company and stating the exact coverage and period of time for which the coverage is applicable in accordance with requirements of the Contract Documents.

Certificate of Occupancy
A written document issued by the governing authority in accordance with the provisions of the Building Permit. The Certificate of Occupancy indicates that the project, in the opinion of the building official, has been completed in accordance with the building code. This document gives permission of authorities for the owner to occupy and use the premises for the intended purpose.

Certificate of Payment
Used in association with Application for Payment, signed by the design professional, this document certifies a specific amount that is due and payable to the contractor.

Certified Construction Specifier
A construction professional who by experience and examination by the Construction Specifications Institute has been certified as proficient in

the knowledge and art of preparing technical specifications for the construction process.

Change Order
A written document signed by the owner, design professional and contractor, detailing a change or modification to the Contract for Construction.

Civil Rights Act
Legislation enacted by the Congress of the United States in 1964, and amended in subsequent years. The Civil Rights Act prohibits any act that would discriminate against an individual for any reason, but particularly because of sex, race, age, ethnic origin or religion.

Clayton Act
Legislation enacted by Congress in 1914. The Clayton Act was intended to lessen the negative effects of the Sherman Anti-Trust Act by allowing labor to organize for purposes of negotiating with a single employer.

Closed Bidding
A common term meaning Closed Competitive Selection.

Closed Competitive Selection
The preferred term for Closed Bidding, a process of competitive bidding whereby the private owner limits the list of bidders to persons he has selected and invited to bid.

Closed Shop
A term applied to a trade or skill that requires membership in a particular union to the exclusion of non-union members.

Committee for Industrial Organizations (CIO)
A labor union organized in 1935 for the purpose of representing industrial workers. The CIO was created as a result of a dispute with the AFL. John L. Lewis, president of United Mine Workers, a member of the CIO, was instrumental in merging the AFL and CIO in 1955.

Conditions of the Contract
A document detailing the rights, responsibilities and relationships of the parties to the Contract for Construction.

Consideration
A term used to describe the compensation that shall be paid to one party to a contract by another party in return for services and/or products rendered.

Construction Administrator
One who oversees the fulfillment of the responsibilities of all parties to the Contract for Construction, for the primary benefit of the owner. In the typical project, construction administration is usually provided by the design professional. However, the owner, at his option, may employ a separate professional entity for this purpose.

Construction Drawings
Portion of the Contract Documents which are graphic representations of the work to be done in the construction of a project.

Construction Manager
One who directs the process of construction, either as the agent of the owner, as the agent of the contractor, or as one who, for a fee, directs and coordinates construction activity carried out under separate or multiple-prime contracts.

Constructor

One who is in the business of constructing elements of the "built" environment. A contractor is a constructor who is acting under the terms of a Contract for Construction.

Consulting Engineer

A licensed engineer, employed by the design professional for the purpose of performing specific tasks of engineering design for portions of a project.

Contingency

An amount included in the budget for construction, uncommitted for any specific purpose. This amount is intended to cover the cost of unforeseen factors related to construction, but not specifically addressed in the budget.

Contingency Allowance

A specified sum, included in the Contract Sum. A contingency allowance is intended to be used, at the owner's discretion, and with his approval, to pay for any element or service related to the construction that is desirable to the owner, but not specifically required of the contractor by the construction documents.

Continuing Education

A term applied to a regimen of attendance and application of special study toward specific subject matter. Continuing education may be pursued through accredited professional seminars, college curriculum and other forms of organized study which promote knowledge of the "state of the art" of professional endeavors.

Contract

An agreement between two or more individuals where mutual assent occurs, giving rise to a specified promise or series of promises to be performed, for which consideration is given.

Contract Documents

A term applied to any combination of related documents that collectively define the extent of an agreement between two or more parties. As regards the Contract for Construction, the Contract Documents generally consist of the Agreement (Contract), the Bonds, the Certificates, the Conditions of the Contract, the Specifications, the Drawings and the Modifications.

Contract for Construction

An agreement between owner and contractor whereby the contractor agrees to construct the owner's building or other described project in accordance with the Contract Documents within a specified amount of time for consideration to be paid by the owner as mutually agreed.

Contractor

A constructor who is a party to the Contract for Construction, pledged to the owner to perform the work of construction in accordance with the Contract Documents.

Contractor's Qualification Statement

A statement of the contractor's qualifications, experience, financial condition, business history, and staff composition. This statement, together with listed business and professional references, provides evidence of the contractor's competence to perform the Work and assume the responsibilities required by the Contract Documents.

Contract Sum
An amount representing the total consideration in money to be paid the contractor for services performed under the Contract for Construction.

Contributory Negligence
A term used to describe legal responsibility for an error or fault by one or more parties who have allegedly contributed in whole or part to a loss or damage suffered by another party as a result of a specific occurrence.

Corporation
An association of individuals established under certain legal requirements. A corporation exists independently of its members, and has powers and liabilities distinct and apart from its members.

Covenant
A term used to describe one or more specific points of agreement that may be set forth in a Contract.

Critical Path
A term used to describe the order of events (each of a particular duration) that results in the least amount of time required to complete a project.

Davis-Bacon Act
An act by the Congress of the United States, enacted into law in 1931. The Davis-Bacon Act provides that wages and fringe benefits paid to workers employed by contractors under contract with the federal government be no less than the prevailing rate for each particular trade for that location.

Deductible
A term used to describe a specified amount that would be deducted from compensation paid in event of loss covered under an insurance policy.

Descriptive Specification
A type of specification that provides a detailed description of the required properties of a product, material, or piece of equipment, and the workmanship required for its proper installation.

Design Professional
A term used to describe either an architect or an engineer, or both, duly licensed by state government for professional practice, who may be employed by an owner for the purpose of designing a building or other project.

Diazo
A group of chemical compounds such as benzenediazo hydroxide or diazomethene generally used as a light sensitive emulsion on a support such as paper or plastic. When this material is exposed, as in a photographic process, by the passage of light through an original drawing, and developed by reaction of a coupler, either an acid compound or alkaline agent, an image called a "whiteprint" is produced.

Direct Selection
A process whereby the owner selects a constructor for the purpose of constructing a project. The selection is made at the owner's discretion based on the contractor's experience, availability, and capability. The terms of the contract for construction are reached by negotiation rather than through the process of competitive bidding.

Endorsement

A document, supplemental to an insurance policy covering a specified loss; an endorsement modifies the conditions of the contract terms stated on the face of the insurance policy.

Engineer

A design professional, who by education, experience and examination is duly licensed by one or more state governments for practice in the profession of engineering. This practice may be limited to one or more specific disciplines of engineering. Construction-related engineering disciplines may be civil, structural, mechanical, or electrical systems design.

Equal Employment Opportunity Commission (EEOC)

An agency of the United States Government under the administration of the Department of Labor. This agency is dedicated to enforcing the provisions of Title IV of the Civil Rights Act of 1964 which forbids discrimination by an employer on the basis of race, color, religion, sex or national origin of a potential employee.

Escrow

A legal device used in conjunction with a contract, where something of value is placed with a third party acting as trustee. The escrow serves as a guarantee of performance to the conditions of the contract.

Estimator

One who is capable of predicting the probable cost of a building project.

Exclusionary Provision

A provision stated in an insurance policy covering potential loss where specific types or origins of loss are specifically excluded (by description) from the coverage provided.

Fair Labor Standards Act

An act of the Congress of the United States enacted in 1936, and the subject of numerous amendments to the present day. This act is commonly referred to as the Minimum Wage Law; it establishes a minimum wage for all workers with the exception of agricultural workers, and additionally provides a maximum of a 40 hour work week for straight time pay for employees earning hourly wages.

Fast Track

A term used to describe the construction process whereby a project is constructed in phases—each phase is negotiated as a separate contract. Each phase is dependent upon the completion of the previous phase. Construction time can be shortened because Construction Documents related to each phase or contract can be created during construction of the previous phase.

Federal Mediation and Conciliation Service

An agency of the United States Department of Labor which acts as a mediator in the settlement of disputes as provided in the National Labor Relations Act of 1935 and the Labor Management Relations Act of 1947.

Field Order

A written modification to the Contract for Construction, made by the design professional, the construction administrator, or the construction manager. A field order documents a change to the contract documents in anticipation of the issuance of a formal Change Order signed by owner, design professional and contractor.

General Conditions of the Contract for Construction
The part of the contract documents that defines the rights, responsibilities, and the relationships between the parties to the contract.

General Contractor
A constructor whose chief business activity is the primary responsibility for construction under contract with various owners.

General Obligation Bonds
An instrument of obligation which by permission of the public through Referendum, is in turn issued to investors by a subdivision of government. These bonds promise incremental payment of principal and interest from revenues collected annually by the government. In return, funds are supplied by investors and are used to pay for the construction of publicly owned buildings or other public works projects.

General Requirements
Division 1 of 16 divisions of the specifications when organized under the Construction Specifications Institute's (CSI) Masterformat. The General Requirements, in sequential sections, detail the general administrative requirements of the project in careful coordination with the various Conditions of the Contract for Construction.

Generic
A term used to generally describe a material, product, assembly or piece of equipment, as in the Descriptive Specification, rather than by naming a specific trade name or source of manufacture or distribution.

Guarantee
A warrant, pledge or formal assurance given as a pledge that another's debt or obligation will be fulfilled.

Guaranteed Maximum Cost Contract
A Contract for Construction wherein the contractor's compensation is stated as a combination of accountable cost plus a fee, with guarantee by the contractor that the total compensation will be limited to a specific amount. This type of contract may also have possible optional provisions for additional financial reward to the contractor for performance that causes total compensation to be less than the guaranteed maximum amount.

Inclusive Coverage
A provision in an insurance policy covering potential loss where specific types or origins of loss are specifically included by description under the coverage provided.

Industry Standard
Readily available information in the form of published specifications, technical reports and disclosures, test procedures and results, codes and other technical information and data. Such data should be verifiable and professionally endorsed, with general acceptance and proven use by the construction industry.

Industry Standard Specification
A published specification meeting the general definition of an Industry Standard.

Instructions to Bidders
A document, part of the Bidding Requirements, usually prepared by the Design Professional. Instructions to Bidders set forth specific instructions to candidate constructors on procedures, expectations of

the owner, disclaimers of the owner, and other necessary information for the preparation of proposals for consideration by the owner for a competitive bid.

Insurance
Coverage by contract in which one party agrees to indemnify or reimburse another for any loss that may occur within the terms of the Insurance Policy.

Insurance Policy
A contract which provides Insurance against specific loss.

Invitation To Bid
A written notice of an owner's intention to receive competitive bids for a construction project wherein a select group of candidate constructors are invited to submit proposals.

Joint Venture
A joining of two or more individuals, partnerships or corporations for the single purpose of jointly sharing the responsibility for and compensation from a single endeavor, such as a building project.

Journeyman
The second or intermediate level of development of proficiency in a particular trade or skill. As related to building construction, a journeyman's license, earned by a combination of education, supervised experience and examination, is required in many areas for those employed as intermediate level mechanics in certain trades (e.g., plumbing, mechanical, and electrical work).

Judgment
A judicial decision rendered as a result of a course of action in a court of law.

Labor Union
An organization or confederation of workers with the same or similar skills who are joined in a common cause (such as collective bargaining) with management or other employers for work place conditions, wage rates and/or employee benefits.

Landrum-Griffin Act
Enacted by Congress in 1959, this act requires labor union management to be subject to audit for the funds of union members for which they are responsible.

Legal Notice
A covenant, often incorporated in the language of an agreement between two or more parties, that requires communication in writing, serving notice from one party to the other in accordance with terms of the agreement.

Liability
Exposure to potential claim by which a first party may be subject to pay compensation to a second party in the case of loss or damage occurring to the second party for acts attributable to the responsibility of the first party.

Lien
A legal means of establishing or giving notice of a claim or an unsatisfied charge in the form of a debt, obligation or duty. A lien is filed with government authorities against title to real property. Liens must be adjudicated or satisfied before title can be transferred.

Life Cycle
A term often used to describe the period of time that a building can be expected to actively and adequately serve its intended function.

Litigation
Legal action or process in a court of law.

Loss of Use Insurance
A type of insurance coverage that compensates the owner for the loss of the use of his property in the case of a mishap such as fire or other damage.

Lump Sum
An amount used in a contract or bid representing the total cost of an item of work, or project.

Mark-Up
A percentage of other sums that may be added to the total of all direct costs to determine a final price or contract sum. In construction practice, the mark-up usually represents two factors important to the contractor. The first factor may be the estimated cost of indirect expense often referred to as ''overhead''. The second factor is an amount for the anticipated profit for the contractor.

Master
A term applied to the third and highest level of achievement for a tradesman or mechanic who by supervision, experience, and examination has earned a master's license attesting that he is a master of the trade and no longer requires supervision of his work as is the case with the journeyman and apprentice levels.

Master Builder
A term applied to one who performs the functions of both design and construction. The master builder approach to building construction has been a practice commonplace in much of the world for many centuries. In the United States, design and construction are traditionally seen as two separate and distinct functions.

Masterformat
The name owned and created by the Construction Specifications Institute (CSI) of the United States and Construction Specifications Canada (CSC) denoting a numerical system of organization for construction-related information and data, based on a 16 division format.

Materialman
A term applied to one through whom the contractor may obtain the materials of construction. The materialman may be a manufacturer's representative or he may be a distributor or salesman of the tools, products, materials, assemblies and equipment vital to the process of construction.

Mechanic's Lien
A type of lien filed by one who has performed work related to the real property for which compensation is either in dispute or remains unsatisfied.

Mediumscope
A term established by the Construction Specifications Institute to denote a section of the specifications that describes a family of related or integrated materials and workmanship requirements. (Narrowscope

specifications denote a single product; broadscope specifications denote a section describing differing materials used in a related manner.)

Minimum Wage Law
Common term used to describe the Fair Labor Standards Act enacted by Congress in 1938. This act establishes a minimum wage for workers and the 40-hour work week.

Mock-Up
Materials and products assembled as a sample or demonstration faithful to the finished product in terms of color, texture, manufacture and/or workmanship, as it will be installed into the building. Mock-ups are useful for review and approval of the owner, design professional or others.

Model Codes
Professionally prepared building regulations and codes, regularly attended and revised, designed to be adopted by municipalities and appropriate political subdivisions by ordinance for use in regulating building construction for the welfare and safety of the general public.

Modifications
Term applied to changes that may be made from time to time to the Contract Documents and/or the Contract for Construction. Modifications made prior to award of contract are called Addenda; modifications made after the contract is in force are called Change Orders.

Multiple Prime Contract
This type of contract is used in a situation where one or more constructors are employed under separate contracts to perform work on the same project—either in a sequence or coincidentally.

Mutual Companies
Insurance companies owned by many individuals who are also the insured. The "pooling" of this combined capital is a form of mutual assurance.

Narrowscope
A term established by the C.S.I. to denote a section of the specifications that describes a single product. (See also Mediumscope and Broadscope.)

National Labor Relations Act
An act of Congress sometimes known as the Wagner Act, enacted in 1935. This act mandated a framework of procedure and regulation by which management-labor relations are to be conducted.

Negotiation
A process used to determine a mutually satisfactory Contract Sum, and terms to be included in the Contract for Construction. In negotiations, the owner directly selects the constructor and the two, often with assistance of the design professional, derive by compromise and meeting of minds the scope of the project and its cost.

Network Schedule
A method of scheduling the construction process where various related events are programmed into a sequential network on the basis of starting and finishing dates.

Non-Restrictive Specification
A type of specification which is written so as not to restrict the product to a particular manufacturer or material supplier.

Norris-LaGuardia Act
Enacted by Congress in 1932, this act was the first piece of major legislation designed to diminish the power of management over labor.

Obligation
A result of custom, law or agreement by which an individual is duty bound to fulfill an act or other responsibility.

Occupational Safety and Health Act (OSHA)
Enacted by Congress in 1970, this act is sometimes referred to as the Williams-Steiger Act. It was designed to improve job safety under administration of the U.S. Department of Labor, with provision of fines and penalties for non-compliance.

Office of Federal Contract Compliance (OFCC)
An agency of the United States Department of Labor charged with administration of Executive Order 11246, issued by U. S. President Lyndon B. Johnson. This agency requires affirmative action on the part of contractors for federal projects in providing equal rights for employees under the provisions of Title IV of the Civil Rights Act of 1964 which forbids discrimination by an employer on the basis of race, color, religion, sex, or national origin.

OPC Relationship
The relationship that normally exists between owner, (design) professional and contractor during the construction process.

Open Bidding
A common, colloquial term meaning the process of constructor selection known as Competitive Selection.

Open Competitive Selection
The proper term for Competitive Bidding—a process of constructor selection whereby an Advertisement to Bidders is published in the news media notifying qualified constructors of the owner's intention to receive and consider sealed competitive bids leading to the award of a Contract for Construction (usually to the qualified bidder submitting the lowest responsible bid with other considerations being given in accordance with published Instructions to Bidders).

Ordinance
An authoritative rule of law, public decree or regulation enacted by a municipality or other political subdivision fully enforceable through the courts system of the municipality or other political subdivision.

Outline Specification
An abbreviated or preliminary form of specification, intended for preliminary evaluation, stating basic but not necessarily complete descriptions of the products, materials and workmanship upon which the Contract for Construction will eventually be based.

Overtime
A term applied to the numbers of hours worked in excess of eight in any one day or more than forty in any one week.

Partnership
The joining of two or more individuals for a business purpose whereby profits and liabilities are shared.

Payment Bond

A form of security purchased by the contractor from a surety, which is provided to guarantee that the contractor will pay all costs of labor, materials and other services related to the project for which he is responsible under the Contract for Construction.

Payments Withheld

A provision of AIA Document A201—*General Conditions of the Contract for Construction*, Paragraph 9.6, which provides that the owner may withhold payments to the contractor if, in the opinion of the design professional, the work falls behind the schedule of construction, or in the event that the work deviates from the provisions of the Contract Documents.

Performance

(1) A term meaning fulfillment of a promise made by one party to a contract or agreement in return for compensation.
(2) The manner in which or the efficiency with which something acts or reacts in the manner in which it is intended.

Performance Bond

A form of security purchased by the contractor from a surety, which is provided to guarantee that the contractor will satisfactorily perform all work and other services related to the project for which he is responsible under the Contract for Construction.

Performance Specification

A description of the desired results or performance of a product, material, assembly, or piece of equipment with criteria for verifying compliance.

Plan Rooms

A service provided by construction industry organizations or service companies, sometimes available to interested constructors, materialmen, vendors and manufacturers. Plan rooms provide access to contract documents for projects currently in the process of receiving competitive or negotiated bids.

Primary Subcontractors

Subcontractors who may perform major portions of the work in a construction project such as installation of plumbing, mechanical or electrical systems.

Prime Professional Service

The chief among multiple professional entities (each under separate contracts with the prime professional) responsible for providing services to an owner.

Principal

(1) The principal authority or person responsible for a business such as architecture, engineering, or construction.
(2) The capital amount of a loan or other obligation as distinguished from the interest.

Product Data

Information furnished and certified by the manufacturer of a product which offers technical data as to the composition of the product or material, recommended use or application, test data, advantages and disadvantages of use, physical properties and characteristics, guarantees and warranties normally provided by the manufacturer and other specific information that may be requested by the design professional.

Professional Corporation

A corporation created expressly for the purpose of providing professional practice and related services which may have special requirements under the law, as opposed to requirements for corporations in general.

Profit Sharing

Provisions in special agreements or contracts for construction where the contractor, as an incentive to save money for the owner, is paid, in addition to the final contract sum, some percentage of any net savings he may achieve if he is able to deliver the finished project to the owner's satisfaction at a total cost which is below a specified limiting amount, which may or may not have been guaranteed by the contractor.

Program

An orderly statement and explanation of the requirements of space and function that are the major considerations to be applied or incorporated to the design of a project.

Progress Schedule

A schedule showing the time relationships of various elements of the construction process. A progress schedule serves to verify whether or not a project under construction, is progressing on schedule.

Project

A term used to describe something that is contemplated, planned, devised or intended to be produced. In construction terms, the total intention of the work of construction to be done such as a building, real estate improvement, or structure.

Project Manual

A bound booklet which (with the possible exception of drawings of large size which may be bound separately) contains the Contract Documents and if appropriate, the Bidding Requirements related to the Contract for Construction.

Project Record Documents

The documents, certificates, and other information relating to the work, materials, products, assemblies, and equipment that the contractor is required to accumulate during construction and convey to the owner for use prior to final payment and project closeout.

Project Team

A collection of professional entities directed and otherwise coordinated to perform work or services for a project.

Promissory Note

A legal instrument, agreement or contract made between a lender and a borrower by which the lender conveys to the borrower a sum or other consideration known as *principal* for which the borrower promises repayment of the principal plus interest under conditions set forth in the agreement.

Proprietary

The naming of a product manufacturer as in a Proprietary Specification.

Proprietary Specification

A type of specification which describes a product, material, assembly or piece of equipment by trade name and/or by naming the manufacturer or manufacturers who may produce products acceptable to the owner or design professional.

Protocol
A procedure or practice established by long or traditional usage and currently accepted by a majority of practitioners in similar professions or trades. Protocol represents the generally accepted method of action or reaction that may be expected to be followed in a transaction.

Punch List
A list of items within a project, prepared by the contractor, confirmed by the owner or his representative, which may remain to be replaced or completed in accordance with the requirements of the Contract for Construction at the time of Substantial Completion.

Purchase Order
A written contract or similar agreement made between a buyer and seller that details the items to be purchased, the price of such items, and the method and responsibility for delivery and acceptance of the items. A purchase order also formalizes the intentions of both parties to the transaction.

Receipt of Bids
The official action of an owner in receiving sealed bids that have been invited or advertised in accordance with the owner's intention to award a contract for construction.

Reference Standards
Professionally prepared generic specifications and technical data compiled and published by competent organizations generally recognized and accepted by the construction industry. These standards are sometimes used as criteria by which the acceptability and/or performance of a product, material, assembly or piece of equipment can be judged.

Reference Standard Specification
A type of non-proprietary specification that relies on accepted reference standards to describe a product, material, assembly or piece of equipment to be incorporated into a project.

Referendum
A special election subdivision which establishes public approval (e.g., for elected officials to sell General Obligation Bonds as a means of financing a public project).

Risk Management
An approach to management and procedure designed to prevent occurrence of culpability, potential liability, contravention of law or other potential risk that could bring about loss in the process of building construction.

Samples
Physical examples of materials, products, equipment or workmanship that establish standards by which the work will be judged.

Schedule of Values
A listing of the elements, systems, items, or other subdivisions of the work, establishing a value for each, the total of which equals the Contract Sum. The Schedule of Values is used for establishing the cash flow of a project.

Seal
A legal term used to describe the signature or other representation of an individual agreeing to the terms and conditions of an agreement or contract.

Secondary Subcontractor
A subcontractor employed by the contractor to complete minor portions of the work, or a subcontractor other than those identified as Primary Subcontractors.

Selective Bidding
A process of competitive bidding for award of the Contract for Construction whereby the owner selects the constructors who are invited to bid to the exclusion of others as in the process of Open Bidding.

Separate Contracts
A procedure whereby an owner may issue separate contracts, each for different portions of the work leading to the completion of a project.

Sherman Anti-Trust Act
Enacted by Congress in 1890, to prevent the unchecked growth of "big" business by preventing companies or individuals from holding a monopoly or controlling prices in certain areas of commerce.

Shop Drawings
Drawings created by a contractor, subcontractor, vendor, manufacturer, or other entity that illustrate construction, materials, dimensions, installation and other pertinent information for the incorporation of an element or item into the construction.

Single Prime Contractor
Term describing a constructor acting alone to fulfill the contractor's responsibility under the Contract for Construction.

Spec Data Sheet
A copyrighted name, owned by the Construction Specifications Institute (CSI), for a document, written or approved and published by CSI, presenting all pertinent properties and technical data related to a particular product. The spec data sheet is useful to contractors and specifiers in the preparation of specifications for the construction process.

Specifications
Documents that define the qualitative requirements for products, materials, and workmanship upon which the Contract for Construction is based.

Specifier
One who writes or prepares the specifications.

Statutes of Limitation
Provision of law establishing a certain time limit from an occurrence during which a judgment may be sought from a court of law.

Statutory Requirements
Requirements that are embodied in the law.

Stock Companies
Insurance companies owned by a group of stockholders for the purpose of selling insurance.

Subcontract
An agreement between a prime contractor and a contractor (specializing in a particular trade) for the completion of a portion of the work for which the prime contractor is responsible.

Subcontractor

One under contract to a prime contractor by subcontract for completion of a portion of the work for which the prime contractor is responsible.

Sub-subcontractor

One under contract to a subcontractor for completion of a portion of the work for which the subcontractor is responsible.

Submittal

A sample, manufacturer's data, shop drawing or other such item submitted to the owner or the design professional by the contractor for the purpose of approval or other action, usually a requirement of the contract documents.

Substantial Completion

The condition when the work of the project is substantially complete, ready for owner acceptance and occupancy. Any items remaining to be completed should, at this point, be duly noted or stipulated in writing.

Superintendent

Title usually applied to one who is the senior supervisor of the work at a construction site, acting on behalf of the contractor.

Supplemental General Conditions

Written modifications to the General Conditions that become part of the Contract Documents.

Supplemental Instructions to Bidders

Written modifications to the Instructions to Bidders that become part of the Bidding Requirements.

Surety

An individual or company that provides a bond or pledge to guarantee that another individual or company will perform in accordance with the terms of an agreement or contract.

Taft-Hartley Act

An act of the Congress of the United States of 1947, introduced by Senator Taft and Representative Hartley, and titled the Labor Management Relations Act. This legislation lessened the power of management over labor and provided that labor participate in some management decisions.

Testing

Action whereby a portion or sample of a material is subjected to procedures designed to prove performance characteristics.

Test Case

A term used by legal practitioners to refer to a trial whose pleadings and merits have, or possess the potential to form a precedence for future judgments in similar cases.

Title

A legal term meaning the right to property, such as real estate.

Transmittal

A form or letter conveying the action to be taken on an item being transmitted from one party to another.

Trial

Term commonly applied to an action in a court of law.

Turn Key

A contract that provides all of the services required to produce a building or other construction project.

Unit Cost Contract
A contract for construction where compensation is based on a stipulated cost per unit of measure for the volume of work produced.

Value Engineering
A science that studies the relative value of various materials and construction techniques. Value engineering considers the initial cost of construction, coupled with the estimated cost of maintenance, energy use, life expectancy, and replacement cost.

Warranty
Manufacturer's certification of quality and performance that may include a limited guarantee of satisfaction.

White Print
A reproduction of a drawing or other document that is a positive image of the original; a reproduction produced by the exposure of light to paper treated with a diazo compound developed in ammonia fumes.

Worker's Compensation Insurance
Insurance carried by employers, mandated by law, that provides compensation for bodily injury and loss of wages for a work-related accident.